PACIFIC INSTITUTE SERIES ON FORENSIC PSYCHOLOGY

METHAMPHETAMINE USE

Clinical and Forensic Aspects

PACIFIC INSTITUTE SERIES ON FORENSIC PSYCHOLOGY
Edited by Harold V. Hall

With the support of Pacific Institute for the Study of Conflict and Aggression, Kamuela, Hawaii

Titles in this Series

Understanding and Preventing Violence: The Psychology of Human Destructiveness
Leighton C. Whitaker

Detecting Malingering and Deception: Forensic Distortion Analysis, Second Edition
Harold V. Hall and Joseph Poirer

Endangered Children: Neonaticide, Infanticide, and Filicide
Lita Linzer Schwartz and Natalie K. Isser

Methamphetamine Use: Clinical and Forensic Aspects
Errol Yudko, Harold V. Hall, and Sandra B. McPherson

PACIFIC INSTITUTE SERIES ON FORENSIC PSYCHOLOGY

METHAMPHETAMINE USE
Clinical and Forensic Aspects

Errol Yudko • Harold V. Hall
Sandra B. McPherson

CRC PRESS

Boca Raton   London   New York   Washington, D.C.

Library of Congress Cataloging-in-Publication Data

Yudko, Errol.
　　Methamphetamine use: clinical and forensic aspects / Errol Yudko, Harold V. Hall, Sandra B. McPherson.
　　　　p. cm. — (Pacific Institute series on forensic psychology)
　　Includes bibliographical references and index.
　　ISBN 0-8493-1477-1 (alk. paper)
　　1. Methamphetamine abuse. 2. Methamphetamine. I. Hall, Harold V. II. McPherson, Sandra B. III. Title. IV. Series.
　　HV5822.A5M483 2003
　　362.29'9—dc21

2003043555

This book contains information obtained from authentic and highly regarded sources. Reprinted material is quoted with permission, and sources are indicated. A wide variety of references are listed. Reasonable efforts have been made to publish reliable data and information, but the author and the publisher cannot assume responsibility for the validity of all materials or for the consequences of their use.

Neither this book nor any part may be reproduced or transmitted in any form or by any means, electronic or mechanical, including photocopying, microfilming, and recording, or by any information storage or retrieval system, without prior permission in writing from the publisher.

The consent of CRC Press LLC does not extend to copying for general distribution, for promotion, for creating new works, or for resale. Specific permission must be obtained in writing from CRC Press LLC for such copying.

Direct all inquiries to CRC Press LLC, 2000 N.W. Corporate Blvd., Boca Raton, Florida 33431.

Trademark Notice: Product or corporate names may be trademarks or registered trademarks, and are used only for identification and explanation, without intent to infringe.

Visit the CRC Press Web site at www.crcpress.com

© 2003 by CRC Press LLC

No claim to original U.S. Government works
International Standard Book Number 0-8493-1477-1
Library of Congress Card Number 2003043555
Printed in the United States of America　1　2　3　4　5　6　7　8　9　0
Printed on acid-free paper

Table of Contents

The Authors xi
Acknowledgments xiii
Introduction xv

Section I   History and Epidemiology

1   History of Methamphetamine 3

    Ephedra 5
    The Spread of Methamphetamine Use in the U.S. 6
    Hawaii and Ice 7
    Current Trends 9
    References 10

2   Epidemiology 13

    References 14

3   Methamphetamine and the Middle East 15

    Introduction 15
    Geopolitical Interconnections 16
    Government Complicity as a Factor 18
    Business Aspects: Ecstasy as a Case in Point 19
    Cultural Factors and Treatment Implications 19
    Comparative Drug Use Patterns 21
    Treatment Approaches 21
    Conclusion 22
    References 23

4   MDMA 25

Myths about MDMA Use 25
Neurotoxic Properties of MDMA in Nonhuman Animals 26
Neurotoxic Properties of MDMA in Humans 27
Conclusions 29
References 30

Section II   Physiology, Effects, and Diagnosis of Methamphetamine Use

5   Physiology 37

Neurotransmitter Action 37
Control of Neurotransmitter Levels 38
Physiological Effects of Amphetamine 38
Tolerance and Sensitization 40
Neurotoxicity 40
Neuropharmacology of Amphetamines 41
References 42

6   Effects of Methamphetamine Use 47

Cerebral Injury and Death from Methamphetamine Use 47
The Unpredictable Effects of Methamphetamine 48
References 51

7   Diagnosis of Methamphetamine Use 55

The Symptomatic Patterns 55
Diagnosing Methamphetamine Syndromes 59
References 62

Section III   Aggression

8   Anecdotal Evidence of the Effects of Amphetamine on Aggression 67

References 69

9   Empirical Evidence of the Effects of Amphetamine on Aggression 71

Administration of Amphetamines to Rodent Subjects 71
    Behavioral Observations 72
    Dose-Dependent Effects 73
        Acute Administration 73
        Chronic Administration 74
Methodological Problems: Distinguishing between Aggressive and Defensive Reactions 75
Amphetamines and Their Effects on Dominance Hierarchy in Primates 76
    Differences of Effects between Ranks 76
    Dose-Dependent Effects 77
Amphetamines and Their Effects on Human Aggressive Behavior 78
    Subjective Analysis 78
    Observed Behavior 79
Concluding Remarks 80
References 81

Section IV   Methamphetamine and the Courts

10   Expert Testimony 85

U.S. Supreme Court Decisions Regarding Methamphetamine 85
Daubert Issues: Who May Testify as Experts? 87
References 95

11   Mitigation in Sentencing 97

Statutory and Case Law Relative to Substance Abuse and Mitigation in Sentencing 97
    State Codes and Cases 97
    Federal Sentencing Scheme 102
Evaluation of Defendants and Context 103
    Purposes of Evaluation 103
    Risk Analysis 104
    Malingering 107
    Procedures 109
        Interview 109

  Psychometrics 110
  Context 113
   Categories of TPI 114
 Reporting to the Court 115
 Pre-Sentence Investigation Reports 117
 Survey of Methamphetamine Cases Evaluated
 in a Court Clinic 119
  Case "AB" 120
  Case "CD" 121
  Case "EF" 122
  Case "GH" 123
  Case "IJ" 124
  Case "KL" 125
  Case "MN" 126
  Conclusions 127
 Special Case of Death Penalty Sentencing 128
 Treatment as a Sentencing Consideration 131
 Review of Treatment Center Cases 139
  Procedure 139
  Results 140
  Discussion 143
 Resources for the Sentencing Process 143
 Chapter Summary 144
 References 144

12 Mitigation to Murder 149

 Reference 150

13 Methamphetamine and Pregnancy 151

 Legal Issues and Status 152
  Maternal Rights against Self-Incrimination
  and Vulnerability to Punishment Based on Drug Testing
  by Hospitals 152
  Maternal Custody Rights 152
  Paternal Custody Rights 153
  Culture 156
  Rights of the Fetus 156
  Legal Perspectives — Summary Statement 157
 The Effect of Methamphetamine on the Fetus 158
  Putative Effects of Methamphetamine 159

What Is Known about the Effects of Methamphetamine
  on the Fetus 160
Conclusion 161
References 162

Section V Forensics

14 *Miranda* Rights, Interrogation, and Competency to Confess 167

Miranda Rights and Methamphetamine 167
Interrogation and Methamphetamine Use 168
Methamphetamine Abuse and Competency to Proceed 170
References 174

15 Criminal Responsibility 177

References 194

16 Dangerousness Prediction in Methamphetamine Cases 195

Summary and Recommendations 197
References 198

Section VI Treatment

17 Treatment of Methamphetamine Abuse — Lack of Evidence for the Efficacy of Any of the Models Currently in Use 203

NIDA Treatment Guidelines 203
Matrix Model of Outpatient Treatment 204
  Basic Elements of the Matrix Model 204
  Components of the Matrix Model 205
  Evidence of the Effectiveness of the Matrix Model 206
Haight Ashbury Outpatient Model 207
Conclusions 209

References		209
Bibliography		**211**
Glossary		**223**
Appendix I	Treatment Facility Checklist	305
Appendix II	Pacific Institute for the Study of Conflict and Aggression Statement of Purpose	307
Appendix III	Verbatim History of a Crystal Methamphetamine Abuser	311
Appendix IV	Temporal Characteristics of Methamphetamine with Forensic Implications	325
Appendix V	Safety Tips for Approaching a Tweaker	327
Index		**329**

The Authors

Errol Yudko, Ph.D., is an Assistant Professor of Psychology at the University of Hawaii at Hilo. He has worked as a consultant to the Big Island Substance Abuse Counsel where he supervised and trained substance abuse counselors. Dr. Yudko is also an advisory board member of the Pacific Institute for the Study of Conflict and Aggression.

Dr. Yudko received a B.A. in biological sciences from the University of California at Irvine, and both M.A. and Ph.D. degrees in behavioral neuroscience from the University of Hawaii at Manoa. Dr. Yudko's postdoctoral research was performed at the Laboratory of Psychopharmacology, University of Hawaii at Manoa. As a student, Dr. Yudko worked as a research assistant for the Center for Memory and Learning at the University of California, Irvine, as a research pharmacologist for the Department of Cognitive Neuroscience for Wyeth Research in the United Kingdom, and as an ethopharmacologist for the Pacific Biomedical Research Center at the University of Hawaii at Manoa.

Dr. Yudko's research interests include the effects of pharmacological agents on aggressive and defensive behavior in both humans and animals, models of substance abuse prevention in adolescents, and violence prediction in adolescents. He has published or presented more than 30 professional papers. He is frequently called upon to provide training for educators, counselors, and others interested in learning about substance abuse in the county of Hawaii. Dr. Yudko is an *ad hoc* reviewer for the *Journal of Studies on Alcohol*.

Harold V. Hall, Ph.D., A.B.P.P., a forensic neuropsychologist, is the Director of the Pacific Institute for the Study of Conflict and Aggression. He has diplomate status in both forensic and clinical psychology from the American Board of Professional Psychology, and is a Fellow of the American Psychological Association.

Dr. Hall's Ph.D. was awarded in clinical psychology from Brigham Young University after which he worked as an intern in clinical psychology at Atascadero State Hospital, California. He later worked as an extern in forensic neuropsychology at Hawaii State Hospital, Kaneohe, and as a Fellow in

Clinical Neuropsychology at the University of Rochester School of Medicine/Strong Memorial Hospital, Rochester, New York.

He served as a consultant to the FBI on Hawaii's first serial rape murder case, the U.S. Secret Service on the profiling of the Unabomber, the National Bureau of Prisons on its witness protection programs, and the Honolulu Office of the Prosecuting Attorney on the Xerox mass-murder case, *State of Hawaii v. Byran Uyesugi*. He has authored or edited six books and more than 40 peer-reviewed articles in violence-related areas. He was elected to the National Academy of Practice in Psychology as a Distinguished Practitioner.

Sandra B. McPherson, Ph.D., A.B.P.P., has diplomate status in both clinical and forensic psychology from the American Board of Professional Psychology. Dr. McPherson has a forensic practice in Cleveland, Ohio. She also teaches for the Fielding Institute School of Psychology, which is based in Santa Barbara, California. Dr. McPherson's Ph.D. was awarded by Case Western University. Her internships were spent at the Cleveland Guidance Center and Brecksville V.A. Hospital.

She has developed special expertise in death penalty mitigation, having worked with many defendants currently on Ohio's death row. Her work in this area began with the first case to be brought under the state's revised capital punishment statute. In addition to the other areas of criminal responsibility work, she is particularly active in domestic relations cases, with special emphasis on problems of sexual abuse allegations and the development of court-worthy psychological evaluations.

She has worked as a consultant to industry, educational institutions, and government. The governmental agencies she has consulted for include the V.A., the FBI, and local police forces. She has published or presented more than 30 professional papers. She is a member of the American Psychological Association and the Ohio Psychological Association, of which she has served as president. She is a former president of the State Board of Psychology.

Acknowledgments

Parts of this book have been provided by the Pacific Institute for the Study of Conflict and Aggression, 65-1230 Mamalahoa Highway, Carter Professional Center, C-21, Post Office Box 819, Kamuela, Hawaii, 96743, telephone (808)885-9800, fax (808)885-6776, e-mail hvhall@ilhawaii.net. All previous forms of this information are obsolete.

Special thanks to contributing authors Farshid Afsarifard, Tiffany Gagnet, Paul Midson, Lori Murray-Bridges, Stuart W. Twemlow, and Sherrlee Watson-Hauanio.

The authors wish to acknowledge and thank the many professionals who reviewed and provided comments on *Methamphetamine Use: Clinical and Forensic Aspects* Listed in alphabetical order, they are as follows:

   Francis Akamine, Esq., Public Defender, Hilo, Hawaii
   Sally Barlow, Ph.D., Associate Professor, Brigham Young University, Provo, Utah
   The late Lucien Buck, Ph.D., Professor, Dowling College, Oakdale, New York
   Ian Cate, Esq., Deputy Prosecuting Attorney, Hilo, Hawaii
   Darwin Ching, Esq., Honolulu, Hawaii
   Claudia Clayton, Ph.D., Assistant Professor, Brigham Young University, Provo, Utah
   Patrick Cook, Ph.D., Forensic Psychologist, Tallahassee, Florida
   Robert Eme, Ph.D., Clinical Professor, Illinois School of Professional Psychology, Roll Meadows, Illinois
   Theodore Feldmann, M.D., Associate Professor, University of Louisville School of Medicine, Louisville, Kentucky
   Charles Golden, Ph.D., Director, Center for Psychological Studies, Nova Southwestern University, Fort Lauderdale, Florida
   Jerilynn Ono Hall, Esq., Kohala, Hawaii
   Jean M. Ireton, Esq., Deputy Prosecuting Attorney, Honolulu, Hawaii
   Gary Jackson, Ph.D., Vice President and Director of Research and Development, Psychological Assessment Resources, Lutz, Florida
   Rosalie Matzkin, Ed.D., Assistant Professor, Pennsylvania State University, Ogontz Campus, Abington, Pennsylvania
   Frank Sacco, Ph.D., Clinical Psychologist, Topeka, Kansas

Lita Linzer Schwartz, Ph.D., Distinguished Professor Emerita, Pennsylvania State University, Ogontz Campus, Abington, Pennsylvania

Rom Trader, Esq., Deputy Prosecuting Attorney, Honolulu, Hawaii

Leighton Whitaker, Ph.D., Adjunct Clinical Professor, Widener University, Wallingford, Pennsylvania

Introduction

Since 1620, when the Puritans arrived on the *Mayflower,* Americans have been ambiguous in their attitudes and beliefs about drugs. It began with alcohol. A quote from the *Mayflower* log reads, "We could not now take time for further search or consideration, our victuals having been much spent, specifically our beer." On board ship the Puritans carried 42 tons of beer, 10,000 gallons of wine, and 14 tons of water (Lee, 1963). However, in 1629, the first laws concerning the use of alcohol in the New World were introduced by the Virginia Colonial Assembly (Cherrington, 1920): "Ministers shall not give themselves to excess in drinkinge, or riott, or spending their tyme idellye day or night." In 1633, Plymouth Colony prohibited the sale of more than 2 pence worth of spirits to "anyone but strangers just arrived." In 1637, Massachusetts ordered that "no persons shall remain in any tavern longer than necessary occasions." Despite these laws, by 1640 the first distillery had been built on Dutch-owned Staten Island.

Thus, from our beginnings we have had this love/hate relationship with drugs. The first settlers arrived with tons of alcohol and almost immediately began to legislate against its use. Then they started building distilleries. This ambiguous behavior continued for centuries. The Revenue Act of 1791 called for taxation on whiskey, which incited the Whiskey Rebellion of 1791. The Revenue Act was repealed in 1802. The first temperance movement began in 1826. The basic philosophy was that beer was good and whiskey was bad. The second temperance movement, 1874, decreed that all alcohol is "evil." Meanwhile, whiskey and brandy were considered by both physicians and the populace as medicinal drinks. Prohibition was enacted in 1920 and repealed in 1933.

Good vs. Bad Drugs

Americans have a tendency to see all things in black and white. Drugs are good or bad. In 1874 beer was good, whiskey was bad. In today's world, natural is good, synthetic is bad. We develop these ideas by listening to our teachers, clergy, parents, politicians, and the media. However, no matter what we believe, it's all the same chemicals. There is only one periodic table. The elements combine together to form compounds. It does not matter how they combine; the effect will be the same. In biochemistry, function is determined by shape. If the right shape is present, then a chemical will have some sort of physiological effect.

Good vs. Evil States

We can observe this phenomenon — our basic desire to label all things as either positive or negative — in our current political dealings with the world. Nations are seen by Americans as either our allies or part of the "axis of evil." Diplomacy is all but forgotten in our current desire to strike out at the "Evil Doers" of the world. Few stop to think that in the countries that we are currently planning to wage war upon there are those who consider Americans the "Evil Ones." Few stop to consider that the very same thought patterns (seeing the world in black and white) are what led to a group of terrorists being able to rationalize the attack on American soil that began the current crisis.

Objectivity

Currently we watch television ads that suggest that illicit drug use supports terrorism. There are a number of fundamental problems with the use of these ads intended to reduce illicit drug use.

First, were the ads ever tested for their effectiveness? The likely answer is that they were not (like the "just say no" and "this is your brain on drugs" ads that came before them). What good could we do if we took the enormous amount of money invested in these ads and put them to use researching how to reduce illicit drug use?

Second, these ads suggest that drugs support terrorism, but what about diamonds and oil? Does not our use of these commodities support terrorism. Bill Mahre, in his new book *When You Ride Alone You Ride with Bin Laden: What the Government Should Be Telling Us to Help Fight the War on Terrorism* seems to be the only member of the media with the courage to address these issues.

Third, who is really being supported by the drug trade? Didn't we learn that it was the U.S. that was trafficking drugs during the Iran-Contra affair? Wasn't it the Taliban who put a stop to the heroin trade in Afghanistan? Hasn't that trade returned since the overthrow of the Taliban?

Science is an attempt to understand the universe objectively. We cannot afford to look at problems from a single perspective. Both science and politics function better when the practitioners understand their opposition. In politics, it is essential to understand your opponent if you ever hope to reach a compromise with him or her or if you wish to best that opponent in a political arena.

Effects vs. Side Effects

In science we must view our world from every possible perspective. We must understand that there may be multiple causes of any phenomenon. Moreover, we must understand that there may be many more *possible* causes of any phenomenon. From that perspective it becomes the job of scientists to design experiments that will allow them to rule out each *possible* cause until only one cause remains.

Thus, the scientist cannot afford to believe in "Good" or "Bad." The scientist must remain objective. In the case of pharmacology, that means we cannot evaluate a drug as either good or bad. We must evaluate it in terms of its effects vs. its side effects.

All drugs have positive effects and negative side effects. If you watch television for any length of time you will see an ad for a pharmaceutical compound. It may be a drug that will reduce your acne, increase your sex drive, or make your depression go away. Whatever the case, at the end of that advertisement you will be presented with a list of possible negative side effects.

The decision of whether or not a drug should be used needs to be based on a careful evaluation of effect vs. side effect. For example, if a physician considers prescribing amphetamine to treat obesity, that physician needs to consider whether the desired effect (appetite suppression) outweighs the negative side effects (sleeplessness, irritability, addiction, etc.). In most cases of this sort, the physician will likely decide not to prescribe the drug. But that should be the decision of the physician, who is an expert in the drug's medicinal qualities, not agents of the federal government, who base decisions on the belief that some drugs are good and some drugs are bad.

Governmental Regulations

Our government has been in the habit, since the passage of the Harrison Act of 1914, of classifying any drug that it does not understand that has any possibility for abuse as Schedule I. Thus, the government makes research on the drug nearly impossible and any medical use out of reach. This behavior has little to do with our scientific understanding of the effects of the drug. Rather, the decision to classify a drug as illegal is almost always an emotional decision. In 1937, a man by the name of Anslinger appealed to Congress to pass legislation to prohibit the use of marijuana based on his unsubstantiated statements that it caused black men to rape white women. This emotional appeal led to the reclassification of marijuana, a substance that is far less harmful than tobacco or alcohol, as an illicit substance with no medical use (a designation that is finally being called into question today).

This emotional decision making of our governmental bodies does not end with the designation of a drug as good or bad. It also extends into how we deal with the drug problems faced by the nation. This is not the place to embark on a lengthy discussion about how the current "war on drugs" makes the problem worse. In brief, upsetting the supply-and-demand equation causes an increase in the value of drugs. This leads to increased incentive to sell illicit drugs and an increase in crime associated with illicit drug use; a lesson that should have been learned during Prohibition. A viable alternative to the current "war" would be to increase our attempts to prevent drug use by dealing with the social causes of drug use (i.e., employment, educational, and family problems). However, even when the government tries to do the right thing and develop substance abuse prevention programs it tends to make the problem worse.

The current trend in substance abuse prevention is to use community coalitions to develop strategies to reduce drug use. The rationale is that if you bring the community together you will inspire politicians to release funds for the cause. However, a recent study (Hallfors et al., 2002) shows that these coalitions can actually make the problem worse. The authors of the paper concluded:

> Not only were effects related to community and youth goals null, but coalitions that targeted adults actually did worse on related indicators over time compared to matched controls. Coalitions that were more comprehensive in their strategies did not show any superior benefit; when coalitions focused high doses of funding and staff time on specific strategies, this produced an inverse relationship with desired outcomes (Hallfors et al., 2002).

One possible solution to this problem would be to allow our experts to do what it is that they do best with minimal interference.

This book is an attempt to evaluate our current knowledge about the effects and side effects of methamphetamine. The use of this drug has been highly politicized in recent years. In a time when the U.S. Drug Enforcement Agency (DEA) and political leaders need to be educated about this drug, they have decided that they are the experts. The DEA and local governments have come together to develop "summits" in which politicians make speeches and spread unsubstantiated information, and in which community members try to brainstorm effective ways to deal with a very complex problem. In this book we attempt to perform this evaluation with little or no bias, which may ruffle some feathers. We attempt to analyze social problems from all possible perspectives. We analyze the effects of methamphetamine from historical, political, clinical, and forensic aspects.

This work is divided into six parts. Section I focuses on the history and epidemiology of methamphetamine use. Section II describes the physiology, effects, and diagnosis of methamphetamine use. Section III analyzes what we know about the effect of methamphetamine on aggression. Section IV examines the interaction between methamphetamine and the criminal justice system. Section V describes issues that pertain to forensic psychologists. Section VI examines the issues regarding treatment and the effectiveness of current treatments.

Note: References within the text may be found either in the chapter reference list or in the bibliography at the end of the book.

Errol Yudko

References

Cherrington, E. H. (1920). *The Evolution of Prohibition in the United States of America*, Westerville, OH: American Issue Press.

Hallfors, D., Cho, S., Livert, D., and Kadushin, C. (2002). Fighting back against substance abuse: Are community coalitions winning? *Am. J. Prev. Med.*, 23(4), 237–245.

Lee, H. (1963). *How Dry We Were: Prohibition Revisited*, Englewood, Cliffs, NJ: Prentice Hall.

Section I

History and Epidemiology

History of Methamphetamine

**ERROL YUDKO
LORI MURRAY-BRIDGES
SHERRLEE WATSON-HAUANIO**

Stimulants have been used medicinally for thousands of years. Chinese physicians have used ma haung, a tea made from the herb *Ephedra vulgaris*, as a medicinal herb for 5000 years. Chat, another stimulant, was used 2000 years ago by Roman gladiators to overcome fatigue and thus fight longer during contests (Wadler, 1994). Coffee has been in existence since at least A.D. 900, when an Arabian medical book referred to it as useful for a variety of indications, including measles and lust reduction. Coffee drinking was so widespread that coffeehouses were common in England, Arabia, and France as early as the 1600s (Ray and Ksir, 2002).

Other drugs used historically for medicinal purposes include opiates, alcohol, and marijuana. Opiates were used as early as the third century B.C. as analgesics, to treat anxiety and psychotic disorders, and were even given to children to ease colic. Fermented honey (mead) may have been used since 8000 B.C. By 6400 B.C., beer and berry wine were being used by Neolithic humans (Ray and Ksir, 2002). Alcohol was also used to reduce anxiety and to help insomnia sufferers fall asleep (Doweiko, 1999).

By the 1500s, drugs were big business. Prior to the arrival of the Spanish in South America in 1518, the coca leaf had been chewed by the Incas in their religious ceremonies and was used as a medium for barter (Byck, 1987; Ray and Ksir, 2002). As Spanish landlords realized that chewing the coca leaf reduced thirst, hunger, fatigue, and increased productivity, the practice of chewing the leaves was encouraged and soon became widespread (Mann, 1994) Cocaine was extracted in 1859. Combined with the invention of the syringe in 1853 cocaine use began to increase in popularity. The extracts from the coca leaf were used in a range of medicinal drinks including Coca-Cola. Cocaine use was widespread; users included many prominent people, among them Sigmund Freud, who was one of cocaine's greatest proponents (Doweiko, 1999).

Opiates, cocaine, and alcohol were so widely used that, by the early 1900s, when there was great concern with drug use, many patented medicines containing these drugs were sold on the streets by peddlers. The ingredients of these snake oil concoctions were kept secret. No agency existed to regulate the contents or claims made about these drug cordials. When the medical community began to question the claims made about these elixirs, the conflict led to the Pure Food and Drug Act of 1906, which prohibited the distribution of food and drugs that were misbranded (Ray and Ksir, 2002).

Another law that passed in the effort to control the manufacture and distribution of opiates was the Harrison Act of 1914. Dr Hamilton Wright thought that the U.S. would improve its trading status with China by helping the Chinese control the importation of opium. In 1912, an international conference was held; at that time, Great Britain wanted to include controlling the importation of morphine, heroin, and cocaine as well. When all talks and compromises were over, the Harrison Act of 1914 was born; its intent was "to provide for the registration of, with collectors of internal revenue, and to impose a special tax upon all persons who produce, import, manufacture, compound, deal in, dispense, or give away opium or coca leaves, their cults, derivatives or preparation, and for other purposes" (Terry and Pellens, 1928). The Harrison Act was meant to be solely a tax law and did not prevent the use or distribution of such drugs (Ray and Ksir, 2002).

In the 1820s a "new drug" called marijuana (which had been used to make rope and clothing since George Washington grew it) came to the attention of Congress. Medicinal use of marijuana can be historically dated to the year 2737 B.C. when Emperor Shen Nung wrote a pharmacy book recommending the use of marijuana to treat "female weakness, gout, rheumatism, ben ben, constipation, and absent mindedness" (Snyder, 1970). There is also a documented case of physicians using marijuana on a rabies patient to control the terror and excitement that the patient suffered (Elliot, 1992). In the 1800s, American and European physicians used marijuana as a hypnotic, anticonvulsant, analgesic, and as treatment for migraine headaches (Ray and Ksir, 2002; Grinspoon and Bakalar, 1992, 1993, 1995). It was not until the 1920s that marijuana became a concern in the U.S. In 1926, newspaper articles began associating marijuana use with violent crime (no evidence of this existed). Harry Aslinger, who was the U.S. Commissioner of Narcotics, reported in 1931 that marijuana use was not a problem. However, in a Congressional hearing in 1937, Aslinger reported that marijuana trafficking had increased at such an alarming rate "that it has come to be the cause for the greatest national concern" (Ray and Ksir, 2002). By this time, newspaper and magazine reports of marijuana had burgeoned to include, not only violent crimes being committed, but also police interviews stating as much (Ray and Ksir, 2002). These reports were believed by the public but, in fact, there was no evidence provided to support their validity. This concern led to the passage of the Marijuana Tax Act in 1937. This act required the registration and taxation of those importing, buying, or selling marijuana, but did not make the possession of marijuana illegal (Ray and Ksir, 2002).

Ephedra

In 1927, the U.S. medical community began to use ephedrine, which is the active ingredient in ma haung, to open bronchial passages in patients with asthma. As the supplies of *Ephedra vulgaris* began to dwindle, pharmaceutical companies began to search for a synthetic alternative. Amphetamine was first synthesized in 1887, but because there was very little interest in it, the substance went unnoticed until it became the alternative to ephedrine (Feldman et al., 1997). By the 1930s, all the major effects of amphetamine were known. While researching the effects, it was discovered that amphetamines could awaken dogs that were under anesthesia. This discovery led to the use of amphetamines, in pill form, to treat narcolepsy (Feldman et al., 1997). Amphetamines were also rumored to have been used in Japan, Britain, Germany, and the U.S. during World War II (Brecher 1972; Lovett, 1994; Feldman et al., 1997). U.S. and Japanese army personnel are said to have used amphetamines to stay awake and alert while assigned to especially long periods on duty (Feldman et al., 1997). Because of the use of amphetamines by Japanese soldiers, Japan "suffered a serious methamphetamine problem during early postwar years" (Suwaki, 1991).

Amphetamine use became so common that college students in the 1950s and 1960s used amphetamines to stay awake all night to study for exams. Long-haul truckers named their routes after how much amphetamine was needed to make the trip. To get halfway across the U.S., truckers used "St. Louie," and for a transcontinental truck run, "West Coast turnabouts" were used (Feldman et al., 1997).

In the 1960s, California users of amphetamine began using speedballs, which are a combination of amphetamine and heroin taken intravenously. Physicians of the Haight-Ashbury Free Clinic in San Francisco tried to warn the public of the dangers of amphetamines by coining the term "speed kills." Dr. D. Smith of the Haight-Ashbury Free Clinic said:

> In the 1970s the Haight-Ashbury area, of San Francisco, turned into one of the most violent areas of the city. It was a direct result of the amphetamine epidemic. In addition, we saw a great deal of amphetamine psychosis,

from high doses of amphetamine producing paranoia, auditory, and visual hallucinations. We started getting a feel that the medical and the psychiatric system did not know how to handle drug epidemics. For example, I was also running the alcohol and drug abuse-screening unit at San Francisco General Hospital where with the diagnosis of paranoid schizophrenia you treat with long-term psychotropic medication. With amphetamine psychosis you detoxify them and use a short-term course of psychotropic medication and get them into recovery.

By the 1980s, amphetamine use dropped because of increased control of its legal manufacture, which, however, led to an increase in the illegal manufacture of methamphetamine. In the 1980s, youth in Hawaii reported smoking methamphetamine and it soon spread to California (Ray and Ksir, 2002). Long-term users in Hawaii have reported to these authors that smokeable methamphetamine dates from at least 1979 in Nanakuli, Oahu.

There are different types of methamphetamine. "Crank" refers to methamphetamine sulfate and has been in use since the 1960s. "Crystal" refers to methamphetamine hydrochloride (Ray and Ksir, 2002), and "ice" is a colorless and odorless concentration of methamphetamine. Ice is manufactured from legally obtained chemicals and is cheaper than crack cocaine. Doweiko suggests that there is historical evidence that ice was brought to Hawaii from Japan by army troops during World War II. The use of ice went unnoticed until the West Coast news media began to report it in the 1970s; a newspaper article quoted an unnamed San Diego police officer who stated that ice was being used in Hawaii.

The Spread of Methamphetamine Use in the U.S.

After the withdrawal of Desoxyn and methedrine from the pharmaceutical market, illicit methamphetamine laboratories emerged in San Francisco late in 1962. Motorcycle gangs took over the manufacture and distribution of methamphetamine in the mid-1960s spreading it north and south along the Pacific Coast. By the 1970s the use of methamphetamine had spread from the blue-collar workers to include college students, young professionals, minorities, and women.

By the 1980s intensified law enforcement efforts that targeted the biker subculture, together with new, easier ways of producing methamphetamine, caused the production and distribution to move to the San Diego area. With the move to San Diego, Mexican traffickers became involved in the manufacture and distribution. Large amounts of the illicitly produced methamphetamine and precursor chemicals were smuggled in from Mexico to California, and distributed not only to the traditional market, but also to the southwestern and midwestern states (Anglin et al., 2000).

Hawaii and Ice

During the 1980s there was a surge in Hawaii of methamphetamine use when a smokeable, highly pure form of D-MA-hydrochloride (ice) became available, imported from Far East sources in the Philippines, Japan, Korea, and Taiwan (Laidler and Morgan, 1997). During the 1990s use of ice in the Hawaiian Islands became rampant. The distribution of methamphetamine in Hawaii was gradually dominated by Mexico- and California-based trafficking organizations. These crime groups are supplemented in Hawaii by extended kinship networks, which sometimes include whole families or neighborhoods (Laidler and Morgan, 1997).

> The use of ice in Honolulu had led to particularly serious physical and psychological problems and significant social disruption in poor working communities where it replaced marijuana which had become scarce and expensive due to eradication policies (NIDA, 1991–1994, summary).

There are thought to be several influences on the tremendous growth of ice in Honolulu after 1987. Residents were pushed away from marijuana, their staple drug of choice, and pulled toward ice by a well-organized marketing campaign by Asian distributors. Also, the overwhelming drug of choice, marijuana, which had been grown and used throughout the islands for many years, became the target of a government eradication campaign. This drove up prices and left locals without their customary smoke. Also very important, many locals derived either part of or their entire livelihood from marijuana production. Thus, when a new, easy-to-use smokeable product entered the market, one that at first seemed nonthreatening to youthful novitiates, i.e., ice, it was readily accepted. Initial users were likely to think of it as a substitute of sorts for marijuana (NIDA, 1991–1994, p. 22). As one respondent reported:

> The ice use on the Waianae coast is greater than a lot of other places in the state. This is like a central distribution center for ice. It's a known fact among the drug

addicts and users on the island. It's [ice] easier to get than marijuana. It's not much more expensive than marijuana either. The amount of people here that use ice is increasing because people who couldn't find marijuana were starting to find ice easier. Plenty of guys I know started using ice because they can't get marijuana. I'd rather see them smoking marijuana because they were mellow, nice people. On ice, they change into robbing houses and carrying guns in less than one month (NIDA, 1991–1994, p. 123).

Methamphetamine continues to be a major problem in Hawaii. Methamphetamine is readily available, with the majority of it converted into ice before it is distributed. In the past few years, ice-related crimes have increased as the drug has increased in popularity and availability. The Arrestee Drug Abuse Monitoring Program in 2001 revealed that 35.9% of males arrested from January to September 2001 tested positive for methamphetamine abuse. Further tests showed arrested males and females in Honolulu tested positive for methamphetamine at a higher rate than for marijuana (28.8%) and for cocaine (11.2%). Among 37 metropolitan areas, Honolulu has the highest percentage of arrested males testing positive for methamphetamine, according to a report from the U.S. Department of Justice. No other city approached 30%. Cities participating in the survey ranged from New York City and Philadelphia to San Diego and Seattle. "The connection between property and violent crimes and ice comes up time and time again. Some of the people we interviewed said crystal meth destroyed their lives," said Major Darryl Perry, Honolulu Police Department Narcotics/Vice Division. Three fourths of the Honolulu Police Department's Narcotics/Vice Division resources go to narcotics investigations dealing primarily with ice, Perry said (*Honolulu Star-Bulletin*, June 12, 2002).

Kat Brady, Community Alliance on Prisons coordinator, believes marijuana eradication efforts forced drug users to turn to methamphetamine. "I think that Green Harvest has had a devastating effect on Hawaii," she said. Brady praises the law approved this year (2002) that includes ice users in a program to send nonviolent, first-time offenders to drug treatment instead of prison (*Honolulu Star-Bulletin*, June 12, 2002).

Pound quantities of crystal methamphetamine arrive in Hawaii from the southwest regions of the U.S., smuggled by couriers and by private post such as FedEx and DHL. Local addicts can purchase ice from a variety of sources; dealers are abundant throughout the state. Most of the methamphetamine labs that are seized in Hawaii are capable of producing ounce quantities. In 2001, there were 30.0 kg of methamphetamine seized in the State of Hawaii by Drug Enforcement Agency (DEA) agents, and only 7.9 kg of marijuana seized (U.S. DEA, 2002).

Current Trends

Methamphetamine is no longer just a big-city problem. Methamphetamine has become the most dangerous drug of small-town America. Methamphetamine is being made and distributed in some of the country's most rural areas. Children 12 to 14 years old who live in smaller towns are 104% more likely to use methamphetamine than those who live in larger cities. One of the reasons that methamphetamine is such a threat in rural areas is because it is easy and cheap to make. Drugs that can be bought over the counter at local stores are mixed with common ingredients to make methamphetamine. Small labs to cook the drug can be set up in kitchens, on countertops, in garages, or just about anyplace. Although superlabs with sophisticated traffickers still supply the majority of methamphetamine, these smaller tabletop labs have increased exponentially in the last decade, setting an alarming trend. More than 20% of the methamphetamine labs seized in 2001 had children present (U.S. DEA, 2002).

Use is increasing among men who have sex with men and use other drugs, young adults who attend "raves" or go to private clubs, homeless and runaway youth, commercial sex workers, members of motorcycle gangs, and people in occupations that demand long hours, mental alertness, and physical endurance. Emerging evidence indicates that users increasingly are administering methamphetamine intravenously. Injecting the drug puts the user at increased risk of contracting HIV/AIDS, hepatitis, and other infectious diseases (NIDA, 1999).

Amphetamine treatment admissions are on the rise. In 1993, amphetamine treatment rates were high in California, Oregon, and Nevada. By 1999, high treatment admission rates were reported in most states west of the Mississippi. Methamphetamine accounted for 94% of all amphetamine treatment admissions reported to the Treatment Episode Data Set (TEDS) in 1999. In 1993, the admission rate for primary methamphetamine abuse was 14 admissions per 100,000 in the U.S. age 12 or older. In 1996, the admission rate for methamphetamine abuse was 24 per 100,000 age 12 and older in the U.S. In 1999, the admission rate for methamphetamine abuse was 32 per 100,000 age 12 and older in the U.S.(DASIS, 2001).

In the Drug Abuse Warning Network (DAWN) 2002 report on emergency department (ED) visits related to the abuse of club drugs, methamphetamine accounted for the largest share of ED mentions. The highest rate of cases of ED visits involving methamphetamine was found in patients age 26 to 29.

DAWN estimated almost 15,000 mentions of methamphetamine visits. The term *club drugs* comes from the association with raves and dance clubs (DAWN, 2002).

During 1999, 4.3% of the U.S. population reported trying methamphetamine at least once. The highest rate of methamphetamine use was among the 18 to 25 age group, with 5.3% of them reporting lifetime use during 1999. In the age group between 12 and 17, 1.4% reported trying methamphetamine, and for those 26 and over lifetime use of methamphetamine was 4.5%.

In 2000 among high school seniors 7.9% had tried methamphetamine in their lifetime (down from 8.3% in 1999). Lifetime use among 8th and 10th graders was 4.2 and 6.9%, respectively. Also in 2000 4.3% of high school seniors had used methamphetamine in the last year and 1.9% had used in the past month (Hawaii Conference on Methamphetamine "ICE" Epidemic, 2002).

References

Anglin, D., Burke, C., Perrochet, B., Stamper, E., and Dawud-Noursi, S. (2000). History of the methamphetamine problem. *J. Psychoactive Drugs*, 32(2), 138–139.

Brecher, E.M. (1972). *Licit and Illicit Drugs*. Boston: Little Brown.

Brethen, P. and Stimsom, J. (2002). Hawaii Conference on Methamphetamine "ICE" Epidemic.

Byck, R. (1987). Cocaine use and research: three histories. In S. Fisher, A. Rashkin, and E.H. Unlenhuth, Eds., *Cocaine: Clinical and Behavioral Aspects*. New York: Oxford University Press.

DASIS (2001). Drug and Alcohol Services Information System, Nov. 16.

DAWN (2002). Report. Drug Abuse Warning Network, Oct.

Doweiko, H.E. (1999). *Concepts of Chemical Dependency*. Pacific Grove, CA: Brooks/Cole.

Elliot, F.A. (1992). Violence. *Arch. Neuro.*, 49, 595–603.

Feldman, R.S., Meyer, J.S., and Quenzer, L.F. (1997). *Principles of Neuropsychopharmacology*. Sunderland, MA: Sinauer Associates, Inc.

Graedon, J. and Graedon, T. (1991). *Graedon's Best Medicine*. New York: Bantam Books.

Grinspoon, L. and Bakalar, J.B. (1992). Marijuana. In L.H Lowinson, P. Ruiz, R.B. Miliman, and J.G. Langrod, Eds., *Substance Abuse: A Comprehensive Textbook*, 2nd ed. Baltimore, MD: Williams & Wilkins.

Grinspoon, L. and Bakalar, J.B. (1993). *Marijuana: The Forgotten Medicine*. New Haven, CT: Yale University Press.

Grinspoon, L. and Bakalar, J.B (1995). Marijuana as medicine. *J. Am. Med. Assoc.*, 273, 1875–1876.

Honolulu Star-Bulletin. (2002). Arrested males on "ice" top 35%, Honolulu outpaces 36 other big cities in its incidence of "ice" use. Wednesday, June 12.

Karch, S.B. (1996). *The Pathology of Drug Abuse*, 2nd ed. Boca Raton, FL: CRC Press.

Laidler, K. and Morgan, P. (1997). Kinship and the community; the ice crisis in Hawaii. In H. Klee, Ed., *Amphetamines Misuse; International Perspectives on Current Trends*. Reading U.K.: Harwood International.

Lingeman, R.R. (1974). *Drugs from A to Z: A Dictionary.* New York: McGraw-Hill.

Lovett, A.R. (1994, May 5). Wired in California. *Rolling Stone*, 39–40.

Mann, J. (1994). *Murder, Magic and Medicine.* New York: Oxford University Press.

NIDA (1991–1994). National Institute on Drug Abuse Final Report: Ice and Other Methamphetamines Use; An Exploratory Study, summary and p. 22, p. 125.

NIDA (1999). Methamphetamine Abuse Alert. *National Institute on Drug Abuse Notes*, 13(6).

Ray, O. and Ksir, C. (2002). *Drugs Society and Human Behavior*, 9th ed. New York: McGraw-Hill.

Snyder, S. (1970). *Uses of Marijuana*, New York: Oxford University Press.

Suwaki, H. (1991). Methamphetamine abuse in Japan. *NIDA Res. Monogr.*, 115, 84–98.

Terry, C.E. and Pellens, M. (1928). *The Opium Problem.* Bureau of Social Hygiene of New York.

U.S. DEA (2002). Drug Enforcement Administration Briefs and Background, Drug and Drug Abuse, State Factsheet, Hawaii. Available at www.usdoj.gov/dea/pubs/states/hawaii.html.

Wadler, G.I. (1994). Drug use update. *Med. Clin. North Am.*, 78(2), 439–455.

Epidemiology

2

HAROLD V. HALL
SANDRA B. MCPHERSON
STUART W. TWEMLOW
ERROL YUDKO

Methamphetamine abuse is fast becoming ubiquitous. Various studies by the United Nations show that methamphetamine is consumed in almost every region of the world, is fast outstripping cocaine and heroin as the drug of choice, and is the single most frequently reported illicitly manufactured drug (United Nations, 1997). Since the mid-1980s, the world in general and the Pacific region in particular have experienced a huge increase in methamphetamine abuse, with nine times the quantity seized in 1993 as was seized in 1978 (United Nations, 1997). In the U.S., as of 1990, an estimated 5.2 million persons 12 years of age and older reported using methamphetamine at least once (National Household Survey on Drug Abuse, 1991). In 1991, 7% of respondents in a large survey reported using methamphetamine at least once, with the highest use in the 18- to 25-year-old age group (Kaplan et al., 1994).

U.S. Department of Justice statistics show that, for the period from 1990 to 1996, 64% of high school seniors could easily obtain methamphetamine. Step-by-step instructions to manufacture methamphetamine are on the Internet. Nearly half of all methamphetamine users will develop cardiovascular symptoms, with the percentage higher in chronic abusers (Lynch and House, 1992; Beebe and Walley, 1995). One third of heavy users will develop bizarre, frankly psychotic behavior and will suffer hallucinations (Griffith, Cavanaugh, and Oats, 1969; Bell, 1973). As illustrated in Figure 2.1, brain deterioration in heavy users may continue for months after abstinence. Psychosis can occur after only one dose (Ando et al., 1986). Ando et al. observed signs in individuals they evaluated that are strongly suggestive of brain damage after a single usage.

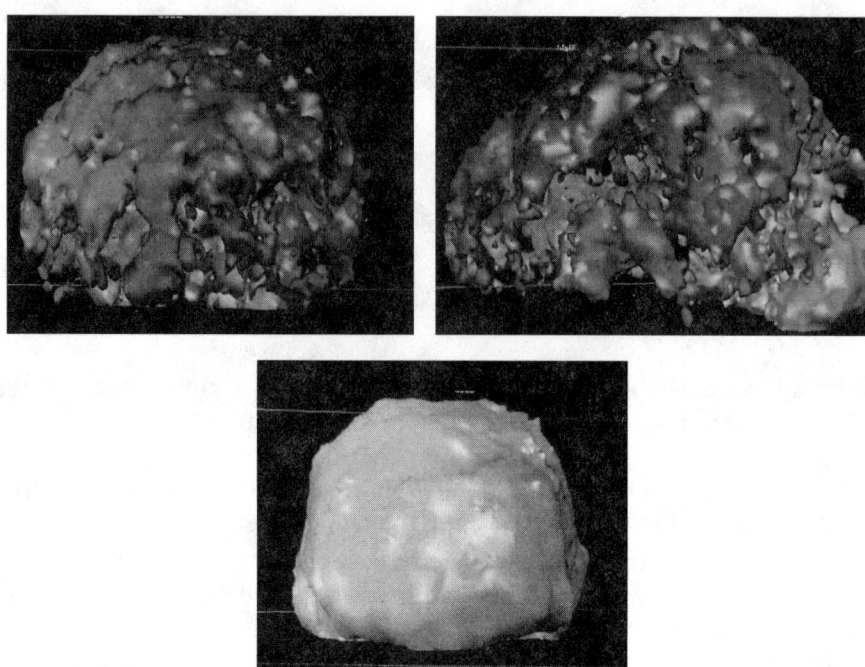

Figure 2.1 Top left: frontal view of brain of young, adult male. No more "ice" use but progressive damage four months later (March 1996). Top right: lateral view of same individual. Bottom: normal brain of young adult male. (Scans courtesy of Queen's Medical Center, Honolulu, Hawaii.)

References

Ando, K., Hironaka, N., and Yanagita, T. (1986). Psychotic manifestations in amphetamine abuse — experimental study on the mechanism of psychotic recurrence. *Psychopharmacol. Bull.*, 22(3), 763–767.

Beebe, D.K. and Walley, E. (1995). Smokeable methamphetamine ("ice"): an old drug in a different form. *Am. Fam. Phys.*, 51(2), 449–453.

Bell, D.S. (1973). The experimental reproduction of amphetamine psychosis. *Arch. Gen. Psych.*, 29, 35–40.

Griffith, J.D., Cavanaugh, J., and Oats, J. (1969). Schizophrenic psychosis induced by large dose administration of diamphetamine. *J. Psychadelic Drugs*, 2, 42–48.

Kaplan, H.I., Sadock, B.J., and Grebb, J.A. (1994). *Synopsis of Psychiatry*, 7th ed. Baltimore: Williams & Wilkins.

Lynch, J. and House, M.A. (1992). Cardiovascular effects of methamphetamine. *J. Cardiovasc. Nurs.*, 6(2), 12–18).

National Household Survey on Drug Abuse. (1995). Reported in Subcommittee on Crime of the Committee on the Judiciary, House of Representatives, 104th Congress, First Session, October 26, 1995 (Serial No. 49), Rising Scourge of Methamphetamine in America.

State v. Monte Louis Young, First Circuit Court, Cr. No. 97–1 1 94 (May 7, 1998).

United Nations (1997). Drug Control Programme.

Methamphetamine and the Middle East

3

SANDRA B. McPHERSON
FARSHID AFSARIFARD

Introduction

Although the focus of this book is forensic applications associated with methamphetamine abuse in the U.S., the substance is produced and marketed globally. Accordingly, it is appropriate to consider issues relating to international levels of abuse, as well as to appreciate the interweaving of local, national, international, political, and ethnic factors that play a role in the spread of methamphetamine.

Both authors of this chapter have had experience in the Middle Eastern and Northern African region. Farshid Afsarifard, born and raised in Iran, has lived in the U.S. since 1976, and recently returned to Iran to provide mental health and substance abuse education to government and mental health institutions in that country. Sandra McPherson has spent time in Gaza, the West Bank, Israel, and Egypt, evaluating health-related issues from a human rights perspective, with an emphasis on mental health and substance abuse and on the treatment programs established to serve the Palestinians in 1990.

Although there are strong prohibitions against alcohol and drug use in the Islamic world and those areas influenced by the traditional force of that religion, problems related to substance abuse have never been unknown and, in fact, have shown significant increases in recent years, especially from the 1960s forward. Furthermore, although the long-standing link between the production of heroin and narcotics in Central Asia and their export to the West has been known as a prime factor in some of the earliest identified serious drug abuse problems in the U.S., the ongoing global aspect of drug production, drug trade, and drug use in the case of methamphetamine has not been adequately appreciated. The constituent parts of methamphetamine have been tracked in transit to and from the U.S. and abroad. Ecstasy abuse, in particular, is a phenomenon that has spread throughout the world (United Nations, 2000; see also Seper, 2002; Trickey and Kennedy, 2002).

Whenever there is a global trade in any substance, licit or illicit, political as well as social implications intertwine. The situation with methamphetamine is no exception. Problems involving methamphetamine use of the type detailed throughout this book have been noted in Thailand, Spain, Germany, Canada, the U.K., Australia, the Czech Republic, Iran, Palestine, Israel, India, and Egypt, among others. A search of major news releases for 2000 to 2002 produced 196 articles detailing methamphetamine-related events in countries throughout the world (see "Battle against ecstasy," 2001; Sot, 2001; Tremlett, 2001; "Woman nabbed," 2001; Chu, 2002; Russo, 2002). Ecstasy is viewed as a global trade commodity. Politically, the emergent issue of terrorism and its link to drugs, which was initially spotlighted in the U.S. press as a way terrorist organizations in the Middle East are funded, is becoming recognized as having much more complex sociopolitical aspects (see especially articles by Bruce, 2002; Klein, 2002; Krikorian, 2002; Solomon, 2002). Drug rings that have been identified as Israeli organized crime based operate out of a country generally viewed as an ally of the U.S. ("Israelis said at head," May 3, 2001). The universality of the drug trade then allows competing national and political interests to selectively perceive their opponents as supporting the use of drugs as a way to engage in hostile interventions in the ongoing struggle.

Interestingly, a peace initiative in Gaza and the Territories involved a meeting of Israeli and Palestinian addictions and mental health specialists. Supported by the U.S. government, the conference sought more adequate programs of intervention. Although it was marred by difficulties with Israeli regulations, which initially hampered attendance, the conference resulted in reduction of misperceptions and the establishment of a more adequate basis for treatment, as well as mutual recognition of the problems that the contemporary drug trade was creating for both peoples (Isralowitz et al., 2001). *Ha'aretz* has documented, for example, the problems of ecstasy in Israeli society with its association to violent criminal acts, including gang rape ("A long night of horror," May 11, 2001; "Four charged with gang rape," May 17, 2001).

Geopolitical Interconnections

Current information available through government and other sources clearly illustrates that methamphetamine, in common with other drugs, is embedded in a complex multilevel international set of factors and connections. In effect, there are multiplex networks that disseminate information about illicit drugs and facilitate the distribution and trade in the substances (see, for example, "War on Drugs," January 23, 2001). This network has been facilitated by existing connections and routes established during the colonial period of the 1700s and 1800s and also reflects current competing or converging interests of governments and criminal organizations (United Nations, 2000).

One of the precursors of today's methamphetamine distribution network was the poppy trade out of Iran, Afghanistan, and Pakistan. The primary conduit to Europe and the U.S. was through Turkey, which remains to this day a preferred route to move heroin and hashish/cannabis (United Nations, 2000). It is hypothesized that these connections are no longer one-way, but rather represent a complex of international highways. Thus, although methamphetamine in its various forms is created in laboratories throughout the world, most ecstasy has been produced in the Netherlands and secondarily in Belgium and then shipped elsewhere. The spread of ecstasy into Southeast Asia has followed some of the original European colonialization routes and has been facilitated primarily by Israeli criminal organizations. In Western and Eastern Europe, the criminal organizations primarily responsible for distribution and trade have been Russian (United Nations, 2000).

Ecstasy as a form of methamphetamine has an interesting history in and of itself. It was first created in Germany in 1912 for use as an appetite suppressant. It was subsequently discovered by psychotherapy practitioners in the U.S. and seen as a facilitator of that process, at least for a short while. However, by 1988, it had become a Schedule I controlled substance. Even earlier, in 1977, it had been so classified in the U.K. Ecstasy has consistently been misrepresented as a drug that has no serious physical impacts, essentially an innocuous recreational substance. Its availability serendipitously co-occurred with the rise of so-called acid house and techno music and a young people's fad of staying up all night and dancing. That fad, incidentally, began on the Spanish island of Ibiza, also known as XTC Island, and thus the name of the drug. In 1988, the "summer of love" unfolded in the U.K. with young people thronging to music and laser light parties in fields and warehouses. Ecstasy was the primary enhancer and maintainer of the frenetic activity (United Nations, 2000).

A study of Turkey's place in the general international drug trade is nicely illustrative of the way various interests are addressed and is certainly similar to the situation in South America. Thus, criminally based organizations, which have facilitated the movement of drugs through Turkey since the days of the Afghanistan/Pakistani/Iran Triangle, are well established and covertly supportive of and supported by the Turkish government. Assassination of human rights activists and other persons critical of the government is part of the *quid pro quo* that takes place, and it is not uncommon for people with drug connections to be publicly overt about their occupations or identity. The government has granted private armies connected to these organizations control of whole regions (United Nations, 2000). If, as is likely, the same conduits that send drugs from Central Asia to the West now also facilitate the movement of ecstasy from Western Europe into Iran, a certain irony but a practical reality is illustrated.

The continuation of interwoven history, geography, and politics is also illustrated in the immediate Turkish situation. Turkey, which historically had some economic dependence on the drug trade, is now even more committed to that source of revenue as a consequence of the Gulf War of 1991. That war closed Turkey's access to Iraqi oil, with the result that there was an immediate and ongoing increment in the degree to which the government was supportive of the drug trade. Interestingly, just as the U.S. and Western Europe have not significantly pressured Turkey to end its persecution of the Kurds and the destruction of their villages, they have taken relatively little notice of the enhanced Turkish activity facilitating the drug trade (United Nations, 2000).

Finally, there is a clear link established between the operation of terrorist organizations and the ongoing drug trade operations. Given the current world situation and the multinational efforts to identify and control terrorist groups, hidden money sources have become extremely desirable. Drug money is one such hidden source. Accordingly, drug ring financing of terrorist groups has been extensively documented (see, among others, Klein, 2002; Roberts and Marin, 2002; Solomon, 2002).

Government Complicity as a Factor

It is reasonable to understand that while drugs have always exercised a certain controlling influence outstripping the desires of societies to end their abuse by virtue of addictive potentials of human beings, it also needs to be understood that the profit motive has never been far from the drug dealer's operations. That statement can be validated in terms of legitimate as well as nonlegitimate drug operations. Furthermore, in the case of nonlegitimate operations, some degree of covert or overt government complicity becomes an issue. Thus, the behavior of the Turkish regime is an obvious example of significant government support for drug-related operations that have international implications. Similarly, the operations in Colombia have been closely tied to more legitimate political levels. Even Israel has only recently made money-laundering illegal in drug-related cases (United Nations, 2000). Given that for some years a major source of the trafficking and delivery systems has been Israeli-based criminal organizations, the lack of concern for reducing the profit level through forfeiture is at least an omission of significance. In other words, even if not intended, Israel became in fact a hidden support for the trade.

In general, countries in the Middle East have deemed any substance involvement, including alcohol, illegal and immoral. Nonetheless, in these same nations, upper-status persons engage in such behavior and rarely suffer legal consequences. In addition to selective enforcement, it can be hypothesized that highly authority-driven government systems may derive a benefit from drug use in their populations. With the development of computer technology, there is easy access to major sources of nongovernment-approved information. Having large segments of the younger and more-likely-to-rebel population self-absorbed and using drugs may be viewed as a desirable way to eliminate challenges to the power base. Such a strategy might underlie differential enforcement and also may be reflected in the lack of extensive support for substance abuse treatment programs.

Business Aspects: Ecstasy as a Case in Point

Production costs for ecstasy (or MDMA) vs. revenues obtained represents an extremely favorable ratio. The history, production, and use patterns of ecstasy as they have occurred across the world scene illustrate effective business operations. The substance moved from an intended therapeutic drug to become a recreational drug. Controls were attempted in U.S. and Western Europe by labeling it a controlled substance and making possession and use illegal. Consistent with the experience of Prohibition, Ecstasy's popularity rose dramatically starting in the late 1980s and increasing throughout the 1990s as a favorable climate of youthful extremism, popular music, and erroneous belief systems combined to make a ready market for a drug whose profit margin was excellent. Throughout Europe ecstasy has been effectively "advertised" as a harmless drug. It is often combined with other drugs to create a variety of effects (notably cocaine and alcohol). Based on seizure patterns, by 1999, there was a serious increase in its use and it had become the second most commonly abused drug (after forms of cannabis) in the European market. Large-scale producers created pills imprinted with pop logos such as smiley faces and car brand signs, all of which were consistent with the notion that the pill was relatively harmless. These makers would also customize logos for large orders (United Nations, 2000). The described business patterns are those well known to any legitimate marketing and production organization.

Cultural Factors and Treatment Implications

Historically, the Arab and Islamic cultures have had a more advanced view of mental health issues in general than was found in Western practice and literature. As early as 1900 B.C.E., original papyri included discussions of mental illness as a somatic phenomenon (of course, hysteria was considered the effect of an inappropriately wandering uterus, but that was not particularly different from some of the much later notions in the Western world as well; methods of intervention, although logically based in their theory and having no true physiologic accuracy, would nonetheless have been fairly successful as hypnotic/suggestion interventions). The Koran defines madness using words that imply supernatural spirits, both good and bad, and emphasizes the importance of respect. Furthermore, the prophets were often viewed as having conditions that were characterized by mental health symptoms of modern parlance but which were considered to make them able to properly innovate and help society. Persons seeking religious ecstasy, not to be confused with the drug, often manifested symptoms that were psychotic-like, a phenomenon not dissimilar from the history of certain religious groups in the 1800s in the U.S. and, prior to that, during medieval times. However, the Islamic explanation for mental illness has consistently emphasized the unity of body and psyche, thus anticipating the very contemporary bio/psycho/social approach to both mental health and substance abuse (Okasha, 1999).

Some specifics regarding different countries may be illustrative of the widespread problems that are now occurring throughout the world. Most recently, the second author received a phone call from one of the Iranian mental health professionals with whom he maintains contact. This psychiatrist asked whether there was anything known about methamphetamine because it appeared in his practice that it was becoming a drug of choice among upper-class and upper-middle-class people. (Users were identifying it as harmless. The inquirer was uncertain of its negative potentials.)

The Iranian government has published reports indicating that there are 3 million addicts and alcoholics in the country. However, unofficial estimates are much higher, suggesting that close to 10% of the population of 60 million is addicted. Given that two thirds of the Iranian population is under the age of 30, these figures would indicate that drug use is epidemic among the youth (see also "Iran faces," 2001). In spite of the strong religious prohibitions against such indulgence, the author has observed that in most major cities in Iran the street level of drug trafficking is rampant and obvious. It is difficult to pass a street corner without being propositioned to purchase drugs. Although there are major economic problems related to very high unemployment and high inflation, drug cost has remained inexpensive. Alcohol that is manufactured illegally (in bootleg settings) is also rather inexpensive (however, brand name liquor is quite costly).

Interestingly, it is known that alcohol use in the Gulf countries is more problematic than it is in Egypt where the Islamic link to governmental control is far weaker (Okasha, 1996). From the standpoint of the U.S., of course, there was the infamous Iran Contra scandal that involved illegal international trades in arms, money, and influence with complex interrelationships to drug trafficking in spite of ongoing antidrug policies (Hartung, 1994).

Comparative Drug Use Patterns

Okasha (1999) indicated that the 1980s saw an increase in the abuse of heroin and narcotics in the Middle East. In addition, contemporary reports based on seizure patterns and other data support the presence of a strong methamphetamine use trend occurring throughout the 1990s in all parts of the world. Ecstasy in particular has been at the forefront of increased use (United Nations, 2000).

A potent factor in use patterns involves intercultural experience. For example, persons from North Africa and the Middle East living in Rome who became involved in drug use and drug treatment showed multiple use patterns, including injection habits that led to HIV seropositivity. The duration of their residence in Rome was a significant factor in drug use patterns (Spizzichino et al., 1995).

Treatment Approaches

Addiction treatment in Iran, as observed by the second author, is becoming more popular. However, there is emphasis on the physical aspects of treatment as overseen by a physician, usually a psychiatrist, including detoxification and titration of the addict from the drug of choice. Opiates are still the most common substances abused, and often longer-acting opiates are used for the treatment process and then not discontinued, thus creating an ongoing use picture. The practice has become a major source of income for some physicians who thus have a major incentive to continue to operate in that fashion. To the extent that a psychosocial aspect is included, a 12-step recovery model similar to that found in the U.S. is in place. Addicts and alcoholics usually enter treatment either due to major medical consequences or extreme family situations. Social pressures that often result in intervention in the U.S. are not commonly noted. Legal problems and being caught by authorities for alcohol- and drug-related offenses are dealt with by the courts and there is no direct connection between treatment and the judicial system.

In Egypt, as the mental health system has developed and modernized, the availability of treatment for drug abuse as well as mental health problems has become much more adequate in the cities. There are modern facilities and medical and nursing schools. However, most people in these regions remain more comfortable with either traditional healers or with trying to cope themselves with aberrant behavior among relatives. There are both shame and religious or cultural prohibitions against modern forms of psychotherapy, for example. Interventions need to be revised and developed that were culturally consistent, to be at all acceptable to identified patients. Following acute care in Egypt, it was even more difficult to gain acceptance for aftercare. In the cities, there were aftercare facilities but they were sparse if available and rarely used outside the more sophisticated urban settings. Obviously, from the standpoint of the treatment of drug abuse, the resistance of the population and the lack of facilities for those who would accept treatment considerably impact the long-range potential for treatment effectiveness (Okasha, 1999).

Observations by the first author in 1990 in Gaza and the West Bank indicated that most of the mental health professionals were Western trained, usually U.S., but also U.K., and returned to their homeland to provide service. Cultural sensitivities, if observed, could facilitate therapeutic interventions. Thus, a woman could be treated for depression or related problems only if she came for treatment with her mother-in-law, or possibly if her mother-in-law came for the information necessary to treat the daughter-in-law. The joint project described above mounted by Israel and Palestine from 1997 to 1999, which involved support for research on prevalence and development of treatment options, indicated not only the achievement of an unusual peace initiative, but also the accessibility of the populations involved to treatment when it was proposed under culturally sound conditions (Isralowitz et al., 2001).

Conclusion

In this short exposition, some important principles have been developed that are integral to an understanding of methamphetamine as a current and increasingly important drug of abuse in the Middle East.

- Methamphetamine use is a global phenomenon.
- Methamphetamine use is supported by pop culture and developmental (adolescent) vulnerability.
- Methamphetamine use is facilitated by propagandistic and misleading marketing.
- Methamphetamine use is maintained by individual addictive potentials.
- Methamphetamine use serves competing and cooperative power interests.

Consistently, the most effective approaches to dealing with methamphetamine abuse will need to engage not only modern treatment programming appropriately adapted to varying cultural contexts, but also a prevention strategy that considers multiple world interests and interrelationships. The only reasonable context for such prevention programming is one of international organization, respect, cooperation, and an end to unilateralism.

References

Battle against ecstasy. (2001). *Ha'aretz* (Israel), March 2.

Bruce, I. (2002). Bombers backed by U.S. drug ring; profits of addiction sent to Middle East groups. *The Herald* (Glasgow), September 3, p. 14.

Chu, L. (2002). New drug from Thailand seeping into West Coast communities. *Associated Press Worldstream*, October 26.

Four charged with gang rape of teen in Rishon (2001). *Ha'aretz* (Israel), May 17.

Hartung, W.D. (1994). *And Weapons for All.* New York: HarperCollins.

Iran faces growing drug problem (2001). *Agence France Presse*, Vienna, February 21.

Israelis said at head of 4-nation drug ring (2001). *Ha'aretz* (Israel), May 3.

Isralowitz, R., Sussman, G., Afifi, M., Rawson, R., Babor, T., and Monteiro, M. (2001). Substance abuse policy and peace in the Middle East: a Palestinian and Israeli partnership. *Addiction*, 96, 973–980.

Klein, R. (2002) Terrorists cash in on drug trade. *The Times Educational Supplement*, June 21, p. 4.

Krikorian, G. (2002). Terrorists received drug money, U.S. says. *Los Angeles Times*, May 10, p. 22.

A long night of horror in the grove (2001). *Ha'aretz* (Israel), May 11.

Okasha, A. (1996). Combat and management of drug abuse: means and challenges. An Egyptian perspective. Plenary Lecture to the First International Conference on Addiction and Drug Dependence, Cairo, March.

Okasha, A. (1999). Mental health in the Middle East: an Egyptian perspective. *Clin. Psychol. Rev.*, 19(8), 917–933.

Roberts, J. and Marin, C. (2002). Drug ring's profits may be linked to terrorism. *CBS News Transcripts, CBS Evening News*, January 10. New York: CBS.

Russo, R. (2002, January 11). Canada feeding speed habit; U.S. drug cops say lax laws make Canada top supplier of chemical for methamphetamine. *The Hamilton Spectator*, January 11, p. B1.

Seper, J. (2002). DEA takes down 2 major meth rings; agency probes for link with terrorists. *The Washington Times*, January 11, p. A8.

Solomon, J. (2002). DEA officials say profits from illegal drug rings in the U.S. linked to terrorist groups. *Chattanooga Times/Chattanooga Free Press*, September 2, p. A-1.

Sot, M. (2001). Myanmar-run methamphetamine lab found on Thai side of border. *Associated Press Worldstream*, September 9.

Spizzichino, L., Gattari, P., Zaccarelli, M., Casella, P., Valenzi, C., and Rezza, G. (1995). HIV infection among injecting drug users from North Africa and the Middle East living in Rome. *Addiction Res.*, 3(1), 57–62.

Tremlett, G. (2001). Spanish drug arrest leads police to Middle East Mafia: investigation into lucrative global ecstasy trade claims a dramatic breakthrough. *The Guardian* (London), August 21, p. 9.

Trickey, M. and Kennedy, M. (2002). Canada fuels U.S. market for drugs: lax laws fail to track supplies of key chemical in 'speed.' *The Ottawa Citizen*, January 11.

United Nations (2000). UN World Report on Drugs.

U.S. drug ring tied to aid for Hezbollah (2002). *The New York Times*, September 3, p. A-16.

War on drugs (2001). *Nottingham Evening Post*, January 23, pp. 6–7.

Woman nabbed for possessing ecstasy (2001). *The Jakarta Post*, July 28.

MDMA

4

ERROL YUDKO

(±)3,4-Methylenedioxymethamphetamine (MDMA, "Ecstasy," E, Adam, X, XTC) is a methamphetamine analogue. It has hallucinogenic, psychostimulant, and multiple behavior-altering activities (Green et al., 1995). Although it was discovered serendipitously in 1912 by Merck Pharmaceuticals, its use as a psychotherapeutic/recreational drug was unknown until the late 1970s. By the early 1980s, as the popularity of the "rave party" increased so did use of MDMA. In 1985, prior to its classification as a Schedule I drug, it was being evaluated for its use in psychotherapy. A fearful Congress and Drug Enforcement Administration (DEA) successfully petitioned for its classification as a Schedule I compound with no evidence that it was at all harmful.

Recreational use of MDMA has been on the rise for the past 20 years (Peroutka, 1987; Schuster et al., 1998; Pope et al., 2001). Increases in the rate of MDMA use have continued despite reductions in the use of other substances (Johnston et al., 2001a,b). This is an international trend (Abraham et al., 1998; Hibell et al., 2000; McPherson and Afsarifard, Chapter 3 of this book).

Although there have been occasional deaths indirectly caused by the use of MDMA (Henry et al., 1992), it is widely considered by its users to be a "safe" drug. The illusion of safety stems from lack of the obvious negative effects that other amphetamine-type compounds induce. MDMA does not cause an increase in aggressive behavior, and its users do not experience paranoid schizophrenia. According to the Drug Abuse Warning Network (DAWN) less than 0.3% of drug-related emergency room visits are due to MDMA. In fact, most users are normal adolescents. The problems with MDMA are far subtler than those associated with methamphetamine. MDMA is neurotoxic, and the observable long-term behavioral effects seem to be specifically linked to impairments of memory and attention in a subpopulation of individuals, which are difficult to detect.

Myths about MDMA Use

Before discussing the known and suspected effects of MDMA it is important to dispel the myths about its use:

1. MDMA drains your spinal fluid.
2. MDMA causes Parkinson's disease (PD).
3. MDMA is an aphrodisiac.
4. MDMA is a "date rape drug."

First, no known pharmacological agent drains spinal fluid.

Second, MPTP is the chemical agent that was featured in the film *The Frozen Addict*. When made improperly, that drug becomes a very potent neurotoxin that can cause brain damage that may cause a syndrome similar to PD. Because it has four letters and starts with an *M*, MPTP is often confused with MDMA. There has never been a single research report that suggests that MDMA causes PD.

Third, MDMA is not an aphrodisiac. Although MDMA use is correlated with high-risk sexual behavior (Klitzman et al., 2002) it is not known to be causal. In fact, it may reduce sexual functioning (Milani, et al., 2000).

Fourth, a date rape drug is difficult to define. There are certain drugs (alcohol, barbiturates, benzodiazepines, and disassociate anesthetics) that have been used by certain unscrupulous individuals or groups to intoxicate a woman to the point where she could not defend herself from, or even remember, a rape. MDMA does not have the characteristics of any of these compounds. Users are conscious and aware. There is no reason to believe that MDMA is a "date rape" drug.

Neurotoxic Properties of MDMA in Nonhuman Animals

Accumulating evidence has documented that MDMA is a selective serotonergic neurotoxin in rodents and nonhuman primates (Stone et al., 1986; Battaglia et al., 1988; Ricaurte et al., 1992). MDMA has been shown to be neurotoxic in rats (Stone et al., 1986; Schmidt and Taylor, 1987), pigeons (LeSage et al., 1993), and nonhuman primates (Ricaurte et al., 1992). MDMA-induced serotonergic neurotoxicity exhibits with four characteristic features:

1. Reduced levels of serotonin and its metabolite, 5-hydroxyindole acetic acid (5-HIAA) (Schmidt and Taylor, 1987) indicate that serotonin is being both released and "turned over" (broken down and reused) less frequently.
2. Reduced numbers of serotonin reuptake transporters (Battaglia et al., 1988) indicate that at the same time serotonin release and reuse is inhibited the molecular mechanism that recycles it is also inhibited.

3. Reduction in tryptophan hydroxylase (TPH) activity (Stone et al., 1986) indicates that the enzyme that synthesizes serotonin is also inhibited.
4. MDMA produces a loss of serotonin-containing neurons (Commins et al., 1987; Slikker et al., 1988).

Similar to the mechanism by which methamphetamine is neurotoxic, there is evidence that MDMA may indirectly cause neurodegeneration by promoting dopamine (DA) release. In Chapter 5 we discuss the mechanisms by which methamphetamine causes DA release. These are calcium-dependent and calcium-independent processes: Ca^{2+}-dependent release is regulated by the firing of an action potential; Ca^{2+}-independent release is spontaneous. MDMA can also release DA by the same two mechanisms, a calcium-dependent process (Gudelsky et al., 1994) and a calcium-independent nonvesicular transporter-mediated process (Nash and Brodkin, 1991; Shankaran et al., 1999). Drugs that block DA transmission have been shown to be effective in attenuating the neurotoxic effects of MDMA. For example, depletion of DA stores by inhibiting the enzyme that makes DA, tyrosine hydroxylase, and blockade of the protein that transports DA both protect serotonergic terminals from MDMA neurotoxicity (Nash and Brodkin, 1991).

The exact mechanism responsible for MDMA-induced neurotoxicity is not known. The two prominent theories are that it may be induced by oxidative stress caused by the increased DA release (Sprague and Nichols, 1995) or by hyperthermia (Malberg et al., 1996).

Neurotoxic Properties of MDMA in Humans

The evidence for a neurotoxic effect of MDMA in humans has been much more controversial than for methamphetamine. Ethical and methodological problems have made evaluation of the effects of MDMA on humans difficult. These difficulties include the inability of researchers to be sure what drug was taken, and how much of it was taken, by a research participant. Ecstasy tablets can contain from 40 to 150 mg of MDMA as well as a variety of other psychotropic compounds. Researchers have to rely on self-report by subjects, which can be contaminated by misdirection (the user could be lying), problems with recall (the user may not remember how much drug he or she took), or simply misinformation (the user may be misinformed about what drug he or she took).

Perhaps the most important methodological issue has to do with studies that include poor control groups. Most MDMA users also use other drugs. For this reason, any study that tries to evaluate the effect of MDMA on human subjects should have two control groups. One of these groups should be a traditional control group of individuals that use no drugs. The other should be a polydrug-use group of individuals that use a variety of drugs but not MDMA. This way the effects of MDMA could be separated from the effects of other drugs. Very few studies of the effects of MDMA have been appropriately controlled. A recent review identified three types of studies that have been used to examine the neurotoxic effects of MDMA in humans (Curran, 2000).

The first type is neurobiological research. Consonant with the animal research described above, the concentration of 5-HIAA in the cerebrospinal fluid of MDMA users is reduced compared with that of non-MDMA-using controls (Ricaurte et al., 1990; McCann et al., 1994). This indicates reduced serotonergic turnover as described above. Further, the literature on humans has also provided a measure of reduced serotonergic reuptake transporters. In one such study (the most direct connection between MDMA and altered serotonergic function in humans) the PET scans of 14 self-affirmed MDMA users who had been abstinent from the drug for 21 days were compared with those of 15 non-drug-using controls. This study indicated that there were fewer serotonin transporters (the molecules that are responsible for serotonergic reuptake into the presynaptic neuron; see Chapter 5) in the brains of the drug users than in the brains of the control group. Human studies that examine the effect of MDMA on tryptophan hydroxylase (TPH) activity and serotonergic cell loss have not been conducted.

The second type of research focuses on psychological functioning. Acute effects of MDMA tend to be positive (Greer and Tolbert, 1986). These effects include intimacy with others, euphoria, heightened sensual awareness, and increased physical and emotional energy. Prior to concerns about the potential neurotoxicity of MDMA, it was hoped that the drug could be used for couples therapy. However, the long-term effects may be very negative. Frequent recreational users of MDMA exhibit poor performance on neurocognitive measures (McCann et al., 1999; Morgan, 1999; Rodgers, 2000; Gouzoulis-Mayfrank et al., 2000; Bhattachary and Powell, 2001; Verkes et al., 2001). Specifically, memory and attention seem to be impaired by MDMA use (for review, see Morgan, 2000; Parrott, 2000). Chronic MDMA abuse has been shown to cause deficits in the following areas: recall (Morgan, 1999); visual and verbal memory in low intellectually functioning males, but not in females or in high intellectually functioning males (Bolla et al., 1998); working memory (Wareing, Fisk, and Murphy, 2000); and complex tests of attention (McCann, 1999). These deficits may (McCann et al., 1999; Morgan, 1999; Gouzoulis-Mayfrank et al., 2000; Bhattachary and Powell, 2001) or may not (Fischer et al., 1995) be permanent. Special note should be made of the work by Bolla et al. (1998). In that study the sex and IQ of the participants were measured. The authors determined that the negative effects of MDMA use may be observed only in lower intellectually functioning males. Females and higher intellectually functioning males may be protected.

The third type of research focuses on psychiatric symptomatology. Serotonin is involved in most psychopathology, and MDMA alters the serotonergic system. Thus, MDMA should have some effect on psychiatric functioning. This literature, however, is impossible to evaluate because most studies have examined only polydrug users with inappropriate control groups, completely confounding the effects of MDMA with those of other drugs.

Conclusions

There have been numerous criticisms of the research that has evaluated the effects of MDMA. One such criticism is that the doses of MDMA given to animals for experimental purposes are far higher than the doses taken by recreational users (Saunders, 1995). However, when the metabolic rates of the animals tested were taken into account, it was determined that the dosages that were neurotoxic to animals were equivalent to the dosages used recreationally by humans (Ricaurte et al., 2000). Some drugs do affect human and nonhuman animals differently. The only way to know is through experimentation.

The available evidence from studies of human MDMA users suggests but cannot prove conclusively that there is a direct relationship between MDMA use and alterations of serotonergic neurotransmission and cognitive impairment. The MDMA users who are typically studied are polydrug users. They have used drugs prior to, during the time of, and after the studies that have evaluated their performance. Many of the drugs that are commonly used (marijuana, alcohol, and methamphetamine, to name but a few) by today's adolescents can cause both serotonergic alterations and cognitive deficits. Recent studies provide conflicting evidence about the relative contributions of MDMA and cannabis to both serotonergic alterations and cognitive deficits (Rodgers, 2000; Croft et al., 2001). Because of ethical concerns (we cannot give humans drugs that we believe may cause neurodegenerative damage), it has been impossible to design a study that would prove conclusively that MDMA causes this type of damage. We have had to rely on correlational studies and analogous animal models to elucidate the effects of MDMA. These studies have tended to support the role of MDMA as a neurotoxin.

Many proponents of MDMA still argue that the potential benefits of its controlled use outweigh any negative effects that it may have (J. Holland, Congressional testimony, 2001). These proponents suggest that under controlled clinical use the drug is not neurotoxic. They suggest that the negative effects occur only after repeated chronic use. However, there is a growing body of evidence that suggests that observable (i.e., behavioral) deficits occur much later than physiological deficits (i.e., brain alterations) (Frederick et al., 1998; Taffe et al., 2001; Winsauer et al., 2002).

References

Abraham, M.D., Cohen, P.D.A., Jan van Til, R., and Langemeijer, M.P.S. (1998). *Licit and Illicit Drug Use in Amsterdam. III: Developments in Drug Use 1987–1997.* Amsterdam: CEDRO.

Battaglia, S., Yeh, Y., and Desouza, E.B. (1988). MDMA-induced neurotoxicity — parameters of degeneration and recovery of brain-serotonin neurons. *Biochem. Behav.*, 29, 269–274.

Bhattachary, S. and Powell, J.H. (2001). Recreational use of 3,4-methylenedioxymethamphetamine (MDMA) or "ecstasy": evidence for cognitive impairment. *Psychol. Med.*, 31, 647–658.

Bolla, K.I., McCann, U.D., and Ricaurte, G.A. (1998). Memory impairment in abstinent MDMA ("ecstasy") users. *Neurology*, 51 1532–1537.

Colado, M.I., O'Shea, E., Granados, R., Esteban, B., Martin, A.B., and Green, A.R. (1999). Studies on the role of dopamine in the degeneration of 5-HT nerve endings in the brain of Dark Agouti rats following 3,4-methylenedioxymethamphetamine (MDMA or "ecstasy") administration. *Br. J. Pharmacol.*, 126, 911–924.

Commins, D.L., Vosmer, G., Virus, R.M., Woolverton, W.L., Schuster, C.R., and Seiden, L.S. (1987). Biochemical and histological evidence that methylenedioxymethylamphetamine (MDMA) is toxic to neurons in the rat brain. *J. Pharmacol. Exp. Ther.*, 241, 338–345.

Croft, R.J., Mackay, A.J., Mills, A.T., and Gruzelier, J.G. (2001). The relative contributions of ecstasy and cannabis to cognitive impairment. *Psychopharmacology* (Berlin), 153, 373–379.

Curran, H.V. (2000). Is MDMA (Ecstasy) neurotoxic in humans? An overview of evidence and of methodological problems in research. *Neuropsychobiology*, 42(1), 34–41.

Fischer, C., Hatzidimitriou, G., Wlos, J., Katz, J., and Ricaurte, G. (1995). Reorganization of ascending 5-HT axon projections in animals previously exposed to the recreational drug (±)3,4-methylenedioxymethamphetamine (MDMA, "ecstasy"). *J. Neurosci.*, 15, 5476–5485.

Fischer, J.F. and Cho, A.K. (1979). Chemical release of dopamine from striatal homogenates: evidence for an exchange diffusion model. *J. Pharmacol. Exp. Ther.*, 208, 203–209.

Frederick, D.L., Ali, S.F., Gillam, M.P., Gossett, J., Slikker, W., and Paule, M.G. (1998). Acute effects of dexfenfluramine (d-FEN) and methylenedioxymethamphetamine (MDMA) before and after short-course, high-dose treatment. *Ann. N.Y. Acad. Sci.*, 844, 183–190.

Gouzoulis-Mayfrank, E., Daumann, J., Tuchtenhagen, F., Pelz, S., Becker, S., Kunert, H.J., Fimm, B., and Sass, H. (2000). Impaired cognitive performance in drug free users of recreational ecstasy (MDMA). *J. Neurol. Neurosurg. Psychiatr.*, 68, 719–725.

Green, A.R., Cross, A.J., and Goodwin, G.M. (1995). Review of the pharmacology and clinical pharmacology of 3,4-methylenedioxymethamphetamine (MDMA or "ecstasy"). *Psychopharmacology*, 119, 247–260.

Greer, G. and Tolbert, R. (1986). Subjective reports of the effects of MDMA in a clinical setting. *J. Psychoactive Drugs*, 18(4), 319–327.

Gudelsky, G.A., Yamamoto, B.K., and Nash, J.F. (1994). Potentiation of 3,4-methylenedioxymethamphetamine-induced dopamine release and serotonin neurotoxicity by 5-HT2 agonists. *Eur. J. Pharmacol.*, 264, 325–330.

Henry, J.A., Jeffreys, J.A., and Dawling, S. (1992). Toxicity and deaths from 3,4-methylenedioxymethamphetamine (ecstasy). *Lancet*, 340, 384–387.

Hibell, B., Andersson, B., Ahlstrom, S., Balakireva, O., Bjarnason, T., Kokkevi, A., and Morgan, M. (2000). *The 1999 ESPAD Report: Alcohol and Other Drug Use among Students in 30 European Countries (Summary)*. Stockholm, Sweden: Swedish National Institute of Public Health.

Insel, T.R., Battaglia, G., Johannessen, J.N., Marra, S., and De Souza, E.B. (1989). 3,4-Methylenedioxymethamphetamine ("ecstasy") selectively destroys brain serotonin terminals in rhesus monkeys. *J. Pharmacol. Exp. Ther.*, 249, 713–720.

Johnston, L.D., O'Malley, P.M., and Bachman, J.G. (2001a). Monitoring the Future: National Survey Results on Drug Use, 1975–2000. Vol. I: Secondary School Students (NIH Publ. 01-4924). National Institute on Drug Abuse, Bethesda, MD.

Johnston, L.D., O'Malley, P.M., and Bachman, J.G. (2001b). Monitoring the Future: National Survey Results on Drug Use, 1975–2000. Vol. II: College Students and Adults Ages 19–40 (NIH Publ.). National Institute of Drug Abuse, Bethesda, MD.

Klitzman, R.L., Greenberg, J.D., Pollack, L.M., and Dolezal, C. (2002). MDMA ("ecstasy") use, and its association with high risk behaviors, mental health, and other factors among gay/bisexual men in New York City. *Drug Alcohol Dependence*, 66(2), 115–125.

LeSage, M., Clark, R., and Poling, A. (1993). MDMA and memory: the acute and chronic effects of MDMA in pigeons performing under a delayed-matching-to-sample procedure. *Psychopharmacology*, 110, 327–332.

Malberg, J.E., Sabol, K.E., and Seiden, L.S. (1996). Co-administration of MDMA with drugs that protect against MDMA neurotoxicity produces different effects on body temperature in the rat. *J. Pharmacol. Exp. Ther.*, 278, 258–267.

McCann, U.D., Ridenour, A., Shaham, Y., and Ricaurte, G.A. (1994). Serotonin neurotoxicity after MDMA: a controlled study in humans. *Neuropsychopharmacology*, 10, 129–138.

McCann, U.D., Mertl, M., Eligulashvili, V., and Ricaurte, G.A. (1999). Cognitive performance in (±)3,4-methylenedioxymethamphetamine (MDMA, "ecstasy") users: a controlled study. *Psychopharmacology* (Berlin), 143, 417–425.

Milani, R., Turner, J.J.D., and Parrott, A.C. (2000). Recreational drug use and psychobiological problems, collaborative UK/Italy study (2): Rome and Padua findings. *J. Psychopharmacol.*, 14, a14.

Morgan, M.J. (1999). Memory deficits associated with recreational use of "ecstasy" (MDMA). *Psychopharmacology* (Berlin), 141, 30–36.

Morgan, M.J. (2000). Ecstasy (MDMA): a review of its possible persistent psychological effects. *Psychopharmacology* (Berlin), 152, 230–248.

Nash, J.F. and Brodkin, J. (1991). Microdialysis studies on 3,4-methylenedioxymethamphetamine-induced dopamine release: effect of dopamine uptake inhibitors. *J. Pharmacol. Exp. Ther.*, 259, 820–825.

O'Hearn, E., Battaglia, G., DeSouza, E.B., Kuhar, M.J., and Molliver, M.E. (1988). Methylenedioxyamphetamine (MDA) and 3,4-methylenedioxymethamphetamine (MDMA) cause selective ablation of serotonergic axon terminals in forebrain: Immunocytochemical evidence for neurotoxicity. *J. Neurosci.*, 8(8), 2788–2803.

Parrott, A.C. (2000). Human research on MDMA (3,4-methylene-dioxymethamphetamine) neurotoxicity: cognitive and behavioural indices of change. *Neuropsychobiology*, 42, 17–24.

Peroutka, S.J. (1987). Incidence of recreational use of 3,4-methylenedimethoxymethamphetamine (MDMA, "ecstasy") on an undergraduate campus. *N. Engl. J. Med.*, 317, 1542–1543 [letter].

Pope, H.G., Jr., Ionescu-Pioggia, M., and Pope, K.W. (2001). Drug use and life style among college undergraduates: a 30-year longitudinal study. *Am. J. Psychiatr.*, 158, 1519–1521.

Reneman, L., Booij, J., Schmand, B., van den Brink, W., and Gunning, B. (2000). Memory disturbances in "ecstasy" users are correlated with an altered brain serotonin neurotransmission. *Psychopharmacology* (Berlin), 148, 322–324.

Reneman, L., Lavalaye, J., Schmand, B., de Wolff, F.A., van den Brink, W., den Heeten, G.J., and Booij, J. (2001). Cortical serotonin transporter density and verbal memory in individuals who stopped using 3,4-methylenedioxymethamphetamine (MDMA or "ecstasy"): preliminary findings. *Arch. Gen. Psychiatr.*, 58, 901–906.

Ricaurte, G.A. and McCann, U.D. (1992). Neurotoxic amphetamine analogues: effects in monkeys and implications for humans. *Ann. N.Y. Acad. Sci.*, 648, 371–382.

Ricaurte, G.A., Bryan, G., Strauss, L., Seiden, L., and Schuster, C.R. (1985). Hallucinogenic amphetamine selectively destroys brain serotonin nerve terminals. *Science*, 229, 986–988.

Ricaurte, G.A., Finnegan, K.T., Irwin, I., and Langston, J.W. (1990). Aminergic metabolites in cerebrospinal fluid of humans previously exposed to MDMA: Preliminary observations. *Ann. N.Y. Acad. Sci.*, 600, 699–710.

Ricaurte, G.A., Martello, A.L., Katz, J.L., and Martello, M.B. (1992). Lasting effects of (±)3,4-methylenedioxymethamphetamine (MDMA) on central serotonergic neurons in non human primates: neurochemical observations. *J. Pharmacol. Exp. Ther.*, 261, 616–621.

Ricaurte, G.A., McCann, U.D., Szabo, Z., and Scheffel, U. (2000). Toxicodynamics and long-term toxicity of the recreational drug 3,4-methylenedioxymethamphetamine (MDMA, Ecstasy), *Toxicol. Lett.*, March 15, 112–113, 143–146.

Rodgers, J. (2000). Cognitive performance amongst recreational users of "ecstasy." *Psychopharmacology* (Berlin), 151, 19–24.

Saunders, N. (1995). *Ecstasy and the Dance Culture*, London: Neal's Yard Desktop Publishing.

Schmidt, C.J. and Taylor, V.L. (1987). Depression of rat brain tryptophan hydroxylase activity following the acute administration of methylenedioxymethamphetamine. *Biochem. Pharmacol.*, 36, 4095–4102.

Schuster, P., Lieb, R., Lamertz, C., and Wittchen, H.U. (1998). Is the use of ecstasy and hallucinogens increasing? Results from a community study. *Eur. Addict Res.*, 4, 75–82.

Semple, D.M., Ebmeier, K.P., Glabus, M.F., O'Carroll, R.E., and Johnstone, E.C. (1999). Reduced *in vivo* binding to the serotonin transporter in the cerebral cortex of MDMA ("ecstasy") users. *Br. J. Psychiatr.*, 175, 63–69.

Shankaran, M., Yamamoto, B.K., and Gudelsky, G.A. (1999). Mazindol attenuates the 3,4-methylenedioxymethamphetamine-induced formation of hydroxyl radicals and long-term depletion of serotonin in the striatum. *J. Neurochem.*, 72, 2516–2522.

Simantov, R. and Tauber, M. (1997). The abused drug MDMA (ecstasy) induced programmed death of human serotonergic cells. *FASEB J.*, 11, 141–146.

Slikker, W., Jr., Ali, S.F., Scallet, A.C., Frith, C.H., Newport, G.D., and Bailey, J.R. (1988). Neurochemical and neurohistological alterations in the rat and monkey produced by orally administered methylenedioxy-methamphetamine (MDMA). *Toxicol. Appl. Pharmacol.*, 94, 448–57.

Sprague, J.E. and Nichols, D.E. (1995). The monoamine oxidase-B inhibitor L-deprenyl protects against 3,4-methylenedioxymethamphetamine-induced lipid peroxidation and long-term serotonergic deficits. *J. Pharmacol. Exp. Ther.*, 273, 667–673.

Stone, D.M., Stahl, D.C., Hanson, G.R., and Gibb, J.W. (1986). The effects of 3,4-methylenedioxyamphetamine (MDA) and 3,4-methylenedioxymethamphetamine (MDMA) on monoaminergic systems in the rat brain. *Eur.J. Pharmacol.*, 128, 41–48.

Taffe, M.A., Weed, M.R., Davis, S., Huitron-Resendiz, S., Schroeder, R., Parsons, L.H., Henriksen, S.J., and Gold, L.H. (2001). Functional consequences of repeated (±)3,4-methylenedioxymethamphetamine (MDMA) treatment in rhesus monkeys. *Neuropsychopharmacology*, 24, 230–239.

Verkes, R.J., Gijsman, H.J., Pieters, M.S., Schoemaker, R.C., de Visser, S., Kuijpers, M., Pennings, E.J., de Bruin, D., Van de Wijngaart, G., Van Gerven, J.M., and Cohen, A.F. (2001). Cognitive performance and serotonergic function in users of ecstasy. *Psychopharmacology* (Berlin), 153, 196–202.

Wareing, M., Fisk, J.E., and Murphy, P.N. (2000). Working memory deficits in current and previous users of MDMA ("ecstasy"). *Br. J. Psychol.*, 91, 181–189.

Winsauer, P.J., McCann, U.D., Yuan, J.J., Delatte, M.S., Stevenson, M.W., Ricaurte, G.A., and Moerschbaecher, J.M. (2002). Effects of fenfluramine, m-CPP and triazolam on repeated-acquisition in squirrel monkeys before and after neurotoxic MDMA administration. *Psychopharmacology* (Berlin), 159, 388–396.

Section II

Physiology, Effects, and Diagnosis of Methamphetamine Use

Physiology

5

ERROL YUDKO
HAROLD V. HALL
SANDRA B. McPHERSON
STUART W. TWEMLOW

Neurotransmitter Action

Understanding the mechanism of action of methamphetamine requires some understanding of neurophysiology. Because the discussion here is brief, readers who wish to further their knowledge of neurophysiology are referred to Pinel (1997). In short, the active unit of the nervous system is the neuron (Schwann, 1839; Cajal, 1917). A neuron is an elongated cell (up to 2 m) that sends messages to other cells through the process of electrochemical signaling (Sherrington, 1987; Bernstein, 1902; Adrian, 1913; Loewi, 1921; Dale, 1914). That is, an electrical impulse, called an action potential, travels the length of the cell to initiate the release of a chemical messenger, called a neurotransmitter. The neurotransmitter substance diffuses across a gap between the cells, called a synapse, where it is chemically bound to a protein called a receptor. The binding of the neurotransmitter to the receptor is equivalent to the receipt of the message.

The process of release of the neurotransmitter from the presynaptic neuron, the neuron on the sending side of the synapse (the neuron on the receiving side is called the postsynaptic receptor), is called exocytosis. Neurotransmitter substances are generally packaged in vesicles (De Robertis et al., 1962). These vesicles sometimes have protein units, known as transporters, that can extract neurotransmitter substances from the cell cytoplasm, the viscous fluid on the inside of the cell, and package them on the inside of the vesicle. In response to an action potential, the vesicle fuses with the cell membrane and releases neurotransmitter into the synapse (Fatt and Katz, 1952). The process of exocytosis is calcium dependent (for review, see Smith and Augustine, 1988). That is, it occurs only in the presence of calcium.

After it has been released, the neurotransmitter diffuses across the synapse and binds to a receptor on the postsynaptic membrane. The message of the neurotransmitter depends on the function of the receptor. Some common messages are "produce an action potential," "suppress an action potential," or "begin a long-term change by activating specific proteins." As long as the neurotransmitter substance remains in the synapse, its message will be received by the postsynaptic neuron. Thus, a mechanism must exist to remove the neurotransmitter. There are, in fact, several such mechanisms. One such mechanism is through the degradation of the neurotransmitter. Another, more important to the present discussion, is through the reuptake of the neurotransmitter into the presynaptic neuron.

Control of Neurotransmitter Levels

In addition to degradation and reuptake, negative feedback and end-product inhibition are two other ways that the cell has available to control the levels of neurotransmitter released into the synapse. Some cells have autoreceptors, which are responsible for negative feedback. That is, a receptor on the presynaptic neuron (called an autoreceptor or presynaptic receptor) acts to turn off a cell when enough neurotransmitter has accumulated in the synapse to activate it. This mechanism prevents the cell from releasing "too much" neurotransmitter at one time. End-product inhibition is the mechanism by which the neuron regulates the amount of neurotransmitter that it synthesizes. When enough product (neurotransmitter) is available, the product itself deactivates the enzymes responsible for its production.

A psychoactive drug can have an effect at any or all of the above-mentioned processes (receptor binding, degradation, synthesis, release, packaging, and reuptake). The most common site of action for a psychoactive drug is at the postsynaptic receptor. However, psychoactive drugs can affect both postsynaptic receptors and presynaptic receptors. Further, these drugs can affect the mechanisms responsible for neurotransmitter synthesis, release, packaging, reuptake, and degradation.

Physiological Effects of Amphetamine

Neurotransmitters can be classified as large or small. Large-molecule neurotransmitters include the peptide transmitters such as the opiates. Small-molecule transmitters include the monoamines and the amino acid transmitters. The monoamines can be further subdivided into the catecholamines and the indolamines. The present discussion focuses on the monoamines. The catecholamines include the neurotransmitters norepinephrine (NE), epinephrine (Epi), and dopamine (DA). The only indolamine is serotonin (5-HT).

Early studies hypothesized that methamphetamine inhibited the reuptake of NE, DA (Harris and Baldessarini, 1973; Azzaro et al., 1974), and 5-HT (Taylor and Ho, 1978). More importantly, methamphetamine also acts as a potent DA-releasing agent (Azzaro et al., 1974; Raiteri et al., 1975; Arnold et al., 1977) and NE-releasing agent (Kuczenski and Segal, 1992). Most of the research attempting to elucidate the mechanism of methamphetamine action has focused on DA because the DA system, which regulates feelings of reward, motor coordination, motivation, and hormonal release, is thought to be primarily responsible for the behavioral changes observed in methamphetamine use.

DA is synthesized in the cytoplasm and transported into vesicles. From the vesicles it is released into the synapse in both Ca^{2+}-dependent and -independent manners. Ca^{2+}-dependent release is regulated by the firing of an action potential. Ca^{2+}-independent release is spontaneous. One major effect of amphetamine is to cause an increase in the amount of DA released spontaneously from the neuron (Robertson et al., 1991).

Amphetamine causes this increase in spontaneously released DA by reversing the activity of the DA reuptake transporter (Bonisch, 1984). This was shown by observing the activity of radioactively labeled amphetamine applied to the terminus region of a dopaminergic neuron (Zaczek et al., 1991). Further, amphetamine-stimulated DA release is inhibited by drugs that block the reuptake of DA (Fischer and Cho, 1979; Raiteri et al., 1979; Liang and Rutledge, 1982). Finally, amphetamine has no effect in genetically engineered mice that do not have the gene that codes for the DA reuptake transporter. Taken together, these findings lead to the exchange diffusion model of amphetamine action. In this model, the amphetamine molecule binds to the reuptake transporter and is taken up into the cell. The transporter is turned around in the process and begins to pump DA out of the cell instead of into the cell.

The weak base model is a second potential mechanism for the spontaneous release of DA in the presence of amphetamine. This model proposes that at high doses amphetamine actually diffuses into the neuron where it interacts with the vesicle (by changing its pH — thus, the name "weak base") and causes DA to leak into the cytoplasm of the cell, thereby providing more cytoplasmic DA to be pumped out into the synapse via the exchange diffusion model (Sulzer and Rayport, 1990; Sulzer et al., 1993).

Amphetamine has several other effects on the DA system as well:

1. Low concentrations of amphetamine enhance the synthesis of DA. This is thought to occur because amphetamine causes the cell to become DA deficient. The cell responds by producing more DA.

2. High concentrations of amphetamine inhibit DA synthesis by binding to presynaptic autoreceptors.
3. Amphetamine also inhibits the enzyme (monoamine oxidase) that degrades DA.

Tolerance and Sensitization

Tolerance is defined as a diminished response to a drug after repeated administration of all effects of a drug exhibit tolerance. In the case of amphetamine, tolerance to the anorexic, hypothermic, cardiovascular, and reinforcing effects has been reported (Lewander, 1971; Miller and Gold, 1989, Perez-Reyes et al., 1991). Reports from chronic amphetamine users confirm a significant amount of tolerance to the euphoric effects of amphetamines (Kramer et al., 1967; Grinspoon and Hedblom, 1975), which tends to result in tremendous dose increases by chronic abusers. The physiological mechanism for tolerance to amphetamine use is unclear, but seems to occur at the cellular level.

An interesting effect of chronic amphetamine abuse is reverse tolerance, or sensitization. That is, use of the drug leads to a stronger subjective effect of the drug at a later time. Repeated, intermittent use or a single use seems to lead to this phenomenon. The use of the drug amphetamine can lead to cross-sensitization, which was originally defined as a hypersensitivity to stress (Robinson and Becker, 1986), but has come to be associated with hypersensitivity to a number of drugs as well.

Neurotoxicity

Methamphetamine neurotoxicity has been well documented in animals (Koda and Gibb, 1973; Seiden et al., 1975; Ellison et al., 1978) but is less clear in humans (Ernst et al., 2000). However, a recent study (Buffenstein et al., 1997) used SPECT scanning to show brain deterioration in methamphetamine abusers that continued for months after abstinence (see Figure 2.1). Methamphetamine seems to be toxic to dopaminergic neurons (Wagner et al., 1980; Ricaurte et al., 1988; Ricaurte, Seiden, and Schuster, 1984) and serotinergic neurons (Hotchkiss and Gibb, 1980; Morgan and Gibb, 1980), but not noradrenergic, cholinergic, and GABAergic neurons (Hotchkiss et al., 1979; Morgan and Gibb, 1980; Wagner et al., 1980). The mechanism for DA neurotoxicity is better understood than the mechanism for 5HT neurotoxicity and may involve methamphetamine triggering the release of large quanta of DA (O'Dell et al., 1991). In fact, drugs that block DA protect against methamphetamine neurotoxicity (Fuller and Hemrick-Luecke, 1980; Hotchkiss and Gibb, 1980; Ricaurte, Seiden, and Schuster, 1984).

Drugs with chemical compositions similar to amphetamine and methamphetamine tend also to be neurotoxic. MDMA (also known as ecstasy, XTC, X, and E) is one such compound. MDMA has been shown to be neurotoxic in rats (Stone et al., 1986; Schmidt, 1987), pigeons (LeSage et al., 1993), and nonhuman primates (Ricaurte et al., 1988). The evidence for a neurotoxic effect in humans has been much more controversial (Holland, 1999). It has been suggested that the doses of MDMA given to animals were far higher than the doses taken by recreational users. However, when the metabolic rates of the animals tested were taken into account, it was determined that the dosages that were neurotoxic to animals were equivalent to the dosages used recreationally by humans (Ricaurte et al., 2000). Chronic MDMA abuse has been shown to cause deficits in the following areas: recall (Morgan, 1999); visual and verbal memory in low intellectually functioning males, but not females or high intellectually functioning males (Bolla, McCann, and Ricaurte, 1998); working memory (Wareing, Fisk, and Murphy, 2000); and complex tests of attention (McCann, 1998). The damage seems to be related to 5-HT neuronal injury (Reneman et al., 2000).

Neuropharmacology of Amphetamines

Amphetamines are rapidly absorbed orally and have a rapid onset of action, usually within 30 to 40 minutes of oral ingestion. Methamphetamine may also be taken intravenously, whereupon it has an immediate effect. Certain forms, the so-called designer amphetamines, may be inhaled. Crystal methamphetamine, the smokable form of this drug, which is primarily found in Hawaii, has an onset time of between 5 and 20 minutes, a subjective feeling of intoxication for up to 8 hours, and a half-life of 12 to 36 hours. Demethylation, or the biochemical breakdown process caused by the presence of methamphetamine in the body, is conclusive evidence that methamphetamine is being detected and not some harmless analogue.

Tolerance, the requirement of progressively higher doses over time to obtain the same effect, occurs with all forms of amphetamines. This phenomenon, in part, accounts for the addictive nature of methamphetamine. Increases in methamphetamine doses from 5 to 1000 mg per day in a single year are not uncommon as a reflection of rapid tissue tolerance in methamphetamine users (Trustees of Indiana University, 1995). As a result of tolerance in long-term abusers, doses as high as 20 times the initial dose may be needed to achieve the same high (Haight-Ashbury Training Manual, 1997). This suggests that knowledge of the behavioral indicia of intoxication, abuse, and dependence, in addition to an understanding of the neuropharmacology of methamphetamine, is indispensable. When compared with other psychostimulants, such as cocaine, methamphetamine has been shown to be less physically addictive in animal studies (Dackis and Gold, 1990). Nevertheless, the psychological addictive potential of methamphetamine is extremely high; many abusers continue their use despite knowing that their abuse is likely to cause florid psychotic symptomatology, such as command hallucinations and disorganized cognition.

The primary effects of methamphetamine are related to the release of catecholamine, particularly DA, from presynaptic neurons in the brain. The drug appears to exert its greatest effect on dopaminergic neurons projecting from the ventral tegmental area to the cerebral cortex and the limbic system, nerve bundles commonly referred to as the "reward pathway" that is thought to be implicated in the addictive potential of methamphetamine (Kaplan et al., 1994).

The designer amphetamines (e.g., MDMA, MDEA, MMDA, DOM) release DA, norepinephrine, and serotonin. As a result of their effect, individuals ingesting these substances experience both stimulant and hallucinogenic effects. Thus, the designer amphetamines exert a broader spectrum of effects than methamphetamine itself.

References

Adrian, E.D. (1913). Wedensky inhibition in relation to the all-or-none principle in nerve, *J. Physiol.* London, 46, 384–412.

Arnold, E.B., Molinoff, P.B., and Rutledge, C.O. (1977). The release of endogenous norepinephrine and dopamine from cerebral cortex by amphetamine. *J. Pharmacol.*, 202, 544–557.

Azzaro, A.J., Ziance, R.J., and Rutledge, C.O. (1974). The importance of neuronal uptake of amines for amphetamine induced release of H-norepinephrine from isolated brain tissue. *J. Pharmacol. Exp. Ther.*, 189, 110–118.

Bernstein, J. (1902). *Pflügers Arch. ges. Physiol.*, 92, 521–562.

Bolla, K., McCann, U.D., and Ricaurte, G.A. (1998). Memory impairment in abstinent MDMA ("Ecstasy") users. *Neurology*, 51, 1532–1537.

Bonisch, H. (1984). The transport of (-)-amphetamine by the neuronal noradrenaline carrier. *Naunyn Schmiedebergs Arch. Pharmacol.*, 327, 267–272.

Buffenstein, A., Coel, M., and Combs, B. (1997). Functional Neuroimaging of Chronic Crystal Methamphetamine Users. Unpublished grant application, University of Hawaii, John A. Burns School of Medicine.

Cajal, S.R. (1917). *Recuerdos de mi vida, Vol. 2: Historia de mi labor cientifica*. Madrid: Moya. There is an English translation: Recollections of my life (translated by E.H. Craigie with the assistance of J. Cano), Philadelphia, American Philosophical Society, 1937). Reprinted Cambridge, MA, MIT Press, 1989.

De Robertis, E., Rodrigues de Lores Arnaiz, H., and Pallegrini de Iraldi, A. (1962). Isolation of synaptic vesicles from nerve endings in rat brain. *Nature*, 194, 794–795.

Dackis, C.A. and Gold, M.S. (1990). Addictiveness of central stimulants. *Adv. Alcohol Substance Abuse*, 9, 9.

Dale, H.H. (1914). *J. Pharmacol. Exp. Ther.*, 6, 147–190.

Ellison, G., Eison, M.S., Huberman, H.S., and Daniel, F. (1978). Long-term changes in dopaminergic innervation of caudate nucleus after continuous amphetamine administration. *Science*, 201, 276–278.

Ernst, T., Chang, L., Leonido-Yee, M., and Speck, O. (2000). Evidence for long-term neurotoxicity associated with methamphetamine abuse: A 1H MRS study. *Neurology*, 54(6), 1344–1349.

Fatt, P. and Katz, B. (1952). Spontaneous subthreshold activity of motor nerve endings. *J. Physiol.* (London), 117, 109–128.

Fischer, J.F. and Cho, A.K. (1979). Chemical release of dopamine from striatal homogenates: evidence for an exchange diffusion model. *J. Pharmacol. Exp. Ther.*, 208, 203–209.

Fuller, R.W. and Hemrick-Luecke, S. (1980). Long-lasting depletion of striatal dopamine by a single injection of amphetamine in iprindole-treated rats. *Science*, 209, 305–307.

Grinspoon, L. and Hedblom, P. (1975). *The Speed Culture: Amphetamine Use and Abuse in America*. Cambridge, MA: Harvard University Press.

Haight-Ashbury Training Manual. (1997). In D. Inaba and W. Cohen, *Uppers, Downers, and All Arounders*. Ashland, OR: Cinemed, Inc.

Harris, J.E. and Baldessarini, R.J. (1973). Uptake of [3H]-catecholamines by homogenates of rat corpus striatum and cerebral cortex: effects of amphetamine analogues. *Neuropharmacology*, 12, 669–679.

Holland, J. (1999). Positron emission tomography findings in heavy users of MDMA. *Lancet*, 353, 592–593.

Hotchkiss, A.J. and Gibb, J.W. (1980). Long-term effects of multiple doses of methamphetamine on tryptophan hydroxylase and tyrosine hydroxylase activity in rat brain. *J. Pharmacol. Exp. Ther.*, 214, 257–262.

Hotchkiss, A.J., Morgan, M.E., and Gibb, J.W. (1979). The long-term effects of multiple doses of methamphetamine in neostriatal tryptophan hydroxylase and tyrosine hydroxylase, choline acetyltransferase and glutamate decarboxylase activities. *Life Sci.*, 25, 1373–1378.

Kaplan, H.I., Sadock, B.J., and Grebb, J.A. (1994). *Synopsis of Psychiatry*. 7th ed. Baltimore: Williams & Wilkins, 1994, 411–428.

Koda, L.Y. and Gibb, J.W. (1973). Adrenal and striatal tyrosine hydroxylase activity after methamphetamine. *J. Pharmacol. Exp. Ther.*, 185, 42–48.

Kramer, J.C., Fischman, V.S., and Littlfield, D.C. (1967). Amphetamine abuse: pattern and effects of high doses taken intravenously. *J. Am. Med. Assoc.*, 201, 89–93.

Kuczenski, R. and Segal, D.S. (1992). Differential effects of amphetamine and dopamine uptake blockers (cocaine, nomifensine) on caudate and accumbens dialysate dopamine and 3-methoxytyramine. *J. Pharmacol. Exp. Ther.*, 262, 1085–1094.

LeSage, M., Clark, R., and Poling, A. (1993). MDMA and memory: the acute and chronic effects of MDMA in pigeons performing under a delayed-matching-to-sample procedure. *Psychopharmacology*, 110, 327–332.

Lewander, T. (1971). A mechanism for the development of tolerance in rats. *Psychopharmacologia*, 21, 17–31.

Liang, N.Y. and Rutledge, C.O. (1982). Comparison of the release of [3H]dopamine from isolated corpus striatum by amphetamine, fenfluramine and unlabelled dopamine. *Biochem. Pharmacol.*, 31(6), 983–992.

Loewi, O. (1921). *Pflügers Arch.*, 189, 239–242.

McCann, J.T. (1998). Broadening the typology of false confessions. *Am. Psychol.*, 53(3), 319–320.

Melga, W.P., Lacan, G., Harvey, D.C., Huang, S.C., and Phelpes, M.E. (1998). Dizocilpine and reduced body temperature do not prevent methamphetamine-induced neurotoxicity in the vervet monkey: [11C]WIN 35,428 — positron emission tomography studies. *Neurosci. Lett.*, 258(1),17–20.

Melega, W.P., Lacan, G., Desalles, A.A., and Phelps, M.E. (2000). Long-term methamphetamine-induced decreases of binding in striatum are reduced by GDNF: PET studies in the vervet monkey. *Synapse*, 35(4), 243–249.

Miller, N.S. and Gold, M.S. (1989). The diagnosis of marijuana (*Cannabis*) dependence. *J. Substance Abuse Treat.*, 6, 183–192.

Morgan, M.J. (1999). Memory deficits associated with recreational use of "ecstasy" (MDMA). *Psychopharmacology*, 141, 30–36.

Morgan, M.E. and Gibb, J.W. (1980). Short-term and long-term effects of methamphetamine on biogenic amine metabolism on extra-striatal dopaminergic nuclei. *Neuropharmacology*, 19, 989–995.

O'Dell, S.J., Weihmuller, F.B., and Marshall, J.F. (1991). Multiple methamphetamine injections induce marked increases in extracellular striatal dopamine which correlates with subsequent neurotoxicity. *Brain Res.*, 564, 256–260.

Perez-Reyes, M., White, W.R., McDonald, S.A., Hicks, R.E., Jeffcoat, A.R., Hill, J.M., and Cook, C.E. (1991). Clinical effects of daily methamphetamine administration. *Clin. Neuropharmacol.*, 14, 352–358.

Pinel, J.P.J. (1997). *Biopsychology.* Boston: Allyn & Bacon.

Raiteri, M., Bertollini, A., Angelini, F., and Levi, G. (1975). Dopamine as a releaser or reuptake inhibitor of biogenic amines in synaptosomes. *Eur.J. Pharmacol.*, 34, 189–195.

Reneman, L., Booij, J., Schmand, R., van den Brink, W., and Gunning, B. (2000). Memory disturbances in "Ecstasy" users are or related with an altered brain serotonin neurotransmission. *Psychopharmacology (Berlin)*, 148, 322–324.

Ricaurte, G.A., Forno, L.S., Wilson, M.A., DeLanney, L.E., Irwin, L., Molliver, M.E., and Langston, J.W. (1988). (±)3,4-Methylene-dioxymethamphetamine selectively damages central serotonergic neurons in non-human primates. *J. Am. Med. Assoc.*, 260, 51–55.

Ricaurte, G.A., Seiden, L.S., and Schuster, C.R. (1984). Further evidence that amphetamine produce long-lasting dopamine neurochemical deficits by destroying dopamine nerve fibers. *Brain Res.*, 303(2), 359-364.

Ricaurte, G.A., Yuan, J., and McCann, U.D. (2000). (±)3,4- Methylenedioxymethamphetamine ("ecstasy")-induced serotonin neurotoxicity: studies in animals. *Neuropsychobiology*, 42(1), 5–10.

Robertson, G.S., Damsma, G., and Fibiger, H.C. (1991). Characterization of dopamine release in the substantia nigra by *in vivo* microdialysis in freely moving rats. *J. Neurosci.*, 11, 2209–2216.

Schmidt, C.J. (1987). Neurotoxicity of the psychedelic amphetamine, methylenedioxymethamphetamine. *J. Pharmacol. Exp. Ther.*, 240, 1–7.

Schwann, T. (1839) *Mikroskopische Untersuchungen*, Sander, Berlin; English translation by H. Smith (1847), Sydenham Soc., London.

Seiden, L.S., Fischman, M.W., and Schuster, C.R. (1975). Long-term methamphetamine-induced changes in brain catecholamines on tolerant rhesus monkeys. *Drug Alcohol Depend.*, 1, 215–219.

Sherrington, C.S. (1987). *The Central Nervous System*. In volume III of Michael Foster, *A Textbook of Physiology*. 7th ed. London.

Smith, S.J. and Augustine, G.J. (1988). Calcium ions, active zones and synaptic transmitter release. *Trends Neurosci.*, 11(10), 458–464.

Stone, D.M., Stahl, D.S., Hanson, G.L., and Gibbs, J.W. (1986). The effects of 3,4-methylenedioxymethamphetamine (MDMA) and 3,4-methylenedioxyamphetamine (MDA) in monoaminergic systems in the rat brain. *Eur. J. Pharmacol.*, 128, 41–48.

Sulzer, D., Maidment, N.T., and Rayport, S. (1993). Amphetamine and other weak bases act to promote reverse transport of dopamine in ventral midbrain neurons. *J. Neurochem.*, 60(2), 527–535.

Sulzer, D. and Rayport, S. (1990). Amphetamine and other psychostimulants reduce pH gradients in midbrain dopaminergic neurons and chromaffin granules: a mechanism of action. *Neuron*, 5(6), 797–808.

Taylor, D.P. and Ho, B.T. (1978). Comparison of inhibition of monoamine uptake by cocaine, methylphenidate, and amphetamine. *Res. Commun. Chem. Pathol. Pharmacol.*, 21, 67–75.

Villemagne V., Yuan, J., Wong, D.F., Dannals, R.F., Hatzidimitriou, G., Mathews, W.B., Ravert, H.T., Musachio, J., McCann, U.D., and Ricaurte, G.A. (1998). Brain dopamine neurotoxicity in baboons treated with doses of methamphetamine comparable to those recreationally abused by humans: evidence from positron emission tomography studies and direct *in vitro* determinations. *J. Neurosci.*, 18(1), 419–427.

Wagner, G.C., Ricuarte, G.A., Seiden, L.S., Schuster, C.R., Miller, R.J., and Westley, J. (1980). Long-lasting depletions of striatal dopamine and loss of dopamine uptake sites following repeated administration of methamphetamine. *Brain Res.*, 181, 151–160.

Wareing, M., Fisk, J.E., and Murphy, P.N. (2000). Working memory deficits in current and previous users of MDMA, *British Journal of Psychology*, 91(2), 181–188.

Zaczek, R., Culp, S., and DeSouza, E.B. (1991). Interactions of amphetamine with rat brain synaptosomes. II. Active transport. *J. Pharmacol. Exp. Ther.*, 257, 830–835.

Effects of Methamphetamine Use

HAROLD V. HALL
SANDRA B. McPHERSON
STUART W. TREMLOW
ERROL YUDKO

Cerebral Injury and Death from Methamphetamine Use

The cerebral damage caused by methamphetamine intoxication can be formidable. Prolonged use is associated with injury to the dopamine system. Essentially, continued methamphetamine use likely leads to axonic degeneration of the dopamine axon terminals in the striatum, frontal cortex, nucleus accumbens, and amygdala. Hypersensitization of neurons occurs, for example, in increasing sensitivity of D-1 receptors. It is important to note that changes in catecholamines alone cannot explain behavior in humans when they are methamphetamine intoxicated.

Animal studies across several species demonstrate that high dosages of methamphetamine damage nerve cells (Swan, 1997). In rats, one high dose is enough to cause damage to neurons; prolonged administration increases the number of neurons that are killed off (Swan, 1997). In squirrels, a single dose of MDMA (which is structurally similar to methamphetamine and mescaline) in only slight doses significantly damages brain neurons that produce serotonin. Twelve to 18 months after exposure, serotonin-producing nerves grow abnormally or not at all. MDMA selectively damages serotonin neurons in virtually all species (Fischer et al., 1995). Buffenstein et al. (1997) showed through SPECT scanning of methamphetamine abusers in Hawaii that brain deterioration continues for months after abstinence, a finding that, if consistently cross-validated, suggests another unique and pathological feature of methamphetamine.

Not surprisingly, high doses of methamphetamine can cause death. A male under arrest died with a blood content greater than 60 mg per liter after swallowing a "baggie" of methamphetamine (Logan et al., 1996). A toxic reaction in humans can occur at levels as low as 50 mg of pure methamphetamine for nontolerant users. Ischemic stroke is associated with methamphetamine inhalation (Rothrock et al., 1998). Massive strokes are fairly common. The second author conducted a neuropsychological evaluation of a 30-year-old, previously normal, federal employee who suffered multiple strokes and a vascularizing dementia after a single methamphetamine intoxication. Although a family history of strokes for members in their 60s and 70s was revealed, representing a possible vulnerability for the client, methamphetamine appeared to cause the client's strokes long before they would normally be expected, given his family history. Methamphetamine taken intranasally has caused caudal thalamic infarctions in an abuser (Sachdeva and Woodward, 1989). Ischemic stroke is associated with methamphetamine inhalation (Rothrock et al., 1997). More ominously, and as discussed above, preliminary data show continued destruction of brain tissue in humans several months after abstinence from methamphetamine (Buffenstein et al., 1997).

In sum, much of the data suggest there is no way of establishing a "safe" or "unsafe" level of methamphetamine for a particular person, or even for the same person with repeated doses. With other drugs, and certainly with alcohol, use of the particular substance must continue for a given time period (e.g., 12 months) and be accompanied by maladaptive behavior to qualify for a DSM-IV diagnosis of substance abuse. Preliminary data suggest that this is in marked contrast to methamphetamine abuse where a small number of intoxications can create catastrophic changes in physical and mental functioning.

The Unpredictable Effects of Methamphetamine

There are multiple factors, in addition to its untoward effects on nontolerant users, that cause the effects of methamphetamine to be unpredictable. The properties of methamphetamine itself can create unpredictable reactions. Further, there may be impurities in the drug. Methamphetamine manufactured in clandestine labs is frequently impure (Kram et al., 1977; Sinnema and Verweij, 1981). Methamphetamine can be used to "cut" other drugs, which means that interactive effects must be considered. Also, a variety of toxic chemicals can be used as the precursors from which methamphetamine can be formed (e.g., ephedrine and pseudoephedrine, benzyl chloride, benzyl cyanide, methylamine); or as reagents, substances that react with precursors (e.g., hydriodic acid, iodine, mercuric chloride, sodium cyanohydridoborate); or as solvents (e.g., ethanol, ethyl chloroform, acetone). Residues of these substances may contaminate the final product.

There are two basic methods for producing methamphetamine, each of which requires 2 to 4 days to produce a batch. One method involves the reaction of phenyl-2-propanone (P-2-P), phenylacetine, and methylamine. The other method uses ephedrine as a precursor chemical, which does not necessitate use of a controlled precursor. This method, referred to as the ephedrine/red phosphorus method, requires the use of hydrogenator. Red phosphorus is on the list of less restricted chemicals in many states, and information that this chemical can be obtained from the fireworks and matchmaking industries has been widely disseminated on the Internet since 1996 (e.g., see deadlock@paranoia.com). The striking pad on match covers is about 40% red phosphorus and 30% antimony sulfide, with lesser amounts of glue, iron oxide, manganese dioxide, and glass powder. Some of these chemicals, alone or in combination, can cause toxic reactions in the methamphetamine user. In addition, the ephedrine/red phosphorus method often produces "garbage" methamphetamine. Unless simple precautions are followed, which are typically not followed by makers who are often chronic methamphetamine users themselves, high amounts of iodoephedrine and azirine are produced as contaminants.

Most methamphetamine is not the clear, pure hydrochloride salt we typically associate with the drug, but contains impurities that can be identified by their color as follows:

- Red: Methamphetamine from pseudoephedrine; the red coloring of the tablet was not washed away.
- Orange: Ephedrine sulfate was used; the sulfate was reduced to sulfur.
- Purple: The iodine from the phosphorus-iodine reaction was not chemically washed.
- Green: Copper somehow made its way into the mixture, possibly because of the mixing vessel.
- Brown: A tablating agent or oxidized red coloring was present in the reduction.

Use of drugs other than methamphetamine affects the user's response to methamphetamine. Cocaine intoxication causes cross-tolerance to discriminative and reinforcing effects of methamphetamine in animal studies (Peltier et al., 1996). It is important to understand that although the terms to describe cross-reverse tolerance (i.e., sensitivity) vary as shown in Table 6.1, they refer to the same concept; the terms can be gleaned from the animal and human literature, DSM-IV (1994) and DSM-IV-TR (2000), and other sources.

Polydrug abuse is the rule rather than the exception in adult offenders (Kassebaum and Chandler, 1994). Repeated use of methamphetamine alone can decrease sensitivity and increase tolerance to more methamphetamine (Ando et al., 1996). Even innocuous foods can cause cross-reverse tolerance (i.e., sensitivity) to methamphetamine. In many users, caffeine increases sensitivity to the effects of methamphetamine (Ando et al., 1986). Cocaine, L-dopa, and a variety of other substances have been associated with cross-reverse

Table 6.1 Terms Used to Describe Methamphetamine-Like Effects by Another Substance Following Termination of Methamphetamine[a]

	Term	Source
1.	Supersensitivity, Recurrence	Ando, Hironaka, and Yanagita (1986), *Psychopharmacology Bulletin*
2.	Sensitivity	Asami, Kuribara, and Tadokoro (1986), *Yakubutsu Seishin Kodo*
3.	Transferable Effects	Kuribara and Tadokoro (1989), *Japanese Journal of Pharmacology*
4.	Cross-Reverse Tolerance	Fujii, Kuribara, and Tadokoro (1990), *Japanese Journal of Pharmacology*
5.	Cross-Reverse Tolerance	Fujii, Kuribara, and Tadokoro (1990), *Japanese Journal of Pharmacology*
6.	Response Generalization	Oliveto, Bickel, Hughes, Terry, Higgins and Badger (1993), *Behavioral Pharmacology*
7.	Unlabeled, refers to methamphetamine-like action (e.g., diet pills, khat)	American Psychiatric Association (2000), like action (e.g., diet pills, khat), *Diagnostic and Statistical Manual of Mental Disorders* (4th edition, text revision)

Note: Substances producing methamphetamine-like effects reported in the literature include caffeine, phenobarbitol (an antiseizure medication), theophylline (a stimulant found in tea), methylphenidate (a compound commonly found in diet pills which is structurally different from methamphetamine but with methamphetamine-like stimulant properties), L-dopa (used in treatment of Parkinson's Disease), bromocriptine (a compound with antidepressant properties), morphine, benzphetamine (a mixture of benzadrine and other methamphetamine compounds), ephedrine (a component of methamphetamine), and cocaine.

[a] Based on a partial review of the literature. Other journals include *Life Sciences*, *Psychophamol*, *Pharmacol Biochem Behavior*.

tolerance. Most abusers are aware of this phenomenon and will deliberately attempt to recreate the effects of methamphetamine by using these substances when methamphetamine is unavailable. Alcohol, a central nervous system suppressant, is commonly used by addicts to decrease the effects of amphetamines, especially during withdrawal periods. In *State vs. Michael Lawrence* (2001), the defendant drank coffee to reexperience a methamphetamine-like "rush," including on the day he dismembered the murder victim, a Kirby vacuum cleaner salesman who came to his house. Table 6.2 lists some of the many studies from the empirical literature involving both humans and animals that show the association between caffeine and methamphetamine.

The common theme from the literature is that methamphetamine causes a lasting sensitivity to relapse. Various animal studies cited above (e.g., see Ando et al., 1986) suggest that relapse into states resembling methamphetamine intoxication can be triggered by environmental stress. These findings have not been generalized to humans. Replication of these findings for humans would suggest that the sudden onset of a state resembling a paranoid state could occur months or even years after an individual's last intoxication from methamphetamine.

Table 6.2 Caffeine and Methamphetamine-Like Effects[a] (studies by date of publication)

		Subjects
1.	White and Keller (1984)	Rodents
2.	Ando, Hironaka, and Yanagita (1986)	Mice, rats
3.	Holtzman (1987)	Rats
4.	Chait and Johanson (1988)	Humans
5.	Kuribara and Tadokoro (1989)	Mice
6.	Fujii, Kuribara, and Tadokoro (1990)	Mice
7.	Stern, Chait, and Johanson (1989)	Humans
8.	Griffiths, Evans, Heishman, Preston, Sannerud, Wolf, and Woodson (1990)	Humans
9.	Oliveto, Bickel, Hughes, Shea, Higgins, and Fenwick (1992)	Humans
10.	Oliveto, Bickel, Hughes, Terry, Higgins, and Badger (1993)	Humans
11.	Mumford, Evans, Kaminski, Preston, Sannerud, Silverman, and Griffiths (1994)	Humans
12.	Kuribara (1994)	Mice
13.	Kuribara (1994)	Mice

[a] Based on a partial review of the literature. Other sources of information include (a) the clinical-forensic evaluation/treatment of methamphetamine abusers by Harold V. Hall, Ph.D, ABPP (1988–2001); (b) consultation with Errol Yudko, Ph.D, Assistant Professor, Department of Psychology, University of Hawaii, Hilo, and consultant to Big Island Substance Abuse Center; (c) a special report of the Pacific Institute for the Study of Conflict and Aggression entitled "methamphetamine use and the mental health expert witness in criminal-forensic contexts," by H. V. Hall, S.B. Twemlow, and S.B. McPherson (January 1999); and (d) the defendant in State of Hawaii v. Michael Lawrence (September 1, 1999 evaluation).

References

Ando, K., Hironaka, N., and Yanagita, T. (1986). Psychotic manifestations in amphetamine abuse — experimental study on the mechanism of psychotic recurrence. *Psychopharmacol. Bull.*, 22(3), 763–767.

Buffenstein, A., Coel, M., and Combs, B. (1997). Functional Neuroimaging of Chronic Crystal Methamphetamine Users. Unpublished grant application, University of Hawaii, John A. Burns School of Medicine.

Chait, L.D. and Johanson, C.E. (1988). Discriminative stimulus effects of caffeine and benzphetamine in amphetamine-trained volunteers. *Psychopharmacology*, 96(3), 302–308.

Diagnostic and Statistical Manual of Mental Disorders, 4th ed. (DSM-IV), published by the American Psychiatric Association, Washington, D.C., 1994.

Diagnostic and Statistical Manual of Mental Disorders, 4th ed. (DSM-IV), Text Revision (DSM-IV-TR), published by the American Psychiatric Association, Washington, D.C., 2000.

Fischer, C., Hatzidimitriou, G., Wlos, J., Katz, J., and Ricaurte, G. (1995). Reorganization of ascending 5-HT axon projections in animals previously exposed to recreational drug 3,4-methylenedioxymethamphetamine (MDMA, "Ecstasy"). *J. Neuroscience*, 15, 5476–5485.

Fujii, T., Kuribara, H., and Tadokoro, S. (1990). Interaction between caffeine and methamphetamine by means of ambulatory activity in mice. *Yakubutsu Seishin Kodo*, 9(2), 225–231.

Griffiths, R.R., Evans, S.M., Heishman, S.J., Preston, K.L., Sannerud, C.A., Wolf, B., and Woodson, P.P. (1990). Low-dose caffeine discrimination in humans. *J. Pharmacol. Exp. Ther.*, 252(3), 970–978.

Holtzman, S.G. (1987). Discriminative stimulus effects of caffeine: tolerance and cross-tolerance with methylphenidate. *Life Sci.*, 40(4), 381–389.

Kassebaum, G. and Chandler, S.M. (1994). Polydrug use and self control among men and women in prison. *J. Drug Educ.*, 24(4), 333–350.

Kram, T.C., Kruegel, B.S., and Kruegel, A.V. (1977). The identification of impurities in illicit methamphetamine exhibits by gas chromatography/mass spectrometry and nuclear magnetic resonance spectroscopy. *J. Forensic Sci.*, 22, 40–52.

Kuribara, H. (1994). Caffeine enhances the stimulant effect of methamphetamine, but may not affect induction of methamphetamine sensitization of ambulation in mice. *Psychopharmacology*, 116(2), 125–129.

Kuribara, H. (1994). Modification by caffeine of the sensitization to methamphetamine and cocaine in terms of ambulation in mice. *Life Sci.*, 55(12), 933–940.

Kuribara, H. and Tadokoro, S. (1989). Reverse tolerance to ambulation-increasing effects of methamphetamine and morphine in six mouse strains. *Jpn. J. Pharmacol.*, 49(2), 197–203.

Lawrence Michael Borchardt v. State of Maryland, No. 55, Sept. Term, 2000, *App v. New Jersey*, 530 US 566.

Logan, B.K., Weiss, E.L., and Harruff, R.C. (1996). Case report: distribution of methamphetamine in a massive fatal ingestion. *J. Forensic Sci.*, 41(2), 322–323.

Mumford, G.K., Evans, S.M., Kaminski, B.J., Preston, K.L., Sannerud, C.A., Silverman, K., and Griffiths, R.R. (1994). Discriminative stimulus and subjective effects of theobromine and caffeine in humans. *Psychopharmacology*, 115(1–2), 1–8.

Oliveto, A.H., Bickel, W.K., Hughes, J.R., Shea, S.Y., Higgins, S.T., and Fenwick, J.W., (1992). Caffeine drug discrimination in humans: acquisition, specificity and correlation with self-reports. *J. Pharmacol. Exp. Ther.*, 261(3), 885–894.

Oliveto, A.H., Bickel, W.K., Hughes, J.R., Terry, S.Y., Higgins, S.T., and Badger, G.J. (1993). Pharmacological specificity of the caffeine discriminative stimulus in humans: effects of theophylline, methylphenidate and buspirone. *Behav. Pharmacol.*, 4(3), 237–246.

Peltier, R.L., Li, D.H., Lytle, D., Taylor, C.M., and Emmett-Oglesby, M.W. (1996). Chronic d-amphetamine or methamphetamine produces cross-tolerance to the discriminative and reinforcing stimulus effects of cocaine. *J. Pharmacol. Exp. Ther.*, 277(1), 212–218.

Rothrock, J.F., Rubenstein, R., and Lyden, P.D. (1988). Ischemic stroke associated with methamphetamine inhalation. *Neurology*, 38(4), 589–592.

Sachdeva, K. and Woodward, K.G. (1989). Caudal thalamic infarction following intranasal methamphetamine use. *Neurology*, 39(2/1), 305–306.

Sinnema, A. and Verweij, A.M.A. (1981). Impurities in illicit amphetamine: a review. United Nations Office of Drug Use and Crime, 37–54.

Stern, K.N., Chait, L.D., and Johanson, C.E. (1989). Reinforcing and subjective effects of caffeine in normal human volunteers. *Psychopharmacology*, 98(1), 81–88.

Swan, N. (1997). Response to Escalating Methamphetamine Abuse Builds on NIDA-Funded Research. Available at http:\\165.112.78.61/NIDA-Notes/NNVol1 1 N5/ Escalating .html.

White, B.C. and Keller, G.E. (1984). Caffeine pretreatment: enhancement and attenuation of d-amphetamine-induced activity. *Pharmacol. Biochem. Behav.*, 20, 383–386.

Diagnosis of Methamphetamine Use

7

HAROLD V. HALL
SANDRA B. McPHERSON
STUART W. TWEMLOW
ERROL YUDKO

The Symptomatic Patterns

The clinical symptoms of methamphetamine use are primarily sympathomimetic in nature and are well documented in the literature on humans and animals (Tadokoro and Kuribara, 1986; Rothrock et al., 1988; Sachdeva and Woodward, 1989; DeVito and Wagner, 1989; Tohhara et al., 1990; Beebe and Walley, 1995; Ando et al., 1996; Ashizawa et al., 1996; Chuck et al., 1996; Logan et al., 1996; Peltier et al., 1996; Wolkoff, 1997). At low doses, methamphetamine causes generally positive effects, such as increased alertness, energy, euphoria, elevated self-confidence, persistent activity and work, increased talkativeness, increased sexual pleasure and hypersexuality, a sense of well-being, increased strength, and a loss of appetite. The ego-syntonic, pleasurable nature of methamphetamine intoxication explains its persistence as well as the addictive cycle that usually emerges.

Table 7.1 depicts methamphetamine intoxication and its general effects on violence potential and reality testing. The increase in violence potential and the decrease in reality testing are associated with increasing dosages. Note that reality testing in homicides may be preserved under mild effects of methamphetamine, but that delusional homicides are the hallmark of severe impairment as a result of this drug.

Higher doses of methamphetamine may result in negative symptoms such as disorganized or purposeless physical activity, tremors, muscle tics, slurred speech, muscle spasms (hyperflexia), motor instability, incoordination, gait ataxia, bruxism (i.e., teeth grinding), and athetosis (e.g., strange motor movements). Affective symptoms include agitation, restlessness, rage, panic, and anxiety. Somatic sensations include numbness of the skin and limbs. Hallucinations may occur as well as strong feelings of paranoia with

Table 7.1 Impact of Changing Dose of Methamphetamine Across Several Dimensions

Duration/Dose	Methamphetamine Intoxication	Methamphetamine Delirium	Violent Potential	Methamphetamine Delusions	Impairment Reality Testing
Low dose	Euphoria	Anxiety and irritability sometimes resulting in extreme paranoia or panic-like delirium	Violent increases as a function of dose	Occurs in many chronic users	Impairment increases as a function of dose
	Initial decreased anxiety Disinhabition Heightened interest in the environment				
	Feelings of increased competence Increased self-esteem Clear sensorium without cognitive confusion or hallucinations			Note that paranoid delusions can be experimentally induced by prolonged amphetamine administration	
Medium dose	Extreme impulsiveness including violence	Panic attack sympathetic discharge with fear of impending death			

Irresponsibility or disinhibition		Delusions are related to amount and duration rather then subjects' predisposition to psychosis
Impaired judgment Grandiosity Atypical generosity Hypersexuality	Disorientation similar to organic delirium with alternate in perception of time, place, and person	
Hypervigilance		Reality testing may be preserved if the effect is mild but delusional homicides do exist when reality testing is severely impaired
Compulsive repetitive actions Mania Psychosis or Bipolar Affective Disorder	Stimulant overdose	Delusions last longer than for cocaine, often for several days
High dose		

Source: Adapted from Gabbard, G.O., Ed., *Treatment of Psychiatric Disorders*, 2nd ed., Vol. 1, American Psychiatric Press, Washington, D.C., 1995, 706–720.

a severe amphetamine-induced psychosis. Most high doses of methamphetamine are associated with a clear sensorium. Violent behavior toward others with increased risk-taking behavior has been observed frequently. Hyperthermia (extreme rise in body temperature) is common. At high dosages, difficulty with urination, irregular heartbeat, convulsions, stroke, coma, and death have occurred.

The period following intoxication ("coming down" or "on the crash") is characterized initially by restlessness, irritability, and a craving for the drug, along with fatigue and long periods of sleep. Confusion, disorientation, and hunger are common during this period.

Chronic symptoms of methamphetamine use include motor problems, depression, irritability, fatigue, exhaustion, and formication (delusions of insects crawling on the skin). Persisting neuropsychological symptoms associated with chronic methamphetamine use have been noted in animal and human investigations. Such symptomology includes visual-spatial disturbances, memory encoding and retrieval problems, lowered attention and concentration (especially selective attention), and executive dysfunction such as delayed responses and perseveration. A long-lasting amotivational syndrome, probably associated with dopamine depletion, often sets in. Circadian variations upset the sleep–wakefulness cycle. Flashbacks associated with threatening stimuli have been noted. Symptoms similar to paranoid schizophrenia, a disorganized lifestyle, persistent delusions, poor judgment, and irresponsibility have been observed. As discussed earlier, the user may realize that visual and auditory hallucinations stem from methamphetamine use, but will continue with the pathological behavior anyway. A diminished social life with compromised coping abilities is a natural consequence. Fatal liver, heart, kidney, and lung disorders, as well as brain injury due to cerebral bleeds and other factors, have been implicated. There is a lowered resistance to disease. Acne, sores, corneal ulcerations, and skin disorders such as dry, itchy skin may occur. As alluded to earlier, a chronic reverse tolerance (i.e., sensitivity) to a variety of chemicals including cocaine, ephedrine, L-dopa, and morphine often ensues. Relevant to forensic issues, methamphetamine users may use such drugs as a substitute for methamphetamine and amphetamine psychosis may be induced or exacerbated by such drugs (Tadororo and Kuribara, 1986). Weight loss is usually striking, along with malnutrition, avitaminosis, and other problems in nutrition and appetite.

Table 7.2 presents the symptoms of methamphetamine withdrawal. The effects on the user's mood during this period are considerable. Violence potential is increased during withdrawal, furthered by an entrenched delusional system and compromised ability to cope.

Table 7.2

Duration and Dose	Acute Withdrawal: the Crash	Chronic Withdrawal and Mood Dysfunction[a]	Violence Potential
Low dose	Recovery in most low-dose first-time users	Decreased capacity to perceive reward or pleasure	Violent potential increases as dose increases
		Follows several hours to 3 days after the crash after a period of hypersomnolence	
	Mildly depressed mood and anxiety	Increased anxiety	
		Inactivation	
Medium dose	Craving with sometimes commission of crimes to obtain money	Irritability	
		Restricted feelings of pleasure in drug-free life	
	A wish to escape from the hyperstimulated dysphasia with increased use of sedative drugs and alcohol to induce sleep	High anxiety	
		Severe depression	
	Hypersomnolence and hyperphagia	Loss of temper	
High dose	Unipolar depression in some, withdrawal and chronic mood dysfunction in chronic abusers	Mood disorders	

[a] Methamphetamine is physiologically as well as psychologically addictive but the symptoms are primarily expressed psychologically.

Source: Adapted from Gabbard, G.O., Ed., *Treatment of Psychiatric Disorders*, 2nd ed., Vol. 1, American Psychiatric Press,, Washington, D.C., 1995, 708–720.

Diagnosing Methamphetamine Syndromes

Terms used by mental health experts have diverse meanings and one should not assume that one understands the meaning of expert testimony unless those terms are defined explicitly. The expert should employ the *Diagnostic and Statistical Manual,* Fourth Edition (DSM-IV, American Psychiatric Association, 1994) classification system to differentiate among methamphetamine intoxication, abuse, dependence, and withdrawal or other special symptoms of methamphetamine-induced conditions.

Absent combinations of drugs (e.g., polysubstance dependence), the possibilities for methamphetamine-related diagnoses in DSM-IV (listed under Amphetamine or Amphetamine-like disorders because of common properties and general arousal effects) are as follows:

Code	Term
304.40	Amphetamine Dependence
305.70	Amphetamine Abuse
292.89	Amphetamine Intoxication
292.0	Amphetamine Withdrawal
292.81	Amphetamine Intoxication Delirium
292. xx	Amphetamine-Induced Psychotic Disorder
.11	With Delusions
.12	With Hallucinations
292.84	Amphetamine-Induced Mood Disorder
292.89	Amphetamine-Induced Anxiety Disorder
292.89	Amphetamine-Induced Sexual Dysfunction
292.89	Amphetamine-Induced Sleep Disorder
292.9	Amphetamine-Related Disorder Not Otherwise Specified (NOS)

Only two of these conditions (Codes 292.89 and 292.81) denote methamphetamine intoxication at a particular time. An expert's diagnosis of methamphetamine abuse or dependence for the time of an alleged offense, for example, does not imply that the affected person was methamphetamine intoxicated before or during the commission of that alleged crime. Both abuse and dependence refer to the emergence of a maladaptive pattern within a 12-month period but, as has been seen, that pattern may be triggered by short-term usage.

As a caveat, although these diagnoses are helpful, they can imply greater precision than is, in fact, present. Standards should be improved to specify the degree of change and to separate normal alterations of consciousness from pathological states. Until that occurs, we are left with a rudimentary classification system. Using DSM IV criteria, a diagnosis of methamphetamine intoxication for a particular time requires that the following occur:

A. Methamphetamine use shortly before or during a relevant event. An altered state of consciousness must be present, even though metabolites may still be in the body from previous methamphetamine use or from other substances.

B. Clinically significant maladaptive behavioral or psychological changes (e.g., euphoria or affective blunting; changes in sociability; hypervigilance; interpersonal sensitivity; anxiety, tension, or anger; stereotyped behaviors; impaired judgment; or impaired social or occupational functioning) that developed during, or shortly after, ingestion of methamphetamine.
C. Two (or more) of the following, developing during, or shortly after, ingestion of methamphetamine:
  (1) Tachycardia or bradycardia
  (2) Pupillary dilation
  (3) Elevated or lowered blood pressure
  (4) Perspiration or chills
  (5) Nausea or vomiting
  (6) Evidence of weight loss
  (7) Psychomotor agitation or retardation
  (8) Muscular weakness, respiratory depression, chest pain, or cardiac arrhythmias
  (9) Confusion, seizures, dyskinesias, dystonias, or coma
D. The symptoms are not due to a general medical condition and are not better accounted for by another mental disorder.

According to DSM-IV, the diagnosis should specify whether delusions or perceptual disturbances (e.g., hallucinations, sensory illusions) occurred in the absence of delirium. Again, these are not precisely separable from normal levels of suspicion or normal mild sensory distortion. Sensory interpretation — including distortion — is fundamental to all perception. By convention (and assuming the accuracy of the defendant's report), intact reality testing means that the accused knew that the perceptual disturbances were induced by methamphetamine.

When perceptual disturbances occur in the absence of such knowledge, a diagnosis of Methamphetamine-Induced Psychotic Disorder, with Hallucinations (or sensory illusions) should be made, as methamphetamine psychosis closely resembles paranoid schizophrenia. The clinical experiences of some of the reviewers of this book (see Appendix II) indicate that delusions and hallucinations are not the equivalent of loss of contact with reality (e.g., many schizophrenics and methamphetamine abusers suffering from psychotic symptoms can shift immediately from delusional and/or hallucinatory activity to respond to the realistic requirements of a situation).

The diagnoses of Methamphetamine-Induced Psychotic Disorder, Mood Disorder, Anxiety Disorder, Sexual Dysfunction, Sleep Disorder, and NOS conditions (as in other symptoms not included in the above conditions) imply intoxication or withdrawal from methamphetamine when the symptoms are in excess of those usually associated with the intoxication or withdrawal symptoms but only when the symptoms are sufficiently severe to warrant independent clinical attention. For clarity, the evaluator must specify whether those methamphetamine conditions occurred with onset during intoxication or with onset during withdrawal.

References

American Psychiatric Association. (1994). *Diagnostic and Statistical Manual of Mental Disorders* (DSM-IV), 4th ed.. Washington, D.C.: American Psychiatric Association.

Ando, K., Hironaka, N., and Yanagita, T. (1996). Psychotic manifestations in amphetamine abuse — experimental study on the mechanism of psychotic recurrence. *Psychopharmacol. Bull.*, 22(3), 763–767.

Ashizawa, T., Saito, T., Yamamoto, M., Shichinohe, S., Ishikawa, H., Maeda, H. , Toki, S., Ozawa, H., Watanabe, M., and Takahata, N. (1996). A case of amotivational syndrome as a residual symptom after methamphetamine abuse. *Nihon Arukoru Yakabutsu gakkai Zasshi*, 31(5), 451–461.

Beebe, D.K. and Walley, E. (1995). Smokeable methamphetamine ("Ice"): An old drug in a different form. *Am. Fam. Phy.*, 51(2), 449–453.

Chuck, R.S., Williams, J.M., Goldberg, M.A., and Lubniewski, A.J. (1996). Recurrent corneal ulcerations associated with smokeable methamphetamine abuse. *Am. J. Ophthalmol.*, 121(5), 571–572.

DeVito, M.J. and Wagner, G.C. (1989a). Functional consequences following methamphetamine-induced neuronal damage. *Psychopharmacology*, 28(a), 432–435.

Logan, B.K., Weiss, E.L., and Harruff, R.C. (1996). Case report: distribution of methamphetamine in a massive fatal ingestion. *J. Forensic Sci.*, 41(2), 322–323.

Peltier, R.L., Li, D.H., Lytle, D., Taylor, C.M., and Emmett-Oglesby, M.W. (1996). Chronic D-amphetamine or methamphetamine produces cross-tolerance to the discriminative and reinforcing stimulus effects of cocaine. *J. Pharmacol. Exp. Ther.*, 277(1), 212–218.

Rothrock, J.F., Rubenstein, R., and Lyden, P.D. (1988). Ischemic stroke associated with methamphetamine inhalation. *Neurology*, 38(4), 589–592.

Sachdeva, K. and Woodward, K.G. (1989). Caudal thalamic infarction following intranasal methamphetamine use. *Neurology*, 39(2/1), 305–306.

Tadokoro, S. and Kuribara, H. (1986). Reverse tolerance to the ambulation-increasing effect of methamphetamine in mice as an animal model of amphetamine psychosis. *Psychopharmacol. Bull.*, 22(3), 757–762.

Tohhara, S., Kato, A., and Nakajima, T. (1990). Methamphetamine abuse by smoking. *Arukoku Kenkyuoto Yakubutsu Ison*, 25(6), 467–474.

Wolkoff, D.A. (1997). Methamphetamine abuse: An overview for health care professionals. *Hawaii Med. J.*, 56(2), 34–66.

Section III

Aggression

Anecdotal Evidence of the Effects of Amphetamine on Aggression

8

HAROLD V. HALL

The association between methamphetamine and violence has been observed repeatedly. In a recent murder case in Hawaii, a forensic psychologist testified that San Diego is considered the methamphetamine capital of the world, with methamphetamine found in the system of 90% of violent defendants or being part of the precipitating events (*State v. Monte Louis Young*, 1997). The theme of violence runs through all operations associated with the manufacture, sale, and consumption of methamphetamine.

Congressional testimony before the 104th Congress (Subcommittee on Crime, House of Representatives, 1995) provided examples of the strong connection between methamphetamine and violence:

> Some of the problems in dealing with this particular drug ... are the high violence potential. I run a tactical team that does high violence entries of primarily clandestine drug lab type entries. There are only several teams that will do this mainly because of the hazards involved. The atmosphere can become very poisonous, explosion, chemical contamination, and violence potential, from the weapon problem with the suspects inside. So, this is one of the things that become very important to what I'm doing. There's, again, weapons involvement. There normally is always high velocity type weapon involvement — Mack 10s, Tech-9s, Uzis, mini Uzis, street sweepers, which is an automatic 12 gauge shotgun, these type of things (pp. 37–38).

In addition, the violence associated with methamphetamine is unparalleled. Some examples of this violence:

- Phoenix, Arizona, police say methamphetamine is largely responsible for the 40% jump in homicides in 1994.
- In Contra Costa County, near San Francisco, police have found that methamphetamine is involved in 89% of domestic disputes in that county.
- In San Diego, rival methamphetamine-smuggling rings were responsible for a series of killings that resulted in 26 deaths. Also in San Diego County, the percentage of methamphetamine detections in [arrestees] rose from 23% in the first half of 1991, to 45% during the same period in 1994.
- In San Luis Obispo, California [in May 1995], local authorities requested DEA assistance in confronting spiraling violence that involved 13 drug-related homicides, committed by gangs engaged in the production and distribution of methamphetamine in that count[y].
- In Tacoma, Washington, police reported that half a dozen homicides were related to a methamphetamine organization which, among other things, pipe bombed the residence of a narcotics detective.

A key question is whether previous violence associated with methamphetamine, especially when it is similar to the instant offense, was the result of a habitual set of violent acts or an isolated event. Historical instances of violence should be examined in terms of variables such as frequency, severity, recency, acceleration, triggering stimuli, opportunity factors, and inhibitions to aggression.

Historical factors that have traditionally indicated willfulness to commit violence in methamphetamine cases include the following:

- Lengthy time delays between triggers to violence and the instant crime
- Performance of complex chains of behaviors in order to execute the violent behavior
- Flexibility of response (e.g., when the perpetrator has multiple weapons with which to inflict harm)
- Predatory vs. reactive violence

Key forensic questions can be formulated as follows:

- Should the defendant have known the likely outcome of the chain of behavioral events culminating in violence?

- Did the defendant know that methamphetamine intoxication in this situation, based on the defendant's history, would likely result in his or her violence to another?

References

State v. Monte Louis Young, First Circuit Court, Cr. No. 97-1 1 94 (May 7, 1998).

Subcommittee on Crime of the Committee on the Judiciary, House of Representatives, 104th Congress, First Session, October 26, 1995 (Ser. No. 49), Rising Scourge of Methamphetamine in America.

Empirical Evidence of the Effects of Amphetamine on Aggression

9

ERROL YUDKO
PAUL MIDSON

The effect of methamphetamine (MA) on aggressive behavior has not been studied. However, anecdotal evidence provided by numerous judicial and clinical workers suggests a high correlation between aggressive acts and the use of drugs, most prominently stimulants such as MA. The effects of the D- and L-isomers of amphetamine on aggressive behavior have been studied in rats, mice, humans, and nonhuman primates. In this chapter we assume that the effects of MA on aggressive behavior are similar to the effects of amphetamine. This is most likely, but not necessarily the case. Speculation has been made that the potential combination of the induced psychoactive effects of amphetamines can lead to dangerous and aggressive behavior (Wright and Klee, 2001). However, there is a body of research suggesting that high doses of amphetamine essentially reduce aggressive behavior (antiaggressive effects), while lower doses may potentiate aggressive responses. Rodents and primates are frequently used as analogous models for humans in experimentation because ethical considerations preclude the use of human subjects. Further, the brain structures of these animals are similar enough to those of humans to allow us to gather a great deal of insight into the human condition by understanding the effects of drugs in nonhuman animals. It has been shown that continued and consistent amphetamine use can sometimes result in paranoia and delusions, accompanied by other latent conditions such as mood swings and depression. It is the goal of this chapter, therefore, to illustrate the relationships between amphetamine use and intraspecies aggressive behavior.

Administration of Amphetamines to Rodent Subjects

As mentioned above, ethical concerns preclude the use of humans in many experimental situations; however, we can understand many features of the human central nervous system by understanding the brains of other animals. The animal most widely used in the area of amphetamine experimentation is the rodent, which has an analogous, rather than homologous, brain structure to humans. In the following sections, we examine the modification of aggressive behavior in rodents by amphetamines. The various aspects of aggressive behavior include the tendency for provoked attack, the influence of environment on behavior, social factors, and the neurological basis of aggression.

Behavioral Observations

When using nonhuman subjects to study aggressive behavior, the typical research methodologies most usually employed by experimenters include pain-, isolation-, and brain stimulation-induced aggression. However, when making a comparison between animals of different species the outcomes of these tests yield varying and somewhat contradictory results, which in turn hampers one's ability to generalize to the human population. Additionally, it has been found that the most important aspects of amphetamine-stimulated aggressive and defensive responses vary with the nature of the species involved, the stimulus situation, prior experience with these certain behaviors, and the dosage and chronicity of drug exposure; the last is of primary concern (Miczek and Tidey, 1989).

When observing the effects of amphetamines on the aggressive responses of rodent subjects, the behavioral categories most commonly analyzed are nonsocial exploration, social exploration, immobility, threat/attack, escape/avoidance, and defensive/submissive reactions. The nonsocial exploration category includes behavioral elements such as exploring the surroundings. It has been shown in various studies that acute doses — single or intermittent doses rather than chronic daily doses — of amphetamine increase significantly the occurrence of such exploratory behavior (Moro et al., 1997).

In the mouse, social exploration involves crawling over and under other mice, grooming, sniffing, and other social interactions. Increased social activity in response to amphetamine is dose dependent. In other words, as the dose of the drug increases, the amount of behavior observed also increases. In the case of amphetamine, as the dose of the drug is increased in mice, social exploration increases as well (Moro et al., 1996); however, no noticeable effect has been observed in subjects treated intermittently — two injections a week or injections on alternating days (Moro et al., 1997). Thus, the chronicity of administration clearly has an effect on the behavioral consequence. This suggests that a single dose of amphetamine can have effects very different from chronic doses.

Squatting, crouching, and a general lack of movement comprise immobility and are typically used as an index of fear (Blanchard et al., 1969). Previous literature shows that both the frequency and the mean duration of this behavior are significantly reduced after amphetamine administration (Moro et al., 1996). This means that treated mice spend considerably less time motionless with shorter intervals between the periods of movement, which clearly indicates a direct relationship between the administration of *d*-amphetamine (dextroamphetamine) and the rate of motor activity. It also suggests that amphetamine may have the effect of reducing fear. However, the effects of amphetamine seem to be complex. Flight from a potentially dangerous conspecific can also be a sign of fear. Whereas acute and intermittent administration of amphetamine causes an increase in flight from a conspecific, chronic administration causes a reduction in flight (Moro et al., 1997).

Threat/attack behaviors consist of upright, offensive stances, lunging, attacking, and chasing. Moro et al. (1996) found that the total duration of time spent in threat postures was increased by a low acute dose of amphetamine (0.25 mg/kg); however, the total duration of attacks was reduced significantly in comparison with a saline-treated control group at intermediate (1.5 mg/kg) or high (3 mg/kg) dose ranges (Moro et al., 1996; 1997). Furthermore, intervals between the attacks were considerably shorter for amphetamine-treated animals, resulting in a higher rate of attack (Moro et al., 1996). Taken together with the biphasic effect of amphetamine on the duration of attack, this result suggests that amphetamine changes the quality of attack in a dose-dependent manner.

Dose-Dependent Effects

Acute Administration

The administration of amphetamine causes dose-dependent changes in either the type of behavior observed or the intensity of the behavior observed. As described in the previous section, higher doses of amphetamine can result in a disruption in the patterns of aggressive behavior displayed by male mice (Miczek and Tidey, 1989; Moro et al., 1996). This effect was evidenced by (1) repeated attacks separated by shorter time periods and (2) treated mice showing less sensitivity to their opponents' displays of submission, which, consequently, caused continued attack (Moro et al., 1996). Other studies have shown that distorted perceptions of social signals caused a decrease in the attack and threat behavior of dominant animals to subordinates, in territoriality toward intruders, and in lactating mothers defending their litters (Miczek and Tidey, 1989).

There is a common belief among health-care workers and workers in the criminal justice system that amphetamine has a dose-dependent effect on aggressive behavior. Research shows, however, that *d*-amphetamine has quite different effects that vary in accordance with species, dose of amphetamine, and the type of stimuli used. Miczek and Tidey (1989) suggest that pain-induced aggressive or defensive reactions in rats and mice were noticeably increased after the administration of low doses of amphetamine. However, at intermediate to high dose levels these effects were reduced or disrupted, along with a decrease in isolation- and extinction-induced aggressive behavior. Moro et al. (1996) obtained similar results in an isolation-induced aggression experiment using 52 male mice. It was found that lower doses (less than 4 mg/kg) increased the occurrence of threat and attack behaviors (especially at 0.25 mg/kg) and produced other ambiguous outcomes, whereas intermediate to high doses (above 4 mg/kg) yielded clear antiaggressive effects. These findings consequently strengthened the principle of rate dependency or dose dependency, which is the idea that varying quantities of amphetamine will have diverse effects on the treated subject, otherwise known as *biphasic* effects. It is interesting to note that the frequency of escape and defensive responses to threat during times of social conflict was increased in a dose-dependent manner in a much less ambiguous way (Miczek and Tidey, 1989). Aggressive and defensive responses are mediated by very different neurological systems. Thus, one possible explanation for the perception that amphetamine leads to aggressive behavior may be a misperception of the nature of aggressive behavior. Caseworkers may be calling "defensive" responses "aggressive" responses.

Chronic Administration

Chronic administration — repeated or regular administration over a certain time period — of a drug can have very different effects when compared with acute administration. This is because neurochemical changes occur in the brain after repeated drug administration. Thus, chronic administration of a drug can lead to behavioral changes even when the user is not actively under the influence of the drug. Acute effects of a drug that has been administered chronically (i.e., when a chronic user stops using for a period of time and then starts again) can also have effects different from acute effects of a drug that has not been administered chronically. This sequence occurs potentially because the drug can alleviate withdrawal.

Tolerance to the antiaggressive effects of amphetamine has been shown with a daily dose of 1.5 mg/kg for 7 days (Moro et al., 1997). Chronic and acute administration of amphetamine led to increases in defensive and escape behaviors, and no statistically significant differences were discovered between one group of mice that had received seven daily injections of amphetamine and another that had received the same dosage of saline (Moro et al., 1997).

Note: By using selective antagonists it has been shown that dopamine receptors of the D2 subtype (see Chapter 5 on Physiology) are most effective in reducing the increased motor activity brought on by amphetamine intoxication (Miczek and Tidey, 1989). This inhibition does not, however, carry over to the disruptive effects on social and aggressive behavior. It would appear that agonism of the D2 receptor is most likely not associated with amphetamine control of aggressive behavior. Other dopamine receptor antagonists such as haloperidol and chlorpromazine have been found to reduce aggressive and social behavior, yet none has reversed the effects of amphetamine on these actions (Miczek and Tidey, 1989).

Methodological Problems: Distinguishing between Aggressive and Defensive Reactions

A persistent problem in the pursuit of information regarding aggressive behavior is the ways in which the data are gathered and analyzed. As mentioned before, the typical methods of experimentation are isolation-induced and pain-induced aggression, as well as intruder–resident models. The problem is that both fear and anger can elicit attack. Pain-induced aggressive behavior is fear induced and thus neurologically very specific. Intruder-induced aggressive behavior is anger induced and thus neurologically very different from pain-induced aggressive behavior. There is no reason to predict that amphetamine would affect pain-induced aggressive behavior the same way it affects intruder-induced aggressive behavior.

Another difficulty worth mentioning is the interaction between behavioral categories and the confounding that may consequentially occur. One example is the decrease in immobility that is associated with amphetamine administration and the corresponding increase of escape/avoidance behaviors that may possibly arise from such escalation in locomotor activity. It seems reasonable that the stimulant effects of amphetamine could perhaps cause a sensation of irritability that would lead to higher rates of occurrence for defensive/offensive categories and otherwise confound the results for additional behavioral comparisons. It has been shown, however, that these amphetamine-related increases in motor activity are significant in regard to behavioral transitions such as avoidance and nonsocial exploration, but are not significant when transitions of attack are involved (Moro et al., 1996).

Amphetamines and Their Effects on Dominance Hierarchy in Primates

Humans are primates, as are monkeys and apes. Evolution tends to be very conservative and so the brains of humans are very similar to our cousins. In fact, genetically we are about 98% the same as our primate cousins. Although research that involves monkeys demonstrates the same dose-dependent effects of amphetamine as shown with rodent subjects, the resultant effects on aggressive behavior favor a positive rather than negative relationship (Smith and Byrd, 1984; Martin et al., 1990). Primarily, the effects that amphetamine has on primates' dominance rank have been examined. Analysis has suggested that these effects are a function of social status and group dynamics (Smith and Byrd, 1984).

Differences of Effects between Ranks

The behavior of dominant animals differs drastically from that of subordinate animals (for review, see Yudko, 1998). We tend to categorize dominant styles of behavior as aggressive and subordinate styles of behavior as defensive. Dominant and subordinate animals also differ from each other neurochemically and hormonally. We can identify the rank of a primate within its hierarchy by observing behavior. When amphetamine is administered to monkeys of different social status within an established colony, the subjects express behavior dependent on their position in the hierarchy. For example, treatment of d-amphetamine causes an increase in aggressive behavior — open mouth threats, biting, chasing — in low- and high-ranking monkeys, with little or no effect on those in the mid-ranks (Smith and Byrd, 1984). Similar effects were observed when measuring rates of affiliative behaviors — grooming, holding, huddling — between the subjects: high-ranking monkeys showed decreases in affiliation with little variance, low-ranking monkeys also displayed reductions but with a larger range of variance, and mid-ranking monkeys conveyed no significant decline in affiliative behaviors (Smith and Byrd, 1984). These findings are extremely important. They suggest that the effect of amphetamine on aggressive behavior is linked to the initial level of aggressiveness of the individual.

Additional discoveries have been made that further illustrate the diverse effects amphetamine has on the dynamics and hierarchy of primate interaction. Along with the fact that low- and high-ranking monkeys are principally affected comes a certain directionality of their aggressive displays. High-ranking subjects treated with d-amphetamine were more aggressive to adults and other superior members of the group, whereas those in the lower ranks displayed greater aggression to juveniles and those with inferior positions in the dominance hierarchy (Martin et al., 1990).

This type of effect, a drug causing individuals to act differently depending on preexisting personality traits, is not unique to amphetamine. A comparison of the animal and human literature on the effects of alcohol on aggressive behavior yields a similar result (Yudko et al., 1997). In fact, the effect of alcohol on aggressive behavior may be bidirectional. In other words, alcohol can cause aggressive behavior in a subclass of the population (i.e., in highly aggressive individuals but not in low to moderately aggressive individuals) and alcohol use can be caused by the need of the highly aggressive individual to self-medicate (this theory assumes that being very aggressive causes increased levels of stress and that alcohol is used by these individuals to alleviate that stress). This type of behavior can lead to a cyclic pattern in which the highly aggressive individual becomes involved in situations that cause stress. This person then drinks alcohol to alleviate that stress. The alcohol causes that person to become more aggressive, which causes more problems in the individual's life (brought about by aggressive behavior leading to negative outcomes), which causes more stress, which leads to more drinking. These results taken together with the above analysis of the effect of amphetamine on primate behavior suggest that the reports of human aggressive behavior being increased by amphetamine use are simply an artifact of highly aggressive individuals tending to take and be made more noticeably aggressive by amphetamine.

Dose-Dependent Effects

In contrast to the results reported from rodent research, greater rates of aggressive behavior were observed in correspondence with increases in dosage. Low doses (0.01 mg/kg) produced very little change in aggression whereas a rapid escalation was observed with subsequent increases (up to 1 mg/kg; Martin et al., 1990). In Smith and Byrd's (1984) study, the highest-ranking monkey displayed the largest increase in aggressive behavior in direct relation to the increase in dose, with rates of more than 30 times that of the control group at the highest dose (0.56 mg/kg). According to previous literature and current speculation, an adequately broad range of doses will yield an inverted U-shaped dose-effect curve that is typical of the behavioral effects of psychomotor stimulants (Martin et al., 1990). This finding indicates that increasingly larger doses of amphetamine would eventually lead to the reduction of aggressive behavior.

In regard to affiliative behaviors, one notices a dose-dependent effect on the rate of occurrence that almost parallels that of aggressive behavior. Over a range of doses (0.003 to 0.56 mg/kg) a considerable majority of subjects demonstrate a dose-related pattern of affiliative behavior with little or no effect at lower doses and large decreases at higher levels (0.3 to 0.56 mg/kg; Smith and Byrd, 1984). These results are also contrary to those found in rodent experimentation, where clear increases of social exploration were observed in male mice following acute doses of amphetamine.

Amphetamines and Their Effects on Human Aggressive Behavior

Because the possession, use, and distribution of amphetamine are illegal and because the compound causes brain damage, ethical concerns have prevented experimental research on the behavioral effects of amphetamine. Thus, the available literature on the effects of amphetamine in human participants is all correlational. Although there have been reports of high correlations between violent crime and amphetamine use, these studies may be confounded because other drugs such as alcohol are often involved and users that commit these acts sometimes have aggressive tendencies beforehand (Wright and Klee, 2001). The existing literature does give some indication regarding the effects of various doses and the possible predictions one can make concerning the long-term effects on mental health, but until more research can be performed we are limited in our understanding the relationship of amphetamine with human aggressive behavior.

Subjective Analysis

The advantage of experiments involving human subjects is that people have the ability to describe their immediate emotional states and report their feelings and thoughts. However, these subjective analyses can sometimes be inaccurate, and in a sense become "contaminated" because of participants' biases or reservations concerning the personal information they disclose, especially if it involves substance abuse. In a self-report study involving amphetamine users from a metropolitan city in Australia, Vincent et al. (1998) reported that more than one third of the sample comprising 100 participants had experienced symptoms of depression and anxiety prior to their amphetamine use, and nearly one third had experienced previous mood swings and aggressive outbursts. In addition, some of the participants believed that their usage had intensified these conditions, and almost a quarter of the subjects felt symptoms of depression and anxiety attacks for the first time after they started using the drug, although not all of them associated these symptoms with their amphetamine use. Other research shows decreases in fatigue, increases in vigor, no significant changes in anger or confusion, and a moderate decrease in depression (Cherek et al., 1986). Different subjects from separate studies also show signs of excessive confidence and delusional paranoia (Wright and Klee, 2001).

In subjective experiments, it is important that the participants understand completely what it is that they are analyzing in order to obtain accurate results. When studying the effects of amphetamine on human aggressive behavior, it is essential that we distinguish this aggression from negligent, violent crime. Although there is no clear-cut line that separates the two, we can think of violent crime as forceful and offensive acts that violate the norm and possibly lead to malevolent physical violence, whereas aggression is a "hostile or destructive tendency or behavior" (Wright and Klee, 2001). One could therefore generalize from this distinction that violence has a more social, and perhaps even economic, connotation, whereas aggression appears to be associated more closely with psychological factors. In Wright and Klee's (2001) study the respondents were asked about any ongoing problems they may have been experiencing with amphetamine-related aggression, and were "encouraged to include in their response incidents that did not result in physical harm to others, but which had produced a conscious awareness of their own hostility." By making such a distinction, one can acquire accurate data that are more representative of the population.

Observed Behavior

Experiments have been carried out that use positive and negative reinforcement to examine the effects of amphetamine on aggressive behavior. In one such study, subjects were given the opportunity to gain points that were redeemable for a monetary reward by pressing an assigned button. This was the non-aggressive response. Their point values were systematically reduced by a fictitious partner from whom they could subtract points by pressing a different button, which was the aggressive response. Biphasic results similar to those reported in nonhuman research were observed, with lower doses (5 and 10 mg/70 kg) of d-amphetamine increasing the rate of aggressive responses and higher doses (20 mg/70 kg) reducing these occurrences to levels found after placebo administration (Cherek et al., 1986). Another noteworthy outcome was that while the rate of aggressive responses was decreased at the highest dose, the amount of non-aggressive responses remained unaltered.

Referring back to the Vincent et al. (1998) study, one can extrapolate generalized correlations between amphetamine use and the behavior and health of the user. One of the outcomes of this analysis was that symptoms such as depression and anxiety were likely to be intensified, and additional problems including paranoia and aggression could possibly arise with continued use. Furthermore, it was determined that a direct relationship existed between increasing severity of dependence and mental and physical health deficits, which was consistent with the fact that the sample used in the study had considerably poorer mental and physical health and emotional functioning when compared to the general South Australian population. These data support the popular opinion that amphetamines can have severe and detrimental effects on both physical and mental performance.

Concluding Remarks

Research shows that the effects of amphetamine on aggressive behavior are complex and are dependent on the types of variables involved. One such variable would be the kind of species used for experimentation. It can be difficult to make comparisons between species, as they tend to produce differing results and have unique brain structures. For example, in experiments involving rodent subjects, higher doses of amphetamine lead to a decrease in aggressive behavior, whereas higher doses in monkeys cause an escalation in aggression. In addition, the affiliative behavior of primate subjects clearly has biphasic effects, with rates of occurrence decreasing steadily as the dose increases (Smith and Byrd, 1984), whereas rodent subjects exhibit clear increases in social exploration along the same scale (Moro et al., 1996). Such diversity between species often makes it difficult to generalize to the human population, and so carefully organized experimentation may be necessary to understand this variance.

Another complexity is the biphasic effects that amphetamine has on behavior. This dose-dependent condition can sometimes lead to difficulties in predictability since there is no clearly defined linear relationship. Even intraspecies effects can have large degrees of variance and so extensive sample sizes are necessary to gain a better perspective. It is interesting, however, that these biphasic results seemingly contradict the common belief that larger doses of amphetamine cause increases in aggressive behavior, when, in fact, it is smaller doses that elicit this condition.

When studying the effects of amphetamine on human behavior, several factors must be taken into consideration before any assumptions can be made. For example, the history of drug use of a patient, the patient's lifestyle, and the patient's social status and interactions are all possible influences on his or her drug habits and aggressive patterns of behavior. Wright and Klee (2001) report some interesting points in the area of amphetamine-related human aggressive behavior. For instance, correlations between amphetamine use and aggression are strongly associated with drug dealing rather than intoxication. Moreover, in regard to the subjects' patterns of amphetamine use, there were no significant differences between those who reported aggression and the rest of the sample, and no straightforward relationship could be found between amphetamine use and one's potential for aggressive behavior.

As one can see, the connection between amphetamine use and aggressive behavior is ambiguous and complex, with no easily discernible results. Since it is an illicit substance, the opportunities for human experimentation and research using this compound are extremely limited. Unfortunately, the only way we can obtain additional information regarding the subject is to increase the volume of current research and use larger sample sizes to enhance external validity and gain a broader perspective.

References

Blanchard, R.V. and Blanchard, D.C. (1969). Crouching as an index of fear. *J. Comp. Psychiol. Psychol.*, 67, 370–375.

Cherek, D.R., Steinberg, J.L., Kelly, T.H., and Robinson, D.E. (1986). Effects of *d*-amphetamine on human aggressive behavior. *Psychopharmacology*, 88, 381–386.

Feldman, R.S., Meyer, J.S., and Quenzer, L.F. (1997). *Principles of Neuropsychopharmacology*. Sunderland, MA: Sinauer Associates.

Martin, S.P., Smith, E.O., and Byrd, L.D. (1990). Effects of dominance rank on *d*-amphetamine-induced increases in aggression. *Pharmacol. Biochem. Behav.*, 37, 493–496.

Miczek, K.A. and Tidey, J.W. (1989). Amphetamines: aggressive and social behavior. *NIDA Res. Monogr. Ser.*, 94, 68–100.

Moro, M., Salvador, A., and Simon, V.M. (1996). Changes in the structure of the agonistic behavior of mice produced by *d*-amphetamine. *Pharmacol. Biochem. Behav.*, 56(1), 47–54.

Moro, M., Salvador, A., and Simon, V.M. (1997). Effects of repeated administration of amphetamine on agonistic behaviour of isolated male mice. *Behav. Pharmacol.*, 8, 309–318.

Navarro, J.F. and Maldonado, E. (1999). Behavioral profile of 3,4-methylenedioxymethamphetamine (MDMA) in agonistic encounters between male mice. *Prog. Neuro-Psychopharmacol. Biol. Psychiatr.*, 23, 327–334.

Smith, E.O. and Byrd, L.D. (1984). Contrasting effects of *d*-amphetamine on affiliation and aggression in monkeys. *Pharmacol. Biochem. Behav.*, 20, 255–260.

Vincent, N., Shoobridge, J., Ask, A., Allsop, S., and Ali, R. (1998). Physical and mental health problems in amphetamine users from metropolitan Adelaide, Australia. *Drug Alcohol Rev.*, 17, 187–195.

Wright, S. and Klee, H. (2001). Violent crime, aggression and amphetamine: what are the implications for drug treatment services? *Drugs Educ. Prev. Policy*, 8(1), 73–90.

Yudko, E., Blanchard, R.J., and Blanchard, D.C. (1997). Pre-clinical models of alcohol and aggressive behavior. *J. Alcohol Stud.*

Yudko, E., Blanchard, R.J., and Blanchard, D.C. (1998). The effect of subordination on hormonal and behavioral indices in Long Evans rats. *Diss. Abstr.*

Section IV

Methamphetamine and the Courts

Expert Testimony

10

HAROLD V. HALL
SANDRA B. MCPHERSON
STUART W. TWEMLOW
ERROL YUDKO

U.S. Supreme Court Decisions Regarding Methamphetamine

A search for U.S. Supreme Court cases involving methamphetamine usage reveals a decidedly conservative stance, although dissenting opinions reflect support for defendants' and Constitutional rights. The few cases uncovered involved sentencing guidelines, entrapment procedures, waiver of plea bargain discussion inadmissibility and coercion in the plea bargaining process, hearsay evidence, and the right to cross-examination.

For example, in *Fowner v. United States* (1992), the Court upheld the lower court's ruling that sentencing based on the amount of a drug could reflect not just the amount for which the defendant was found guilty but also additional material that constituted a nondrug waste product. Similarly, in *Kinder v. United States* (1992), the lower court was upheld in applying a sentence that reflected an amount of a drug that the defendant had referred to in the course of discussions but was higher than the amount specified in the plea bargaining that allowed a conviction.

Significant issues arise in the area of entrapment. Investigation of conspiracies to manufacture and sell drugs often involves undercover work and so-called sting operations. In such efforts, enforcement agents participate in criminal enterprises as part of obtaining court-worthy evidence. A substantial issue focuses on the individual's predisposition to commit a given crime. The question involves whether, but for the activity of the government agent, the individual would have remained a law-abiding citizen. The original case involved a reversal of a conviction during the prohibition era (*Sorrells v. United States*, 1932). However, in *United States v. Russell* (1973), an agent provided an essential and extremely hard-to-obtain ingredient (phenyl-2-propanone), which is a necessary component used only for the production of methamphetamine.

There had been considerable efforts by law enforcement authorities to end or discourage its sale even to persons licensed to possess it. The Court held that because the defendant was not an unwary person but, in fact, was a very active criminal, his claim of entrapment was without merit. Therefore, the initial appeal that reversed his conviction was itself reversed and the defendant's conviction was upheld.

It was noted that the issue should center not on the predisposition of the defendant but rather on the behavior of the government. The dissent took the position that "it is the Government's duty to prevent crime, not to promote it." Interestingly, the controlling factor for the dissent was the relative unavailability of this ingredient. The government had argued that this very unavailability demonstrated the awareness and intent of the defendant who had not been able to find it elsewhere until its provision by the government agent.

Plea bargaining is the known vehicle for much of U.S. justice. Certain rules pertain to plea discussions, including that the contents of those plea bargaining discussions may not be later used against the defendant unless that person enters into a waiver. The question then becomes whether or not entering into such a waiver is voluntary and knowing or is in some way coerced. Given the stakes, the potential for relatively powerful coercive factors to enter the picture clearly exists. It was on these grounds that the Court considered *United States v. Mezzanatto* (1995). The *Mezzanatto* Court ruled that as long as the defendant made the waiver in a knowing and voluntary fashion, no Constitutional guarantees or procedural rules that exist to support the plea bargain process were violated. The dissent was instructive in that it was noted that the next steps might allow defendants to waive their rights against self-incrimination with their statements being used as affirmative evidence against them at trial. In the *Mezzanatto* case, the waiver consisted of an agreement that statements made during the plea bargaining process could be used to impeach the defendant should his testimony at trial warrant same (presuming that the plea bargain failed). No plea bargain was struck. Mezzanatto's statements then were used to impeach his subsequent presentation. (He claimed he was not really involved in the methamphetamine production and thought that the other party was using a laboratory to provide the CIA with plastic explosives. Since the investigation included an undercover officer who had provided him with materials that he took to that laboratory, and because he had talked with that officer about those materials and their nature and purpose, this somewhat creative defense at trial did not serve the defendant well.) Cross-examination included references to statements the defendant had earlier made in the course of the plea bargain process that bolstered the government's case regarding his awareness of and role in the operation.

Expert Testimony

Another admissibility issue challenged the confrontation clause included in the Sixth Amendment to the Constitution. Hearsay evidence is generally excluded from the courtroom because there can be no cross-examination of the declarant of the statements. The right of cross-examination is basic to the adversary process. However, exceptions to the hearsay rule have been allowed under certain conditions, including unavailability of a witness and trustworthiness of the statement. In *United States v. Inadi* (1986), the government had recorded statements of a co-conspirator who subsequently failed to appear at trial. Furthermore, defense did not make any effort to obtain the presence of this individual. The Supreme Court took the position that the co-conspirator's statements were admissible on two grounds: the confrontation clause has, as one of its purposes, the pursuit of truth; and delays and other practical matters may make witnesses unavailable and place an undue burden on the government.

A number of cogent points were raised by the dissent. First, it was noted that co-conspirators, themselves engaged in criminal enterprise, may or may not be factual in their communications and that there is certainly no reason to presume that they are such. In fact, criminals may communicate with each other to mislead. The fact that they are discussing an enterprise does not mean that either one of them speaks the truth. Additionally, both criminals and noncriminals speak in casual and often ambiguous fashion, and the particular evidence of this case contained many ambiguous statements. Absent the opportunity to cross-examine the individual making the statements, there was no chance to properly clarify the meanings that those statements might have had.

As the above decisions illustrate, the posture of the Court, when dealing with amphetamine-related cases, leans toward conservatism and support for law and order at the expense of concern for defendants' rights or dangers of Constitutional erosion.

Daubert Issues: Who May Testify as Experts?

In *Daubert v. Merrell Dow Pharmaceuticals, Inc.* (1993, 1995), the U.S. Supreme Court considered an appeal from the Ninth Circuit Court of Appeals regarding the admission of expert testimony on the issue of whether or not maternal use of Bendectin caused human birth defects. The plaintiffs were two minors who claimed that they suffered limb reduction birth defects because their mothers had taken Bendectin for morning sickness. The district court had determined that the plaintiffs failed to meet the "*Frye* test" of "general acceptance" for admission of expert testimony and granted summary judgment in favor of the defendants on the basis of their expert's affidavit stating that Bendectin had not been shown to be a risk factor for human birth defects. The plaintiffs sought to introduce affidavits from eight other scientists on the correlation between Bendectin and limb defects. The Ninth Circuit, relying on *Frye*, affirmed the district court's ruling (1991).

On appeal, the U.S. Supreme Court overruled *Frye v. United States* (1923), in which it had been held that expert opinion based on scientific technique is inadmissible unless the technique is "generally accepted" as reliable in the relevant scientific community. The Court held that the *Frye* decision was superseded by the adoption of the Federal Rules of Evidence, in particular Rule 702, which provides that expert testimony is admissible "if scientific, technical, or other specialized knowledge will assist the trier of fact to understand the evidence or to determine a fact in issue." Rule 702 does not require "general acceptance" as a prerequisite to admissibility.

Under Rule 702, "the trial judge must ensure that any and all scientific testimony or evidence admitted is not only relevant, but reliable" (*Daubert*, 509 U.S. at 589). When faced with a proffer of expert scientific testimony, the trial judge must first determine, pursuant to Rule 104(a) of the Federal Rules of Evidence, "whether the expert is proposing to testify to (1) scientific evidence that (2) will assist the trier of fact to understand or determine a fact in issue. This entails a preliminary assessment of whether the reasoning or methodology underlying the testimony is scientifically valid and whether that reasoning or methodology can be properly applied to the facts in issue" (*Id.* at 592–593). Among the factors to be considered in making this determination are (1) whether a theory or technique can be and has been tested; (2) whether the theory or technique has been subjected to peer review and publication; (3) the known or potential rate of error and the existence and maintenance of standards controlling the technique's operation; and (4) whether the theory or technique is generally accepted within a relevant scientific community (*Id.* at 593–594). The focus of the court's inquiry "must be solely on principles and methodology, not on the conclusions that they generate" (*Id.* at 595). The Supreme Court remanded the case to the Ninth Circuit for application of the two-part test to determine whether or not the expert testimony was properly admissible on the question of whether Bendectin caused the plaintiffs' limb defects.

On remand, the Ninth Circuit noted that, pursuant to the Supreme Court's ruling, the court:

> Must engage in a difficult, two-part analysis. First, we must determine nothing less than whether the experts' testimony reflects "scientific knowledge," whether their findings are "derived by the scientific method," and whether their work product amounts to "good science."

> Second we must ensure that the proposed expert testimony is "relevant to the task at hand," i.e., that it logically advances a material aspect of the proposed party's case. The Supreme Court referred to this second prong of the analysis as the "fit requirement" (43.F.3d 1311, 1315 (1995), quoting *Daubert*, 509 U.S. 579; internal citations omitted).

The court's task was "to analyze not what the experts say, but what basis they have for saying it" (*Id.* at 1316). To perform their "gatekeeping role," courts must satisfy themselves that scientific evidence meets a certain standard of reliability before it is admitted. This means that the expert's bald assurance of validity is not enough. Rather, the party presenting the expert must show that the expert's findings are based on sound science, and this will require some objective, independent validation of the expert's methodology (*Id.* at 1316). The Ninth Circuit noted that:

> One very significant fact to be considered is whether the experts are proposing to testify about matters growing naturally and directly out of research they have conducted independently of the litigation, or whether they have developed their opinions expressly for purposes of testifying. That an expert testifies for money does not necessarily cast doubt on the reliability of his testimony, as few experts appear in court merely as an eleemosynary gesture. But in determining whether proposed expert testimony amounts to good science, we may not ignore the fact that a scientist's normal workplace is the lab or the field, not the courtroom or the lawyer's office (*Id.* at 1317).

The fact that an expert's testimony is based on research conducted independently of the litigation "provides important, objective proof that the research comports with the dictates of good science" (*Id.*). If the proffered expert testimony is not based on independent research, the party proffering the testimony must come forward with other objective, verifiable evidence that the testimony is based on "scientifically valid principles" (*Id.*).

In sum, experts need to subscribe to the notion that scientific methodology is based on hypotheses testing, distinguishing it from other fields of human inquiry. In *Daubert*, the Supreme Court stated that vigorous cross-examination, presentation of contrary evidence, and careful instruction on the burden of proof are the traditional and appropriate means of attacking

Table 10.1 *Daubert* Questions for Experts Regarding Methamphetamine

1. Using your methods of generating findings from your database, what is the rate of error in coming to conclusions for each of the procedures employed? If you do not have these statistics, why don't you have them?
2. Have you published any articles on the theory or clinical practice on methamphetamine abuse? Have you published any peer-reviewed books or articles?
3. Are you aware of the literature on the effects of methamphetamine on memory and perception? If so, cite several empirical articles.
4. In coming to conclusions in this case, what are the reliability, validity, and relevance of your findings?
5. Are you testifying based on scientific knowledge and methodology that is scientifically valid? Doesn't that imply that you are aware of the scientific investigation in methamphetamine abuse for studies that have used a sound methodology to connect the literature to this particular case?
6. What is a decision path? Doesn't a decision path illustrate retrospectively that the expert reasoned his or her way from the database to ultimate conclusions? What is your decision path in this case? What is the accuracy of that decision path?
7. What data do you have to support the competing hypothesis that the witness/defendant/victim in this case was methamphetamine intoxicated and therefore may have affected your findings?
8. Isn't it true that one way to validate competing hypotheses is by examination of corroborating data? Have you done that in this case? What data in this case suggest that you are wrong in your conclusions? Isn't it true that all experts should consider competing hypotheses? Isn't hypothesis testing the essence of science?
9. Isn't it true that the literature states that the purity of methamphetamine can vary widely as a function of precursor agents, additives, and other chemicals? To your knowledge, which precursor agents and additives were associated with the methamphetamine this person abused?
10. Did you cross-validate the memory of the witness in this case? How would you do that?
11. Isn't another way of evaluating the impact of methamphetamine abuse to look at behavioral effects? What behavioral effects do you see in this case?
12. Given all of the above, how confident are you that you exhibited in coming to your conclusions a sound methodology and that you demonstrated a connection between the methodology and the facts of this case?
13. Isn't it true that your conclusions regarding methamphetamine in this case may be faulty if the database on which you relied is incomplete or flawed in some other way? You did not interview family members who had knowledge of his drug habit. What assumptions are you making in failing to consider that data?

shaky, but admissible, evidence presented by the expert. Table 10.1 presents sample *Daubert* questions for experts regarding methamphetamine.

As an example of a case in which *Daubert* was applied, in *United States v. Sylva, Saya, and Burke* (1996), the U.S. attorney successfully argued that the defendant's expert, G.B., a psychiatrist/attorney in Honolulu, used improper methodology to reach conclusions concerning the effects of prolonged and active polysubstance abuse on the credibility of the government's chief witness, Alfredo Bunag. Dr. B. "intended to testify how Bunag's polysubstance abuse with particular concentration on his crystal methamphetamine use affect[ed his] 'ability to remember, relate, and distinguish historical events.'" In an Order Denying Defendant Sylva's Proffer of Expert Testimony for Failure to Meet the Daubert Standard, filed December 12, 1996 in the above-referenced case, the Court noted that under *Daubert*, "if a party objects and raises a material dispute as to the admissibility of expert scientific evidence, the district court must hold an *in limine* hearing (a so-called Daubert hearing) to consider the conflicting evidence and make findings about the soundness and reliability of the methodology employed by the scientific experts" (Order at pp. 2–3, quoting *Daubert*, 43 F.3d at 1318, n. 10).

In concluding that Dr. B.'s opinions did not fulfill any of the factors set forth in *Daubert*, the Court reasoned as follows:

> First, Dr. [B.'s] opinion is not supported by scientific methodology and procedures. Dr. [B.] never conducted a direct psychological examination of Bunag. Nor did Dr. [B.] conduct neuropsychologic testing on Bunag which would have involved corroborating Bunag's memory with other reliable sources. Dr. [B.] did not even witness Bunag's testimony in this case nor listen to recordings of his pre-arrest conversations nor read any transcripts of his testimony. Rather, Dr. [B.] planned to base his testimony on an affidavit containing hearsay accounts of Bunag's drug use by four unknown "witnesses." The affidavit did not even suggest the amount of polysubstance abuse other than with respect to ice. Not only is such evidence inherently unreliable; but Dr. [B.] admitted, it is a methodology unendorsed by any scientific survey, literature or publication. In fact, Dr. [H., another psychiatrist] went so far as to say that experts in the field could not reasonably rely on such testimony to render an opinion. Accordingly, the Court finds that Dr. [B.] employed unreliable methodology in forming his expert opinion.
>
> Assuming Dr. [B.'s] methodology was accurate, moreover, Dr. [B.] failed to cite with particularity any articles supporting his underlying thesis: that prolonged crystal methamphetamine use has any effect on memory. The government's witness, Dr. [H.], explained this omission by testifying that there is no literature at present

which holds that methamphetamine use has any effect on memory. Accordingly, the Defendant also failed to establish that Dr. [B.'s] theory or technique has been subjected to peer review and publication [Footnote omitted].

Even if methamphetamine use did affect one's memory, both expert witnesses testified that a number of individual variables such as stress, intellect, varying tolerances to the drug, and other health factors must be considered before truly determining the effects of the drug. Here, Dr. [B.] knows nothing about Bunag's individual characteristics. Accordingly, without some consideration of Bunag's characteristics, Dr. [B.'s] opinion would be unreliable. Moreover, Dr. [H.] testified that the predictability of the impact of sustained usage of ice is not reliable.

The presence of individual characteristics goes to another factor in Daubert: the known or potential rate of error. Defendant, however, put forward no evidence on the rate of error in predicting the effects of crystal methamphetamine on memory loss.

In sum, all the Defendant has put forward is Dr. [B.'s] own testimony concerning the reliability of his opinion. However, "bald assurances of validity" simply do not suffice for Daubert (*Daubert v. Merrell Dow Pharmaceuticals*, 43 F.3d 1311, 1315 (9th Cir. 1995)).

The Court concluded that Dr. B.'s testimony did not concern scientific knowledge for purposes of *Daubert*. The Court also ruled that Dr. B.'s testimony failed to meet the second prong of *Daubert* that the testimony must aid the trier of fact. The Court noted that the jury "had ample opportunity to evaluate the memory and credibility of Bunag" during his 3 days of testimony, which included aggressive cross-examination on his drug use and his memory. Dr. B would also have been able to compare his testimony to tapes of pre-arrest conversations. Because the jurors' exposure to Bunag for over 30 hours would allow them to evaluate his memory and credibility, Dr. B.'s further testimony would not aid the trier of fact in determining whether or not Bunag had the capacity to "remember, relate and distinguish historical events."

The Court also noted the absence of cases in which expert testimony concerning the effect of drug use on a witness's ability to perceive and recall was allowed. In fact, in *United States v. Rohrer* (1983), the Court stated that such testimony "threatens to usurp the jury's function of determining guilt." Agreeing with the caveat in *Rohrer*, the Court reasoned:

> Confronted with an "expert," the Court fears that the jury would give undue deference to Dr. [B.'s] testimony and forfeit their own role of determining credibility. Therefore, even if Dr. [B.'s] testimony did fulfill Daubert, the Court would exclude it under Fed. R. Evid. § 403 because its probative value is substantially outweighed by the danger of unfair prejudice and confusion and the possibility that it would mislead the jury.

Dr. B. presented findings based on an almost non-existent database, consisting of affidavits of two men, themselves methamphetamine abusers, who supposedly knew the government's witness. Had Dr. B. not made that connection between his knowledge of methamphetamine and the case at hand, his actions may have been allowed and he could have avoided the pitfalls described above.

In *State v. Cachola* (1993), the defendant was charged, among other things, with attempted murder of a man who testified that he (the victim) was intoxicated on methamphetamine. Expert testimony was rendered without the benefit of interviewing the victim. The difference between *Cachola* and *Sylva* was that, in the former case, testimony was based on the expert's clinical training, experience, and findings from the methamphetamine studies. No person-specific conclusions were proffered.

In *Cachola*, the second author was qualified as an expert in forensic psychology. The court allowed opinions regarding the effect of methamphetamine on memory and perception. In addition, hypotheticals were permitted, which then allowed the defense attorney to apply findings about methamphetamine to the alleged victim's memory and perception of events. *Cachola* was acquitted of the attempted murder charge. The reader is referred to *State v. Fukusaku* (1997) for an additional discussion about the admissibility of scientific evidence and expert opinions and witness credibility.

Table 10.2 presents general strategies for cross-examining experts in methamphetamine cases.

Table 10.2 Expert Witness Cross-Examination Tactics for Methamphetamine Abuse Cases

Method	Principle/Example	Counteraction by Expert
1. Make the expert your witness	If you have a strong case on methamphetamine causation, create an ally instead of an adversary (e.g., "You say he was severely addicted to methamphetamine?")	Anticipate and amplify on leading words/questions of cross-examiner; be familiar with literature showing the opposite findings
2. Attack the expert's field	Question his entire discipline (e.g., "'As a psychologist, you know nothing about the metabolism of methamphetamine by the human body, do you?")	Use as opportunity for educating the trier of fact on the behavioral and neuropsychological effects of methamphetamine
3. Attack the expert's qualifications	No matter how well trained or experienced the expert, there are always areas where he/she lacks knowledge	Admit your level of experience to the court, which it is hoped includes knowledge of intoxication; become better trained
4. Expose the expert's bias.	The expert's integrity may be for sale if he or she spends much time in court or charges large fees	Know court experience/outcomes of cases and present them to the court
5. Attack the expert's (second-order) facts	Particularly suited for experts who do no factual investigation but rely on the reports of others	Directly assess defendant, victim, or witness or do not comment on them; answer hypothetical
6. Vary the hypothetical	Must have a factual basis; this method reveals the decision path of the expert	Know the decision path leading to your conclusions and therefore how varying data changes conclusions
7. Impeach with a treatise	If an expert differs with others in his field, the expert may be wrong; easy to do in methamphetamine cases as state of the art is primitive	Do not accept a proffered treatise as authoritative, especially in a rudimentary field like methamphetamine abuse
8. Attack the expert	The only direct method, this is dangerous and should be avoided in favor of above tactics	Be thoroughly prepared; meet with your attorney prior to court

Source: Adapted from McEthaney, J., *J. Am. Bar Assoc.*, 9, 99, 1989. The last column was adapted from H. Hall and R. Thordone, *Disorders of Executive Function: Civil and Criminal Law Applications*. Boca Raton, FL: St. Lucie Press, 1993.

References

Casey v. United States, 276 U.S. 413 (1928).

Daubert v. Merrell Dow Pharmaceuticals, Inc., 113 S.Ct. 2786 (1993), on remand, 43 F.3s 1311(9th Cir. 1995).

Fowner v. United States, 504 U.S. 933 (1992).

Frye v. United States, 293 F. 1013 (D.C. Cir. 1923).

Kinder v. United States, 504 U.S. 946 (1992).

State v. Cachola, First Circuit Court, Cr. No. 92–01 93 (Oct. 11, 1993).

State v. Fukusaku, 85 Haw. 462, 946 P.2d 32, recon. denied, addendum remanding case (1997).

United States v. Inadi, 475 U.S. 387 (1986).

United States v. Mezzanatto, 513 U.S. 196 (1995).

United States v. Sorrels, 287 U.S. 435 (1932).

United States v. Russell, 411 U.S. 423 (1973).

United States v. Rohrer, 708 F. 2d 429 (9th Cir. 1983).

United States v. Sylva, Saya, and Burke, U.S. District Court for the District of Hawaii, Cr. No. 95-01065(02) ACK (1996).

Mitigation in Sentencing

11

SANDRA B. MCPHERSON
FARSHID AFSARIFARD

In the eyes of many, substance abuse is a matter of personal poor judgment in decision making. In spite of significant popular and scientific literature suggesting that addiction is a condition that has at least some organic and genetic inputs, having a drug or alcohol problem still equates with having a character deficiency. The law reflects this not uncommon perspective in that "being under the influence" of mind-altering substances is not exculpatory unless involuntary ingestion is involved. Furthermore, as is seen below, substance abuse may lead to enhancement of sentence severity. However, substance abuse has also been mitigating for sentencing purposes, ranging from an explicit affirmative defense in California of "diminished actuality" to nebulous so-called "wastebasket" mitigation clauses that permit the defendant to raise any factors of possible consequence. Forensic evaluation focused on the sentencing phase thus takes place in a complex and often uncertain legal context.

Statutory and Case Law Relative to Substance Abuse and Mitigation in Sentencing

Two major levels of consideration pertain when it comes to sentencing schemes. One involves state codes and the case law that defines and guides their implementation by judges. The second is the federal law and a very special ongoing operation that has created a complex but not particularly flexible decision-making process. Aspects of how these levels operate with respect to substance abuse, particularly methamphetamine abuse, and sentencing are detailed below.

State Codes and Cases

In the state sentencing processes, somewhat greater potentials for mitigatory findings are evident. Cases in Ohio from 1997 to the present that have had appellate review were accessed. Table 11.1 provides information regarding the types of cases, issues involved, and outcomes.

Table 11.1 Methamphetamine and Sentencing: Ohio Appeals 1996–2002 Cases

Citation	Type	Major Issue	Outcome
State ex rel, Wright v. Ohio Adult Parole Authority 75 OS3d 82 661 N.E. 2d728, 1996	Revocation of conditional release	Restrictions in search and seizure; under prior precedent unreasonably obtained evidence not admissible	Evidence obtained unreasonably is admissible
State v. Cossin 110 Ohio App. 3d79673 N.E. 2d 647, 1996	Revocation of conditional release	Use of probationer's statements as evidence	*Miranda* not required; statements admissible
State v. Hawkins 120 Ohio App. 3d277 697 N.E. 2d 1045, 1997	Suppression of evidence	Appellant claimed search warrant not adequate	Trial court upheld
State v. Perry 1997 Ohio App. LEXIS 4309, 9/15/97	Suppression of search evidence	Defendant claimed he had ingested methamphetamine and was therefore incompetent to permit the search	Trial court upheld
In re Wilds 997 Ohio App. LEXIS 4934, 10/24/97	Custody case	Appellant felt he should have been able to extend hearing and given custody in spite of his drug convictions	Trial court upheld
In re Josslin 1998 Ohio App LEXIS 2008, 5/4/98	Custody case	Appellant wanted custody, which had been given to her sister and husband due to neglect and violence with methamphetamine use	Trial court upheld
State v. Robinette 80 Ohio St. 3d 234 685 N.2d 762, 5/13/98	Possession of methamphetamine	Defendant consented to car search; methamphetamine found; defendant claimed lack of knowledge and therefore invalid consent	Trial court upheld
State v. Trumbull 1998 Ohio App. LEXIS 4268, 9/17/98	Possession of methamphetamine	Defendant agreed to search then later said he didn't know he had a choice; methamphetamine found	Trial court upheld

Mitigation in Sentencing

Case	Charge	Details	Outcome
State v. Wise 1998 Ohio APP. LEXIS 5121, 10/1/98	Possession of methamphetamine	Defendant stated search exceeded scope of warrant; methamphetamine found	Trial court upheld
State v. Signs 1998 Ohio App. LEXIS 5468, 11/20/98	Possession and trafficking in methamphetamine	Defendant originally pled no contest; possessed and transported methamphetamine	Trial court upheld
State v. Lewis 1999 Ohio App. LEXIS 5485, 11/19/99	Methamphetamine sale	Defendant wanted to suppress statements of witness to methamphetamine sales	Trial court upheld
State v. Hughbanks 1999 Ohio App. LEXIS 5789, 12/3/99	Death penalty homicide; multiple issues methamphetamine involved	(See discussion below)	Trial court upheld
State v. McNamee 139 Ohio App. 3d 875745.n.2.d 1147, 11/9/00	Possession	Appeal warranted search; "ecstasy" obtained	Trial court upheld
State v. Cates 2000 Ohio App. LEXIS 5387, 11/21/00	Methamphetamine sale	Defendant sold methamphetamine near a school; appealed sentence	Trial court upheld
Saterfield v. Saterfield 2001 Ohio App. LEXIS 2592, 6/13/01	Custody	Appellant contested custody to stepmother; biological mother disqualified due to methamphetamine use	Trial court upheld
State v. Gough 2001 Ohio App. LEXIS 3331, 7/23/01	Drug trafficking	Defendant sought suppression of evidence — primarily cocaine, some methamphetamine	Trial court upheld
State v. Callahan 2001 Ohio App. LEXIS 4633, 10/17/01	Manslaughter; weapon under disability; conspiracy to manufacture methamphetamine	Defendant appealed the conviction based on what he felt was insufficient evidence; the materials involved were methamphetamine ingredients	Trial court upheld for all but conspiracy to manufacture
State v. Ridgeway 2001 Ohio App. 6057 LEXIS 6057, 11/21/01	Methamphetamine sale case	Law enforcement had informant	Trial court upheld

As the table reflects, a significant emphasis involved issues of search and seizure with defendants attempting to obtain reversals or remands based on the illegal gathering of evidence against them. In one of the more innovative of such defenses, the defendant indicated he had been high on methamphetamine at the time of his arrest and therefore had not been competent to agree to the search of the premises that ultimately resulted in the evidence against him. The Court of Appeals was unimpressed and affirmed the judgment against him.

Some of the issues of these cases involve difficult legal concepts. The notion of conspiracy requires that the state prove an agreement existed to achieve a specific illicit goal, that the parties knew of that agreement and the goal, and that at least one of them committed on overt act in the furthering of the agreement (Davis and Vitullo, 2001). Prosecutors have been accused of padding charges by adding conspiracy when evidence constituting proof of these elements was lacking and unlikely to be found. However, juries have not necessarily been able to deal adequately with the legally complex conspiracy arguments. In *State v. Callahan* (2001), the appeals court found in favor of the defendant on the basis that the conspiracy element was not adequately founded. However, the rest of the case stood.*

In *United States of America v. Thomas Conne James* (2001), a defendant alleged that there was differential selection of persons for federal- vs. state-level charges, the impact of which was to create an arbitrary and discriminatory application of the law. Although the defendant was not upheld in his petition, it is true that state sentencing schemes are more flexible and less likely to result in the degree of severity that the federal guidelines have imposed in federal cases. Thus, for example, in Ohio judges are explicitly given some discretion to raise or lower expected sentencing levels for crimes committed. There are a number of factors that are articulated in the law as suggesting greater or lesser seriousness and therefore meriting greater or lesser outcomes. Among the aggravating factors is a "pattern of drug or alcohol abuse that is related to the offense and the offender refuses to

---

* Conspiracy has been viewed by the government as a difficult charge to prove in part because of the limitations imposed by the *Cruz* ruling (*U.S. v. Cruz*, 12cr7 F3d 791,795, 1997). On January 21, 2003, the Supreme Court reviewed a conspiracy case and reversed *Cruz*. up until January 21, for example, defendants could be found guilty of conspiracy (which is an important component in drug cases for obvious reasons) only if they believed they were in the conspiracy before it was ended by police action. In *United States of America v. Francisco Jiminez Recio and v. Adrian Lopez-Meza*, the Ninth Circuit ruled that *Cruz* pertained; even though the judges expressed repugnance for the *Cruz* ruling (270 F.3d 845, 2001 U.S. App. LEXIS 23404, 2001), they followed it. However, in the ruling on the 21st, the Supreme Court reversed *Cruz* on the point of whether the conspiracy had to be ongoing and not stopped by police for defendants enrolled in actions pursuant to the crime to be charged as co-conspirators (the police had spotted the vehicles, arrested the initiators, and set up a sting to catch the two people the initiators called to pick up the truck).

acknowledge that the offender has demonstrated that pattern, or the offender refuses treatment for the drug or alcohol abuse" (ORC 2929.12 (d)(4)).

Case law in Ohio, however, has given rise to some interesting and varied precedents. Thus, for example, in a 1984 case, *State v. Burkholder,* evidence obtained in an illegal search was allowed in a probation revocation proceeding. However, in 1996, under *State ex rel, Wright v. Ohio Adult Parole Authority,* the use of illegally obtained evidence was considered inadmissible. Interestingly, drug use may or may not be considered a probation violation depending on the conditions under which it occurred and the conditions that prior existed for the probation. However, the use of illicit drugs usually involves criminal charges, which then become the basis for revocation. In the case of the death penalty, aggravating and mitigating circumstances are articulated, as is usually the case across the country. Drug use is not an aggravating factor but statutory mitigating factors do not include it either. The statute, however, explicitly indicates that the defendant "shall be given great latitude in presence of evidence." Case law, especially *Lockett v. Ohio* (1978), assures that in relevant situations drug use, abuse, and dependency may be presented as part of the mitigating picture.

A review of some other state approaches is consistent with the situation in Ohio. In Hawaii there are specific factors to be considered and the trial court is given significant and explicit discretion. With respect to probation, the court may require drug testing regardless of whether drugs were part of the offense. The court may consider the defendant's past history of use and the possible contribution that drug use might make to recidivism in ordering the testing procedure.

The approach in California is consistent. It does, however, specifically mention heroin, cocaine, and "any analog of these substances" as meriting enhancement of sentence (Article 11353.1 California Health and Safety Code). The code section further specifies that if the offense involves the substances and takes place close to children's facilities and certain other kinds of community settings, that enhancement is desirable. In that regard, the California code is somewhat similar to the federal sentencing guidelines. Interpretations of the California approach have suggested that the court must consider alcohol dependence as mitigatory and should not consider it as an aggravating aspect. On the other hand, the court does not have to consider drug use as having mitigation value where that use did not directly predispose to the commission of the crime.

During the 1990s at the state and federal levels, three strikes laws were passed. California's three strikes law was particularly Draconian in drug-related cases, leading to life terms for minor possession convictions. Under the California statute, crimes usually considered misdemeanors could become felonies leading to long-term incarceration. The "upgrade" of misdemeanor to felony provision for sentencing purposes has been found unconstitutional by a circuit court of appeals, but the state appealed and the matter has been set for Supreme Court review (Gearan, 2002).*

Federal Sentencing Scheme

From the perspectives of sentencing in federal court, relatively recent socio-legal history has to be considered. In 1984, the Sentencing Reform Act set up the machinery for federal sentencing guidelines to be drafted and then subsequently amended by the U.S. Sentencing Commission. The interaction between Congress and its own creature (the commission) became an interesting process. There was a Supreme Court challenge to the validity of the Sentencing Commission. However, the functioning of this organ was upheld (*Mistretta v. U.S.*, 1989; Parker and Block, 2001).

The overall purpose of the act and of the subsequent guidelines was stated to be an improvement in "honesty, uniformity, and proportionality" (Ruback and Wroblewski, 2001, p. 744). However, it can also be viewed as part of the trend toward a more conservative and punishment-oriented system of justice. Illustratively, the purposes of sentencing were articulated to be just punishment, deterrence, incapacitation, and rehabilitation, in that order. Even as Congress passed this act and then established the Sentencing Commission, Congress continued, however, to amend the sentencing process with specifics that amounted to a "micro-managing" of the process. The Crime Control Act of 1990 included sentencing guidelines specific to methamphetamine offenses, and the Comprehensive Methamphetamine Control Act of 1996 increased those penalties.

Not surprisingly, the U.S. Sentencing Guidelines as they have developed out of this history fulfill the priority placed on punishment. The guidelines involve a highly complex system of levels with rules for enhancement or reduction (upward or downward adjustment). With respect to methamphetamine, the emphasis is quite clear. Methamphetamine leads to a vulnerability to enhancement of any penalty range that is mandated for given crimes. The guidelines are explicit in this regard, and methamphetamine has been singled out as a drug-among-drugs that can lead to upward adjustments. Special tables exist for amounts that are associated with such adjustments. The guidelines also reflect the current awareness that the production of methamphetamine is dangerous to nonparticipants and the environment generally (see Vogt, 2001). Thus, methamphetamine manufacturing leads to very specific enhanced penalties with quantity, manner of disposition, including

---

* On March 5, 2003, in Lockyer, *Attorney General of California v. Ardrade*, the Supreme Court upheld the constitution of the California statute (http://www.findlaw.com/us/000/01-1127.html).

"likelihood of release into the environment of hazardous or toxic substances," duration and extent of manufacturing, and location of the laboratory (enhancements are based on whether the facility is near children or other persons who are relatively defenseless) (Federal Sentencing Commission, Guidelines Manual, 2001).

Thus, methamphetamine, rather than having mitigatory potential, can be an explicit basis for upward departure increasing sentence severity. Consistently, a diminished capacity plea at sentencing under the current guidelines is specifically disallowed if voluntary drug ingestion is involved.

Evaluation of Defendants and Context

Purposes of Evaluation

All forensic evaluation and analysis takes place within a legal context and properly focuses on the questions before the court. As the foregoing section illustrated, there are relevant precedents that constrain both questions and variables, which may be entertained by the court. It is within that context that evaluation takes place.

Mitigation in sentencing involves the notion that some agreed-upon level of punishment for the crime committed can be adjusted in the direction of leniency if factors particular to the person and situation warrant such consideration. Mitigation is a basic part of all legal codes and has been present either in content (by defining offenses according to some set of standard factors to be greater or lesser) or by reference to modifying conditions (the Code of Hammurabi written about 1700 B.C.E. contained such specifics) (Danesh-Khoshdoo, 1991).

More currently, the resurrection of capital punishment after *Furman* (1972) created sets of definitions of mitigatory factors and a body of case law further elaborating what could or should be brought to the attention of the jury or judge. Following *Lockett v. U.S* (1978), inclusion of individually based information resulted in drug related factors being placed in evidence at trial levels and subsequently becoming a focus in appeals.

In any mitigatory evaluation, forensic psychologists need to develop information on factors relevant to the likely outcomes of available sentencing alternatives. To provide the court with valid input, it is necessary to focus on both actuarial and individual case-related data. Risk analyses (see below) provide a valid basis for making predictions in instant cases. Such analyses are only as good as the large-scale studies on which they are based and on the degree to which the individual being evaluated is properly considered as a member of the reference group of those studies.

While substitution of clinical impressions for properly constructed actuarial predictions has been criticized on scientific grounds (Meehl, 1996; Grove and Meehl, 1996; Ruback and Wroblewski, 2001), even statistically based techniques include measures of dynamic, or potentially changeable, factors. Furthermore, within the limits provided by statistical analyses, more detailed and individualized assessment allows insight into factors of relevance to the treatment process that themselves may have actuarial implications. For example, completion of sexual offender treatment has been shown in some but not all studies to reduce recidivism potential (Hanson and Busière, 1998; McConaghy, 1999).

Risk Analysis

Even with a judge predisposed to consider sentencing from a rehabilitative justice perspective, there is a duty to engage in an assessment of the factors that are part of protecting society vs. the factors that favor a less restrictive type of outcome. In those jurists who are not predisposed to consider rehabilitation as a primary purpose, administration of justice, the importance of victim impact, and the need to send a message of disapproval by way of punishment of offenders will outweigh offender potentials for rehabilitation. However, regardless of the underlying philosophy of justice that a court may hold, that part of the decision making that is based on an assessment of the needs of society for protection may be impacted by an appropriate risk analysis.

Because that is true, most, if not all, pre-sentence investigation reports include outright or implicit risk analyses. However, what can also be said is that pre-sentence investigation reports do not reflect a high level of scientifically informed assessments and basically incorporate what have been statutorily or by regulation determined to be the relevant risk factors. Thus, in Ohio, the following areas are typically found in pre-sentence reports: basic demographics, identifying information, family information, arrest history, gang affiliation, health (physical and mental) status, drug/alcohol use, military service, financial information, employment history, and defendant's perspective on the instant offense.

By contrast, the current level of risk analysis is well past that point when Monahan (1981) was warning against psychologists' involvement on the basis that the insecurity and unreliability of such analyses made that activity unethical. At this point, three generations of scientific work later, certain assertions can be stated with respect to risk analysis:

- There are legitimate actuarially based approaches to risk analysis that do provide valid information about low base rate behavior and that have now been tested for long enough periods that reasonably

Mitigation in Sentencing

informed decision making can take place on the basis of the data yielded in the individual cases. Further, there are refined statistical methods for dealing with that data (Hall, 2000).

- Actuarial assessment alone, however, has been possibly misapplied in the criminal justice system depending on the level of sophistication of the examiner. Actuarially based instruments include both static and dynamic factors. To the extent that an instrument is based only on static (unchangeable) qualities, the implications are negative for rehabilitation — in effect, a self-fulfilling prophecy that will never change because the items upon which it is based are themselves immutable and the outcome has been fixed (McConaghy, 1999; Mulvey and Lidz, 1985, 1995; Rice et al., 1991; Quinsey et al., 1998).
- However, it is clear that tampering with an actuarial system on the basis of clinical intuition not only offends *Daubert* (1993), but has also been appropriately criticized because it does not show any reasonable promise of scientific adequacy (Grove and Meehl, 1996).
- The current generation of statistically based risk analysis includes instruments (Table 11.2) that involve both static and dynamic aspects, which can be used not only to provide scientifically reasonable predictions, but also to suggest appropriate intervention modes such that risk levels may be reduced, depending on subsequent behavior and outcome of intervention.

A review of the content of the instruments listed in Table 11.2 shows that drug abuse is only sometimes one of the factors used in prediction. It is, of course, considered a dynamic factor because it can be, at least theoretically, altered as a function of treatment or situational input. However, none of the instruments differentiates the use of amphetamine derivatives, including methamphetamine, from other drugs. Some instruments have isolated opiate and heroin use as specific predictors. In Hall's approach (see Chapter 16) an effort has been made to isolate the factors that are specific to this particular drug and their implications for risk analysis. It appears that methamphetamine operates to potentiate violence in persons with a history of violence. A cyclic pattern is typical in chronic methamphetamine addiction and its action as a releaser for violence. General forensic principles with respect to violence prediction should be followed, along with an appreciation for specific mechanisms that can operate in the case of methamphetamine intoxication or a use history for that substance. An assessment of methamphetamine use and its relationship to offenses committed can be a basis for recommending treatment that may reduce violence potentials. However, the research is yet to be done that allows methamphetamine use per se

Table 11.2 Risk Analysis Instrumentation

Instrument	Purpose/Limitations	Bibliography
Client Management Classification System (CMC)	Developed in Wisconsin, involves semistructured interview, which explores specific "criminogenic" factors; allows a set of treatment specifications that has been associated with reduced risk in 18-month follow-up studies; follow-up research is quite insecure	Eisenberg and Markley (1987); McManuis, Stagg, and McDuffie (1988); Dhaliwal, Porporino, and Ross (1994)
Hare Psychopathy Check List — Revised and Screening Version (PCL-R; PCL:SV)	20 items (PCL-R) or 12 (PSL:SV); static and dynamic factors involve significant experience and training needed to use adequately; substantial research backing as a general predictor of violence recidivism and also for sexual violence	Hare, Harpur, Hakstian, Forth, Hart, and Newman (1990); Hart, Cox, and Hare (1995); see also other publications
Level of Surfaces Inventory — Revised (LSI-R)	54 items, Yes/No format, static and dynamic variables; good support for prediction and monitoring of risk levels	Andrews and Bonta (1998)
Minnesota Sex Offender's Screening Tool — Revised (MnSOST-R)	12 items with associated scores, which reflect positive and negative correlations with recidivism and include both historical and static variables for use only with persons who have been incarcerated and are being considered for release	Epperson, Kaul, and Hesselton (1999)
Offender Group Reconviction Scale (OGRS)	Developed in England and Wales, scale is rapidly being implemented in pre-sentence investigation throughout those parts of the U.K.; consists of six items; has been shown to predict reconviction within 2 years in 83% of cases	Copas and Marshall (1998); Cooke and Michie (1998)
Rapid Risk Assessment for Sexual Offense Recidivism (RRASOR)	Four items with liability and validity data; developed in Canada; static factors	Hanson (1997, 1998)
Risk of Reconviction Scale (ROR)	Developed in England and Wales to predict suitability for parole; six items with weighted positive and negative scores reflecting positive and negative correlations of the items, and differentiated for general re-offending and serious re-offending (see also OGRS)	Copas and Marshall (1998)

(continued)

Mitigation in Sentencing

Table 11.2 Risk Analysis Instrumentation (Continued)

Instrument	Purpose/Limitations	Bibliography
Salient Factor Scale (SFS)	Developed by U.S. Parole Commission; six items; static and dynamic factors, including specified heroin/opiate dependence	Gottfredson, Wilkins, and Hoffman (1978); Hoffman (1994)
Sexual Offender Risk Appraisal Guide (SORAG)	Developed out of the MacArthur studies and work on the VRAG; 14 variables; not significantly better than the VRAG for prediction of violent recidivism in the sexual offender population	Quinsey, Harris, Rice and Cormier (1998)
Sexual Violence Risk–20 (SVR-20)	20 factors with static and dynamic aspects; evaluator determines risk level on the basis of experience with the population; factors are empirically valid, but instrument has not been statistically validated	Boer, Wilson, Gauthier, and Hart (1997)
Static 99	Refinement of the RRASOR; 10 items, all static, coded present or absent	Hanson and Thornton (2000)
Violence Risk Appraisal Guide (VRAG)	12 items; includes the PCLR score, thus reflecting all of those variables and implicitly counting certain items twice; empirically based, with ongoing research	Quinsey, Harris, Rice, and Cormier (1998)

to be treated as a statistically based predictor in the absence of other established indicators.

A specific pattern of lethal aggression involves homicide–suicide, the co-occurrence of aggression directed toward the self and others. Trained police officers know that dealing with persons who are actively threatening suicide can be dangerous because of the potential to redirect the aggression toward the officer. Specific studies of behavior involving acts of aggression against self and others have not included methamphetamine or other stimulants but have identified that opiates and alcohol may be predictors. Given the dynamics of methamphetamine and its potential for mood destabilization as well as reduced executive function, further research into all aspects of aggression directed both inward and outward needs to specify in more detail substance abuse patterns, including especially methamphetamine (Hillbrand, 2001).

Malingering

At all phases of the forensic evaluation, malingering is a significant issue because motivation to present in a fully disclosing and honest fashion is generally less likely than would be the case in other contexts. As indicated by Hall and Pritchard (1996), evaluation of malingering in methamphetamine cases is complicated because methamphetamine genuinely impacts cognitive function causing both short-term and more subtle or chronic long-term defects. Furthermore, acute and chronic impacts of methamphetamine can produce psychotic-like mentation. Finally, in individuals who are predisposed or have preexisting mental illness, the use of methamphetamine may worsen the symptom picture.

Legal context obviously has an impact on impression management approaches. It is not uncommon for methamphetamine users to deny or minimize the part played by the drug in an instant case, since they usually know or are told by defense counsel that voluntary ingestion of substances is not exculpatory (Hall, Chapter 14). In the case of a postconviction evaluation, there is also likely to be significant interest in being seen in a sympathetic light. Therefore, the motivation to consciously emphasize psychopathology, and to attribute it to mental illness, is often present. From an affective standpoint, there may be depressive reactivity by virtue of the situational factors being faced (prospects of extended time in prison), and there may also be an underlying biochemical basis for depressive reactivity due to the extended withdrawal.

For the most part, psychological instrumentation is not at the level necessary to definitively evaluate the percentages to which given symptoms may reflect malingering. It is also very difficult to determine, in the case of an actual psychotic-like presentation, whether the cognitive distortions are methamphetamine residua or symptoms of an underlying, preexisting, and ongoing mental illness of a schizophrenic or similar type. Differentiating "real" vs. "manufactured" mental problems involving either cognitive or emotional illness can be problematic and certainly requires data beyond that of the presentation and products of the defendant.

Evaluation of malingering has been further complicated by case decisions that have defined conscious attempts at distortion in the course of such evaluations to be indicators for upward adjustment to sentencing guidelines (see, for example, *United States v. Pineda*, 1992). A double-edged scientific and legal dilemma presents. The responsible forensic practitioner is under an ethical obligation to acknowledge and investigate malingering potentials. However, the identification of malingering not only assists the psychologist and court in assigning weight to psychological findings, but also potentially affects the defendant harmfully. Malingering as a condition is hard to diagnose or "prove." Therefore, the practitioner is under an obligation to come to this conclusion only by careful development of supportive data (Melton et al., 1997; Rogers, 1997).

Some approaches that can be helpful in dealing with this dilemma are the following:

Mitigation in Sentencing

- Repetition of cognitive assessment for comparison to that done closer to the time of the act, perhaps as a function of a defense expert's evaluation or a court-ordered evaluation due to questions of reduced or exculpatory status.
- Review of historical data using records produced prior to the instant offense; prior records of mental illness.
- Interviews of family, employers, or school personnel. School records, especially from pupil personnel sources or from schools where actual narrative reports of behavior are maintained, may be of assistance.
- Defendant retrospective of the crime. A close to verbatim account of the criminal activity can be evaluated against independent evidence in the record and other interviews and interrogation to determine whether significant minimization or distortions can be identified. Patterns of distortion can be evaluated for known impacts of methamphetamine use on time perception and memory function.

Procedures

Interview

Interviewing allows a behavior sample that itself can be interpreted. It also provides information that a defendant is willing or able to share. Methamphetamine is known to impact cognitive functioning in a variety of ways but is not determinative of either content or type of distortions that may occur in instant cases. As is always the case in interviewing individuals accused or found guilty of crimes, issues of malingering arise. However, in chronic methamphetamine users, organically based misrepresentation of facts also needs to be considered.

The interview needs to gather the usual materials in a clinical assessment (personal history, family history, health status and history, educational and vocational background, legal history, mental status functioning, and obviously a history of drug/alcohol abuse including onset and patterns of use). The specifics thus obtained can be evaluated against available third-party and record information, providing insight into the degree of consistency and possibly identifying patterns of dissimulation (self-aggrandizement, omissions, projection of responsibility). The use of some type of underlying structure at least for coverage of topics can be recommended.

A retrospective on the instant crime may or may not be obtained. Even after a finding of guilt, some defendants maintain innocence and look to the appeals process for vindication. Defendants may be instructed not to discuss the crime by counsel. On the other hand, in some cases, counsel will urge the clients to review in entirety and with honesty their memory of events as they transpired. This material may be of substantial value in the sentencing process (it may illustrate remorse and insight, for example) or it may significantly affect risk analyses (for example, the PCL-R). It allows specialized inquiries into unusual aspects including analysis of the relationship of the defendant to weapons — Meloy's (1992) Weapons Assessment can be used where appropriate — or to distorted thinking, especially in sex crimes. It may provide examples of the impact of the drug on cognitive functioning, referencing a sense of rapidly occurring events that actually took far longer (time distortion) and problems around detail recovery (encoding and retrieval memory problems). See Chapter 14 for a fuller discussion of factors of cognitive distortion vs. malingering.

In obtaining a retrospective from the defendant, the use of an inverted triangle model of interviewing, with an emphasis on the devices of the cognitive interview (Fisher and Geiselman, 1992; Milne and Bull, 1999), is recommended. Initial inquiry is open ended: "Tell me what happened. Begin at the beginning and give me as much detail as you can remember." After the defendant provides an account (with nonspecific encouragement: "What happened next?" "Just tell me what you remember"), one can focus on specific aspects and ask for particular details of what was experienced ("Describe for me what it looked like when …" "I wonder exactly what you could see when…" "I wonder if you could hear anything going on when …"). Ask about how long sequences took where that information is not spontaneously provided.

This type of extended inquiry into the criminal behavior is not always either possible or desirable. However, when it is undertaken, using auditory taping can be of significant help in obtaining the kind of very specific response information that lends itself to forensic analysis. In some jails, it is possible to arrange in advance permission to do such recording; many facilities will not allow it without such permission and it would be hazardous to attempt it without checking on local rules. Sometimes a court order is necessary for a recorded interview. Learning a highly adequate form of shorthand is a boon to any forensic evaluation.

Data obtained in the course of the interview may be applicable to an understanding of the offense and motivational state, which are clearly relevant to the sentencing process. It allows insight into characterologic features, which are often a focus at this stage of criminal justice. Treatment or other rehabilitation efforts may be enhanced by the findings.

Psychometrics

A review of current literature produced little in the way of specific patterns associated with methamphetamine abuse. Most research has been done on the impact of alcohol, cocaine, or polysubstance abuse. Research on stimulants as a class is also available for extrapolation.

In the area of neuropsychological functioning, there has been some attention paid to impacts on memory, attention, psychomotor measures, and processing variables. Common instruments used for investigations have included the Wechsler Adult Intelligence Scales (currently, the WAIS-III), the Wechsler Memory Scale (R or III), Trailmaking Test, Wisconsin Card Sort Test, and other instruments that reflect variables associated with cognitive deficits.

One recent study looked at memory deficits in MDMA abusers with initial testing and follow-up 1 year later. Results documented other sources of observation, which suggest that ongoing methamphetamine use leads to progressively increasing neurocognitive deficits (Zakzanis and Young, 2001). McKetin (2000) documented poor performance on all indices of the WMS-R for amphetamine dependent persons vs. impairment specific to visual memory tasks for heavy users but not those meeting dependency requirements. Other analyses indicated patterns on attentional tasks by those classified as dependent that were indistinguishable from psychotic and affective conditions. This study, however, may be only suggestive for methamphetamine abusers.

Attention deficit hyperactivity disorder (ADHD) has been a focus of some investigations. Hypotheses that ADHD may be related to inability to profit from standard approaches in substance abuse treatment have been evaluated and only partially supported. Associations between ADHD and substance choice have been considered, especially referencing psychostimulants. However, such studies highlight the differential diagnostic dilemma: underlying and preexisting organic bases for neuropsychological divergence from normal exist along with those deficits that are produced by substance abuse. Similarly, studies of substance abuse and schizophrenia have shown overlaps in patterning on neuropsychological testing (Snyder, 1998; Badgett, 1999). As methamphetamine is known to have impacts on memory, perception, and executive control functioning, as well as presenting substantial issues for identifying and ruling out malingering (particularly of mental illness in order to be seen as less culpable), obtaining standardized data from the defendant, in addition to his or her reports, is an important component to the assessment process. However, it may or may not be possible to do extended neuropsychological screening at the pre-sentence level in many cases. Where interview and other data strongly suggest an organic component, the expense in time and money can be justified. In some cases, neurological assessment (CT scan, MRI) may be possible, but would be rarely approved in the vast majority of such cases.

Instrumentation that can be utilized at a screening level includes WAIS III; Wechsler Memory Scale R or III (argument can be made for use of the older instrument—the third edition contains some statistical anomalies and is so specialized that very occasional use is likely to lead to administration errors); Trailmaking; Rey Figure; Bender Gestalt (although much maligned, as a screening assessment of both gross perceptual motor functions and as an informal means of assessment of task management, it can be helpful — some patterns consistent with psychotic function have been noted in the literature and their presence might bolster ruling out malingered mental illness, presuming other very consistent data as well). All these instruments would have some potential to map strengths and weaknesses of cognitive function that have relevance for capacity to benefit from treatment or the need for special supports in that process.

Personality assessment instruments have also been studied with regard to substance abuse, especially since differentiation of non-substance-related conditions from those produced by use becomes an important issue in recommending treatment interventions. The MMPI contains a number of substance abuse scales (the MacAndrews, the Addiction Potential Scale, and the Addiction Admission Scale can be referenced). Additionally, clinicians know that the Harris and Lingoes subscale Bizarre Sensory Experiences (Sc6) and the Bizarre Mentation Subscales (BIZ1 and BIZ2) can register with substance abusers, especially those who have experienced hallucinatory phenomena.

The strength of the instrument, particularly for forensic purposes, lies in its statistical base and the ongoing production of substantial scientific literature. In regard to issues of malingering, the MMPI tests have built-in validity indicators as well as studies of patterns associated with different impression management styles. In cases of individuals without the capacity to read at approximately a 6th to 8th grade level, it can be administered orally or by tape, but that procedure can be difficult to manage in many criminal justice settings, both for reasons of time and regulations. In general, however, most defendants are capable of taking the test — and most forensic practitioners would have to justify not using it in preference to some other instrumentation, particularly more subjectively based approaches.

The Millon Clinical Multiaxial Inventory (MCMI-III) is a newer but also well-established empirically self-report questionnaire. This test may be of some assistance in identifying specific Axis II configurations and can be helpful as part of the database on which differentiations between likely malingering vs. honest responding have occurred. It is not a good instrument to use to replace the MMPI for Axis I conditions and it overdiagnoses personality disorders such that it should be used where there is reason to believe the individual reasonably has an Axis II condition.

On the MCMI, there have been studies specific to cocaine and more generally to substance abuse that identify patterns of importance, including differentiation of antisocial personality disorder from other personality patterns within the population of substance abusers, the identification of patterns relevant to treatment issues, and the characteristic malingering response modes found in different diagnostic groups (Flynn and MacMahon, 1997; Flynn et al. 1997; Weiss, 1998; Messina, 2000; Messina et al., 2001).

The Personality Assessment Inventory is a relative newcomer. It has a much less substantial scientific base than the MMPI tests, but the literature increasingly cites its usefulness. It requires less time to administer, has a lower reading level, and has a built-in method for looking more continuously than dichotomously at traits. (All tests that are completed by the defendant must be actively proctored by the forensic clinician or a qualified agent who can assure that the test was indeed the product of the defendant's work.)

Projective techniques do have a place in forensic work (some forensic practitioners have subscribed to the contrary). However, their strength lies in the insight they provide into intrapersonal aspects of function. The Exner Rorschach has a substantial base of use in the court system and has been cited in numerous cases as meeting scientific requirements over a period of many years. Under certain specialized circumstances, as with death penalty mitigation, extended ways of dealing with content have some relevance for understanding crime and criminal. A forensic psychologist needs to prepare in advance for possible cross-examination about the reliability and validity of this (as of any) instrumentation used. One of the authors (McPherson) has testified in court about the Rorschach using a step-by-step but brief exposition: the test is made up of inkblots which can be seen as many things; the individual produces responses with an inquiry into why he or she said what was said; the responses including all the reasons used are categorized and a count made of categories and numbers of times used; these numbers are then put into relationships with one another — often ratios — which allow patterns to emerge that are associated in the scientific literature with different personal characteristics. McPherson has never had to go any farther than that in explication.

Other projective techniques have less frequent application to forensic assessment at the pre-sentence level, although any data regarding personality structure and functioning may be of interest and relevance to treatment that may be mandated. Thus, responses to sentence completion techniques or even versions of the Thematic Apperception Test may be included as supportive or illustrative, but not determinative, of the examinee's characteristics.

Context

It is at the level of developing information regarding contextual factors that the most reliance on third-party information (TPI) is likely to occur. As with data produced by way of traditional individual assessment procedures, there is concern with issues of reliability and validity from a scientific standpoint further underscored by *Daubert* (1993) decisions and other rule of evidence precedents. Evaluation of TPI should consider the source of the product and should not presume accuracy due to status of the informant (see discussion in Melton et al., 1997). An attitude of objectivity and skepticism serves well in dealing with these kinds of data.

Categories of TPI

Different data sources with associated concerns follow:

- School Records. Information is not likely to be contaminated by immediate case-related variables. Reliability for academic and intellectual function is high; bias can impact behavioral items, especially if the individual was disliked or identified as a "bad apple."
- Juvenile Records. Information relative to offending is likely to be highly accurate; if anything, the degree of antisocial behavior will be understated since the data cover only those acts for which the defendant was apprehended.
- Adult Criminal Records. Same as above. However, it can be noted that minority and impoverished status predispose to criminal behavior and to winding up in the system to a greater degree than is true for those with higher status and wherewithal in the society. Therefore, the meaning of a significant "rap" sheet might be more indicative of psychopathic character referencing a middle- or upper-middle-class defendant, whereas it may reflect general antisocial behavior in the case of an inner-city gang member.
- Prison Records. Generally good sources for capacity to conform to highly structured environments, these records are a reasonable basis for predicting adjustment to prison in the future. However, disciplinary incidents may or may not reflect potential and actual misbehavior of a defendant. There is corruption by virtue of the power imbalance (Zimbardo et al., 1972), racism, and other factors that can impact a prison record.
- Treatment Records. Records predating the offense may be viewed with confidence regarding mental status, diagnosis, and response to treatment, as well as possibly contain information important to background, family, and other history. Records from a treating professional that postdate the offense may be subject to unconscious bias of the treating therapist who is invested in his or her patient, as well as reflect what the defendant may want to promote.
- Reports from Family Sources. Both positive and negative bias based on highly individual factors of relationship and history has to be considered.
- Police Reports. Generally viewed as highly reliable and valid by the court system, some skepticism is nonetheless warranted, particularly

Mitigation in Sentencing

where racial factors may be involved, or where the police have felt themselves victimized by the defendant or associates. Police brutality is less common than many defendants may believe, but it is not unknown and when it occurs there is motivation to cover it up by attributions of violence to the defendant in the course of confrontations.
- Victim Statements. Again, victim statements have high regard from the court system, but cannot be accepted without some scrutiny. Particularly in cases of sexual offenses, context and motivation of the reporter have to be considered. That said, it must be noted that a false report of sexual abuse is a low base rate phenomenon.
- Crime Scene Data. Information from the investigation of the crime scene can be of particular importance in methamphetamine (or any) cases involving violence. The interest is often in whether the violence was spontaneous and not under good executive control. Crime scene pictures and descriptions can provide important input to that issue.
- Medical Records and Medical Examiner Reports. The information is usually of good quality. However, there have been instances of incompetent or corrupt medical examiners. Recently, in one jurisdiction in Ohio, it was identified that a given period of time involved an essentially automatic classification of questionable infant deaths as accidental rather than raising the possibility of homicide, leading to extended but belated investigations (Sangiacomo, 2002).
- Interrogation Reports and Tapes. Any taped interview or statement has a certain amount of face and real validity. When the entire interrogation is documented, issues of suggestion and coercion can be evaluated, but in the U.S. that is a rare occurrence.

Reporting to the Court

In general, forensic reports follow a format of identifying information, procedure, and results. In many teaching settings, there is a preference expressed for what is known as fully integrated reports where all data are combined into a description of the individual and referenced periodically throughout the body of the report, after which there are diagnostic and conclusion or treatment recommendation sections. The forensic report, however, must withstand the scrutiny of the legal system and there is an obligation to make the data reasonably accessible to the process of examination and cross-examination. Toward that end, the following format is recommended:

- Identifying information. It is important to include birth date and any other specific identifiers that may be an ongoing basis for assuring that the report references the defendant. It is also important to include

a description of the offense. All reports need to be identified as to the purpose of the evaluation.
- Procedure. Sources of information relied upon should be listed. It is particularly true in performing second opinions or assessments for defense counsel that some information available through the court system may not be made accessible to the psychologist. By listing those materials that are used, unnecessary challenges are avoided and necessary ones can be made.
- Detailing results. This section contains results of interviews, including mental status examinations, history as obtained from the defendant, retrospectives, which may be reproduced verbatim at times, and other defendant-generated information. A separate section should be provided that details results from third-party information and provides specific sources for specific items and sections for cognitive and personality assessment, which detail the relevant results from test data. Scores should be included in these reports. It would be rare to include personality profiles with the report although they may be made available upon appropriate demand; however, computer-generated interpretations for personality assessment instruments should never be a part of the report to the court.
- Diagnosis. The DSM-IV system should be used but modifiers that are significant in identifying defendant status can be inserted into the diagnostic presentation. It is desirable to include all five axes but it is necessary to include Axes I through III.
- Summary and recommendations. It is in this section that the foregoing data are integrated into a set of logically connected and scientifically founded conclusions and recommendations. A risk analysis may be part of this section, in which case the particular instrumentation needs to be referenced with the specific outcomes. In methamphetamine-related cases, coverage for substance abuse in the course of the defendant's narrative and any relevant commentary from third-party sources and in the diagnostic section need to appear. Treatment recommendations should be based on the data and should specify needs and parameters that will enhance the potential for treatment success. In most methamphetamine cases, particularly where use has been in any way extended, concern should be raised for neuropsychological functioning and a recommendation made for assessment as appropriate along with inclusion of compensatory work and education in the treatment plan. As is always the case, the forensic report addresses the particular legal questions that are present. Therefore, the instrumentation chosen, as well as the conclusions rendered, often needs to speak to issues of recidivism and the factors that may serve to reduce that potential. Another area that needs to be covered in the

final section and related where appropriate to recommendations is the role that methamphetamine and other substance abuse played in the instant offense. This connection is particularly relevant for recommendations that aim at reducing recidivism potentials.

Final caveat: A good psychological report describes an individual and is written in a way that compels attention. However, it is also well known that the part of the report that is most likely to be read, especially by persons such as probation officers writing pre-sentence investigation reports (PSIs) and judges, who have asked for the information, is the last section. That section must embody all characteristics of good legal writing: clarity, logical structure, and linear reasoning.

Other detailed helpful information for approaching court-related evaluations can be found in Melton et al. (1997).

Pre-Sentence Investigation Reports

Pre-sentence investigation (PSI) reports that are submitted by the probation department are of substantial importance to the sentencing process. However, there is significant variation in content and degree of independent judgment actually exercised by the writers. In some settings, there are guidelines for the collection of data with an expected, almost rote production of the report. In other places and sometimes within settings, there are expectations for individual initiative based on experience and training. Instructions to probation staff can exert a measurable impact on both the content and, ultimately, the outcome of the sentencing process. (In one case in our experience, a political agenda operated to support punishment; the PSI was replete with all the usual markers for probationary eligibility — first offense, restitution made, remorse evident, punishment from other sources already occurred, offender employed and had family responsibilities, support system existed, no personal risky habits — but the usually present recommendation section was not completed, increasing the ability of the prosecutor to obtain a higher severity than was objectively warranted.)

Psychological reports may or may not be referenced in a PSI. Sometimes, such evaluations may be submitted independently by defense counsel or requested by the court. Psychological reports tend to be most valued when they provide a rationale for what the court has determined will take place. To some degree, this is due to the view of clinicians as having an overly liberal bias and being more "soft-hearted" than defendants warrant (Melton et al., 1997).

As has already been documented in the legal literature, a factor of substantial importance in the sentencing process is drug use, particularly where that use may have precipitated aggression. The issue of drugs as precipitating *uncharacteristic* aggressive behavior may be raised as mitigating, but it is as likely as not that the voluntary use of methamphetamine in particular will have an opposite impact on sentencing outcomes. As was seen in *Lopez v. Davis* (2001), the inclination to classify drug use and trafficking as more aggravating than mitigatory extends to eligibility for early release consideration.

One of the authors (McPherson) was present at a sentencing hearing in which the presiding judge accepted a seriously mentally ill defendant's guilty plea to bank robbery. The judge refused to hear any mitigatory testimony on behalf of the defendant and lectured him on his immorality and unworthiness for mental health treatment or other consideration by society. The foundation for the judge's approach was that the defendant had a history of drug involvement and therefore his mental illness, if indeed he had such, was a function of his own doing (the defendant had a clear and independently documented family history of mental illness and exhibited classical symptoms of schizophrenia). A harsh sentence was levied; attempts then had to be initiated in the prison system to obtain the medication to which the defendant had been responding but which was not being prescribed due to the judge's "diagnosis."

Clearly, even with careful use of data and documentation of sources, psychological reports may have an impact different from that intended (or no impact at all). Clinicians who identify substance use as a mitigatory circumstance need to understand that from a legal perspective it is a double-edged sword. They are also providing evidence of a factor that may be seen as cautionary for rehabilitation and subsequent safe release (Melton et al., 1997).

Although a treatment approach for addiction is more likely than a retribution or punishment model to lower recidivism when successfully completed (see below for further notes on treatment characteristics and see also Chapter 17), that fact is little appreciated by many jurists. In a pre-sentence evaluation, the forensic clinician must consider two major aspects:

- To what degree was the crime a function of a correctable and diagnosable condition (for example, methamphetamine dependence), on the basis of which recommendations may be made for treatment? Such recommendations reflect a rehabilitative approach to criminal justice.
- On the other hand, to what extent has an individual operated aggressively while under the influence of methamphetamine? In such cases, a known increased risk of recidivism is present, which may argue for a longer sentence and more caution regarding any conditional release (Miller and Potter-Efron, 1989; Melton et al., 1997).

The actual relationship between crime and drugs is complex and may involve a primary criminal motivation (i.e., money) or may reflect correlations with other factors (e.g., contaminated drugs, characterologic features of the offender, or psychosocial/environmental aspects). Some studies have demonstrated that intake of drugs predisposes individuals to reduce their sense of personal responsibility, to behave impulsively, and then to blame the outcome on the intoxicated state (Lang et al., 1976; Fagan, 1990; Brochu, 1992). Brochu's (1992) review of the literature for the period 1972 to 1992 did not support the conclusion, however, that amphetamine or other stimulants per se were major defining factors to account for violent crime. Rather, the consensus supported the relative importance of contextual factors and multicausal analysis. Similarly, the findings by these writers regarding cases evaluated at a court clinic and cases seen at a hospital (see below for details) supported a complex view of the causes and onset of aggressive behaviors. Thus, both criminological studies and clinical evidence support individual assessment in developing risk estimates (Hart, 2001).

Survey of Methamphetamine Cases Evaluated in a Court Clinic

Although assessment and treatment options in the county from which the below cases were reviewed are better than many, they are generally available only to defendants for whom a mandatory prison sentence is not involved. The general inclination of judges at this court is to refer whenever they perceive questions about treatment-related issues. It is the impression of the court psychologist that defendants referred for a pre-sentence psychological evaluation often are seen as having greater potential for treatment than incarceration.

The focus for psychological evaluations as the psychologist reported it is to develop information relevant to the mitigation and sentencing issues and to the risk of violation of probation where a treatment package is recommended. In his opinion, further evaluation of the substance-related and other treatment aspects of referred defendants should be a component of any ongoing treatment facility.

The major sources of referral are the judges on their own initiatives, motions by defense counsel, or the request of the probation department where initial psychosocial history leads to a question of psychological status. The majority of referred persons with substance-related issues attend outpatient therapy for their drug-related problems, although some undergo inpatient programs prior to outpatient phases. Two major treatment options are typically used. In one setting, the treatment approach is based on the presence of an existing criminal lifestyle associated with the drug use. In the other, the defendant does not appear to have established a criminal lifestyle, but has had some drug treatment with relapse. Most defendants attend the jail treatment program prior to release.

The general procedure involves a screening assessment with an interview, Carlson Psychological Survey, MMPI-2, Substance Abuse Subtle Screening Inventory III (SASSI-III), a Pre-sentence Questionnaire (filled out by the defendant), review of police and prosecutor file reports, and review of prior criminal history record. In some cases, the assessment is done by a substance abuse counselor, with review of the MMPI-2 by a psychologist but reportage only of substance-relevant data from that instrument.

The following cases represent a sample of recent evaluations in methamphetamine-related instances. In the associated commentary, an emphasis on the treatment needs and likely outcomes given treatment opportunities is presented.

Case "AB"

AB was a 44-year-old white male arrested with a codefendant for possession of methamphetamine and involvement in manufacture.

Evaluation found him to show no signs of disturbance on inquiry into mental status, no prior mental health treatment, and a prior criminal history for property crimes. Inquiry of the defendant into substance-related issues resulted in information that he was abusing alcohol twice per week, had had five DUIs (the last occurring 15 years prior), and that he showed tolerance. He admitted to using cocaine during his 30s three to five times in total, and to initial use of amphetamines in high school. This client, in spite of the conditions under which he was arrested, maintained denial for any kind of methamphetamine use.

MMPI-II was defensive but unremarkable for any clinical elevations. Substance-related scales showed a seriously elevated MacAndrews, but no significant findings on the Addiction Potential or Admission Scales. The CPS indicated a profile consistent with a background of family stability but the presence of personal emotional instability, poor judgment, and hostile behavior. Resulting diagnosis was Alcohol Abuse, R/O dependence, and amphetamine abuse referencing the methamphetamine and the denial.

Comment. This defendant is atypical in many respects of persons seen in the court clinic for drug-related problems. His use as detailed, as well as his age and the lack of an ongoing set of criminal acts, referencing the criminal history, makes conclusions and recommendations tentative. The indicators of ongoing extensive methamphetamine use were not evident in the information available, but the overall impact of the history as obtained is consistent with an ongoing and untreated addictions-based lifestyle. The recommendations for the jail treatment program and abstinence are well founded. The likelihood that there will be a recovery status in this case is, however, very low since there has been and probably will be no real focus on the addictions component.

Case "CD"

CD was a 23-year-old white male. He was charged with a felony two possession of drugs, a felony two aggravated possession of drugs, and felony five possession of cocaine.

When initially seen at the jail, he had crying spells and showed significant depressive symptoms but denied suicidality. He was seen again after 3 weeks and his mood state was improved. His substance history included initial use of alcohol at age 12 with tolerance occurring early on. He began drinking beer frequently in junior high school. He reported blackouts, and he indicated that his alcohol use negatively affected his relationships and his work life. At ages 16 and 17, he began the use of marijuana, a quarter ounce every day or eight or nine joints. He began using cocaine laced with opium and hashish. He snorted heroin six times in total. He began crystal methamphetamine at age 18 and used it every day for about 2 years; however, he indicated he had only used it "two or three times" since age 20. He stated he had used LSD about 50 times and was using barbiturates from age 20 to the present on a daily basis. His preferred drug was Valium or Klonopin with alcohol. He also indicated the use of ecstasy once or twice. His criminal record included carrying a concealed weapon and trafficking in cocaine.

Test results indicated significant impacts on his personality and functioning. The MMPI-II was taken in a valid fashion, and he disclosed significant problems. Clinical scales were elevated, especially Scales 2, 4, 6, 7, and 0, which would be consistent with an ongoing depressive picture, withdrawal from positive social contacts, the presence of anxiety, and some underlying characterologic features. The MacAndrews was in the critical range, but the Addiction Potential and Addiction Admission Scales were not highly elevated. The MacAndrews, of course, is the subtle indicator. The SASSI was consistent with substance abuse and/or dependency. The CPS was not remarkable for any specific profile. The diagnosis on the basis of all of the information collected included Axis I: Adjustment Disorder with Depressed Mood, R/O Depressive Disorder, NOS; polysubstance dependence with physiologic dependence and polysubstance abuse; Axis II: Personality Disorder, NOS. Recommendation was for inpatient treatment followed by appropriate outpatient follow-up.

Comment. On the basis of the substance abuse history alone, the clear presence of dependency and primary addiction is indicated. Serious alcohol dependency was already in evidence prior to the maturation of this defendant's brain; it can be reasonably concluded that by the time he reached adulthood, he had significant underlying biological mechanisms involving receptor sites that would support and reinforce all types of substance abuse. The degree of ongoing use that has been characteristic of half of his life would call for a more complete neurological assessment and an extended program should there be any hope for success in rehabilitation.

Case "EF"

EF was a 27-year-old white male arrested for a felony one kidnapping and felony four aggravated burglary.

On the mental status evaluation, there were no signs of any mental illness. The defendant was currently prescribed an SSRI antidepressant. Background history was instructive. He was born and raised in a rural setting, the youngest of five children. He indicated no abuse history. His biological parents had significant marital problems and instability. He reported no problems in school, indicated he had never been diagnosed with ADHD. He did not graduate but did obtain his GED. He indicated he was married, but there were problems including a domestic violence conviction in a different state. He also indicated that he had been identified with minor self-mutilation practices at the age of 14. His domestic violence occurred when on drugs.

Substance abuse-related information included that he began the use of alcohol at the age of 6. He stopped use of that substance at 18 but had restarted 3 years ago at the age of 24. At that point he began consuming half a gallon of whisky every 3 days, and he reported tolerance. He was using LSD regularly, marijuana from the age of 13 to 22, cocaine daily from the ages of 16 to 18 with last use at age 22. His crystal methamphetamine use began at age 18 and continued daily until age 22.

His criminal record included domestic violence, rape of his spouse, four DUIs, theft of a firearm, receiving stolen property, possession of methamphetamine, possession of a controlled substance, possession of drug paraphernalia, possession of narcotics, and possession of a stolen vehicle. The current crime involved a female victim and the sudden eruption of violence on his part. He was resistant at arrest and had to be forcibly controlled. His verbal behavior was replete with profanities. He was amnesic for the events at the time of the crime; he did recall drinking and getting into a verbal fight with his wife just before the incident.

Comment. The above scenario is consistent with observed patterns for persons with heavy methamphetamine use history. The potential to return to extremely violent behavior exists over an extended period of time. The accuracy of his statement that he had not used methamphetamine since age 22 is questionable. If true, his behavior would be consistent with the action of a releaser substance (alcohol is a disinhibiter); predisposition due to methamphetamine impacts rises with the extent and recency of use of that substance.

Test results and other findings from the assessment process included a valid MMPI-II with some minor elevation on Scales 4 and 6, a highly elevated MacAndrews, as well as subclinical elevation on the Addiction Potential Scale and high elevation on Addiction Admission Scale. The PCLR was at 23, which is moderate for psychopathic character traits but the loading was on Factor Two, the primary predictor of violent criminal behavior.

Resulting diagnosis was Axis I — Major Depressive Disorder in remission and polysubstance abuse and Axis II — Antisocial Personality Disorder with histrionic and psychopathic features. History included treatment for his major depression. The recommendations were for an inpatient treatment program and subsequent halfway house and ongoing aftercare, as well as for anger management.

Comment. This case clearly illustrates the individual who is biologically and psychosocially scripted for an addiction lifestyle and an ongoing lifelong vulnerability to substance abuse and dependency. Furthermore, his risk for violent behavior is substantial, particularly under any conditions where he has engaged in the use of substances that reduce executive control. Although he denied serious dysfunctional aspects of his family life, the early onset of substance abuse and the instability of the parental union, along with the noted self-mutilation habits at age 14, would all suggest that there may be some borderline features to his personality integration with specific liabilities when it comes to relationships with women. Therefore, recommendations should have included further assessment of neuropsychological functioning and a specific emphasis on therapy focused on his relational capacity as part of the long-range treatment plans, but presuming an extended period of control over substance use.

Case "GH"

GH was a 20-year-old white female arrested for illegal assembly or possession of chemicals for the manufacture of drugs, a felony three.

Although her current mental status was unremarkable, depression by history was noted with three hospitalizations and an episode of suicidality occurring 1 year prior. At the time of evaluation, she was prescribed an SSRI antidepressant. She had engaged in wrist cutting. Her substance use included occasional use of alcohol with intoxication occurring only once or twice. She denied any tolerance or other problems. She used marijuana in high school "all the time." Until 2 years ago, she was using an eighth to a quarter of an ounce a week. The current crime referenced her involvement in a methamphetamine lab. She indicated she had used cocaine only twice, and that she had been using crystal methamphetamine for 3 weeks to "feel opposite" from her ongoing use of marijuana.

Test results did not show significant psychopathology. The SASSI-III referenced dependency, detachment from feelings, poor insight into feelings, and other attributes often seen in drug users. Her MMPI-II was quite defensive. The resulting protocol was within normal limits, with low points on 7 and 0, referencing a need to present as gregarious and socially adept, and to deny any feelings of discomfort. Neither the MacAndrews nor the Addiction Potential or Admission Scales were at critical levels.

The diagnosis included Depressive Disorder, NOS, referencing especially the clear history in the treatment records, and cannabis dependence and amphetamine abuse. In regard to her methamphetamine use, she maintained that she had only consumed the substance three times, and that she was essentially unaware of the methamphetamine lab in her house (a friend had set up the lab and paid her in marijuana for use of the space). Recommendations of the assessment included the jail treatment program and then postjail abstinence and ongoing substance abuse treatment.

Comment. In all likelihood, she is, as the diagnosis indicated, dependent on marijuana but an occasional user of other substances. A strong educational program about the specific substances and their impacts would need to be part of her substance abuse treatment. However, development of the dual diagnosis component (referencing her underlying depression, for which some of her substance abuse would be self-medicating), as well as detailing her addiction psychology, would be the only way to secure a potential for her to avoid future involvement, both criminally and in relationship to substance abuse. She will be particularly prone to methamphetamine abuse as it would relieve some of the underlying depressive symptomology, which is not addressed adequately by her use of marijuana and may in some cases be enhanced at times. The pattern of denial and minimization is already in place and would need to be a focus of her treatment.

Case "IJ"

IJ was a 21-year-old white male arrested for trafficking in drugs that are not controlled substances, a felony five.

This assessment was completed by a chemical dependency counselor with consultation on the MMPI and diagnosis by a licensed psychologist. The procedure was much more attenuated, including the Pre-sentence Questionnaire, MMPI-II, interview, police report, and hospital data. The MMPI-II was read only for the substance abuse scales.

The defendant expressed remorse, accepted responsibility for what he had done, admitting to the preparation of ecstasy for personal use and for a friend. His psychiatric history included a hospitalization for depression with

Mitigation in Sentencing

suicidal potential occurring after his religious community learned of his drug use. He was placed on Zyprexin, Depakote, and Ativan. He subsequently overdosed on alcohol and Ativan. Aftercare for his substance abuse-related problems was recommended, but he did not follow through. He provided the following substance abuse history. At 17, he was using alcohol and marijuana. At 19, he was using LSD with cocaine and also had used over-the-counter cough syrup. He abstained for a period of about a year, but then relapsed when he became anxious and lonely in his life situation. Relapse was on methamphetamine (ecstasy), which he used five times a day for 3 weeks, until he was out of his supply. His most recent use included marijuana about three times a month, alcohol about three times a month, and abuse of Vicodin and Ativan when he could obtain those substances. He uses alone. He described increasing tolerance. He scored high on a drug dependency test. His family history included a maternal grandfather who was an alcoholic and possibly schizophrenic. His diagnosis was polysubstance abuse, and the recommendations were for intensive outpatient therapy after the jail treatment program.

The MMPI-II was reported only for the substance abuse scales. The MacAndrews was not high. The Addiction Admission Scale was at the critical level; the Addiction Potential Scale was not.

Comment. A review of the MMPI-II data that were not considered by the counselor would indicate the presence of an underlying chronic depression, referencing especially the subscales and other special scales that can reflect conditions not obvious on the main clinical scale profile. Scale 2 is at T64, or certainly at a relevant subclinical level. Scales 7 and 8 are clearly elevated. The 278 configuration is a possible indicator of long-term underlying clinical depression. A diagnosis provided by the CD counselor was Polysubstance Dependency but did not reference the Depressive Disorder. Clearly, the treatment program would need to address the underlying depression as well as the psychosocial components that have supported long-term drug use in the face of severe disapproval by significant to the defendant religious and community authorities. His potential for responding to classical drug treatment alone is limited to non-existent. His likely response to a multimodal and multilevel treatment program would be greater.

Case "KL"

KL was a 41-year-old white male. His crime was aggravated possession of drugs, a felony five.

Interview indicated no problems referencing his mental status. He did have significant health conditions of diabetes and hypertension. He indicated that he used alcohol only minimally because of his medical status, although prior to diagnosis, he said he had been drinking two to three beers a day. He used marijuana at age 15 to 16 but not since. From age 14 forward, he has been an ongoing two to three packs per day cigarette smoker. He indicated he used cocaine twice and crystal methamphetamine twice. He was prescribed Effexor after his arrest for apparent depressive aspects. He was arrested prior to the current charges for domestic violence, which involved sudden dyscontrol, some pushing, and property damage ("I blew up, broke stuff, and pushed her"). At the time, he said there were serious stressors involving both his children and the death of a highly regarded family member. He had also been through a recent divorce.

His MMPI-II was valid, and the main scale profile was within normal limits. However, the configuration would suggest some primary underlying relational problems. The MacAndrews was clearly elevated, as were the Addiction Potential Scale and the Addiction Admission Scale. Diagnosis was Axis I, Adjustment Disorder with depressive traits, amphetamine abuse, and R/O alcohol abuse; Axis II was deferred; Axis III referenced the diabetes and hypertension. The psychologist noted, on the basis of other records as well as the findings from the tests, that there was likely minimization of his use of methamphetamine. He had a pattern, based on the prior record as well as the present, of admitting only that which had been proved, even when the truth was otherwise. The recommendations included outpatient substance as well as the jail treatment program, and some stress management counseling.

Comment. The pattern of denial is one that has been noted as a marker for addiction. In this case, it does not seem to serve the purposes of denial in methamphetamine cases where a hoped-for minimization or exculpation from legal responsibility is involved. However, his capacity to benefit from treatment, and to avoid relapse into addictive behavior, is clearly imperiled by this mode of operating.

Case "MN"

MN was a 25-year-old African-American male arrested for possession of drugs, felony five, and referred for testimony to mitigate penalty.

Prior criminal history included preparation of drugs for sale, attempted possession of drugs, DUI, probation violations, and other drug-related charges. Social history indicated his father had died as a victim of homicide, but he stated he had never been close to that individual. His mother was employed. He had a history of difficulty beginning in adolescence. He was referred for special schooling because of his inability to conform to classroom expectations, including fighting and truancy. He wound up in the juvenile system on burglary and drug abuse charges and spent the better part of a year in a facility where he received some drug treatment. His employment history was inconsistent with gaps.

Substance abuse included marijuana every other day to every day, using four to five, unable to stop. He managed to abstain for a year but then returned to regular use. His other dependence was on ecstasy, which he had used every other weekend for a year. He reported using more and more over time. He had tremors, memory loss, and weight loss as a function of that use. He indicated he used cocaine only once.

Psychological assessment was consistent with the substance abuse history and suggested the presence of dependency. Both the MacAndrews and the Addiction Admission Scale were elevated. Other aspects of the MMPI referenced characterologic features including some significant passive–aggressive potential along with antisocial traits. Dependency was reflected on the SASSI-III. Diagnosis based on the data collected was: Axis I: Cannabis Dependency and Amphetamine Dependency; Axis II: Antisocial Personality Disorder.

Recommendations for both jail treatment program and referral to the program with an emphasis on overcoming a criminal lifestyle were made with a suggestion that prognosis at this point may be poor.

Comment. Unfortunately, the above picture is more usual than not. Nonetheless, efforts to find ways to intervene through long-range and multimodal involvements might well significantly reduce levels of criminal activity in the community. However, given a general inclination and "scripting" for antisocial behavior and the profoundly addictive potential of methamphetamine, along with all the other complications it visits upon its users (in this case, probable long-term central nervous system deficits), the poor prognosis is clearly a warranted conclusion from the data.

Conclusions

The foregoing reports are illustrative of the usual processing of individuals who are arrested for methamphetamine, or for that matter, other substance-related crimes. In this particular court system, some psychological attention is provided for persons with drug-related issues, which is certainly not true across the board. Most persons who commit drug-related crimes do not receive any special attention unless they are processed through drug courts, which have begun to develop across the country, or some features of their crimes or situations warrant special attention. It is not uncommon, of course, for persons of means to obtain drug-related assessments and access treatment in lieu of incarceration, but routine forensic assessment of defendants with drug-related issues or crimes is not the usual practice across the country.

However, as this sampling illustrated, when psychological assessment is undertaken, procedures do not regularly address some of the issues that need to be a focus in methamphetamine-related cases. If maximizing rehabilitation is the goal, which would have the benefit of reducing the cost to society of addictions-based behavior, the following recommendations can be supported:

- There is a need for neuropsychological assessment if not at the time that these screenings and initial assessments are being accomplished, certainly as part of the initial treatment process. Methamphetamine is known to produce ongoing deficits and disinhibitory potentials.
- There is a need for specific education of both defendants and court personnel about the unique impacts of methamphetamine.
- There is a need for an addictions model, which incorporates a biopsychosocial understanding, as the basis of treatment (see below in the discussion of treatment approaches).

Special Case of Death Penalty Sentencing

As detailed in Chapter 14, sentencing implications exist when methamphetamine ingestion is involved in cases where sanity or diminished capacity issues have been raised. The same can be said for the case of capital sentencing. In all states with the death penalty, there is a bifurcated or two-phase trial process. This format grew out of the resumption of capital punishment that took place in the late 1970s and 1980s. Statutes were written to answer the Supreme Court decision in *Furman v. Georgia* (1972), where it was found that the penalty was levied in an unconstitutionally capricious fashion. Separation of the guilt phase from the sentencing phase was the remedy that developed to answer the questions that had been raised in *Furman* and that pertain to the arbitrary and/or discriminative imposition of justice.

The first phase involves a determination of whether the individual is guilty of an act that has resulted in homicide and whether that act meets certain criteria that define it to be deserving of an extreme punishment. If the jury or, in some cases, judge panel finds the aggravating specifications are supported by the evidence, a second trial takes place. That trial usually occurs a short period of time after the first trial, although it is not uncommon for there to be at least a brief hiatus to allow the defendant and the defense team some opportunity to prepare for the second phase.

Nonetheless, death penalty mitigation work cannot possibly be achieved during the time lapse between the ending of the case in chief and the beginning of the sentencing trial. Therefore, most mitigation preparation takes place during the period before the case in chief is even heard and involves evaluation of the defendant and the gathering of information under the assumption that it may be necessary but with the knowledge that indeed it may not be.

Methamphetamine, which is known to cause psychotic behavior and also to create the potential for violence, can become a part of a capital case. The issues that have been discussed in other chapters present in full force when it comes to managing an evaluation and presentation to the courts in death penalty cases. In most states, the expert generally works as a member of the defense team. Results of the evaluation come to the attention of the court only with the agreement of the defendant and counsel. The entire process is protected and confidential, which differentiates it from the evaluation that takes place in the case of a sanity or diminished capacity forensic context. In some states, there is provision for an expert to function at the pre-sentence level in a death penalty case and to be appointed by the court to respond to all parties, including both defense and prosecution. In states where there is that possibility, well-informed defense counsel will carefully motion for their own expert rather than accessing a court-appointed independent expert because of the liabilities involved. For the forensic practitioner, the issue is not one of whether it is appropriate to work for defense. It is the duty of the practitioner to represent fairly and honestly and in a scientifically valid way any data that are developed. Sometimes this can mean that the expert does not testify because the results will not be of assistance to counsel who is representing the defendant. Most of the time, however, even in the case of very socially unacceptable characteristics, an expert who explains the defendant and the crime rather than allowing the jury to continue to see the situation only in terms of the highly offensive act that has occurred, provides some basis for a life as opposed to a death outcome.

Two cases illustrate the role that methamphetamine may play in this particular context. In the case of *State of Ohio v. Gary Hughbanks* (1999), an appeals court reviewed the case and upheld the death penalty. The fact picture involved the defendant fatally stabbing a married couple who came upon him as he was burglarizing their home.

Certain aspects of his fairly extended appeal related to the part played by methamphetamine. When Hughbanks was administered the first polygraph test, he produced rather unusual results. The officer asked him whether he had used drugs and he indicated he had been injecting crystal methamphetamine. The officer testified that the findings from the test were consistent with someone coming down from a methamphetamine high, but he also indicated that Hughbanks did not appear to be under the influence of drugs. Hughbanks informed the officer that he had been treated by a psychiatrist; the officer indicated he did not try to talk with that physician. A second polygraph was administered and results did not show any unusual deviations. At issue in the appeal was the notion that results of the tests and the confession obtained should be suppressed because of duress and mental illness factors that affected Hughbanks' capacity to be Mirandized. The officer testified that the defendant's behavior did not show abnormality indicative of inability to understand and make the decision whether to cooperate. There was a family history for schizophrenia and there was mental illness history on the part of this defendant including auditory hallucinations, for which he had been admitted to the hospital and prescribed antipsychotic medication.

Hughbanks also appealed on the basis that he should have been provided a neuropharmacologist and substance abuse expert among other professionals to assist in his defense. Certain other objections on the basis of which the appeal was submitted did not relate so directly to mental state and the use of drugs. In the affirmation of his death sentence, the appeals court took the position that the alleged failure to provide necessary funds for experts was without merit since the defendant had made no request for additional assistance at the time. It was noted that he did ask and was granted support for a mitigation specialist and a neuropsychologist.

Although it can be noted that his lack of memory for aspects of the event may have been an artifact of his methamphetamine use and some of the atypical results of the polygraph would not be inconsistent with methamphetamine influence, it is just this kind of situation that raises serious problems around the question of malingering. In one of the errors that he raised, the defendant indicated that his motion to suppress the confession should not have been denied because he was under the influence of drugs when he signed his waiver of *Miranda* rights. He also claimed that he was mentally ill. However, the appeals court took the position that he had not presented any indications that he was functioning on an involuntary basis and that neither his drug use nor his mental state resulted in an inability to voluntarily waive rights. Therefore, his appeal on these bases, as well as others, was not upheld.

An interesting issue also was raised regarding the part played by mental illness. In mitigation to the death penalty in Ohio, mental illness is a statutory mitigator if it results in substantial inability to appreciate the wrongfulness of an act or to conform one's conduct. However, the facts as presented not only did not support a not guilty by reason of insanity plea (which would have been precluded in any event by the voluntary ingestion of an illicit substance), but also did not meet the requirement of inability to appreciate wrongfulness. Thus, this case contained many legal concerns that touch on issues of importance in methamphetamine cases, including neuropsychological impacts, voluntariness given the influence of drugs, and the interaction of drugs and preexisting or potential mental illness. All these factors combined, however, did not rise to the level that allowed the appeals court to reverse the death penalty finding.

Although in the *Hughbanks* case apparently there was reasonable effort made to provide him with representation and with a mitigation defense, the same may not be true in many instances. In a 2002 case in Texas involving a man who went on a killing spree following the attack on the World Trade Center, the expeditious and cavalier way of dispensing capital justice seriously contrasts to that which was seen in *Hughbanks*. Stroman was an individual who was apparently in a psychotic state, which was either induced or exacerbated by methamphetamine use. He committed a series of murders based on his belief that foreigners such as his victims needed to die to avenge the 9/11 terrorist attacks. Stroman admitted to the acts and justified them on the basis of his delusional system. The course of the trial, however, is instructive. It took nearly 4 weeks to seat a jury but once that was accomplished, the case in chief began on one morning and was completed in 3 hours. Closing arguments were scheduled for the next day as defense counsel had no witnesses and essentially no defense. The case went to the jury at 10:00 in the morning with a finding of guilty to all specifications by 11:00 A.M. on the same day. The mitigation was scheduled for the next day including impact testimony to be presented by the state. The defense had retained a psychologist to provide mitigation evaluation and testimony and in addition had obtained a neuropsychologist as there was medical evidence of central nervous system damage and a long history of inappropriate behavior. The defendant, incidentally, insisted on coming to his trial dressed in a Harley T-shirt. He maintained his shaved head, which had been his custom for some years, and saw to it that all of his tattoos clearly showed. It was obvious from the outset that he would join the ranks of many others in Texas where the speedy administration of capital justice is the rule and the niceties of defendant rights may be observed in the breach. The jury returned in 5 hours with a recommendation of death (Mary Connell, personal communication, March 2002).

Treatment as a Sentencing Consideration

Although substance abuse in general and methamphetamine abuse in particular have given rise to sentencing enhancement rather than leading to a primary focus on recidivism prevention, the importance of intervention has not been lost in the criminal justice system. Toward that end, as was seen in the review of court cases above, recommendations for treatment as part of probation or conditional release are not uncommon. However, reaching a goal of reducing addictive behavior and the crime that is associated with it depends on having adequate treatment modalities.

Treatment for chemical dependency in general and specifically for methamphetamine has not been uniform around the country. There have been a number of attempts through the National Institute on Drug Abuse (NIDA) and American Society for Addiction Medicine (ASAM) to develop standardized treatment protocols that would act as guidelines to programs that treat addiction. However, the penetration of these algorithms in the provider community has been at best sporadic and fragmented. Many providers continue to use a traditional approach to treatment that is primarily based on the disease concept and follows the Hazleton model. This approach, although effective for many, is more than 30 years old and it has not integrated some of the more recent scientific understanding of addiction and addiction treatment. There continues to be a primary substance-based understanding of addiction as opposed to a more complex model.

A more modern, scientific approach considers addiction as a disorder of activation. Based on this model, there are genetic predispositions to addiction. Those who begin to use mood altering substances activate the addictive tendencies. With frequent and chronic use this pattern becomes solidified and can create major changes in the brain chemistry and the way in which the individual responds to non-drug-induced pleasurable stimuli. The addict will require mood-altering substances to activate certain processes in the brain in order to experience pleasure. With chronic use, there is a shift from attempting to create pleasure (the high), to avoidance of pain, which is caused by withdrawing from the substance. To avoid pain the addict will use whatever means necessary to obtain drugs and the compulsion to use will control multiple aspects of his or her life. Prolonged drug use will affect the physical, social, and psychological functioning of the addict and will result in a downward spiral. The addicted individual who is fortunate enough will "hit bottom" before causing permanent destruction in his or her life; compelled by a sense of desperation, along with external pressures (such as the carrot and stick of court-mandated treatment), the addict may then seek help.

There is a great deal of variability in addiction treatment around the country. If a treatment program is part of a larger behavioral health provider, it is highly likely that it provides a wider range of services than is found as part of a general hospital setting. Such multifactor programs include detoxification and some form of rehabilitation above and beyond simple discharge into a 12-step community-based program.

Comprehensive addiction treatment needs to be multidimensional. This approach to treatment can be highly effective but it tends to be more costly than the more traditional interventions. Because prolonged addiction can create problems in a number of areas, treatment planning needs to consider the various aspects of the individual's adjustment that are affected. A multilayered approach, which allows intervention into physical, social, psychological, and psychiatric problem areas in individually tailored fashion, is necessary.

In the ideal situation, the addict is followed through varying levels of care in the same organization and there is familiarity with the case. However, effective communication between agencies with a consistent treatment philosophy can achieve the same result.

The most acute level of care in addiction treatment is medical detoxification. During this phase the addict is abstinent from drugs of dependency and a state of withdrawal will ensue that must be medically managed. Treatment during this phase often requires medication that reduces withdrawal symptoms by acting on the brain in similar ways as did the substance of abuse. These medications are generally slow-acting substances and do not result in drastic changes in mood.

For most substances, the acute phase of this process lasts less than 4 days. However, there are certain mood-altering substances that tend to have longer-lasting half-lives and can continue to create discomfort and problems associated with withdrawal. Heavy methamphetamine use can result in prolonged chronic withdrawal symptoms, which are physiologically based but psychologically expressed, including anxiety, irritability, and anhedonia (loss of pleasure in life). Sometimes, there is progression to a major depressive state.

Care during acute and early chronic withdrawal involves an extensive medical assessment as many addicts have a history of neglecting their health and often suffer from a variety of health-related problems secondary to their drug use and the lifestyle associated with a drug-abusing subculture. Often addicts, particularly those with an extensive history of alcohol use (and most methamphetamine users are polysubstance abusers with alcohol a frequent component), suffer from malnutrition and medical problems related to vitamin and nutritional deficiency.

Shortly after the detoxification is completed, addiction treatment for most patients can be provided on an outpatient basis. Day treatment and intensive outpatient programs are options that are often used. A subpopulation of patients with coexisting mental health diagnoses may require a more structured treatment immediately after detoxification. A large-scale internationally based study of specific interventions into methamphetamine-induced psychoses is currently in the process of development. The researchers hope to identify the best neuroleptic medications as well as other treatment and prevention components (J. Rathner, personal communication, June 2002). An adequate treatment program needs to consider external problems in areas of work environment, neighborhood, and family that can create significant problems in recovery. While dealing with relapse is part of a modern treatment program, with addicts who have had repeated relapses after detoxification, more structured and highly supervised modes are indicated. Where individuals have co-morbid psychiatric diagnoses, high levels of family conflict, or have high levels of external cues that trigger addictive behavior, treatment-planning teams need to consider a clinically managed residential program with step down available to a more traditional residential program.

The clinically managed residential program is particularly effective with individuals who require psychotropic medications. Often, extensive education and orientation are indicated to prevent dropout from treatment and early termination of medication use.

Long-term therapeutic communities that focus on providing structure, supervision, treatment, and resocialization can be effective in treatment of the more chronic group of individuals who have had a history of difficulties with issues other than addiction. Some communities have developed and implemented prerelease programs for addicts who have been incarcerated for nonviolent drug-related offenses. These programs are designed for those addicts who are highly vulnerable to relapse and require a high degree of external support and structure.

In these programs, the addict is usually provided with incrementally higher levels of responsibility and moves along the continuum of being closely monitored to rather independent living and working in the community. However, these programs usually have limited direct treatment modules such as group or individual therapy. They rely heavily on peer support and use other community resources for treatment of adjustment difficulties that are often present in addicts who are new in recovery. The length of stay in this type of program is relatively high and can range from 90 to 180 days. It is hoped that with the routines that are established during their stay in such programs, addicts will begin to internalize a more structured lifestyle that is conducive to staying sober. In most of these programs there are daily requirements and each resident is mandated to attend 12-step groups.

Short-term residential programs, on the other hand, are designed to integrate the addict into the recovering community (Hubbard et al., 1998). During their stay in these programs, clinical staff and peer support focus on helping addicts develop internal coping skills that enable them to live a sober lifestyle. Participants also are presented with alternative approaches to asking for peer support in 12-step recovery meetings and to expand their sober social support systems. Learning leisure activities that are conducive to staying sober is included to assist in prevention of relapse through avoidance of old "traps."

Generally speaking, an essential aspect of recovery from addiction is active participation in 12-step recovery programs. This process, which includes extensive peer support and following the tradition of using 12 steps in the recovery process, has proved to be relatively effective in promoting and maintaining abstinence in alcoholics and addicts. There is limited scientific scrutiny of the program as it is, by nature, an anonymous group and it does not easily lend itself to empirical investigation. However, intuitively, the values of the 12-step programs are in the structure that they provide for the addict. This type of external sober support is instrumental in relapse prevention and takes the addict out of situations that contain cues that activate drug-seeking desires in the brain and subsequently lead to use.

Effective addiction treatment requires a multidisciplinary team. To be able to perform a comprehensive biopsychosocial assessment of the addict, the team needs to include a physician (an addictionologist or a psychiatrist with addiction treatment specialization), a psychologist, and a chemical dependency counselor. Clinical social workers who provide family and social assessment are essential team members. For treatment to produce optimal results, these professionals must collect data and work together in treatment planning. An attitude of respect for the participant includes an understanding on the part of the treatment team that addicts, like all other patients, are interested in getting better (Demiff et al., 2000).

In order for a substance to affect an individual's mood, it must be able to pass the blood–brain barrier and cause biochemical changes in the brain. The cognitive, emotional, and behavioral effects of these substances mimic those seen in other processes that result from changes in brain chemistry, such as mental illness. It is common that during the active phase of their use, methamphetamine addicts in particular may be diagnosed erroneously as suffering from mental illness. Evaluation must proceed with care or an individual who is abusing substances or addicted to them could be diagnosed with an illness that is chemically induced and may disappear when direct effects of the chemicals dissipate. Kono et al. (2001), in their comparison of individuals who abused nicotine, alcohol, methamphetamines, and inhalants, noted that those who abused methamphetamines displayed a significantly higher intensity of symptoms related to perceptual disturbances, thought disorder, mood disorder, and problems with acting out behaviors, which they categorized as volition disorder.

On the other hand, it is very important to note that there are those addicts or alcoholics who have a coexisting psychiatric condition (patients with dual diagnosis). For individuals who display psychiatric symptoms as a side effect of their substance abuse, there needs to be an active treatment plan for addiction treatment, and a "wait and see" approach toward the psychiatric symptoms. Those individuals who either have a preexisting psychiatric condition or who have developed psychiatric illness during the course of their use of mood-altering chemicals will require a treatment plan that includes psychiatric interventions. Unfortunately, many traditional addiction treatment programs around the country lack appropriate psychiatric services, and this aspect of treatment for those addicts who are most vulnerable is missing.

The usual pattern noted in treatment of these individuals is characterized by repeated relapses and the psychiatric symptoms interfering with ability to benefit from the addiction recovery program. Also, shortly after discharge from these programs, the individual is likely to go back to using drugs in an attempt to self-medicate the psychiatric symptoms. Dual diagnosis treatment needs to be provided by a team of professionals who have expertise for both addiction and psychiatric problems.

The opposite case can also occur. There are psychiatric programs that mistakenly attribute drug-related symptoms to psychiatric conditions and often attempt to medicate the addiction problems away. Ignoring addiction-related issues not uncommonly can lead to prescription of addictive medications for what are withdrawal symptoms.

One of the main problems in the field of addiction treatment is blaming treatment failure on the patient with accusations of "poor motivation" and "being in denial." In making these statements, the clinicians absolve themselves from any responsibility for providing the type of care that is a "good fit" for the patient and thus lose a chance to improve compliance levels. Also, in blaming the patient for treatment failure, a cyclical reward system is set up that promotes the sense of inadequacy and low self-esteem often associated with being an addict. The patient is invalidated and the problem is increased. In research with patients suffering from borderline personality disorder and other patient groups with multiple problems, Linehan (1993) has demonstrated that validation is an effective tool for engaging patients in treatment and therefore obtaining more positive outcomes. The tradition of pejorative labels for patients who have difficulties in navigating a course of treatment has been a significant factor in addiction treatment failures. (For example, a counselor dismissing a patient as a "frequent flyer" is not unknown in the case of so-called resistant participants.) If the patient accepts the view of the counselor, then he or she has incorporated a concept of inability to benefit from treatment. If, on the other hand, the patient disagrees with the assumptions of the counselor, then there is demonstrated "noncompliance," which can lead to termination of treatment (so-called therapeutic discharge).

In treatment planning for addicts it is important that those who provide the treatment take some responsibility for making sure that the addict is motivated to follow the treatment plan. There are certain commitment strategies that can be quite effective in raising levels of participation. Linehan and colleagues (Linehan, 1993) have demonstrated the effectiveness of these strategies in keeping patients with borderline personality disorder engaged in treatment. Treatment dropout can be reduced dramatically when commitment to therapy is defined as a major objective of therapeutic work rather than as a prerequisite on the part of the patient. Thinking about treatment in this way is especially necessary for individuals who have been referred into treatment by the legal system, rather than presenting themselves for assistance.

Completing a comprehensive program is enhanced through evaluation of prior treatment history. The addict must be asked to outline a history of addiction and psychiatric treatment including the reasons for admission to treatment, the center where treatment occurred, the length of treatment, how long sobriety lasted, and what caused the relapse. A great deal of insight can be obtained if further questions on the course of treatment and its completeness are assessed. As mentioned earlier, there is a great deal of variability in how addiction services are provided; however, there are types of treatment that tend to be offered by certain programs and attended by certain types of addicts in order to pacify certain individuals or institutions. For example, in cases of driving under the influence, many individuals, especially first-time offenders, participate in a weekend program that takes place at a local hotel. Educational offerings are the main aspect of this intervention, along with the brief isolation. There are also many individuals who enter a treatment program and are in the process of withdrawal from drugs and alcohol. These individuals are usually detoxified medically, and are presented with certain educational modules regarding alcoholism and addiction. The assumption is made that these addicts can manage the cognitive tasks involved. After a few short days, they are discharged into the community with no meaningful follow-up treatment and are told that they are in a place where they can benefit from community-based 12-step programs.

Therefore, it is important that during the assessment period, questions regarding the extent and type of treatment are asked to determine whether or not the addict has had a true chance at recovery. Issues related to the type of professional involved in treatment and the programmatic aspect of treatment need to be addressed. This aspect of assessment is even more important in forensic situations, because addicts with legal involvement and criminal convictions tend to have fewer financial resources and it is likely that their treatment was provided in community-based agencies that also have limited resources. It also allows some education of the court regarding those factors that were not under the control of the individual and that favor appropriate treatment options.

Given the extensive damage caused by even short-term use of methamphetamines, the issue of deficits associated with brain injury needs to be addressed directly. Certain aspects of this type of deficit clearly interfere with the addict's ability to learn and process information. A great deal of programming at most addiction recovery centers is based on a psychoeducation model. It would be safe to assume that chronic methamphetamine users may have a great deal more difficulty with the learning material presented to them than persons without the central nervous system damage. Given that impulse control and inhibition and management of feelings are difficult for these individuals, frustration enhances dropout potentials as well as leads to acting out in ways that disrupt treatment for themselves or others. If cognitive deficits that result in significant interference with learning are noted, appropriate assessment should be undertaken. It may be important to design treatment interventions that are behavioral in nature and do not involve higher-level cognitive work. At the same time, cognitive rehabilitation measures can be included in the treatment plan that will assist in later mastery of more traditional educative aspects. In fact, the 12-step recovery program has a strong behavioral component that is designed to engage participants in the process even if they do not cognitively appreciate more abstract principles.

Educating the addict's support system can positively affect treatment outcome. Family members, sponsors from 12-step programs, probation officers, and case managers should be informed about the complexities related to how the brain of the addict may be compromised. As a result, the addict's support system is less likely to engage in blaming — and thus unwittingly contribute to treatment failure when cognitive interference leads into treatment lapse.

Individuals with dual diagnosis are significantly more difficult to treat and tend to have a higher rate of relapse in both their psychiatric condition and addiction. This phenomenon generally arises because one or the other aspect of their condition is not treated adequately. As mentioned above, there are major psychological issues and cognitive deficits associated with methamphetamine use. In addition, behavioral problems, often secondary to either premorbid personality or brain damage caused by the destructive force of the substance, make management of these individuals difficult in traditional treatment settings.

The dual diagnosis problem should be assessed prior to making a referral for treatment. Individuals with a history of methamphetamine use and other coexisting conditions require an addiction treatment facility with significant capability to address psychological and psychiatric issues. This combination of expertise is rarely present in even fairly sophisticated treatment settings and is conspicuously absent in programs designed for "treatment" of addicts who have been adjudicated and have been mandated to receive addiction treatment programming as part of their sentencing.

Prerelease programs usually run between 90 to 180 days and are designed to assess the individual's capabilities to live a sober life outside of the structure of a correctional facility. These programs are not designed to provide primary treatment of any type and are often managed by graduated peers. They are usually found in inner-city locations with access to drug-infested neighborhoods. Given the cognitive, emotional, and behavioral vulnerabilities of chronic methamphetamine users, these programs can represent a major risk for "treatment failure" with subsequent categorization as resistant or non-compliant.

Another aspect of treatment for methamphetamine users is related to how rapidly they become addicted to this drug and how quickly their use results in major impairment and subsequent need for treatment (Castro et al., 2000). Hartz et al. (2001) have reported extensively on the intensity of craving for this drug and the cues associated with relapse because of it. In the long run, the emphasis needs to be on prevention because the prognosis for methamphetamine-addicted individuals, given the brain impacts, can be bleak.

Review of Treatment Center Cases

Some of the above observations regarding treatment can be seen in the case characteristics found in a review of methamphetamine cases from a relatively small suburban multimodal psychiatric facility located in northeast Ohio. Laurelwood is a private facility that is part of the larger community of healthcare institutions known as University Hospitals.

Laurelwood has a largely working- or middle-class population with insurance coverage or the capacity to pay for treatment, although *pro bono* service is offered when feasible. As such, the case sample is not representative of the nation at large insofar as drug abuse patterns and responses to treatment are concerned. Given the population skew, the following results from this case survey raise some red flags in spite of the small sample size.

Procedure

Cases admitted to the hospital during the past year were reviewed to obtain a selection where methamphetamine abuse was present; 17 cases were identified (Table 11.3). Information collected included gender, marital status, age, other substances abused, criminal record including arrest, time served, and probation, chemical dependency treatment history, mental health treatment history, presence of agreement for treatment after release, Axis I diagnosis, Axis II diagnosis, Axis III diagnosis, family history for chemical dependency

Table 11.3 Demographic Characteristics

Gender		Mean Age	Age Range	Marital Status				Total
				Single	M	Div	Sep	
M	N = 13	24.85	18–40	10 (77%)	1 (8%)	1 (8%)	1 (8%)	13
F	N = 4	26.75	16–39	2 (50%)	2 (50%)	0	0	4

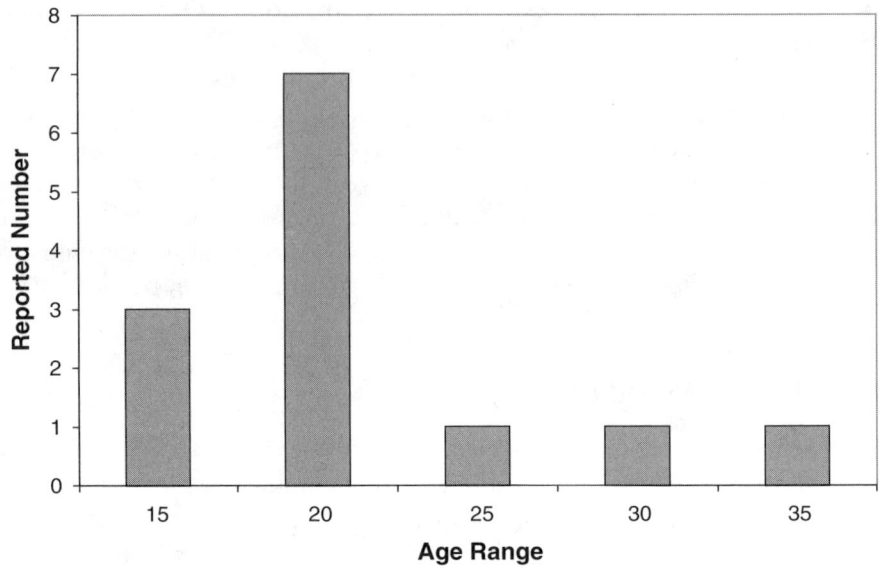

Figure 11.1 Onset of methamphetamine use.

Table 11.4 Reported Criminal Justice Contact (N,%)

Gender	Arrest History	Served Time	Probation
M	8 (47%)	5 (29%)	1 (6%)
F	2 (12%)	1 (6%)	0
Total	10 (59%)	6 (35%)	1 (6%)

or other mental health diagnoses. No identifying information was reported and data have been grouped as indicated below.

Results

This small sample, heavily weighted with males over females, nonetheless has characteristics of significant interest. The age range includes persons who are into middle life years. However, as Figure 11.1 shows, the period of most likely initial use is in the 20s for the 13 states where information about the initial use of methamphetamine was available.

Table 11.4 illustrates the not surprising finding that over half of the sample reported contact with the criminal justice system. Of the 11 patients for whom there was a report of involvement with the criminal justice system, several kinds of offenses were referenced. Of the 11, 9 had at least one charge that involved substance-related activity (possession of drugs or paraphernalia, driving under the influence, under-age consumption). Five had contact

Mitigation in Sentencing

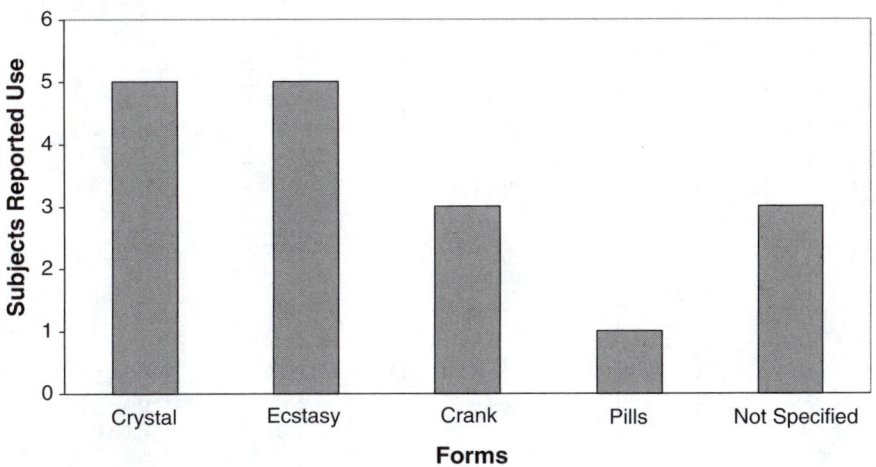

Figure 11.2 Forms of methamphetamine used.

with the criminal justice system secondary to aggressive behavior including domestic violence, disruptive behavior in school, assault charges, and attempted murder.

Table 11.5 clearly illustrates the polysubstance use patterns of this sample, which are characteristic across the board in treatment centers such as this. Alcohol, as might be expected, remains the most likely substance to be abused in addition to other identified chemicals and was found in every one of these methamphetamine users.

Table 11.6 illustrates another facet of the diagnosis and treatment of chemical abuse. There are significant co-morbid conditions; some are induced by the substance abuse but others are preexisting or co-occurring and may themselves be underlying bases for drug/alcohol involvement. Given the short inpatient treatment scope in this setting, most Axis II diagnoses were deferred with only one person identified as having no Axis II vulnerability and only two positively identified with a personality disorder.

Figure 11.2 illustrates the prominence of ecstasy as one of the more important manifestations of methamphetamine abuse in this region.

Other data collected on this sample included information on Axis III conditions: hypothermia, sexually transmitted diseases (STDs), possible lupus, chronic pain, chronic obstructive pulmonary disease, arthritis, possible malnutrition, and asthma. Family history was positive for significant mental health conditions in three records (bipolar affective disorder, schizophrenia, and Alzheimer's) and was significant for alcohol abuse or dependency in 14 of the cases.

Table 11.5 Substance Abuse Status (N, %)

Sex	ETOH	Cocaine	Marijuana	Hallucin	BZPs	Narcotic	Other
M	13(76%)	11(65%)	11(65%)	8(47%)	2(12%)	7(41%)	Inhalent, nicotine, oxydone
F	4(24%)	4(24%)	3(18%)	4(24%)	0	2(12%)	Nicotine, barbiturates, ketamine, Vicodan
Total	17(100%)	15(88%)	14(82%)	12(71%)	2(12%)	9(53%)	

Note: Percentages not exact sums due to rounding errors.

Table 11.6 Axis I Diagnostic Status (N, %)[a]

Sex	Non-Substance-Induced Mood Disorders	Substance-Induced Mood Disorders	Non-Substance-Induced Psychotic Disorders	Substance-Induced Psychotic Disorders	Adjustment Disorders	ADHD	Other
M	2(12%)	1(8%)	2(12%)	2(12%)	2(12%)	2(12%)	Substance Induced (1)
F	3(18%)	2(12%)	0	0	0	0	Oppositional Defiance (1) Anorexia Nervosa
Total[b]	5(29%)	3(18%)	2(12%)	2(12%)	2(12%)	2(12%)	

[a] Rule outs were assumed to be present, consistent with DSM-IV system and were counted. They included one major depression, one substance-induced mood disorder, and one adjustment disorder.
[b] Patients had more than one Axis I condition; numbers do not sum to 17.

Mitigation in Sentencing

Discussion

The fact that methamphetamine cases were relatively uncommon for this population does not diminish the importance of the findings. In effect, there is an early indication of an increasing problem, which is seen in the small sample available for scrutiny. The characteristics of these individuals and their families were consistent with what is repeatedly found in all other areas of substance abuse. There is a family component. Involvement with illicit substances places one at risk for criminal justice contact, and there is a significant likelihood of mental health co-morbidity of a type that requires that the treatment plan include appropriate components. Clearly, this is not a population that can be served by a one-size-fits-all treatment approach, nor is it a population that can be treated in any setting where all use of substances, including psychotropic medication, is not well tolerated. Recent media exposure has featured reports of ecstasy abuse, which has become one of the more common party drugs in the geographic area served by the hospital. The findings of this small study are consistent with alarms that have been raised about the use of this significantly dangerous substance.

Resources for the Sentencing Process

The Substance Abuse and Mental Health Services Administration (SAMHSA, 2001) provides a directory with listings for type of services available at facilities across the country which is issued on a yearly basis. Identified service categories include indication of those programs that are set up to provide for the criminal justice population. A brief phone survey of some of these facilities was initiated using a semistructured inquiry was conducted (see Appendix I). Even given the very limited number of contacts with completed data (N = 20), there was geographic representation across the mainland. Assuming the sample to have some representatives for the national picture, it would appear that there is increasing use being made of cognitive behavioral approaches, often in combination with 12-step programs. Multiservice was the rule. Most had some psychiatric care and almost all indicated dual diagnosis treatment was offered including psychotropic medication. (However, one informant indicated dual diagnosis patients were treated, but also stated no one was allowed to have prescribed medication once the individual entered the program.)

All facilities had social work coverage, about half had psychologists All either had detox units or could access the service. Almost all either had or accessed inpatient, partial hospitalization, or intensive outpatient programs. Almost half had a residential program in place. Ancillary programs, such as occupational and recreational therapy and vocational rehabilitation, were also seen as important components in treatment planning (N = 18, 90%). In a couple of contacts, there was unwillingness to respond to questions about the scope of services and underlying treatment philosophy and there was one facility where no one claimed to know the answers to the questions. On the other hand, there are settings that include specific methamphetamine focus, such as the UCLA Integrated Substance Abuse Program (Cunningham–Rathner, personal communication, June 2002). Clearly, it becomes important to engage in direct person-to-person contact in making referrals.

Chapter Summary

Substance abuse has become a complicating factor at all levels of the American criminal justice system. In the particular case of methamphetamine, use has generated a body of case law and led to specifications in the federal sentencing system. At the state level, it has been incorporated in various ways into sentencing considerations. Forensic assessment has proceeded from a psychological perspective of understanding behavior and designing interventions. The sometimes difficult interface between mental health and law is regularly evident in forensic assessment around methamphetamine cases and particularly in regard to the sentencing process. Issues of risk analysis with its inherent insecurities and yet its important place in supporting the protection of society as well as the rights of the individual have clearly been a part of the processing of methamphetamine cases. While some varieties of substance abuse affect primarily the individual insofar as negative outcomes are concerned, methamphetamine is a drug that is regularly associated with disinhibition and violence. The reduction of violent crime is of high concern to law enforcement and the overall operation of justice. As with all others who seek to serve the best interests of the system of criminal justice, it is necessary to walk a tightrope. This balancing act must take place within the scientific limitations of the data collected, further complexly constraining the practitioner.

References

Badgett, S.A. (1999). Neuropsychological Functioning Subtypes of Schizophrenia and Mood Disorders. Doctoral dissertation, Fordham University, New York.

Brochu, S. (1992). A critical look at the conceptual models explaining drugs and crime. Paper presented at the 3rd Conference of the European Association of Psychology and Law, Oxford, U.K.

Castro, F.G., Barrington, E.H., Walton, M.A., and Rawson, R.A. (2000). Cocaine and methamphetamine differential addiction rates. *Psychol. Addictive Behav.*, 14(4), 390–396.

Danesh-Khoshboo, Y. (1991). *The Civilization of Law: A Commentary on the Laws of Hammurabi and Magna Carta.* Berrien Springs, MI: Vandevere.

Daubert v. Morrell Dow Pharmaceuticals, 509 U.S. 579 (1993).

Davis, B.A. and Vitollo, J. (2001). Federal criminal conspiracy. *Am. Crim. L.R.*, 38, 777–817.

Demiff, L., Rizvi, S.L., Brown, M., and Linehan, M.M. (2000). Dialectical behavior therapy for substance abuse: a pilot application to a methamphetamine dependent woman with borderline personality disorder. *Cogn. Behav. Pract.*, 7, 457–468.

Fagan, J. (1990). Intoxication and aggression. In M. Tonry and J.Q. Wilson, Eds., *Drugs and Crime (Crime and Justice: A Review of Research*, Vol. 13), Chicago, IL: University of Chicago Press.

Fisher, R.P. and Geiselman, R.E. (1992). *Memory-Enhancing Techniques for Investigative Interviewing: The Cognitive Interview.* Springfield, IL: Charles C Thomas.

Flynn, P.M. and McMahon, R.C. (1997). MCMI applications in substance abuse. In T. Millon, Ed., *The Millon Inventories: Clinical and Personality Assessment.* New York: Guilford Press.

Flynn, P.M., McCann, J.T., Luckey, J.W., Rounds-Bryant, J.L., Theisen A.C., Hoffman, J.A., and Koman, J.J. (1997). Drug dependence scale in the Millon Clinical Multiaxial Inventory. *Substance Use Misuse*, 32(6), 733–748.

Furman v. Georgia, 408 U.S. 238 (1972).

Gearan, A. (2002). 3-strikes laws' long sentences to get review. *The Plain Dealer.* p. A6.

Grove, W.M. and Meehl, P. (1996). Comparative efficiency of informal (subjective, impressionistic) and formal (mechanical, algorithmic) prediction procedures: the clinical-statistical controversy. *Psychol. Public Policy Law*, 2(2), 293–323.

Hall, H.V. (2000). Violence Prediction and Risk Analysis. Workshop Manual. Sponsored by The Pacific Institute for the Study of Conflict and Aggression.

Hall, H.V. and Pritchard, D. (1996) *Detecting Malingering and Deception: The Forensic Distortion Analysis (FDA).* Winter Park, FL: St. Lucie Press.

Hanson, R.K. and Bussiere, M.T. (1998). Predicting relapse: a meta-analysis of sexual offender recidivism studies. *J. Consulting Clin. Psychol.*, 66(2), 348–362.

Hart, S.D. (2001). Violence risk assessment. Keynote Address, 11th European Conference of Psychology and Law, June 8, Lisbon, Portugal.

Hartz, D.T., Fredrick-Osborne, S.L., and Galloway, G.P. (2001). Craving predicts use during treatment for methamphetamine dependence: a prospective, repeated-measure, within-subject analysis. *Drug Alcohol Dependence*, 63, 269–276.

Hillbrand, M. (2001). Homicide, suicide and other forms of co-occurring aggression against self and against others. *Prof. Psychol. Res. Pract.*, 32(6), 626–635.

Hubbard, R.L., Carddock, S.G., Flynn, P.M., Anderson, J., and Etheridge, R.M. (1998). Overview of one-year follow-up outcomes in the Drug Abuse Treatment Outcome Study. *Psychol. Addictive Behav.*, 11(4), 291–298.

Kono, J., Miyata, H., Sadanobu, U., Yanagita, T., Miyasato, K., Ikawa, G., and Hukui, K. (2001). Nicotine, alcohol, methamphetamine, and inhalant dependence: a comparison of clinical features with the use of a new clinical evaluation. *Alchohol*, 24, 99–106.

Lang, A.R., Goeckner, D.J., Adesso, V.J., and Marlatt, G.A. (1976). Effects of alcohol on aggression in male social drinkers. *J. Abnormal Psychol.*, 84(5), 508–518.

Linehan, M.M. (1993). *Cognitive Therapy of Borderline Personality Disorder*. New York: Guilford Press.

Linehan, M.M., Armstrong, H.E., Suarez, A., Almari, D., and Heard, H.D. (1991). Cognitive behavioral therapy with chronically borderline suicidal patients. *Arch. Gen. Psychiatr.*, 48, 1060–1064.

Lockett v. Ohio, 438 U.S. 586 (1978).

McConaghy, N. (1999). Methodological issues concerning evaluation of treatment for sexual offenders: randomization, treatment drop-outs, untreated controls, and with treatment studies. *Sexual Abuse*, 11, 183–194.

McKetin, R. (2000). Cognitive Functioning and Psychological Morbidity among Illicit Amphetamine Users. Doctoral dissertation, University of New South Wales, Sydney, Australia.

Meehl, P.E. (1996). *Clinical versus Statistical Prediction: A Theoretical Analysis and a Review of the Literature*. Northvale, NJ: Jason Aronson (original work published in 1954).

Meloy, J.R. (1992). *Violent Attachments*. Northvale, NJ: Jason Aronson.

Melton, G.B., Petrila, J., Poythres, N.G., and Slobogin, C. (1997). *Psychological Evaluations for the Courts: A Handbook for Mental Health Professionals and Lawyers*, 2nd ed. New York: Guilford Press.

Messina, N. (2000) Therapeutic Community Treatment Outcomes for Substance Abusers with Antisocial Personality Disorder. Doctoral dissertation. College Park: University of Maryland.

Messina, N., Wish, E., Hoffman, J., and Nemes, S. (2001). Diagnosing antisocial personality disorder among substance abusers: the SCID versus the MCMI-II. *Am. J. Drug Alcohol Abuse*, 27(4), 699–717.

Miller, M.M. and Potter-Efron, R.T. (1989). Aggression and violence associated with substance abuse. *J. Chem. Dependency Treat.*, 3(1), 1–36.

Milne, R. and Bull, R. (1999). *Investigative Interviewing: Psychology and Practice.* New York: John Wiley & Sons.

Mistretta v. U.S., 488 U.S. 361, 396 (1989).

Monahan, J. (1981). *Predicting Violent Behavior: An Assessment of Clinical Techniques.* Beverly Hills, CA: Sage.

Mulvey, E. and Lidz, C. (1985). Back to basics: a critical analysis of dangerousness research in a new legal environment. *Law Hum. Behav.*, 9, 209–218.

Mulvey, E. and Lidz, C. (1995). Conditional prediction: a model for research on dangerousness to others in a new era. *Int. J. Law Psychiatr.*, 18, 129–143.

Parker, S. and Block, M.K. (2001). The limits of federal criminal sentencing policy; or, confessions of two reformed reformers. *George Mason Law Rev.*, 9, 1001–1125.

Rice, M.E., Quinsey, V.L., and Harris, G.T. (1991). Sexual recidivism among child molesters released from a maximum security psychiatric institution. *J. Consulting Clin. Psychol.*, 59, 381–386.

Rogers, R., Ed. (1997). *Clinical Assessment of Malingering and Deception.* New York: Guilford Press.

Ruback, R.B. and Wroblewski, J. (2001). The federal sentencing guidelines: psychological and policy reasons for simplification. *Psychol. Public Policy Law*, 7(4), 739–775.

SAMHSA (2001). *National Directory of Drug and Alcohol Abuse Treatment Programs*, Department of Health and Human Services, Washington, D.C.

Sangiacomo, M. "Three Dead Infants, 30 Years, No Answers," *The PlainDealer*, February 10, 2002, B2, Cleveland, OH.

State ex rel, Wright v. Ohio Adult Parole Authority, 75 OS3d 82 661 NE2d 728 (1996).

State v. Burkholder, 12 OS 3d 205, 12 OBR 269, 466 NE2d 176 (1984).

State v. Callahan, Ohio App. 6057 LEXIS 6057 (2001).

State v. Hughbanks, Ohio App. LE-XIS 5789, 12/3/1999.

U.S. Sentencing Commission (2001). Federal Sentencing Guidelines Manual. The West Group, Washington, D.C.

United States v. Pineda, 981 F.2d 569 (1st Cir. 1992), Honolulu, HI.

United States v. Thomas Conne James, 257 F.3d 1173, 2001 U.S. App. LEXIS 15938 (2001).

Vogt, A. S. (2001). Comment: the mess left behind: regulating the cleanup of former methamphetamine laboratories. *Idaho Law Rev.*, 38, 251–290.

Zakzanis, K.K. and Young, D.A. (2001). Memory impairment in abstinent MDMA ("ecstasy") users: a longitudinal investigation. *Neurology*, 56(7), 966–969.

Zimbardo, P., Haney, C., Banks, W., and Jaffe, D. (1972). *The Psychology of Imprisonment: Privation, Power, and Pathology.* Unpublished manuscript, Stanford University, Stanford, CA.

Mitigation to Murder

12

HAROLD V. HALL
SANDRA B. MCPHERSON
STUART W. TREMLOW
ERROL YUDKO

The Model Penal Code concept of extreme mental or emotional disturbance, commonly referred to as "extreme emotion," is currently recognized in Hawaii, New York, and Oregon, and to some extent in Pennsylvania, Illinois, New Mexico, and California. Under this schema, the accused can use extreme emotion as a mitigating factor to reduce a murder charge to manslaughter. Hawaii Revised Statutes §707-702(2) states the following:

> In a prosecution for murder in the first and second degrees it is a defense, which reduces the offense to manslaughter, if the defendant was, at the time he caused the death of the other person, under the influence of extreme mental or emotional disturbance for which there is a reasonable explanation. The reasonableness of the explanation shall be determined from the viewpoint of a person in the defendant's situation under the circumstances as he believed them to be.

The Hawaii Revised Statutes adopted the definitions of extreme emotion as articulated in *People v. Shelton* (1976):

> [E]xtreme emotional disturbance is the emotional state of an individual, who (a) has no mental disease or defect that rises to the level established by [Haw. Rev. Stat. §704-400 (1985)]; and (b) is exposed to an extremely unusual and over-whelming stress; and (c) has an extreme emotional reaction to it, as a result of which there is a loss of self-control and reason is overborne by intense feelings, such as passion, anger, distress, guilt, excessive agitation or other similar emotions.

Extreme emotion involves a three-part test as follows and as illustrated below:

1. External stresses impact on the individual
2. Causing cognitive (thinking) and affective (emotional) reactions, which then
3. Lead to a loss of self-control.

Reference

People v. Shelton, 88 Misc. 2d 136, 385 N.Y.S.2d 708 (1976).

Methamphetamine and Pregnancy

13

ERROL YUDKO
SANDRA B. MCPHERSON

> The right of the people to be secure in their persons, houses, papers, and effects, against unreasonable searches and seizures, shall not be violated, and no Warrants shall issue, but upon probable cause, supported by Oath or affirmation, and particularly describing the place to be searched, and the persons or things to be seized.
>
> —The Fourth Amendment of the U.S. Constitution

Few provisions of the Bill of Rights are as utterly American as the Fourth Amendment of the Constitution. This amendment grew from the experience of the colonials in America as well as from their English roots. "Every man's house is his castle." But what of the body of a woman? This chapter evaluates how the courts attempt to balance the rights of a fetus with the rights of its mother. Is it right for the courts or Child Protective Services (CPS) to remove a child from its mother's care if the newborn tests positive for a drug? Many of us would answer this query with an unquestioning "yes." However, we tend to make that decision based on the assumption that the drug itself is damaging to the fetus. For most drugs (including cocaine and methamphetamine) this has been difficult to demonstrate using the scientific method. For some drugs (including alcohol and tobacco) the relationship between use and fetal damage is quite apparent. The problem with the current picture is that CPS is likely to remove a child from its mother's care if there is evidence that the mother was using methamphetamine during her pregnancy, but not tobacco.

Legal Issues and Status

Individual, social, moral, and legal issues converge when addressing the abuse of methamphetamine by pregnant women and the appropriate societal response. In some ways it might seem that the issue is needlessly complex. Methamphetamine abuse is an illegal activity, punishable within the existing range of statutes at state and federal levels. However, the particular problems that arise in the case of abuse of methamphetamine in pregnancy do in fact involve significant legal questions across different legal venues.

A search of federal appeals and Supreme Court activity has identified several areas of focus and some reasonably inferred trends. Major issues included maternal rights against self-incrimination and vulnerability to punishment on the basis of nonpermitted testing at the time of birth of the child; maternal custody rights; paternal custody and/or visitation rights; and individual rights against unreasonable detention.

Maternal Rights against Self-Incrimination and Vulnerability to Punishment Based on Drug Testing by Hospitals

Decisions that have been rendered and, for that matter, statutes that have been passed in various states, have tended to support incursions into the rights of mothers to protect or secure the needs of children. Certainly such decisions rest on a long-established principle that the needs of the youngest members of society are paramount. However, the cases themselves illustrate not only abstract legal issues but also lifestyles and behaviors that are well known in the field of substance abuse. Although methamphetamine use figures in the cases, sometimes very prominently, it is rarely the only basis on which decisions have been rendered.

Although cases reviewed at levels below the Supreme Court have tended to support protection of unborn and newly arrived children, the one Supreme Court case on point is *Ferguson et al. v. the City of Charleston et al.* (2001). In that case, a state hospital had used a urine sample from a mother without her permission to check for cocaine in collaboration with law enforcement to identify cocaine abusers and to obtain evidence against them. The Supreme Court, in a six-to-three decision, considered it to be an unreasonable search, if not an unholy alliance. The purposes and the process, however, distinguished that case from others at lower appeals levels where both state laws and individual actions on the part of law enforcement and other agencies have been upheld.

Maternal Custody Rights

The *Ferguson* case generated significant interest, both from the standpoint of its implications for criminal justice and because of the conflicting issues and

Methamphetamine and Pregnancy

values it addressed. Ely (2001), writing in the *Chicago Daily Law Bulletin*, noted with approval that testing of women and other aspects of their medical care during pregnancy could not be a basis for criminal prosecution. Similarly, in *The Legal Intelligencer*, Mauro (2001) cited Justice Stevens' position that the prosocial motives of the government could not become the basis for the loss of Fourth Amendment protections. However, the limits to which the *Ferguson* decision would be tolerated were illustrated in Flumenbaum and Karp's (2000) review of the case of *Kia P. v. Long Island College Hospital* (2000). Noting the *Ferguson* decision, the authors nonetheless detailed the basis for dismissal of a lawsuit against the hospital by Kia P. who alleged impropriety by the institution for withholding her child Mora following the birth. The hospital acted on a "good faith" basis due to possible methadone withdrawal symptoms and test findings in the newborn which, if present, could be life threatening (and would mean that the mother had abused the drug during her pregnancy). The appeals court finding affirmed the lower court that no violations existed with respect to Fourth Amendment (due process) rights.

Review of Table 13.1 indicates a clear trend to support the needs of a child born or unborn and other children who may be affected as well. Thus, in decisions regarding custody, usually emanating from juvenile court actions and child protection agency motions for termination of parental rights, the appeals courts have generally acted to protect the children. Certain presumptions are made in these cases and are sometimes detailed in the decisions. Those presumptions include the following:

- Ample scientific evidence proves that maternal use of methamphetamine and other substances does, in fact, cause damage to the developing fetus.
- Maternal involvement in lifestyles where illicit drug abuse is a prominent feature usually renders the mother unable to assert adequate responsibility for a child or children.

Very often, courts proceed from a best interest posture rather than one of requiring proof of child endangerment. For example, in two cases, while some aspects of the family situation improved, the children's ages, conditions, and histories were such that placement of them with their biological parents — whose stability was insecure at best — was viewed as an unacceptable experiment (*In the interest of C.E.*, 2001; *In the interest of M.S.D. and M.A.D.*, 2001).

Paternal Custody Rights

Fathers' rights can also be affected by maternal drug use in pregnancy. In *Michael M. v. Arizona* (2002) the mother had used during pregnancy. After

Table 13.1 Cases from Lower Courts of Appeal across Several U.S. Jurisdictions (1994–2002)

Case Name	LEXIS Cite	Trial Court Action[a]	Appeals Court Action[a]	Methamphetamine Factor[b]
Sheriff, Washoe County Nevada v. Cathy Encoe	1994 Nev. LEXIS 156	Mother guilty of child endangerment	Affirmed	C
In re Guardianship of Travis Alexander Zyler	1996 Neb. LEXIS 208	Appointment of guardian	Remanded Direction to Vacate; dissolution pending by mother	MU
In re the matter of Malachi Eugene Ettinger	1996 Ore. App. LEXIS 1380	Denial of motion for TPR	Reversed Remanded for TPR	MU
In re the welfare of D.F. David Bryant	1998 Wash. App. LEXIS 676	TPR	Affirmed	MU C (F)
In re Brittany C.	1999 Cal. App. LEXIS 1058	TPR	Affirmed	Mus
In the matter of Jane Doe	1999 Ida. App. LEXIS 95	TPR	Affirmed	MU C N
In re Bethany M.	1999 Neb. App. LEXIS 118	TPR	Affirmed	MU
In the matter of Christian Wilcox and Savannah Wilcox	1999 Ore. App. LEXIS 1561	Denial of motion for TPR	Reversed Remanded	MU
Connie B. v. Sup. Ct. of San Diego County	2001 Cal. App. LEXIS 1812	TPR	Affirmed	Mus C N

Methamphetamine and Pregnancy

Case	Citation	Court action	Outcome	Code
In re Juanita C.	2001 Cal. App. LEXIS 3789	TPR	Affirmed	MU C
In the interest of M.S.D. and M.A.D.	2001 Iowa App. LEXIS 588	TPR	Affirmed	Mus
In the interest of C.E.	2001 Iowa App. LEXIS 649	Denial of TPR	Reversed remanded	MU
In the matter of the Unborn Child of Julie Starks	2001 Okla. LEXIS 7	Custody of fetus by holding the mother	Vacated order to dismiss	M,F/P
In the matter of Selana Lee Lucas	2001 Ore. App. LEXIS 1589	TPR	Affirmed	MU C
Michael M. v. Arizona Department of Economic Security and Corianna M.	2002 Ariz. App. LEXIS 34	TPR	Affirmed	MU C
Michelle K. v. Sup. Ct. of Los Angeles County	2002 Cal. App. LEXIS 385	TPR	Affirmed	MU
In re Alejandra P.	2002 Cal. App. LEXIS 702	TPR	Affirmed	MU C
Amber A. v. Sup. Ct. of Orange County	2002 Cal. App. LEXIS 2075	TPR	Affirmed	MU C
Fernando C. v. Sup. Ct. of San Diego County	2002 Cal. App. LEXIS 2783	TPR	Affirmed	MU FU

[a] Court actions: TPR = termination of parental rights.

[b] Methamphetamine factors: MU = use in pregnancy; C = child tested positive for methamphetamine at birth; FU = father use of methamphetamine; (F) = father unable to provide for child; M,F/P = production of methamphetamine by mother and father; N = neglect by virtue of use.

birth, the child was placed first in foster care and then with a relative. In the meantime, the father was incarcerated on charges unrelated to drug abuse, but had petitioned for contact with the child. He was denied contact by the children's services department, an action subsequently ordered by the juvenile court. That court also denied him any opportunity to see his child during the court session even though visitation could have been easily accomplished. The court took the position that since the father was in prison, he did not deserve to see his child until he was released and further stated the child would likely be harmed by prison visitation. The appeals court indicated no support for the notion of harm to the child and also noted that a visit at the time of the original court hearing, now moot, had not merited an outright rejection.

Culture

Some cases revolved around rather unusual factors. In one, the appeal of the mother was joined by the Native American tribe to which she belonged. It was asserted that the state had failed to provide an appropriate expert witness at the time restoration of parental rights was refused. There was further assertion that the state should have turned over jurisdiction to the tribe. However, the trial court was affirmed. The reasoning at the appeals level was that no cultural issues presented and therefore the law requiring an expert with Native American cultural background did not apply in this case. The appeals court felt the basic requirements for health and safety and security of the child were not met by the mother and could not be reasonably anticipated to be present in the future (*In the matter of Selana Lee Lucas*, 2001).

Rights of the Fetus

Although most decisions favored termination of parental rights, one illustrated a ruling favoring appellant mother (*In the matter of the unborn child of Julie Starks*, 2001). In that case, the Superior Court of Oklahoma remanded a case on the basis that the unborn fetus was not a child under the Oklahoma Children's Act. This case involved the trial court ordering the detention of the mother through the duration of her pregnancy to prevent her ongoing involvement with methamphetamine from damaging the unborn child. However, the issue of the rights of the fetus was also addressed somewhat earlier in *Sheriff, Washoe County, Nevada v. Cathy Encoe* (1994). There the court reasoned that transmission of methamphetamine through the umbilical cord after birth but prior to its being severed allowed the finding that injury to a child rather than to a fetus had occurred. On that basis, a criminal finding of child endangerment by the mother was affirmed.

Cases involving parental and fetal rights as well as individual freedoms have generated journal commentary. Janssen (2000) directly addressed both methamphetamine cases and the particular balancing of the rights of the different entities that become involved in methamphetamine use in pregnancy. Individuals have been convicted of killing unborn children, but mothers have the right to abort. The issue becomes one of at what point the mother's willful use of a harmful substance and her decision not to abort constitute a basis for action to be taken against her.

In the face of a rising awareness of methamphetamine abuse and the inability to treat the fetus as a child under existing laws, various states have acted to pass legislation protecting the rights of the fetus. In Missouri, the approach was to confer all rights of citizenship of a minor on the unborn child. Other states have been somewhat less generous but the trend is clear. In Iowa, where there had been a restriction against criminal penalties for mothers who used methamphetamine, a movement has surfaced to support stiffer penalties specific to methamphetamine abuse. Cited was a 1994 study that found that 4% of infants born during that year were exposed to illegal substances and that nearly half of all these newborns were born to methamphetamine users. The backlash of punitive reactivity, occasioned by the rise in methamphetamine use and its destructive impacts in the country, is perhaps best illustrated in the following sequence. In 1997, the Georgia Court of Appeals had rejected an attempt to charge a woman in connection with pregnancy drug use. Further, in 1998, a woman who shot herself in an attempt to perform an illegal abortion was successful in having the charges dismissed. In 1999, a case involved a woman who gave birth to twins. One died. The death was attributed to the mother's use of drugs, including specifically amphetamines. She was charged with murder for causing the child's death (Renaud, 1999).

Legal Perspectives — Summary Statement

In effect, a legal, social, and psychological quagmire exists in the case law and statutes that address methamphetamine abuse in pregnancy. Liberals and conservatives rightly can view perilous "slippery slopes" in any attempts to deal with this area in the context of the courts or by statutory remedy. In the meantime, there is an insecure scientific foundation for raising the issues and the application of legal sanctions varies not by degree of scientific foundation but by social attitudes and political practicalities. As can be seen in the following section detailing scientific findings, the methamphetamine impacts on fetal well-being may well be significantly less than use or abuse of legal drugs for which no loss of citizen rights is a consequence.

The Effect of Methamphetamine on the Fetus

Significant work identifying methamphetamine use in relation to different factors associated with fetal development has not yet been accomplished. Much of what is known comes from studies of cocaine abuse during pregnancy. It is well established that some drugs have more negative impacts on the fetus than others. Therefore, conclusions derived from the following cocaine studies have to be viewed as tentative.

In the 1980s the fear of cocaine-addicted babies was extreme in the medical and legal communities. It is now known that the picture of the crack baby with significant brain damage and serious developmental disorders was an exaggeration. There have been some studies that have identified negative effects of cocaine on a developing fetus, but these effects are minor compared with the horrors that the media of the 1980s would have had people believe. Further, many of the studies are filled with methodological flaws that make it impossible to differentiate between the effects of cocaine and the effects of some other substance or behavior. Similarly, the nature of the participants of a study can affect the results of the study, a factor known as selection bias. Many of the studies of the effects of cocaine on the fetus involve women in drug treatment programs or women suspected of substance use by clinical staff (Zuckerman et al., 1995). It is likely that these women exhibited other behaviors (such as cigarette and alcohol use) that may have worsened (or even were the main contributors to) the identified problems with the fetus. Further, many of the studies of the effects of cocaine on the fetus were correlational. A correlational study examines two variables and notes a relationship between them. In other words, if we measure the amount of cocaine used across the population and the number of birth defects exhibited by infants in that population, we will likely find a positive correlation (as cocaine use rises, the number of defects rises as well). The problem is that such a study does not suggest a causal relationship between cocaine use and birth defects. It is likely that tobacco use is positively correlated with both birth anomalies and cocaine use; thus it could be tobacco that causes the anomalies, not cocaine. Finally, there are many factors that can cause the negative effects that have been attributed to cocaine use, including polydrug use, low socioeconomic status, chaotic social environment, poor nutrition, poor prenatal care, and an increased incidence of sexually transmitted diseases (STDs) (Holzman and Paneth, 1994; Zuckerman et al., 1995). A recent review of this literature has been provided in the monthly newsletter of the Illinois Teratogen Information Service (Simi et al., 1998). Cocaine studies focused on specific aspects of fetal function illustrate further what is known and not known in this area.

Putative Effects of Methamphetamine

Spontaneous abortion. Although there have been some studies that have suggested a correlational link between cocaine use and spontaneous abortion, a recent meta-analysis (meta-analysis is a mathematical method of adding the effects of many potentially contradictory studies in order to determine a consensus) suggests that this is only the case when polydrug use is confounded with cocaine use (Lutiger et al., 1991). This is evidence that use of multiple drugs, not just cocaine, is associated with spontaneous abortion.

Placental abruption. Placental abruption occurs when the placenta pulls away from the wall of the uterus before labor begins. As with spontaneous abortion it has been suggested that placental abruption is associated with cocaine use. However, as with spontaneous abortion, several studies have concluded that this condition co-occurs with polydrug use (Keith et al., 1989; MacGregor et al., 1989) but not with cocaine use (Holzman and Paneth, 1994). In fact, in a 1994 review of the literature, Holzman and Paneth suggest that placental abruption is more likely associated with alcohol and tobacco use than with cocaine use.

Pre-term delivery. Holzman and Paneth (1994) also suggest that pre-term delivery may be related to lifestyle rather than to cocaine use. However, they concede that low birth weight, microcephaly, and reduced fetal length have all been observed consistently in cocaine-exposed newborns.

Sudden infant death syndrome. It has also been suggested that cocaine exposure increases the occurrence of sudden infant death syndrome (SIDS). However, a recent meta-analysis found that the risk for SIDS was increased when cocaine-exposed infants were compared with non-drug-exposed controls, but not when compared with polydrug controls (Fares et al., 1997). Once again, the evidence points to a negative effect of polydrug use on the fetus, but not necessarily the use of cocaine on its own.

Behavioral effects in newborns. A pattern of withdrawal has been identified in neonates. This pattern includes tremulousness, irritability, abnormal sleep patterns, poor feeding, high-pitched cry, and muscle rigidity (Chasnoff, 1988). Further, it has been suggested that there is a dose-related risk for poor state regulation, attention, responsiveness, orientation, and motor/tone (Hurt et al., 1995; Richardson et al., 1996; Delany-Black et al., 1996; Eyler et al., 1998).

Structural brain abnormalities. While brain abnormalities have been observed in chronic users of cocaine, no structural brain abnormalities have been observed in those who were exposed prenatally (Behnke et al., 1998; Smith et. al., 2001). However, cocaine-exposed rabbit pups display an abnormal structural and neurochemical development of the anterior cingulate cortex, which persists into adulthood and may cause an attentional deficit (Romano and Harvey, 1998). The data from longitudinal studies on the behavioral and neuroanatomical effects of prenatal cocaine exposure are too contradictory to draw any conclusions from them (Mott et al, 1994; Zuckerman et al., 1995; Landry and Whitney, 1996; Hurt et al., 1997; Loebstein and Koren, 1997).

Taken together, the above data suggest that while cocaine has some effect on the developing fetus, the extent of that effect is far less severe than we initially suspected. Further, due to numerous methodological flaws, it is impossible to differentiate the effects of cocaine from some other drug. In fact, the abnormalities listed above have all been associated with other, very common legal substances including tobacco, which is associated with low birth weight (Cnattingius et al., 1993), spontaneous abortion (Harlap and Shiono, 1980), placental abruption (Raymond and Mills, 1993), perinatal mortality (Werler, 1997), pre-term delivery (Shiono et al., 1986), SIDS (Haglund and Cnattingius, 1990), and deficits in cognitive development (Naeye and Peters, 1984).

What Is Known about the Effects of Methamphetamine on the Fetus

It seems that the lesson of the 1980s is not being applied to methamphetamine. Our knowledge about the effect of methamphetamine on the human fetus is limited. We know far less about the effects of methamphetamine on the developing fetus than we know about the effects of cocaine, alcohol, and tobacco. In fact, the National Institute of Drug Abuse (NIDA) was advertising in the *Journal of the American Medical Association* (*JAMA*) as late as 2000 for researchers who would be interested in examining the effect of methamphetamine on the fetus (Marwick, 2000) in hopes that they could head off the unfounded fears that we experienced with the cocaine scare of the 1980s. Most of what we do know comes from examining the effects of methamphetamine on mouse fetal tissue. This is a very difficult model to use to attempt the understand the human condition, because as discussed in Chapter 4 on MDMA (a compound chemically similar to methamphetamine) the effects of brain damage can proceed very differently in rodent models than in the human animal.

In the mouse, we know that methamphetamine can cross the placenta and affect the embryo (Won et al., 2001). However, we have not observed any anatomical damage resulting from this effect. We have observed changes in the levels of the neurotransmitters serotonin* (Won et al., 2002) and

---

* For the biochemist, reaggregates of mesencephalic-striatal projections prepared from methamphetamine-exposed embryos showed a significant elevation in serotonin levels at all culture ages compared with reaggregates prepared from saline-treated embryos. Levels of 5-HIAA in reaggregates and culture medium were also elevated in 14- and 29-day-old cultures derived from drug-exposed embryos.

dopamine* (Heller et al., 2001) in the rodent neonate, but the consequences of these chemical changes for the adult animal are unclear.

A recent review by Plessinger (1998) concluded that "based on findings in humans and the confirmation of prenatal exposures in animals, amphetamines and methamphetamines increase the risk of an adverse outcome when abused during pregnancy." Plessinger further concluded that clefting, cardiac anomalies, and fetal growth deficits have all been observed in studies of both humans and other animals. However, the effects of prenatal exposure to amphetamines on behavior in humans were confounded by both genetic and environmental factors, which included polydrug abuse. Thus, the study was unable to draw any conclusions about the effect of prenatal methamphetamine exposure on human behavior.

The policy of CPS in Hawaii County is that, if a newborn baby tests positive for methamphetamine exposure,** it will remove the child, and any siblings, from the mother's care. An exception may be made if there is another non-drug-using adult living with the mother who will agree to care for the infant. Hospitals around the island are not obligated to test mother or infant for methamphetamine exposure. Some do and some do not. Those who do not cite the need to assure that new mothers come to the hospital for both pre- and postnatal care (if expectant mothers know that they will be tested for drugs and could lose their children, then they may just decide not to use medical services) and the lack of evidence to support a damaging role of methamphetamine on a fetus.

Conclusion

We have reviewed several lines of evidence suggesting that the current trends that we are observing in court and CPS activity are in fact inconsistent with the present state of science. Science is an ever-changing institution. The scientist believes that when new data appear that discredit a theory then we must change the theory. The scientist is trained to change his or her beliefs very quickly. The courts and CPS, however, are not. The effect of cocaine on the developing fetus has always been a controversial issue. However, we now know that the damaging effects of cocaine on the fetus are far less severe than the damaging effects of tobacco. In regard to cocaine, we jumped the gun in assuming it was more damaging than it really was. Similarly, we do not know

---

* For the biochemist, dopamine levels were elevated in fetal corpus striatum and the rostral mesencephalon following maternal treatment with 40 mg/kg methamphetamine for 7 or 14 days.
** The standard method for testing a newborn for drugs is the meconium test. Meconium is the fetus's first fecal matter. The use of the test is questionable because one report suggests that it yields false positives 43% of the time (Moore et al., 1995).

if methamphetamine causes fetal damage. This uncertainty is of extreme importance because, in decisions regarding custody, the appeals courts have generally acted to protect the children — we have reviewed a body of literature that suggested that the courts have chosen to adopt the point of view that the health of a child is more important than incursion into the rights of mothers. However, if we do not know if methamphetamine is damaging to a fetus, is it appropriate to punish a mother for use of methamphetamine during pregnancy by removing her child from her care? The hypocrisy of both the court system and CPS is clear when we examine the effects of tobacco on the fetus. We do not remove children from the custody of parents because parents smoke tobacco products; even though, we know that tobacco causes severe damage to the developing fetus.

References

Chasnoff, I.J. (1988). Drug use in pregnancy: parameters of risk. *Pediatr. Clin. North Am.*, 35(6), 1403–1412.

Cnattingius, S., Forman, M.R., Austin, D.R., Chen, V., and Heymsfield, S.B. (1993). The effect of age, parity and smoking on pregnancy outcome: a population-based study. *Am. J. Obstet. Gynecol.*, 168(1), 16–21.

Delaney-Black, V., Covington, C., Ostrea, E., Jr., Romero, A., Baker, D., Tagle, M.T., Nordstrom-Klee, B., Silvestre, M.A., Angelilli, M.L., Hack, C., and Long, J. (1996). Prenatal cocaine and neonatal outcome: evaluation of dose-response relationship. *Pediatrics*, 98, 735–740.

Ely, M.L. (2001). These tests belong in medical — not criminal — realm. *Chicago Daily Law Bull.*, April 9, 6.

Eyler, F.D., Behnke, M., Conlon, M., Woods, N.S., and Wobie, K. (1998). Birth outcome from a prospective, matched study of prenatal crack/cocaine use: II. Interactive and dose effects on neurobehavioral assessment. *Pediatrics*, 101(2), 237–241.

Fares, I., McCulloch, K.M., and Raju, T.N. (1997). Intrauterine cocaine exposure and the risk for sudden infant death syndrome: a meta-analysis. *J. Perinatol.*, 17(3), 179–182.

Ferguson v. Charleston (99-936) 532 U.S. 67 (2001) 186 F.3d 469, reversed and remanded. No. 01-278. [1-497], Filed October 24, 2001.

Flumenbaum, M. and Karp, B.S. (2000). Fetal rights, birth mother Fourth Ammendment rights, *New York Law J.*, December 27, 3.

Haglund, B. and Cnattingius, S. (1990). Cigarette smoking as a risk factor for sudden infant death syndrome: a population-based study. *Am. J. Public Health*, 80(1), 29–32.

Harlap, S. and Shiono, P.H. (1980). Alcohol, smoking, and incidence of spontaneous abortions in the first and second trimester. *Lancet*, 2(8187), 173–176.

Heller, A., Bubula, N., Lew, R., Heller, B., and Won, L. (2001). Gender-dependent enhanced adult neurotoxic response to methamphetamine following fetal exposure to the drug. *Journal of Pharmacology and Experimental Therapeutics*, 298, 769–779.

Holzman, C. and Paneth, N. (1994). Maternal cocaine use during pregnancy and perinatal outcomes. *Epidemiol. Rev.*,16(2), 315–334.

Hurt, H., Brodsky, N.L., Betancourt, L., Braitman, L.E., Malmud, E., and Giannetta, J. (1995). Cocaine-exposed children: follow-up through 30 months. *J. Dev. Behav. Pediatr.*, 16(1), 29–35.

In the interest of C.E., Minor Child, C.E., Minor Child, Appellant, J.M., Father, Appellant, Iowa Department of Human Services, Appellant.

In the interest of M.S.D. and M.A.D., Minor Children, M.W.D., Father, Appellant, A.S.D., Mother, Appellant. No. 00-2092. [1-492], Filed September 12, 2001

Janssen, N.D. (2000). Fetal rights and the prosecution of women for using drugs during pregnancy. *Drake Law Rev.*, 48, 741.

Keith, L.G., MacGregor, S., Friedell, S., Rosner, M., Chasnoff, I.J., and Sciarra, J.J. (1989). Substance abuse in pregnant women: recent experience at the Perinatal Center for Chemical Dependence of Northwestern Memorial Hospital. *Obstet. Gynecol.*, 73, 715-720.

Kia, P. v. Long Island College Hospital, U.S. App. LEXIS 31151 (2nd Cir. Dec. 5, 2000).

Landry, S.H. and Whitney, J.A. (1996). The impact of prenatal exposure:studies of the developing infant. *Sem. Perinat.*, 20, 99-106.

Loebstein, R. and Koren, G. (1997). Pharmacokinetic changes during pregnancy and their clinical relevance. *Clin. Pharmacokinet.*, 33(5), 328-343.

Lutiger, B., Graham, K., Einarson, T.R., and Koren, G. (1991). Relationship between gestational cocaine use and pregnancy outcome: a meta-analysis. *Teratology*, 44(4), 405-414.

MacGregor, S.N., Keith, L.G., Bachicha, J.A., and Chasnoff, I.J. (1989). Cocaine abuse during pregnancy: correlation between prenatal care and perinatal outcome. *Obstet. Gynecol.*, 74(6), 882-885.

Marwick, C. (2000). NIDA seeking data on effect of fetal exposure to methamphetamine. *J. Am. Med. Assoc.*, 283(17), 2225-2226.

Mauro, T. (2001). High court: prenatal program violated 4th Amendment. *The Legal Intelligencer*, March 22, p. 4.

Michael M. v Arizona, 2002, Ariz. App. LEXIS 34.

Moore, C., Lewis, D., and Leikin, J. (1995). False-positive and false-negative rates in meconium drug testing. *Clin. Chem.*, 41(11), 1614–1616.

Mott, S.H., Packer, R.J., and Soldin, S.J. (1994). Neurologic manifestations of cocaine exposure in childhood. *Pediatrics*, 93, 557-560.

Naeye, R.L. and Peters, E.C. (1984). Mental development of children whose mothers smoked during pregnancy. *Obstet. Gynecol.*, 64(5), 601-607.

Plessinger, M.A. (1998). Prenatal exposure to amphetamines. Risks and adverse outcomes in pregnancy. *Obstet. Gynecol. Clin. North Am.*, 25(1), 119-138.

Raymond, E.G. and Mills, J.L. (1993). Placental abruption. Maternal risk factors and associated fetal conditions. *Acta Obstet. Gynecol. Scand.*, 72(8), 633-639.

Renaud, T. (1999). Drug-addicted mother faces murder count in newborn's death. *Fulton County Daily Report*, November 17.

Richardson, G.A., Conroy, M.L., and Day, N.L. (1996). Prenatal cocaine exposure: effects on the development of school-age children. *Neurotoxicol. Teratol.*, 18(6), 627-634.

Romano, A.G., Harvey, J.A. (1998). Prenatal cocaine exposure: long-term deficits in learning and motor performance. *Ann NY Acad. Sci.*, 846, 89–108.

Shiono, P.H., Klebanoff, M.A., and Rhoads, G.G. (1986). Smoking and drinking during pregnancy. Their effects on preterm birth. *JAMA*, 255(1), 82-4.

Simi, E., Ormond, K., and Pergament, E. (1998). Cocaine and pregnancy. *Illinois Teratogen Information Service*, Northwestern University Medical School.

Smith, L.M. Chang, L., Yonekura, M.L., Gilbride, K., Kuo, J., Poland, R.E., Walot, I., and Ernst, T. (2001). Brain proton magnetic resonance spectroscopy and imaging in children exposed to cocaine in utero. *Pediatrics*, (2), 227–231.

Werler, M.M. (1997). Smoking and reproductive outcomes. *Teratology*, 55, 382–388.

Won, L., Bubula, N., McCoy, H., and Heller, A. (2001). Methamphetamine concentrations in fetal and maternal brain following prenatal exposure. *Neurotoxicol. Teratol.*, 23(4), 349–354.

Won, L., Bubula, N., and Heller, A. (2002). Fetal exposure to methamphetamine *in utero* stimulates development of serotonergic neurons in three-dimensional reaggregate tissue culture. *Synapse*, 43(2), 139–144.

Zuckerman et al. (1995). Methodological issues in controlled studies on effects of prenatal exposure to drug abuse. *NIDA Res. Monogr.*, 149, 16–38.

Section V

Forensics

Miranda Rights, Interrogation, and Competency to Confess

14

HAROLD V. HALL
SANDRA B. MCPHERSON
STUART W. TWEMLOW
ERROL YUDKO

Miranda Rights and Methamphetamine

Psychological and psychiatric experts are occasionally called upon to assess the ability of the defendant to render incriminating statements. The key *Miranda* question concerns whether a defendant can rationally and intelligently choose to waive or invoke rights to self-incrimination. Methamphetamine intoxication at the time of police questioning or interrogation, to the extent that it interferes with these cognitive capacities, raises the question of voluntariness.

Yet, voluntariness depends on the totality of the circumstances, not just the condition of the accused at the time of the questioning. It includes such factors as the context in which the questioning takes place, the officers' conduct, and the extent to which the officers utilize prior incriminating statements to extract more information. Under this reasoning, it becomes highly relevant whether the questioning officers are aware that the accused is methamphetamine intoxicated.

In State v. Samson Pebria, Jr. (1997), a methamphetamine-intoxicated, recently released prison inmate was questioned at a hospital by the arresting officer, who asked, "Do you know why you are being detained?" The accused responded, "I went grab the girl" and later stated, "I like rape her." One finding of fact from the Intermediate Court of Appeals (ICA, No. 19) was that the noted confusion on the part of the accused did not arise from the questioning by the officer. The confusion arose "because of [Pebria's] inability to recall what had occurred previously because at the time of the incident he was under the influence of ice." Other findings of fact (Nos. 20, 21, 22) included the knowledge on the part of the detective taking the formal statement of the alleged spontaneous statement, an attempt to lead the defendant into making those statements again and to admit the motive for the alleged offense was to rape the victim. The ICA held that the original statements were obtained in violation of *Miranda* and that the later confession was inadmissible under the "fruit of the poisonous tree" doctrine.

What is missing from most interrogations involving methamphetamine intoxication, and what would be most convincing to the expert, is for the arresting officer or (later) a detective to obtain feedback from the defendant regarding whether or not the subject understood and remembered the *Miranda* rights or whether interfering factors substantially prevented competency to confess. The expert should make every attempt to answer these questions in cases in which methamphetamine use is an issue.

Interrogation and Methamphetamine Use

Investigative interviewing takes place under conditions that vary widely in terms of procedure, experience and capacity of the interviewer, and environmental aspects. Studies of the interview procedure have shown considerable impact as a function of the use of leading questions and prebiased interviewer conditions (Loftus and Palmer, 1974; Loftus and Zanni, 1975; Pirolli and Mitterer, 1984; Memon and Kohnken, 1992; Mount and Perlini, 1995). False confessions occur with complex antecedents. They may be entirely voluntary, and some false confessions may reflect mental problems. False confessions may proceed in consequence of certain later-identified personality traits. Specified pressures can lead to false confessions, which have been classified as "coerced-compliant" and "coerced-internalized." In the former, a knowing incorrect admission is made to gain relief from interrogation pressure. In the latter, individuals predisposed to guilt come to falsely believe in and admit to an act they did not commit (Gudjonsson and Petursson, 1991; Gudjonsson, 1992a,b; *Commonwealth v. Cosmello*, 1993; Kassin, 1997, 1998; McCann, 1998; Reitman, 1998).

In investigative interviews in the U.S., certain deceptive procedures are often the rule, including the provision of misinformation in order to obtain confessions by trickery (Inbau et al., 1986). In contrast, in the U.K., police are not allowed to use deceptive methods. All interrogations are videotaped to reduce coercive and illegal methods as well as to secure good evidence when confessions do occur under questioning (Gudjonsson, 1992b). Whether in the U.K. or the U.S., the above studies have shown a limited impact of interview, content, and style of police interrogation on the production of false confessions. In general, although false confessions occur, no convincing data exist that show that guilty parties will confess falsely to crimes in greater numbers than would be expected by chance. Other case factors have been found to be more important, including the evidence, the level of the offense, and the presence of legal advice (Moston et al., 1992). In a few criminal cases, substances have been used to assist in the recovery of details or repressed material, to reduce the capacity to cover up information that has been denied, or to expose false facts that were "admitted" on a malingered basis. In general, the use of drug-assisted interviews is not recommended. Subjects are able to continue to dissimulate when under the influence of various substances, including methamphetamines. However, with methamphetamines, there are more changes in perception. These changes may involve reports of either positive or negative experiences and anxiety. There may be higher levels of attentiveness than are found among those who are given other substances, such as amobarbital. Suggestibility has not been demonstrated for amphetamines, whereas it has been shown with sedatives (Rogers and Wettstein, 1977).

It should be known whether a suspect is methamphetamine intoxicated when he or she is interviewed. At relatively low doses, amphetamines improve one's capacity to attend, cause an inflated sense of self-efficacy and invulnerability, and increase motor and speech activity and anxiety (Dodgen and Shea, 1997). At high doses, the individual becomes cognitively disorganized. Theoretically, vulnerability to coercion may increase. Certainly, a defense attorney should raise this issue. Further study is needed to determine the interaction of suggestibility, anxiety, attentional focus, and coercion. Given the powerful impact of a confession as evidence, any increased potential for false statements poses a risk for miscarriage of justice.

Studies in many contexts have demonstrated that when learning occurs in a chemically altered state, it may not be possible to access that material unless the person is again under the influence of the drug. Methamphetamine has been used in studies of such state-dependent learning. In common with other chemicals, methamphetamine will produce state-dependent retrieval (SDR). However, careful evaluation of studies in this area has shown that SDR occurs on a free-recall basis, but tends to disappear with cued or recognition-based recall regardless of the kind of substance involved (Brown et al., 1998). By extension, if questioning is managed correctly, the presence of methamphetamine in the system of a suspect or a witness may not necessarily damage that person's capacity to describe accurately experienced criminal events. In such cases, the use of cued and recognition tasks, as well as other safeguards as discussed above, should be built into the interrogation strategies. Diminished capacity plea at sentencing under the current guidelines is specifically disallowed if voluntary drug ingestion is involved.

Methamphetamine Abuse and Competency to Proceed

Reviews of the forensic literature on competency to proceed are found in Blau (1984), Curran et al. (1986), Ewing (1985), Gutheil and Appelbaum (1982), Melton et al. (1987), Shapiro (1984), Weiner and Hess (1987), and Ziskin and Faust (1988). Works devoted exclusively to competency to stand trial include those of Grisso (1986, 1988), McGarry (1973), and Roesch and Golding (1980). Although none of these sources deals primarily with methamphetamine abuse, their contents address means to assess and evaluate competency to stand trial based on behavior.

The legal requirement of competency to stand trial is an extension of the general rule that no one should be tried for a crime in his or her absence. If a defendant must be physically present to defend against criminal charges, that defendant must also be "mentally present." Disorders that interfere with the psychological participation of a defendant at trial may render that defendant incompetent to stand trial and require that the proceedings be postponed until effective participation can be assured. Symptoms of methamphetamine use may compromise the defendant's competency to stand trial. As discussed above, chronic methamphetamine abuse may cause severe confusion, apathy, short-term memory problems, executive dysfunction, auditory hallucinations, and other significant problems that may persist for a considerable length of time after abstinence commences.

Several competency questionnaires are available for use in evaluating trial competencies: the Competency Assessment Instrument (Grisso, 1986; 1988), the Interdisciplinary Fitness Interview (Golding et al., 1984), the Competency Screening Test (McGarry, 1973), Georgia Competency Test (Gothard et al., 1995), and MacArthur Competence Assessment Tool — Criminal Adjudication (1996). The forensic evaluator should utilize these methods within a broad-spectrum assessment approach that also evaluates psychopathology, skills, and response styles. Most jurisdictions use a variation of the rule to define competency to stand trial outlined by the U.S. Supreme Court in *Dusky v. United States* (1960). *Dusky* requires that defendants have the ability to (1) understand rationally and factually the legal proceedings and (2) cooperate with their attorney in their defense. A methamphetamine-induced disorder that interferes with either of these capabilities is sufficient to render the defendant incompetent to stand trial. However, incompetency to stand trial is not to be equated with the mere presence of mental illness (*Feguer v. United States*, 1962; *United States v. Adams*, 1969), or amnesia (*United States v. Wilson*, 1966), or of a need for treatment. The claimed disorder must be of the kind and severity that impair the functional capacities outlined in *Dusky*.

Usually, the question of competency to stand trial is raised by the defense attorney, who has the most frequent contact with the defendant and who has the professional and legal obligation to raise the question in appropriate cases. However, case law suggests that the question must be raised, even by the prosecution or the court itself, whenever a "bona fide doubt" exists regarding the defendant's capacity to mount a defense (see *Drope v. Missouri*, 1975). The question of a defendant's competency to proceed may be raised at any time from the defendant's first appearance in court to the time of sentencing.

In actual practice, most mentally disturbed defendants are easily identified by participants in the criminal process. Actively psychotic, demented, and severely mentally retarded persons are usually recognized by arresting officers, jail personnel, and defense attorneys, and they may be transferred to treatment facilities prior to any court appearances. Clinically, the chronic methamphetamine abuser is the defendant who has lost weight; looks malnourished, disheveled, and unhealthy; is reticent or loose in verbal responses; appears aphasic or has word-finding problems; is generally confused; shows impulsiveness with a low frustration tolerance. Often, the individual exhibits a blank stare. Such an abuser is often unable to answer simple questions that require orientation (to person, place, date, and circumstances of the evaluation), attention, and memory.

In *State v. Melvin Hashimoto* (1989), the 30-year-old defendant was charged with holding captive and robbing several people in Mililani. He had smoked ice for $5\frac{1}{2}$ years before, as well as during, the instant offenses. In his Hawaii Revised Statutes (HRS) §707-404 sanity report, the senior author stated:

> The Defendant is presently unfit to proceed. [The Defendant was expressionless and not oriented to date, claiming that it was 2 months earlier.] He claims no recall of his attorney and has no stated idea of possible legal consequences if convicted of the charges. He stated that he is facing the charge of "running away" and [talked about seeing the devil laughing at him in the rearview mirror of the car as he approached the scene of the alleged crime]. He could not recall the function of the judge and the defense attorney, but stated the prosecutor was on his side. He claims no knowledge of the legal process, stating that he has never been to court previously. [Oahu Community Correctional Center] medical records revealed that he is partially stabilized on antidepressant and antipsychotic medication. These same records suggest (a) the reporting of visual and auditory hallucinations, noncommand in quality; (b) anhedonia and depression; (c) distractibility; (d) blank spells; and (e) other psychological symptoms.

The defendant was reexamined 1 year later. He showed a substantial improvement in the criteria for competency and was found to be fit to proceed.

Defendants who are heavy methamphetamine users or who decompensate while awaiting trial often require professional treatment before criminal proceedings can occur. From a fitness perspective, if a person is disorganized and psychotic, it does not matter if the psychosis is secondary to voluntary substance abuse or to some other condition. If the *Dusky* criteria are violated (or if relevant state cases suggest other competency criteria are violated), the expert should report that the defendant is incompetent to stand trial.

Defense attorneys sometimes raise questions of competency to stand trial for their apparently competent clients as a "fishing expedition" to secure a court-ordered professional evaluation of their clients which would otherwise be unavailable. These evaluations usually produce data from the expert relevant to an insanity plea, to the question of mitigation, or to dangerousness factors that may be considered at the time of sentencing. Yet, the vast majority of defendants evaluated for competency to stand trial are found to be competent. This reflects the very basic cognitive and behavioral skills required in *Dusky*. In addition, assuming that the clinical data obtained are valid and reliable, the fishing expedition may actually save the court time and money in the event that these other issues are raised by the defendant or are abandoned as trial strategies. Findings from a competency evaluation may also serve as a basis for a plea bargain as in the aforementioned *State v. Hashimoto* case.

In summary, the question of competency to stand trial in methamphetamine cases involves three separate questions: (1) Does the defendant exhibit methamphetamine symptoms sufficiently severe to justify a finding of incompetency (diagnosis)? (2) Is the defendant unable (a) to understand rationally and factually the legal proceedings, or (b) to assist counsel in defense (incapacity)? (3) Is this incapacity caused by the mental disorder (causation)? The answers to these three questions lead to several possible scenarios:

- Methamphetamine alone or in combination with another mental disorder causes a defendant to be incapacitated.
- Methamphetamine alone or with another mental disorder does not cause a defendant to be incapacitated.
- The defendant has a genuine condition that causes an insufficient incapacity to stand trial (e.g., circumscribed delusions about the "facts" of the alleged crime, but an impairment in trial capacity).
- The defendant has a genuine mental disorder and his or her impaired capacity to stand trial is due to fabrication or exaggeration (e.g., malingering in the context of a genuine disorder), or the defendant may have a genuine mental disorder and be incapable of standing

trial, but the mental disorder is not severe enough to justify a finding of incompetence (e.g., depressed defendant whose guilt over killing his wife leads to disinterest or lack of cooperation in putting on a defense).

In some jurisdictions, a finding of incompetence to stand trial is not restorable and can lead to continuing criminal court jurisdiction in the same way that a "not guilty by reason of insanity" finding allows (see Ohio, Senate Bill 285, effective July 1, 1997). In Hawaii, competency to stand trial (i.e., fitness) is covered in HRS §704-406. Fitness is not defined.

The Hawaii Intermediate Court of Appeals attempted to define, if not operationalize, competency to stand trial in *State v. Silverio Soares* (1996). A threefold test requires that the trial court determine whether or not the defendant (1) has sufficient mental ability to consult with his or her defense counsel with a reasonable degree of rational understanding, (2) has the capacity to assist in preparing a defense, and (3) has a rational, as well as factual, understanding of the proceedings against him or her.

Application of the above test appears to go beyond *Dusky v. United States* (1960), *Drope v. Missouri* (1975), and other cases pertinent to competency to proceed. Moreover, the test appears ripe for application of the empirical findings on methamphetamine as those findings apply to cases where the defendant abused methamphetamine, even a substantial period before the instant offense occurred. The test requires a functional ability to develop a working relationship with one's defense counsel, provide information that can be used to present a coherent defense, and make fundamental defense decisions. These abilities rest on attentional, recall, executive, and other cognitive skills, which are commonly impaired in methamphetamine abusers. The paranoia that results from methamphetamine abuse may cause distrust and withholding of information. Recall of the alleged offense may be distorted and fragmentary. Making fundamental defense decisions requires the synthesis of a wide variety of information, as well as judgment and executive abilities to plan, monitor, and reevaluate legal positions and strategies.

The *Soares* test requires that the defendant have the ability to testify in court, if necessary. Methamphetamine abusers may have significant deficiencies in speech and language processing, as well as in other cognitive dimensions, that could lessen the positive impact of the testimony.

The test also requires that the defendant be able to withstand the pressures of a trial. The data on brain deterioration in methamphetamine abusers suggest that, even after complete abstinence from the drug, the defendant's ability to withstand the pressures of a trial (as well as other stressors) may suffer. This deterioration, if it in fact does compromise the defendant's ability to adapt, may likely affect a broad range of cognitive abilities and may necessitate fitness evaluations at various points in the legal process.

Finally, the *Soares* test requires that the evaluation of fitness to proceed be made with specific reference to the nature of the charge, the complexity of the case, and the gravity of the decisions with which the defendant is faced. Translated into the thinking of forensic mental health experts, this means that no longer can general fitness criteria or standards be applied to specific cases without taking the unique circumstances, strengths, and limitations of the defendant into consideration. This position is reasonably close to the notion that the gravity of the decisions with which the defendant is faced, to take as one example of required skills, be appraised by the evaluator from the viewpoint of the defendant as he or she perceived them to be. Thus, both norm-based and individual (i.e., idiosyncratic) measures may have to be utilized in future evaluations of competency to stand trial where methamphetamine is involved. The *Soares* test, at least in methamphetamine cases, appears to necessitate a thorough forensic neuropsychological or neuropsychiatric evaluation with built-in measures to detect possible malingering and deception. Forensic evaluations of competency to stand trial, rather than reflecting easily measured traits/states of the defendant, should, in methamphetamine cases, at least approximate the "penetrating and comprehensive examination" of the defendant as required by *State v. Kane* (1971).

References

Blau, T. (1984). *The Psychologist as Expert Witness*. New York: John Wiley & Sons.

Brown, D., Scheflin, A.Q., and Hammond, D.C. (1998). *Memory, Trauma Treatment, and the Law*. New York: W. W. Norton.

Commonwealth v. Cosmello, Ct. Common Pleas, Susquehanna, PA (November 15, 1993).

Curran, W., McGarry, A., and Shah, S., Eds. (1986). *Forensic Psychiatry and Psychology: Perspectives and Standards for Interdisciplinary Practice*. Philadelphia: F. A. Davis.

Dodgen, C.E. and Shea, W.M. (1997). *Psychoactive Substance Disorders: A Comprehensive Resource for Clinicians and Researchers*. Florham Park, NJ: C & D Publications.

Drope v. Missouri, 420 U.S. 162 (1975).

Dusky v. United States, 362 U.S. 401 (1960).

Ewing, C.P. (1985). *Psychology, Psychiatry and the Law: A Clinical and Forensic Handbook*. Sarasota, FL: Professional Resource Exchange.

Feguer v. United States, 302 F.2d 214 (1962).

Golding, S.L., Roesch, R., and Schreiber, J. (1984). Assessment and conceptualization of competency to stand trial: Preliminary data on the Interdisciplinary Fitness Interview. *Law Hum. Behav.*, 8, 321–334.

Gothard, S., Rogers, R., and Sewell, K. (1995). Feigning incompetency to stand trial: an investigation of the Georgia Court Competency Test. *Law Hum. Behav.*, 19, 363–373.

Grisso, T. (1986). *Evaluating Competencies: Forensic Assessments and Instruments.* New York: Plenum Press.

Grisso, T. (1988). *Competency to Stand Trial: Evaluations.* Sarasota, FL: Professional Resource Exchange, Inc.

Gudjonsson, G.H. (1992a). The psychology of false confessions and ways to improve the system. *Int. Dig. Hum. Behav. Sci. Law*, 1(2), 49–53.

Gudjonsson, G.H. (1992b). *The Psychology of Interrogations, Confessions, and Testimony.* New York: John Wiley & Sons.

Gudjonsson, G.H. and Petursson, H. (1991). Custodial interrogation: why do suspects confess and how does it relate to their crimes, activities, and personality? *Personality Individual Differences*, 12(3), 295–306.

Gutheil, T. and Appelbaum, P. (1982). *Clinical Handbook of Psychiatry and the Law.* New York: McGraw-Hill.

Inbau, F.E., Reid, J.E., and Buckley, J.P. (1986). *Criminal Interrogation and Confessions.* Baltimore, MD: Williams & Wilkins.

Kassin, S.M. (1997). The psychology of confession evidence. *Am. Psychol.*, 52, 221–233.

Kassin, S.M. (1998). More on the psychology of false confessions. *Am. Psychol.*, 53(3), 320–321.

Loftus, E.P. and Palmer, J.C. (1974). Reconstruction of automobile destruction: an example of the interaction between language and memory. *J. Verbal Learning Verbal Behav.*, 13, 585–589.

Loftus, E. P. and Zanni, G. (1975). Eyewitness testimony: the influence of the wording of a question. *Bull. Psychonomic Soc.*, 5(1), 86–88.

MacArthur Competence Assessment Tool — Criminal Adjudication (1996). Odessa, FL: Psychological Assessment Research, Inc.

McCann, J.T. (1998). Broadening the typology of false confessions. *Am. Psychol.*, 53(3), 319–320.

McGarry, A. (1973). Competency to Stand Trial and Mental Illness (DHEW Publication ADM. 77-103). Rockville, MD: Department of Heath, Education and Welfare.

Melton, G., Petrila, R., Poythress, N., and Slobogin, C. (1987). *Psychological Evaluations for the Courts: A Handbook for Mental Health Professionals and Lawyers.* New York: Guilford Press.

Memon, A. and Kohnken, G. (1992). Helping witness to remember more: the cognitive interview. *Int. Dig. Hum. Behav. Sci. Law*, 1(2), 39–48.

Moston, S., Stephenson, G.M., and Williamson, J. (1992). The effects of case characteristics on suspect behaviour during police questioning. *Br. J. Criminol.*, 32, 23–40.

Mount, M. and Perlini, A.H. (1995). The effects of source credibility and question working on witness recall: a case of the emperor's clothes. Paper presented at the 103rd Annual Convention of the American Psychological Association, New York.

Pirolli, P.J. and Mitterer, J.O. (1984). The effect of leading questions on prior memory: evidence for the coexistence of inconsistent memory traces. *Can. J. Psychol.*, 38(1), 135–141.

Reitman, A. (1998). Social psychology of false confessions: Bern's early contribution. *Am. Psychol.*, 53(3), 320–321.

Roesch, R. and Golding, S. (1980). *Competency to Stand Trial*. Urbana Champaign, IL: University of Illinois Press.

Rogers, R. and Wettstein, R.M. (1977). Drug-assisted interviews to detect malingering and deception. In R. Rogers, Ed. *Chemical Assessment of Malingering and Deception*. New York: Guilford Press.

Shapiro, D. (1984). *Psychological Evaluation and Expert Testimony*. New York: Van Nostrand Reinhold.

State v. Hashimoto, First Circuit Court, Cr. Nos. 89-1537, 90-0054, 90-0022 (1989).

State v. Kane, 52 Haw. 484, 479 P.2d 207 (1971).

State v. Pebria, 85 Haw. 171, 938 P.2d 1190 (1997).

State v. Silverio Soares, First Circuit Court, Cr. No. 90-1068 (May 8, 1996).

United States v. Adams, 297 F. Supp. 596 (1969).

United States v. Wilson, 263 F.Supp. 528 (D.D.C. 1966).

Weiner, I. and Hess, A. (1987). *Handbook of Forensic Psychology*. New York: Wiley & Sons.

Ziskin, J. and Faust, D. (1988). *Coping with Psychiatric and Psychological Testimony*, 4th ed. Los Angeles: Law and Psychology Press.

Criminal Responsibility 15

HAROLD V. HALL
SANDRA B. MCPHERSON
STUART W. TWEMLOW
ERROL YUDKO

The Hawaii Revised Statutes (HRS) defines pathological intoxication as "intoxication *grossly excessive* in degree, given the amount of the intoxicant, to which the defendant *does not know* the defendant is susceptible and which results from a *physical* abnormality of the defendant." HRS §702-230(5)(c) (emphasis added).

Despite frequent attempts by defendants to present voluntary intoxication as pathological intoxication, and therefore as an exculpating factor, the courts have consistently maintained that voluntary intoxication is not admissible to negate state of mind to establish an element of the offense. See *State v. Souza* (1991); *State v. Hall* (1983); *State v. Freitas* (1980); *State v. Nuetzel* (1980).

In *State v. Souza* (1991), the defendant admittedly smoked methamphetamine just before he stabbed the victim in the back with a knife. Souza then repeatedly stabbed the victim as the latter attempted to escape, and then pursued the victim in a car, grazing his leg as the victim jumped into the bushes. Souza was subsequently arrested, charged, and convicted of attempted murder in the second degree and unauthorized control of propelled vehicle. On appeal, the Hawaii Supreme Court held that voluntary intoxication was not admissible and that it was a gratuitous defense that is not constitutionally protected as a defense to criminal conduct.

Psychological and psychiatric experts have not been deterred by the courts' ostensibly clear rulings. In *State v. Romel* (1990), the facts were straightforward. (See *Tradewind Insurance Co., Ltd. v. Stout*, 1997.) On June 30, 1988, 18-year-old Romel shot his summer-school teacher while she was teaching English at Aiea High School. At trial, Romel testified that he had been smoking crystal methamphetamine since his junior year and had smoked "ice" every day of summer school up to the time of the shooting. Prior to the shooting, he smoked ice before going to school with his gun. He further testified that the ice made him feel paranoid, and that he believed that the victim-teacher had been picking on him.

A psychiatrist based in Honolulu testified that ice smokers develop a paranoid psychosis similar to the symptoms of paranoid schizophrenia. In a further restatement of general findings from the literature, she observed that large quantities of ice make a person "very paranoid and delusional." Based on her interview of Romel, she concluded that he had experienced a "severe paranoid hallucinatory or persecutory state," had gotten to the point of "absolute desperation," and "felt he had no recourse but to try to kill [the victim], kill the object of his pain." Unsupported by any statistics or base rate information, she speculated that it "was 99.9 percent that he was not able to choose to stop" taking methamphetamine. She then concluded that the defendant would not have shot the victim had he not been methamphetamine intoxicated.

A clinical psychologist testified that, based on his interview of the defendant and his mother, Romel showed behavior consistent with ice abuse. Based on his interview and police reports, he conjectured that Romel had a minimal history of acting out. He then opined that the chances of the shooting occurring "without some kind of drug involvement would have been negligible, minimal." He then added that ice "was a major, major contributing factor, if not the causal one of what [Romel] did."

The state's expert agreed with the expert psychiatrist's conclusion that, at the time of the shooting, Romel was paranoid and deluded. He then opined that Romel's state of mind "was a classic picture of focused delusion," meaning the false belief directed at a particular set of circumstances. A particular person "is the one responsible for everything and right or wrong[,] everything kind of comes down on that one person." This expert also failed to incorporate the defendant's probable history of violence, especially under methamphetamine. Had such an evaluation been performed, the "focused delusion" may have been found to be directed at parties who placed expectations for performance on the defendant.

The jury in the *Romel* case decided beyond a reasonable doubt that the defendant intended to shoot his teacher. Romel was convicted of attempted murder in the second degree, which meant that, despite the proffered conclusions of the experts on the accused's drug use, the jury believed he had formed the specific intent to kill his teacher.

In the more recent case of *State v. Holbron* (1995), unlike those in the *Romel* case, experts offered diagnoses of multiple mental conditions to explain methamphetamine-related violence. In *Holbron*, on April 21, 1990, the defendant, in what appeared to be heinous conduct, threw a plate of food brought to him by his girlfriend at her head, then threw a radio at her. Holbron then asked her, "You ready to f____ die?" He then poured gasoline on her and attempted to set her afire with a match. The attempt failed, but a second match ignited the gasoline and the victim suffered severe burns trying to extinguish the flames. The defendant ran out of the house and down the street. The house was destroyed by fire.

Holbron did not dispute the facts, but instead offered the defense that he had "potentially suffered a lot of trauma to the head ... and that he has recognized organic difficulties in the way his brain works and the way he functions in a day-to-day situation." One of the defense experts testified that Holbron's right frontal lobe was damaged, which created difficulties in impulse control. A second defense expert diagnosed Holbron's condition as Organic Mental Disorder NOS and an Antisocial Personality Disorder. A third expert diagnosed substance-induced Organic Mental Disorder and Methamphetamine Use.

The defense theory, as argued to the jury on the basis of cerebral damage, was that Holbron's bizarre actions clearly indicated that he did not have the requisite state of mind to commit attempted murder. Obviously referring to the amotivational effects of methamphetamine and brain damage, among other factors, his defense attorney then maintained that Holbron was not sufficiently "aroused" by the events of the alleged crimes to the point where he would have formed the specific intent to cause the victim's death. The defense attorney argued that "if anything, [Holbron] acted recklessly." The trial ended with the return of the jury's guilty verdict after 29 minutes of deliberation.

Pathological intoxication has been successfully used as a defense if, by reason of such intoxication at the time of the alleged offense, the defendant lacked substantial capacity either to appreciate its wrongfulness or to conform his or her conduct to the requirements of the law (HRS §702-230(4) and (5)). In other words, pathological intoxication can assume the status of a mental condition and hence may allow exculpation if a link to a cognitive or volitional impairment can be demonstrated.

Such was the case in *State v. Kuhia* (1992), a landmark case in several respects. Here, the defendant was acquitted by virtue of the affirmative defense of pathological intoxication by methamphetamine, a first in Hawaii, which the defense proved by a preponderance of the evidence. Two important facts were determinative: (1) the defendant was not substance intoxicated at the time he killed the victim; and (2) multiple diagnoses were offered, at least one of which had exculpating potential. In Kuhia, mental health experts, as well as other corroborating evidence, suggested that the defendant suffered from paranoid schizophrenia and an organic delusional disorder, in addition to methamphetamine abuse. The organic delusional disorder was seen as caused by chronic methamphetamine use, impairing his ability to conform his conduct to the requirements of the law.

Kuhia raises the troubling question of the necessity of intoxication at the time of the alleged killing in order to establish pathological intoxication, a clear implication of HRS §702-230. This outcome appears to contradict the general principle limiting the availability of pathological intoxication as a defense in that it permits a defendant to avail himself or herself of a mental condition at the time of the alleged offense that is linked to a history of voluntary self-induced intoxication. Note that in all pre-1998 methamphetamine cases presented in this chapter in which the pathological intoxication defense was unsuccessfully offered, the defendant was methamphetamine intoxicated at the time. Under *Kuhia*, pathological intoxication could be presented as a defense for a defendant who had not ingested methamphetamine for a considerable period of time, perhaps months or years, before the alleged crime.

In *State v. Garringer* (1996), the defendant was convicted of robbery. During trial, Garringer admitted that he and a younger accomplice had planned to rob a Jack-in-the-Box. The minor threatened a worker, pounded the shotgun on the counter, where it discharged, and killed the worker. Garringer then grabbed the money from the cash register and the two males fled in a car stolen by Garringer prior to the robbery. The defendant testified at trial that he had smoked methamphetamine almost every day for about 2 years and that he and the minor had smoked methamphetamine before the robbery and planned to rob the Jack-in-the-Box after running out of drugs. Garringer testified that "despite feeling the symptoms of withdrawal during the incident in question, he had control over what he was doing." He never blamed methamphetamine for the robbery. Garringer was convicted of robbery in the first degree and of firearms-related charges.

Garringer later filed an action for postconviction relief. One of the grounds for the requested relief was ineffective assistance of his trial counsel, who had failed to raise the issue of the defendant's temporary insanity due to the effects of drug usage and had failed to obtain psychiatric evaluations of the defendant prior to trial. The Hawaii Supreme Court held in part that Garringer should have been allowed to clarify his petition by amending it to include factual allegations showing that (1) his appellate counsel omitted an appealable issue, and (2) in light of the entire record, the status of the law, and the space and time limitations inherent in the appellate process, a reasonably competent attorney would not have omitted that issue. The court noted that, despite the fact that the defendant's acquittal in *Kuhia* was based on the affirmative defense of pathological intoxication, Garringer was required to "overcome significant hurdles in order to establish that such a defense was potentially meritorious and that a reasonably competent attorney would not have omitted that issue."* On remand for a hearing to determine

---

* Among these hurdles were Garringer's trial testimony that, despite his use of crystal methamphetamine, he had control over what he was doing, and that he was voluntarily intoxicated at the time of the crime.

the merits of Garringer's ineffective assistance of counsel claim, the circuit court found against him. Garringer has appealed this ruling.

Other cases are of interest in untangling the issues surrounding pathological intoxication. In recent years, the methodology of the sanity examiner has been scrutinized in cases of criminal responsibility in which the role of methamphetamine was minimized, ignored, or misconstrued by the expert. In methamphetamine cases, no longer can it be assumed that a consensus of the three panel §704-404 examiners to the effect that the defendant is mentally incapacitated automatically leads to an acquittal on grounds of physical or mental disease, disorder, or defect.

The key case in Hawaii is *State v. Monte Louis Young* (1998). In that case, on May 10, 1997, shortly before 7 A.M. at the Burger King on University Avenue in Honolulu, Young pulled a hammer from behind his back and began striking the victim, Paul Ulbrich, on the back of the head. The victim's screams could be heard for some distance. After each blow, Young examined his handiwork as if to survey the damage. After the third blow, Young raised the hammer toward a Burger King worker and said, "Get in[side] before I kill you too." Young leapt over a wall, dropped the hammer in the parking lot, and left in his pickup truck.

According to witnesses and the experts, Young had been acting strangely before the killing, and had heavily abused alcohol and marijuana in the weeks before the instant homicide. He had a history of violent acting out within a strong polysubstance abuse pattern extending back at least a decade. His previous abuse of methamphetamine, apparently his drug of choice when available, was extensive. In 1993, Young's father had reported a 10-year history of methamphetamine use by Young. Young last became intoxicated on methamphetamine approximately 2 months before the instant homicide.

Computerized tomography (CT) scanning revealed a small subarachnoid hemorrhage and a cerebral contusion in Young's right parietal area. Based on his strange behavior, evidence of brain damage, and other factors, each of the examiners rendered a diagnosis of Psychotic Disorder NOS, among other diagnoses, and all but one examiner linked that disorder to a substantial impairment in both cognition and volition. The state retained the senior author to comment on the methodology of the sanity examiners pursuant to HRS §704-410. The state also retained the services of a clinical-forensic psychiatrist who had examined Young for the defense 5 years earlier in California.

In its Findings of Fact and Conclusions of Law, the court ruled that Young was guilty of murder in the second degree. The court correctly noted that (1) a condition excluding responsibility is an affirmative defense that must be shown by a preponderance of the evidence; (2) the lack of substantial capacity means "capacity which has been impaired to such a degree that only an extremely limited amount remains"; (3) if Young had "no impairment, or if the impairment was not substantial, a fair-minded [trier of fact] would find the defendant sane beyond a reasonable doubt"; and (4) that Young had "failed to prove by a preponderance of the evidence, that he lacked the substantial capacity either to appreciate the wrongfulness of his conduct or to conform his conduct to the requirements of law." The court also concluded that self-induced intoxication, which is intoxication caused by substances that the defendant knowingly introduces into his body, is prohibited as a defense to any offense, does not constitute a physical or mental disease, disorder, or defect within the meaning of §704-400, and therefore cannot be considered an exculpatory condition that is the product of circumstances that were beyond Young's control.

In applying this reasoning, the court held that the state had proved, beyond a reasonable doubt, that Young knowingly and voluntarily ingested drugs and alcohol both over a prolonged period of time and in the weeks immediately preceding the homicide. The court viewed these two time periods of voluntary substance abuse as having caused Young's several "physical or mental diseases, disorders or defects."

There are remarkable similarities between *Young* and *Kuhia*, including prior substance abuse, which most likely contributed to other diagnosed mental conditions but no methamphetamine intoxication at the time of the alleged offense. It is speculated that *Young* will nullify the impact of *Kuhia* to a substantial degree. The above cases lead to the conclusion that the expert's decision path as well as *Daubert* considerations should be scrutinized closely. The American Law Institute (ALI) test of criminal responsibility leads to a three-part test of insanity: (1) a genuine, sufficiently severe mental disorder; (2) a substantial impairment in the accused's capacity to appreciate the wrongfulness of his acts and/or in his ability to conform his conduct to the requirements of the law; and (3) a link between the two. A heuristic model based on this three-part test for criminal responsibility evaluations was presented by the senior author (1984, 1987) and has direct relevance to methamphetamine cases. This model involves the retrospective analysis of the following:

- The forensic database
- The type of distortion and/or deception shown by the defendant
- The defendant's reconstruction of the instant offense
- Long-term (i.e., historical) vs. instant crime behavior
- The defendant's mental disorder in terms of whether it is sufficiently severe and causally connected to the instant offense
- Self-determination and choice of crime-related behaviors
- Conclusions regarding criminal responsibility

The first recommended step involves the creation of a reliable and valid database, multisourced and interdisciplinary in nature, that forms the basis for all opinions regarding criminal responsibility. The contents of the database are obtained by examining the perpetrator, victim, context of the crime, and other data relevant to the accused's current and past circumstances. The most important part of the forensic analysis concerning methamphetamine abuse may be the database on which the eventual conclusions are based. Criteria for including data in the database are that they are multisourced and interdisciplinary and are based on information drawn from sources other than the client. It is especially important to gather data from sources that the defendant wishes to conceal because of the likelihood of finding unfavorable information concerning methamphetamine abuse (e.g., juvenile records; so-called expunged records, which may be available in unmodified form at government archive centers; interviews with peers, ex-spouses, and mates; military performance reports; and information from other states or countries). It is helpful for the credibility of the expert to base the forensic evaluation on as many database sources as possible.

The notion of a complete database is critical in evaluating criminal responsibility in situations involving methamphetamine. At this juncture in time, the perception of the court, rather than reality, is the important factor. In *Kuhia*, the court appeared satisfied that the mental health experts had an adequate database, which then provided the foundation for later acquittal. In *Garringer*, the defendant asserted in his petition for postconviction relief that he should have been psychiatrically evaluated, thus, in essence, claiming that the court had an incomplete database.

In *Young*, all the defense experts admitted that their proffered findings could be wrong if the database on which each expert had relied was flawed or incomplete. The state then demonstrated through its own experts and through cross-examination that the sanity examiners' database lacked essential information. For example, the three panel examiners failed to take into account or even properly review existing neuropsychological tests from a defense neuropsychological consultant to the effect that Young had average or better cognitive functioning. Thus, a link between a mental condition based on brain damage and a substantial impairment, even if cerebral injury was established, could not be established.

The next step in the decision process concerning criminal responsibility consists of ruling out or accounting for nondeliberate distortion within (1) the evaluator; (2) the reporting person; and (3) the reported event. Nondeliberate distortion due to anxiety, fatigue, or other factors may largely explain both evaluation and crime behavior and is, therefore, considered first. Nondeliberate distortion for the methamphetamine user at the time of the instant offense may consist of several simultaneously operating factors. Time perception is altered, resulting in unreliable estimates of time. Short-term memory problems, including encoding and retrieval difficulties, may be experienced. Other deficiencies in the perpetrator, victim, and witnesses need to be explored as discussed above.

As the next step in the evaluation process, deliberate distortion, if it exists, should be ruled in by a positive and replicable demonstration of misrepresentation. Deliberate distortion may be shown by the defendant and by cross-validating sources. The evaluation of the defendant's self-reports in methamphetamine cases should be scrutinized for misrepresentation by examining third-party reports and material evidence of the crime. Psychometric testing by objective measures, such as the Minnesota Multiphasic Personality Inventory–2 (MMPI-2), California Personality Inventory (CPI), 16-PF, and the Millon Multiaxial Clinical Inventory–III (MCMI-III), are appropriate for assessing distortion due to the embedded scales that accurately measure deception. An inspection of the crime scene is important as much methamphetamine-related violence occurs within a brief time span at a particular site, and an appreciation of the context is helpful to the evaluator. Data derived from the input of significant or knowledgeable others that indicate bias or a given motivational set (e.g., desire for revenge or desire to be reunited with the defendant) should be excluded from the data pool or placed in proper perspective by comparison with other known facts. In the murder and attempted murder cases reviewed above — *Romel, Holbron, Kuhia, Garringer,* and *Young* — the issue of nondeliberate distortion by the defendant was not raised. Considering the significant effects of methamphetamine use on attention, memory, and other cognitive skills, as discussed previously, the accuracy of the defendant's recollection needs to be cross-validated and not merely assumed or left unaided in the province of the jury.

Deliberate distortion — particularly faking bad or malingering in order to feign symptoms and conditions — raised as a significant source of concern in these cases was also not addressed. Yet, the base rate for malingering in state-of-mind defenses for felony cases, in general, is conservatively estimated at 20% (Rogers, 1988). There are compelling reasons to suggest that the incidence of malingering may be higher in methamphetamine cases. First, the chances of malingering increase with genuine deficiencies (Hall and Pritchard, 1996), and methamphetamine creates significant cognitive and psychological deficiencies in many abusers. Second, most defendants know, or have been instructed by their attorneys, that methamphetamine abuse or intoxication does not constitute an exculpating condition, as in virtually all cases the drug was taken knowingly and voluntarily. Thus, the search is on by the defense team, including the retained experts, for a condition that may be sufficiently severe and beyond the control of the defendant (e.g., a thought disorder such as Paranoid Schizophrenia). Methamphetamine mimics this psychosis in many respects and thus would be a natural target for incorrect (but unintentional) diagnosis by defense experts. The defendant may, however, as seen by the authors in a number of cases, deliberately deemphasize methamphetamine use and exaggerate or fabricate psychotic features of their behavior.

After distortion and deception are taken into account, as a third step, a defendant's recollection of an alleged crime is usually helpful to know in inferring his or her state of mind. Even when the defendant does not testify or when state law shifts the burden of rebutting insanity to the government after the defendant has raised the possibility of insanity, presenting the defendant's state of mind through experts is critical to the successful application of the insanity defense. Although state of mind can often be inferred from eyewitness accounts, material evidence, reports of third parties regarding events before and after the crime, and the defendant's own description of events, the expert presents the state of mind of the defendant from a professional, independent vantage point using a well-established DSM-IV classification system. Hence, the impact on the court, especially when unrebutted, can be considerable.

In some methamphetamine cases, the accused may not render spontaneous statements or submit to interrogation shortly after the alleged crime. In such cases, an inspection of the crime scene and interviews of cross-validating sources take on even greater importance. In none of the cases cited above did the mental health experts who examined the defendant visit the scene of the crime. In cases where the accused declines to be evaluated by an expert, that professional must refrain from proffering conclusions relevant to criminal responsibility. The expert may, however, comment on the methodology of the other sanity commissioners, as in *Young*, and present information from the literature on methamphetamine abuse.

The fourth step involves conducting an historical analysis of relevant past behavior and comparing it with that shown during the instant offense. The goal is to determine whether the instant offense is typical or atypical for the defendant. Rare events are most likely triggered by high stress or an unusual combination of environmental or internal events in the absence of history. Common events suggest a habitual pattern and are considered more inculpatory. In methamphetamine cases, repetitive violence associated with abuse of this substance is considered inculpatory because it implies recurring choice to aggress upon others.

A key question is whether basal violence associated with methamphetamine, especially when it is similar to the instant offense, was the result of a habitual set of violent acts or an isolated event. Historical instances of violence should be examined in terms of variables such as frequency, severity, recency, acceleration, triggering stimuli, opportunity factors, and inhibitions to aggression.

Historical factors that have traditionally indicated willfulness to commit violence in methamphetamine cases include the following:

- Lengthy time delays between triggers to violence and the instant crime
- Performance of complex chains of behaviors in order to execute the violent behavior
- Flexibility of response (e.g., when the perpetrator has multiple weapons with which to inflict harm)
- Predatory vs. reactive violence

Key forensic questions can be formulated as follows:

- Should the defendant have known the likely outcome of the chain of behavioral events culminating in violence?
- Did the defendant know that methamphetamine intoxication in this situation, based on the defendant's history, would likely result in violence to another?

Consider the following two courtroom scenarios:

> Prosecutor: Doctor, you testified that the accused suffered a substantial impairment in mental capacity at the time of the alleged offense. You cited a list of neuropsychological and psychological deficits in terms of his ability to self-control and self-monitor his behavior as reasons for the substantial incapacity, including a history of methamphetamine abuse. You did not examine previous violence, focusing instead on behavior during your evaluation and at the time of the alleged crime. Would your conclusion change if you knew the accused engaged in several dozen other very similar acts of previous violence while methamphetamine intoxicated, with rewarding consequences, high-stated self-control, some evidence of planning and rehearsal, and minimal loss of verbal or physical abilities during those violent acts? Why or why not? Cannot one's past violence influence and affect appreciation of wrongdoing and self-control in later violence?

Criminal Responsibility

Let's turn this around for the defense, assuming expert testimony to the effect that there was no substantial impairment for a male defendant who admitted to attacking the victim:

> Defense: Doctor, would you change your mind if you knew that the defendant (a) had no previous violence at all prior to the instant case and, in fact, worked productively and nonviolently in his job at the plantation for 15 years; (b) had an extremely high cumulative stress level for the year before the violence, as measured by several standardized tests and independently by DSM-IV criteria; (c) was borderline retarded with poor coping skills at best; and (d) believed that he had to perpetrate the violence because his life had been placed in danger by the victim? The other examiners considered these facts, why didn't you?

In short, there is no escape from considering historical influences to criminal behavior. This is because mental capacity to a greater or lesser degree is always influenced by previous experiences. Studies have suggested that historical violence accounts for the major portion of the statistical variance in accounting for exhibited violence (Hall et al., 1987). A history of violence or, conversely, a benign past, appears to act as a prepotent force of its own, determining to a large extent whether violence will, or will not, occur. In addition to history, triggers to violence and opportunity factors account for a high incidence of exhibited violence (Hall et al., 1984). This holds true whether or not there is a history of methamphetamine abuse.

Historical influences are discussed throughout the cases cited above. In *Romel*, the examiners noted that the defendant had a history of methamphetamine abuse, but one examiner, who proffered the ultimately unsuccessful opinion that the defendant was mentally incapacitated, failed to uncover a collateral history of violence even though the defendant was methamphetamine intoxicated at the time of the instant homicide. In *Holbron*, the defense attorney unsuccessfully argued that his client had a history of antisocial behavior (which is usually seen as inculpatory), reflected in several mental conditions, which then caused the defendant to be less aroused by the events of the alleged crime (and therefore presumably less responsible). In *Young*, the court noted as instrumental to its conclusions that the defendant had no family history of mental health problems but had a strong individual history of (1) polysubstance abuse and, in particular, methamphetamine abuse; (2) Antisocial Personality Disorder, with long-term behaviors associated with this condition; and (3) violence toward others.

As a fifth step, a diagnosis of the defendant's mental state at the time of the crime usually requires evidence in support of a DSM-IV mental condition. This is the first prong of the traditional three-part test of insanity (i.e., establishing a mental condition). For all practical purposes, sanity examiners, at least in this jurisdiction, offer dual or multiple diagnoses to the court. A diagnosis, such as Methamphetamine Intoxication or Abuse, is rarely offered alone because the examiner who wishes to find lack of criminal responsibility knows that voluntary substance abuse is not effective in achieving a favorable outcome, or because a single diagnosis does not reflect the clinical reality of the case. In *Kuhia*, the eventual acquittal of the defendant was tied to multiple diagnoses, any one of which could have been exculpatory in nature.

Defense attorneys should note that a very high percentage of methamphetamine abusers also have attention deficit hyperactivity disorder (ADHD; Eme, personal communication, 1998). The forensic evaluator must determine whether ADHD should be diagnosed in the instant case and factor these observations into his or her conclusions regarding criminal responsibility.

Any psychiatric condition, alone or in combination with existing conditions (i.e., creating interactive effects), provides the basis for lack of criminal responsibility. The situation is even vaguer when the accused was not methamphetamine intoxicated at the time of the alleged offense but had chronically used methamphetamine sometime in the past. Courts need to know, as in *Young*, that methamphetamine psychosis or methamphetamine-related violence persists for months after abstinence and can be triggered by substances other than methamphetamine to include alcohol, marijuana, cocaine, opiates, and even caffeine. The literature on cross-reversal tolerance (i.e., sensitivity) needs to be shared with the trier of fact.

A proffered diagnosis requires evidence that the condition existed at the time of the crime, regardless of whether or not it also existed prior to or after the crime. Evidence of a chronic mental disorder (e.g., schizophrenia, mental retardation, or cognitive disorder) in existence before the instant offense increases the likelihood that the disorder also existed at the time of the crime, but is not sufficient by itself. Some chronic mental disorders can be in some level of remission or can be controlled with psychotropic medications. Evidence of a mental disorder (e.g., depression, anxiety disorder) that arose after the instant crime is irrelevant to a diagnosis at the time of the offense.

The existence of a mental disorder at the time of the instant offense may or may not shed any light on the (legal) blameworthiness of the defendant. The severity of the disorder and its impairment of critical faculties at the time of the offense mediate its exculpatory effect. As a sixth step, the analysis of self-control and choice by the accused is central to the determination of criminal responsibility. Intact self-control and choice for the time of the alleged crime, which can exist along with delusional or hallucinatory behavior, often lead to a finding of criminal responsibility. Conversely, impaired self-control frequently results in exculpation or mitigation of responsibility for the instant offense. In sum, the evaluator should analyze the instant offense for the defendant's abilities and deficits in areas relevant to behavioral self-regulation. An exclusive focus on limitations, pathology, and deficiencies is a fundamental mistake.

Whether or not methamphetamine use is an issue, parameters to be considered during the alleged commission of the crime by the defendant include the following:

- Coherence and other characteristics of speech suggesting intact verbal expression
- Intensity and appropriateness of affect, especially during portions of the crime sequence that would normally produce strong emotion
- The focus of the crime, ranging from nebulous to markedly specific
- Level of substance intoxication during or shortly before the alleged offense
- Current, long-range mental conditions such as retardation or focal brain damage
- Behaviors requiring immediate, short-term, and historical memory skills of discrete sensory modalities or a combination of modalities
- Gross-motor, fine-motor, perceptual-motor, and motor-sequencing skills
- Presence of bizarre behavior
- Level of anxiety and stress reactions
- Presence of delusions and/or hallucinations
- Presence of depressed or expansive mood
- Planning and preparation
- Cognitive awareness of criminality
- Level of physical activity
- Self-reported control

The defendant's activities during the week (or longer) before the instant offense should be examined for behavioral deterioration, especially in self-care, work productivity, and in the central love relationship. For many of these parameters, quantitative measures on an empirically validated, Likert-scale format can be obtained from the Rogers Criminal Responsibility Scale (Rogers, 1988) and the Schedule of Affective Disorders and Schizophrenia (Spitzer and Endicott, 1978).

Other considerations include the use of a weapon designed for attack, such as a gun, knife, or numchuka, or a tool that could easily inflict harm (e.g., hammer, screwdriver). The presence of any such weapon during an offense would indicate a chain of responses more subject to control (i.e., selecting, obtaining, concealing, carrying, reaching for, and attacking with the weapon). Chains of responses usually call for shifts in behavior programs and lessen the likelihood of impulsivity. The next level of complexity involves use of a weapon that could be used for attack that the perpetrator found at the scene of the crime. A defendant's use of his or her body to club, strangle, or kick a victim suggests a primitive response. An attack with certain parts of the body, such as biting or banging one's head against the victim, suggests an even more primitive level of aggression. Continuing to attack nonvictim entities (e.g., banging the walls) suggests further loss of behavioral self-control.

The accused's flexibility of response and method of attack should also be considered. The use of multiple weapons or shifting back and forth from one method of attack to another suggests that different executive functions were utilized. This suggests the presence of self-control, even in methamphetamine-intoxicated persons.

As an illustration, in *Young*, indicia of self-control and choice were testified to by witnesses and investigators. These included, but were not limited to (1) the lack of erratic or dangerous behavior while in police custody for abuse of a household member 2 days before the homicide and at other times, in contrast to his claim that he was out of control for weeks prior to the killing; (2) just prior to the hammer attack on the victim, showing the ability to drive a truck, asking a third party for the time and attempting to panhandle some money from him, pulling a hammer from a position of concealment and striking the victim with it, and monitoring the effect of his blows. The damning observation from a self-control perspective was a witness's testimony that "after each blow, the defendant would look at Paul's injuries, as if to survey the damage"; and (3) after the fatal attack, showing the ability to threaten but not follow through on another attack on a worker, leaping a wall and running to the truck, driving away, and exhibiting clear and nonerratic cognition and behavior a day after the killing when he was arrested for stealing a boat from Kaneohe Bay.

Defense attorneys should again note the strong association of substance abuse with ADHD. Recognition of this co-morbidity is essential to proper diagnosis and treatment. ADHD is a serious impairment of self-regulation. Because the medical form of methamphetamine — Desoxyn — is effective for the treatment of ADHD, it may be possible that a significant percentage of methamphetamine abusers are self-medicating their ADHD. An individual analysis of self-regulation may reveal whether or not the methamphetamine abuse impairs choice and self-control.

The last step of the heuristic model for criminal responsibility (Hall, 1987) comprises the functional components of the American Law Institute's three-part test, which calls for a connection in the nature of cause and effect between diagnosis and impairment. The evaluator must now compare crime-specific behaviors with the retrospective mental conditions proffered by the experts. A link must be demonstrated between the deficiencies of the defendant (i.e., mental condition) and the criminal behavior (i.e., substantial impairment).

If substantial impairment is found in either cognition or volition, that impairment must result from the proffered mental conditions. All jurisdictions require that there be a demonstrated link between substantial impairments and the accused's diagnosed conditions. Further, the cause must be direct, and not secondary. In most, but not all cases, self-induced alcohol or drug intoxication at the time of the crime may have contributed to the offense but is considered an invalid argument for escaping criminal responsibility. This further decreases the range of behaviors that can be used as the basis for exculpation. The symptom pool is restricted even more by the exclusion of all disorders that were operating at the time of the crime but had little to do with mental capacity interference.

Brain damage, by itself, for example, does not automatically lead to violence. Hall and Sbordone (1993), in an exhaustive review of the literature on brain injury in humans, found that no lesion in any neurological site or system automatically leads to violence. Even with epilepsy, the aggression that has been observed is primitive and defensive in nature, with no intention of inflicting harm on others demonstrated in empirical investigations.

Generally, competent executive behavior is incompatible with loss of self-control due to extreme emotion. "Executive" behavior is a neuropsychological term referring to motor output, self-monitoring, and judgment after sensory and processing functions have been initiated. Skilled executive behavior occurs in a situation where the accused observes and changes his or her behavior simultaneously in response to a fluctuating environment, all in accordance with the goal or desired object of the action sequence. Hypothesis testing is the highest form of effective performance, as when the accused changes his or her own behavior (e.g., threatens the victim, puts a key in a lock) to see the reaction or outcome (e.g., victim acquiescence, the door unlocking) and then changes his own behavior accordingly (e.g., proceeds to assault the victim, proceeds through the door into the bedroom). In essence, this skill taps the defendant's ability to show a concordance between intentions/plans and actions. It is measurable, objective, observable, and incompatible with both extreme emotion and emotional disturbance.

Executive behaviors that tend to rule out extreme mental or emotional disturbance for the time of the instant offense include, but are not limited to, the following:

- Motor or mental rehearsal of the crime sequence
- Demonstration of a variety of violent acts (flexible behavior as with several weapons)
- Ability to orchestrate a multistep or multitask scheme (e.g., long, connected chains of behaviors)
- Ability to show change in principle (e.g., from raping the victim to killing her to eliminate her as a witness)
- Ability to delay violent responses
- Nonstimulus boundedness (acts independent of environmental influences)
- Ability to regulate tempo, intensity, and duration of violent behaviors
- Ability to avoid non-erratic behavior during violence unless that was the planned effect (e.g., deliberately becoming substance intoxicated prior to the instant offense)

The above considerations apply in methamphetamine-related extreme emotion cases. The self-control analysis can benefit the defense or the prosecution, depending on findings. In *State v. Raquepo* (1988), a methamphetamine-intoxicated defendant was charged with attempted murder in the second degree, kidnapping in the first degree, terroristic threatening in the first degree, license to carry firearm, and place to keep firearm in an incident in which the defendant shot a rifle at a roommate/friend. Before trial commenced, the state offered the defendant probation on the basis of a loss of self-control and his disorganization at the time of the offenses. The senior author noted the following deficiencies before, during, and after the offenses:

- The defendant asked for help prior to the offenses. He called for an ambulance, informed his roommate that he could not wait for the ambulance, that he felt dizzy, and that he wanted to go to the hospital immediately. Amnesia commenced from this temporal point with no later data suggesting that he was faking the loss of memory.
- The defendant's behaviors were preceded by strange and perseverative behaviors, such as pacing the floor with a rifle and talking to himself, interspersed with frequent apologies to his friend.
- He shot the rifle in the direction of his friend; this shooting was not in the context of an impaired relationship with the victim.
- A detailed analysis of his background revealed no history of violence toward the victim or anyone else.
- The defendant engaged in disorganized behavior prior to the shooting. He saw the ambulance he was waiting for, but failed to signal the ambulance to stop, provided misdirections when riding in the truck to get help, and other behaviors.

- Delusional thinking, including the thought that he was dying (e.g., he said to his friend, "If you want to save your life, you going to have to save mine because I'm dying, so take me to the hospital."). He wanted to drop off his weapon at the police station prior to proceeding to the hospital. Shooting at his friend may have reflected his fear of abandonment more than intent to kill.
- The defendant showed bizarre behaviors after the offenses. He shot at his friend from the hip in front of others, with no suggestion of secondary gain. There was no chance of escaping detection. After he had left the victim's truck with the keys in it, he asked a stranger to help him by giving him the keys to her truck. He also told this stranger that he had been poisoned and for her to hide his rifle, then threw the firearm onto her lawn. He then proceeded to flag down a police car (with a loaded .45-caliber pistol in his belt) and asked for help, stating that someone was trying to kill him. The bizarreness of his behavior was reflected in the police officers' initial belief that he was the victim of a crime, not the possible perpetrator. The defendant forgot that he had "speed" in his clothes, which was discovered at the police station.

The reader may rightfully question whether or not *Raquepo* constituted a case of voluntary intoxication. Again, the perception of the court and the state or defense in pursuing its case strategy is more critical than actual events.

In *State v. Paned* (1997), the defendant, who had killed an acquaintance with a shotgun, claimed self-defense, but was found guilty of murder in the second degree. A history of methamphetamine-related violence was uncovered, including threatening his grandmother by shoving a gun in her mouth, assaulting various friends, assaulting his wife and striking her with a gun because he suspected her of infidelity, and discharging his shotgun in a reckless manner by shooting at his house. A clear pattern of methamphetamine abuse was shown by bleeding ulcers, paranoia, observations of his behaviors by his family members, and other symptoms. He denied being methamphetamine intoxicated at the time of the killing.

On the night of the murder, the defendant had volunteered to take the victim, a distant relative living at his residence that he suspected of "fooling around" with his wife, to the airport. His behaviors were replete with indicia of choice and self-control, including driving around with the victim, talking to peers and drinking whiskey with them, and calling his mother and instructing her what to tell others if they should call for him. At the scene — a secluded spot in a residential neighborhood — the defendant was in close proximity to the victim when he fired the shotgun twice, fatally shooting the victim in the chest and the right forearm. The defendant sped off in his car and disposed of the shotgun, which was never found. He then drove to his friends' house and instructed them to remove the 12-gauge shotgun shells from the trunk of his car. He then attempted to borrow another car to establish an alibi and eventually went to a hotel to hide out. Despite an initial claim of amnesia for the crime events and for disposing of the shotgun, he presented information suggestive of recall. In sum, there were multiple indications of self-control for the time before, during, or after the violence. These included alibi behavior, ability to delay and execute the killing, and indicia of planning and preparation.

References

Hall, H.V. (1984). Predicting dangerousness for the courts. *Am. J. Forensic Psychol.*, 4, 5–25.

Hall, H.V. (1987). *Violence Prediction: Guidelines for the Forensic Practitioner.* Springfield, IL: Charles C Thomas.

Hall, H.V. and Pritchard, D. (1996). *Detecting Malingering and Deception: The Forensic Distortion Analysis (FDA).* Winter Park, FL: St. Lucie Press.

Hall, H.V. and Sbordone, R. (1993). *Disorders of Executive Functions: Civil and Criminal Law Applications.* Winter Park, FL: St. Lucie Press.

Rogers, R. (1988, 1997). *Clinical Assessment of Malingering and Deception.* New York: Guilford Press.

State v. Freitas, 62 Haw. 17, 608 P.2d 408 (1980).

State v. Garringer, 80 Haw. 327, 909 P.2d 1142 (1996).

State v. Hall, 66 Haw. 400, 660 P.2d 33 (1983).

State v. Holbron, 10 Haw. App. 629, 862 P.2d 1079 (1993).

State v. Kuhia, First Circuit Court, Cr. No. 93-0 1 58 (September 29, 1994).

State v. Nuetzel, 61 Haw. 531, 606 P.2d 920 (1980).

State v. Paned, 85 Haw. 230, 941 P.2d 929 (1997).

State v. Raquero, Second Circuit Court, Wailuku, Maui, Hawaii (1988).

State v. Souza, 72 Haw. 246, 813 P.2d 1384 (1991).

Tradewind Insurance Co., Ltd. v. Stout, 85 Haw. 177, 938 P.2d 1196 (1997).

State v. Monte Louis Young, First Circuit Court, Cr. No. 97-1 1 94 (May 7, 1998).

Dangerousness Prediction in Methamphetamine Cases

16

HAROLD V. HALL
SANDRA B. MCPHERSON
STUART W. TWEMLOW
ERROL YUDKO

Predicting dangerousness involves a three-part process of analyzing the history, triggers, and opportunity to aggress that operate against inhibitions to inflict violence. The three main factors associated with violence, which are also commonly the targets of deception by suspects (Hall, 1982, 1984, 1987; Hall and Pritchard, 1996), including those in methamphetamine cases, are (1) a history of violence; (2) situational and dispositional triggers to violence; and (3) opportunities for violence. Any of the variables associated with violence may be targeted for denial or minimization.

Triggering stimuli, which are short term in duration, intense in impact, and set the violence into motion, are often distorted by offenders. The two most frequently mentioned triggering events, including short-term events, are substance abuse or intoxication and the breakup of a central love relationship (e.g., Bandura, 1973). Other examples are insults to self-esteem (Toch, 1969) and invasion of body space (Kinzel, 1970).

Methamphetamine operates as a powerful trigger to violence in those individuals with a history of violence toward others. When intoxicated, these individuals often lose all sense of empathy, experience a low frustration tolerance, and concomitantly experience a need to aggress upon minimal environmental provocation. On later evaluation, the methamphetamine-intoxicated defendant typically tries to find legitimate reasons for his or her violence.

Opportunity factors, which allow the occurrence of violence or expand the various ways it can be expressed, may also be minimized or denied. Opportunity factors expand the possible severity of exhibited violence or allow its expression. Examples in the former category include availability of a firearm (Berkowitz and LePage, 1967), presence of a physically weaker potential victim (Bandura, 1973), and elevation to positions of authority where violence toward others is institutionally sanctioned (Milgram, 1963; Fromm, 1973). Variables that allow the expression of violence include release from incarceration into the community (Kelly, 1976) and cessation of taking tranquilizing medication (Stone, 1975).

Some associated features of violence are typically affirmed by offenders. These include easily verifiable associations of violence such as convictions, prison incarcerations, and body tattoos with violent themes. Other associations that are usually affirmed include a preference for violent films (TV, movies), books, etc., release from incarceration, and physical prowess in relationship to the (potential) victim. Defendants may blame some factors on others or regard them as irrelevant to violence. The meaning of some features may escape the defendant and hence may not be denied. These include physical abuse as a child, praise or reward by parents for aggression, a violent model in the home, substance abuse by the same-sex parent, and a history of reinforcing outcomes for violence.

Inhibitory variables that lower the chances that violence will occur are typically affirmed by offenders. These variables fall into the lower range of frequency, intensity, severity, or duration of any quantifiable factor that is positively associated with violence. A minimal history of violence may be regarded by a client as a sign of dispositional nonviolence. Therefore, it should not be surprising that many subjects will claim a nonviolent basal history. Because stabilizing psychotropic medication generally acts as an inhibitor to violence, most defendants assert compliance with medication.

Dispositional factors associated with a lower propensity to aggress include high socioeconomic status and high educational level (Kelly, 1976; Monahan, 1981). Offenders may exaggerate their occupational and educational achievement. The opportunity for violence may eliminate or reduce the probability of aggression and some offenders may claim a lack of transportation or a physical disability and therefore raise issues of an alibi and self-defense.

Contextual stimuli include such variables as location of the crime scene and the presence of third parties (Steadman, 1981) and environmental stimuli (Berkowitz, 1983; Horowitz and Willging, 1984). Some persons may therefore emphasize the improbability of violence given eyewitnesses, bright lighting, or other physical "barriers" to violence.

Common mispredictions involving defendants with a history of methamphetamine abuse involve errors in the assessment of dangerousness including the following (Hall, 1987):

- Lack of an adequate forensic database
- Failure to account for retrospective and current distortion

- Prediction of dangerousness in the absence of previous dangerousness
- Reliance on illusory correlations of dangerousness
- Prediction of dangerousness solely from clinical diagnosis
- Failure to consider triggering stimuli
- Failure to take into account opportunity variables
- Failure to evaluate inhibitory factors
- Ignoring relevant base rates
- Failure to formulate circumscribed conclusions.

The disinhibiting effects of methamphetamine intoxication, whether through direct action or through brain damage, can trigger violence if they are coupled with a history of violence. Therefore, for all forensic cases involving violence prediction, the three-part analysis of dangerousness should be performed.

In *State v. Sean Carvalho* (1999), the defendant was convicted of manslaughter for killing his 71-year-old grandmother by striking her with a baseball bat after she refused to give him money for drugs. In offering a prediction of substantial dangerousness, the senior author noted that Carvalho had a substantial history of violence before, during, and after the killing of his grandmother, with methamphetamine abuse or withdrawal a contributing factor. His inhibitions toward violence were weak even in the face of minimal environmental provocation. He had beaten a dog to death with a pipe, made death threats against his grandmother when she refused to comply with his demands, and was involved in three violent fights while in pretrial detention. One attack on another inmate occurred when the inmate informed Carvalho of his work responsibilities.

A critical factor was the severe and frequent methamphetamine abuse in which the defendant had engaged prior to the killing. In fact, he had abused methamphetamine so often that standard intelligence tests showed deterioration from an average to a borderline intellect, along with many neuropsychological signs. Although the senior author's dangerousness predictions extend only a year or two into the future, indicia of violent recidivism for Carvalho were suggested by the long-term effects of methamphetamine.

The reader is referred to Chapter 11 for other details on prediction schemes that can be part of forensic evaluation for a variety or purposes in methamphetamine-related cases.

Summary and Recommendations

Aside from the havoc wreaked by methamphetamine, quite possibly the most damaging substance to humankind in recent memory, a crude phenomenological and epidemiological network of information has been formed that has relevance for experts in forensic settings and situations. Information on methamphetamine that stems from empirical investigation, the most valid and reliable of this information network, needs to form the basis for experts' contributions to the criminal courts and be articulated to the trier of fact. At this rudimentary state of the art, the experts themselves should be questioned closely on their knowledge about methamphetamine. The expert should know the methamphetamine abuse by defendants, victims, and witnesses (in some cases) at the time of the alleged crime. The effects of methamphetamine need to be factored in at every step of the judicial process from interrogation of the suspect to sentencing. Sound, rigorous decision paths for every criminal forensic issue the expert addresses need to be developed to reflect the thinking process of those professionals and to expose possible errors and biases.

References

Bandura, A. (1973). *Aggression: A Social Learning Analysis*. Englewood Cliffs, NJ: Prentice-Hall.

Berkowitz, L. (1983). Aversively stimulated aggression: some parallels and differences in research with animals and humans. *Am. Psychol.*, 38, 1135–1144.

Berkowitz, L. and LePage, A. (1967). Weapons as aggression-eliciting stimuli. *J. Personality Soc. Psychol.*, 7, 202–207.

Fromm, E. (1973). *The Anatomy of Human Destructiveness*. New York: Holt, Rinehart, & Winston.

Hall, H.V. (1982). Dangerousness predictions and the maligned forensic professional: suggestions for detecting distortion of true basal violence. *Criminal Justice Behav.*, 9, 3–12.

Hall, H.V. (1984). Predicting dangerousness for the courts. *Am. J. Forensic Psychol.*, 4, 5–25.

Hall, H.V. (1987). *Violence Prediction: Guidelines for the Forensic Practitioner*. Springfield, IL: Charles C Thomas.

Hall, H.V. and Pritchard, D. (1996). *Detecting Malingering and Deception: The Forensic Distortion Analysis (FDA)*. Winter Park, FL: St. Lucie Press.

Horowitz, I. and Willging, 1. (1984). *The Psychology of Law*. Boston: Little, Brown.

Kelly, C. (1976). Crime in the United States: Uniform Crime Reports. Washington, D.C.: U.S. Government Printing Office.

Kinzel, A. (1970). Body-buffer zones in violent prisoners. *Am. J. Psychiatr.*, 127, 59–64.

Milgram, S. (1963). Behavioral study of obedience. *J. Abnormal Social Psychol.*, 67, 371–378.

Monahan, J. (1981). The Clinical Prediction of Violent Behavior (National Institute of Mental Health, DHHS Publication ADM 81-192). Washington, D.C.: U.S. Government Printing Office.

State v. Carvalho, Haw. App. No. 21701 (Haw. May 20, 1999).

Steadman, H. (1981). A situational approach to violence. *Int. J. Law Psychiatr.*, 5, 171–186.

Stone, A. (1975). Mental Health and the Law: A System in Transition (National Institute of Mental Health, DHEW Publication ADM 76–1 76). Washington, D.C.: U.S. Government Printing Office.

Toch, H. (1969). *Violent Men*. Chicago, IL: Aldine.

Section VI

Treatment

Treatment of Methamphetamine Abuse — Lack of Evidence for the Efficacy of Any of the Models Currently in Use

17

ERROL YUDKO
TIFFANY GAGNET

Traditional treatment programs based on the Minnesota Model (28-day in-patient treatment) have been shown to be ineffective for the treatment of stimulant addiction. Both the National Institute of Drug Abuse (NIDA) and the Center for Substance Abuse Treatment (CSAT) have sponsored research into the efficacy of treatments for methamphetamine (MA) abuse. A third program that has been put forward as a potentially useful model for the treatment of MA abuse is the Haight Ashbury Outpatient Model. Although the program that is currently receiving the greatest national attention, the Matrix Model, has been shown to be promising, none of these models has been effectively evaluated for its efficacy for the treatment of MA abuse.

NIDA Treatment Guidelines

NIDA has published treatment guidelines for stimulant abusers that have been empirically tested and their efficacy validated. However, these manuals were developed and tested on a population of cocaine users. A recent report (Rawson, et al., 2000) identified a variety of differences between MA and cocaine users. MA users report more daily use of marijuana and hallucinogens, more headaches, depression, suicidal thoughts, and hallucinations than cocaine users. Further, MA users report spending less money on stimulants, using less drugs, consuming less alcohol, needing less treatment for co-morbid alcohol use, and, perhaps most importantly, a "significantly shorter length of longest abstinence prior to treatment entry" than do cocaine users. Moreover, MA users report more family problems, more friends who use drugs, and more sex associated with drug use than do cocaine users. Because of these differences, we cannot assume that treatment strategies that work for cocaine users will also work to reduce or eliminate substance use in MA users. Empirical evaluation of the efficacy of this and other models for the treatment of MA use is needed.

Matrix Model of Outpatient Treatment

The Matrix Model of Outpatient Treatment is a 16-week manualized, intensive, nonresidential, directive, non-confrontational, psychosocial approach that was originally developed in response to the cocaine outbreak of the 1980s. The foundation of the model comes from the cognitive behavioral principles and goals. The fundamentals of the model have been recently summarized (Obert et al., 2000). A short summary of that paper appears below.

The goals of the treatment are to stop the drug use, to explore issues regarding addiction and relapse, to educate the family about addiction, to familiarize the individual with the self-help programs available, and to randomly monitor individuals weekly by urine analysis.

Basic Elements of the Matrix Model

To the practitioner of this model the fundamentals of effective treatment are engagement and retention, structure, information, relapse prevention, family involvement, self-help involvement, and urine tests. Engagement and retention are related to the success of the therapist in developing a positive, supportive nurturing relationship, which is fundamental to the success of the treatment. Such a warm environment keeps the patients engaged.

The structural component of the model is comprised of time planning in the early stages of recovery. By helping the addict learn to plan and schedule, the therapist can reduce any open time where the patient could relapse. This activity can be performed individually or in a group setting and is taught as a skill.

The MA user frequently encounters a period of confused emotional affect. Uncontrolled emotions can include paranoia, psychosis, depression, anger, and fear. Information about the emotions and physical states that the client experiences is helpful during the first stages of the treatment. Using standardized psychoeducational lectures the Matrix Model imparts simple, straightforward information about emotion in the early stages of treatment. This information becomes more complex and complete in later phases of treatment.

Relapse prevention entails techniques that teach the individual to recognize situations that may lead to drug use, as well as the coping strategies to effectively deal with those situations. The Matrix Model utilizes the experiences of recovering co-leaders to help patients "struggling with relapse issues."

In the Matrix Model families are involved in treatment. Family can both enhance and interfere with the treatment process (Kaufman, 1992). By teaching the family members about addiction and recovery a practitioner can maximize the benefits that the family brings to treatment and minimize the negatives. The Matrix Model also includes topics designed to familiarize clients with the possible benefits of self-help involvement. Patients are encouraged to utilize community-based programs, such as Narcotics Anonymous (NA) and Alcoholics Anonymous (AA) group meetings. Weekly random urine analysis is important to provide proof of sobriety, and positive tests are viewed as indicators for altering the treatment plan.

Components of the Matrix Model

Treatment components of the Matrix Model consist of individual sessions, early recovery groups, relapse prevention groups, family education sessions, 12-step meetings, social support groups, relapse analysis, and urine testing. There are three 45-minute individual sessions with a therapist. These sessions are used to set goals and verify that they are being met. These sessions can also be combined with other activities such as the inclusion of a family member. Extra sessions can be provided if necessary to deal with crisis intervention or treatment planning.

To reduce expenses, small early recovery groups take the place of holding a significant number of individual counseling sessions. The early recovery groups take place in the first month of treatment. These groups are primarily educational and include the following topics: cognitive tools to reduce craving, time scheduling, discontinuation of any secondary substances, and connecting patients with other community support groups.

Relapse prevention group meetings take place at the beginning and end of each week for the full 16-week program. The goal of these open sessions is to teach the recovering person how to maintain sobriety. These groups are topic centered and always positive. In addition, 12-week family education sessions are presented in a group setting and include slide presentations, videotapes, panels, and group discussion. Topics include neurobiology, conditioning, medical effects of stimulants, and how family relationships are affected by drugs. On-site 12-step meetings are used to ease clients into attending outside meetings on their own initiative.

During their last month of treatment, after completing the family education sessions, the patients attend social support groups. These groups are less structured than the other groups discussed above. They are designed to enable patients to establish relationships with nondrug users. Topics covered are tailored to the specific needs of the individuals in the groups.

Urine tests are done randomly each week, and relapse analysis is provided for patients who relapse. This exercise is designed to evaluate the events that led up to the relapse.

Evidence of the Effectiveness of the Matrix Model

The Matrix Model has been evaluated in five studies over a 15-year period. The first of these evaluations (Rawson et al., 1986) was a quasi-experimental study performed on 83 cocaine abusers. Patients were allowed to select one of three possible treatments. These were self-help groups, 28-day inpatient treatment, or the Matrix Model. Patients who selected the Matrix Model were significantly more likely, measured 8 months after treatment, to recover than the other two groups and significantly more likely to remain in treatment than those who chose the self-help group.

On the surface, this study appears to provide evidence of the effectiveness of the Matrix Model. However, three serious flaws exist in this study. The first is that by its nature a quasi-experimental design is fundamentally flawed. True experimental designs require random assignment of participants into groups. By allowing participants to self-select their group assignment, the researchers in this case confounded the effectiveness of the procedure and the predispositions of the patients. It is impossible to know if a preexisting experience/behavior or something else caused the patients to select one form of treatment over another. Thus, it is impossible to tell if this preexisting condition caused an increased likelihood of recovery. The second flaw is not really a flaw, but a problem with generalizability. This evaluation was conducted on the efficacy of treatment on cocaine abuse, not MA abuse. As we noted above, there are enough differences between cocaine and MA abusers to be suspicious of the effectiveness of a treatment of one that has been evaluated on the other. The third flaw has to do with generalizability as well. Although the Matrix Model in its current form is a 16-week program, the patients treated in the 1986 study received as much as 26 weeks of treatment.

A second study (Rawson et al., 1991), evaluated a larger group of cocaine users. This study was conducted on subjects who received 6 months of treatment. Appropriate scientific controls were still lacking. This study continued to show a high level of efficacy for the Matrix Model for treating cocaine addicts, but no data were collected on MA addicts.

A third study (Rawson et al., 1995) on 100 multiethnic cocaine-dependent subjects was appropriately controlled. These subjects were randomly assigned to either a 6-month Matrix Model group or an "other available community resource group." In this study the Matrix Model participants fared no better than their counterparts who entered a random treatment program. Both groups showed improvement. The authors concluded that the inability of the Matrix Model to yield significantly better results than other forms of treatment was the result of the highly variable treatment experiences of the control participants. From these data it is just as viable to conclude that the Matrix Model is no better than other, traditional methods of treatment.

A fourth study (Huber et al., 1997) used archival data to compare the treatment outcomes of patients who reported MA as their drug of choice with patients who reported cocaine as their drug of choice. All patients received the Matrix Model. There were no significant differences between MA-using and cocaine-using patients. This suggests that the Matrix Model is just as good for treating MA addiction as it is for treating cocaine addiction. But since there have been no empirical studies that support the efficacy of the Matrix Model for treatment of cocaine addiction, it is difficult to accept the Matrix Model for use in the treatment of MA addiction.

Although a number of studies are under way to try to elucidate the effectiveness of the Matrix Model in treating MA addiction (e.g., Galloway et al., 2000), no outcome measures have as yet been reported.

Haight Ashbury Outpatient Model

The Haight Ashbury Model (Inaba and Cohen, 1990) was taken from the Haight Ashbury Drug Detoxification, Rehabilitation and Aftercare Project. This organization has been involved in psychoactive drug treatment and education since 1967. The model consists of four stages, each characterized by an assessment and plan to be developed for that stage. Although the components of this model are based on sound empirical evidence for the effective treatment of substance abuse, the model itself has not been evaluated for its efficacy in the treatment of MA abuse.

The first stage is detoxification, which lasts for the first 3 to 7 days. During stage 1 individuals are assessed to determine whether they need hospitalization, and to determine if they are an emotional risk to harm themselves or others. Further, a physical exam is used to identify any medical emergencies caused by the stimulant abuse. Finally, individuals are assessed for dual diagnosis, and to determine their social and environmental needs. The assessment is followed by a commitment from the client to remain abstinent. Daily outpatient interactions, either group or individual counseling, are scheduled.

The Haight Ashbury model relies heavily on pharmacological mechanisms. If psychosis or speed toxicity is present then haloperdol or other neuroleptic drugs can be used to block the excessive dopamine and catecholamine toxicity. Antidepressant drugs can be prescribed if depression is present. Desipramine (Norparamine), trazadone (Desyrel), and fluoxetine (Prozac) are all typically used as antidepressants. The initial craving is treated with bromocriptine and amantadine (dopamine agonists). Amino acid precursors (e.g., Renew or Tropamine) that can lead to increased levels of the neurotransmitters dopamine, serotonin, adrenalin, noradrenalin, and acetylcholine can also be prescribed.

The second stage of the model, initial abstinence, begins with the first week of the treatment episode and may continue for as long as 3 months. The patient is assessed for dual diagnosis, to fully evaluate any medical needs, to review social and environmental problems and needs, and to identify environmental triggers that may pose a problem for the client.

Abstinence is contracted for 3 months. During this time the patient is required to go to 90 12-step meetings. A structured daily activity plan is developed. A life journal or log of events is maintained. A sober support network is developed. A recovery "sponsor" is found. A personal history of the client's addiction is developed. The client begins this stage with daily meetings with his or her counselor. By the end of the period the client is expected to meet with the counselor three times per week. The client with a dual diagnosis begins psychiatric intervention. The client is taught to identify and to avoid triggers.

Further, during this stage a strategy is developed to address drug cravings. Activities to address this issue may include exercise, proper eating, 12-step meetings, working, meditation, hot or cold baths, or networking with other recovering addicts. Desensitization strategies or deconditioning techniques are used to dispel drug craving in response to triggers.

The third stage, sobriety, usually lasts 3 months to 18 months, and longer in some cases. At this stage psychological and social variables are assessed. Vocational or educational needs of the client are established. The client's recognition of the addiction and recovery processes is assessed. The client's ability to accept the concept of lifelong abstinence from all drugs of abuse is also assessed.

After the third stage assessments are performed, the client must develop plans for a lifetime of sobriety. During this time the client will progressively decrease contact with the program, moving from weekly to monthly visits. Concurrent with a progressive decrease in program visits the client is expected to increase his or her attendance at 12-step meetings.

During stage three clients are required to write a personal history that identifies the effect of drug abuse on their own life and the lives of others. This history includes a list of personal shortcomings, and a list of the people who have been hurt by the user's addiction. The recovering person is instructed to think about how to make restitution to the people who have been hurt. This "history" is then reviewed by others, and input given. This is followed by the development of a list of all of the positive achievements that the individual has made during the recovery process. The completed story is then shared with support groups, counselors, friends, and relatives. Issues from stage two are then revisited before the client moves on to stage four.

Stage four is recovery. This step lasts a lifetime. Continual self-assessments are performed. Plans for abstinence are made. The client must periodically reaffirm his or her decision for lifetime sobriety. The client must also reaffirm that he or she has no interest in drugs and is not questioning the decision to remain drug free. The client will eventually disengage with program services but will continue various recovery support groups.

Conclusions

Although there are a variety of models that have been proposed for the treatment of MA addiction, none has been adequately supported with empirical evidence. All these models have a high level of face validity. That is, they all look good on the surface, but the lack of evidence for their usefulness is troubling. Large sums of public and private monies have been put into developing these models. We must begin to demand outcome measures that support their usefulness.

References

Galloway, G.P., Martinelli-Casey, P., Stalcup, J., Lord, R., Christian, D., Cohen, J., Reiber, C., and Vandersloot, D. (2000). Treatment-as-usual in the methamphetamine treatment project. *J. Psychoactive Drugs*, 32(2), 164–176.

Huber, A., Ling, W., Shoptaw, S., Gulati, V., Brethen, P., and Rawson, R.A. (1997). Integrating treatments for methamphetamine abuse: a psychosocial perspective. *J. Addictive Dis.*, 16, 41–50.

Inaba, D. and Cohen, W.E. (1990). *The Haight Ashbury Training Series*, Vol. 1: *Methamphetamines*. San Francisco: Haight Ashbury Drug Detoxification, Rehabilitation and Aftercare Project and Cinemed, Inc.

Kaufman, E. and Kaufman, P., Eds. (1992). For multiple family therapy to couples therapy. In *Family Therapy of Drug and Alcohol Abuse*, Boston: Allyn and Bacon, 85–93.

Obert, J.L., McCann, M.A., Martinelli-Casey, P., Weiner, A., Minsky, S., Brethen, M.A., and Rawson, R. (2000). The matrix model of outpatient stimulant abuse treatment: history and description. *J. Psychoactive Drugs*, 32(2). 157–164.

Rawson, R.A. (1998). Treatment of stimulant abuse CSAT: TIP 33 (Chair, CSAT Consensus panel). Rockville, MD: DHHS.

Rawson, R.A. (2002). The NIDA Methamphetamine Clinical Trials Group (MCTG): taking research into the field. Paper presented at the Annual ASAM meeting, Los Angeles, CA, April, 2002.

Rawson, R.A., Ed., (2002). Methamphetamine: who uses it, how it is used, and what does it do? *J. Addictive Dis.*, 21, 1.

Rawson, R.A., Obert, J.L., McCann, M.J., Smith, D.P., and Scheffey, E.H. (1989). *The Neurobehavioral Treatment Manual.* Beverly Hills, CA: Matrix.

Rawson, R.A., Shoptaw, S.J., Obert, J.L., McCann, M.J., Hasson, A.L., Marinelli-Casey, P.J., Brethen, P.R., and Ling, W. (1995). An intensive outpatient approach for cocaine abuse treatment: the Matrix Model. *J. Substance Abuse Treat.*, 122, 117–127.

Rawson, R.A., Huber, A., Brethen, P.B., Obert, J.L., Gulati, V., Shoptaw, S., and Ling, W. (2000). Methamphetamine and cocaine users: differences in characteristics and treatment retention. *J. Psychoactive Drugs*, 32, 233–238.

Rawson, R.A., Anglin, M.D., and Ling, W. (2002). Will the methamphetamine problem go away? *J. Addictive Dis.*, 21, 5–19.

Rawson, R.A., Huber, A., Brethen, P., Obert, J.L., Gulati, V., Shoptaw, S., and Ling, W. (2002). Status of methamphetamine users 2–5 years after outpatient treatment. *J. Addictive Dis.*, 21, 107–119.

Rawson, R.A., McCann, M.J., Huber, A., Shoptaw, S., Farabee, D., Reiber, C., and Ling, W. (2002). A comparison of contingency management and cognitive-behavioral approaches for cocaine dependent methadone-maintained individuals. *Arch. Gen. Psychiatr.*, 59(9), 817–824.

Rawson, R.A., McCann, M.J, Shoptaw, S., Miotto, K., Farabee, D., Reiber, C., and Ling, W. (Under review). A comparison of contingency management and cognitive-behavioral approaches for cocaine- and methamphetamine-dependent individuals.

Rawson, R.A., Obert, J.L., McCann, M.J., and Mann, A.J. (1986). Cocaine treatment outcome: cocaine use following inpatient, outpatient and no treatment. CPDD NIDA Res. *Monograph*, 67, 217–277.

Rawson, R. (1991). *Treatment for cocaine abuse: A review of current strategies.* Los Angeles: Drug Abuse Information and Monitoring Project, UCLA Drug Abuse Research Center.

Bibliography

Alm, S. (1998). Personal communication. U.S. Attorneys Office, Honolulu, Hawaii.

American Psychiatric Association (1994). *Diagnostic and Statistical Manual of Mental Disorders* (DSM-IV), Fourth Edition. Washington, D.C.: American Psychiatric Association.

American Psychiatric Association (2000). *Diagnostic and Statistical Manual of Mental Disorders* (DSM-IV-TR) Fourth Edition–Text Revision. Washington, D.C.: American Psychiatric Association.

American Psychological Association, Division 41 (1991). *Speciality Guidelines for Forensic Psychologists*. Washington, D.C.: American Psychological Association.

Ando, K., Hironaka, N., and Yanagita, T. (1986). Psychotic manifestations in amphetamine abuse — experimental study on the mechanism of psychotic recurrence. *Psychopharmacol. Bull.*, 22(3), 763–767.

Andrews, D.A. and Bonta, J. (1998). *The Psychology of Criminal Conduct*, 2nd ed. Cincinnati, OH: Anderson Publishing.

Anglin, D., Burke, C., Perrochet, B., Stamper, E., and Dawud-Noursi, S. (2000). History of the methamphetamine problem. *J. Psychoactive Drugs*, 32(2), 138–139.

Anthony Alexander Campbell v. Burt Rice, 265 F.3d 878; 2001 U.S. App. LEXIS 20321.

Arakawa, L. (1998). Raid uncovers rare lab. *The Honolulu Advertiser*, Aug. 11, B 1.

Arkansas v. Kenneth Andrew Sullivan, 532 U.S. 769 (2001).

Arnold, E.B., Molinoff, P.B., and Rutledge, C.O. (1977). The release of endogenous norepinephrine and dopamine from cerebral cortex by amphetamine. *J. Pharmacol. Exp. Ther.*, 202, 544–557.

Asami, T., Kuribara, H., and Tadokoro, S. (1986). Effects of repeated administration of bromocriptine on ambulatory activity in mice, and changes in methamphetamine sensitivity in bromocriptine-experienced mice. *Yakubutsu Seishin Kodo*, 6(3), 309–317.

Ashizawa, T., Saito, T., Yamamoto, M., Shichinohe, S., Ishikawa, H., Maeda, H., Toki, S., Ozawa, H., Watanabe, M., and Takahata, N. (1996). A case of amotivational syndrome as a residual symptom after methamphetamine abuse. *Nihon Arukoru Yakabutsu Gakkai Zasshi*, 31(5), 451–461.

Atlas, R. (1982). Crime site selection for assaults in four Florida prisons. *Man-Environ. Syst.*, 12, 59–66.

Azzaro, A.J., Ziance, R.J., and Rutledge, C.O. (1974). The importance of neuronal uptake of amines for amphetamine induced release of H-norepinephrine from isolated brain tissue. *J. Pharmacol. Exp. Ther.*, 189, 110–118.

Badgett, S.A. (1999). Neuropsychological Functioning Subtypes of Schizophrenia and Mood Disorders. Doctoral dissertation. New York: Fordham University.

Boer, D.P., Wilson, R.J., Gauthier, C.N., and Hart, S.B. (1997). Assessing risk of sexual violence: guidelines for clinical practice. In C.D. Webster and M.A. Jackson, Eds., *Impulsivity: Theory, Assessment and Treatment*. New York: Guilford Press, 326–341.

Boyle, G.J. and Lennon, T.J. (1994). Examination of the reliability and validity of the Personality Assessment Inventory. *J. Psychopathol. Behav. Assess.*, 18(3), 173–187.

Brecher, E.M. (1972). *Licit and Illicit Drugs*. Boston: Little Brown.

Brochu, S. (1992). A critical look at the conceptual models explaining drug use and crime. Paper presented at the 3rd Conference of the European Association of Psychology and Law, Oxford, U.K.

Brown, D., Scheflin, A.Q., and Hammond, D.C. (1998). *Memory, Trauma Treatment, and the Law*. New York: W.W. Norton.

Budd, K., Poindexter, L., Felix, E., and Naik-Polan, A. (2001). Clinical assessment of parents in child protection cases: an empirical analysis. *Law Hum. Behav.*, 25(1), 93–108.

Byck, R. (1987). Cocaine use and research: three histories. In S. Fisher, A. Rashkin, and E.H. Unlenhuth, Eds., *Cocaine: Clinical and Behavioral Aspects*. New York: Oxford University Press.

California Health and Safety Code, Article 11353.

Cantwell, D.P. (1999). Comorbidity in ADHD and associated outcomes. GRAD-DDA Newsletter, Spring, 1999. Available at http://www.netacc.net/~gradda/Sp99cmo.html.

Castro, F.G., Barrington, E.H., Walton, M.A., and Rawson, R.A. (2000). Cocaine and methamphetamine differential addiction rates. *Psychol. Addictive Behav.*, 14(4), 390–396.

Commonwealth v. Cosmello, Ct. Common Pleas, Susquehanna, PA (November 15, 1993).

Conger, A.J. and Conger, J.C. (1996). Did too, did not! Controversies in the construct validation of the PAI. *J. Psychopathol. Behav. Assess.*, 18(2), 205–212.

Cooke D.J. and Michie, C. (1998). Predicting recidivism in a Scottish prison sample. *Psychol. Crime Law*, 4, 169–211.

Copas, J. and Marshall, P. (1998). The Offender Group Reconviction Scale: a statistical reconviction score for use by probation officers. *Appl. Stat.*, 47, 159–171.

Bibliography

Copas, J., Marshall, P., and Tarling, R. (1996). *Predicting Reoffending for Discretionary Conditional Release*. London: HMSO.

Danesh-Khoshboo, Y. (1991). *The Civilization of Law: A Commentary on the Laws of Hammurabi and Magna Carta*. Berrien Springs, MI: Vandevere.

DASIS (2001). Drug and Alcohol Services Information System, November 16.

Daubert v. Merrell Dow Pharmaceuticals, 509, U.S. 579 (1993).

Davis, B.A. and Vitullo, J. (2001). Federal criminal conspiracy. *Am. Criminal Law Rev.*, 8, 777–817.

DAWN (2002). Report, Drug Abuse Warning Network, October.

Deisinger, J.A. (1995). Exploring the factor structure of the Personality Assessment Inventory. *Assessment*, 2(2), 173–179.

Demiff, L., Rizvi, S.L., Brown, M. and Linehan, M.M. (2000). Dialectical behavior therapy for substance abuse: a pilot application to a methamphetamine dependent woman with borderline personality disorder. *Cogn. Behav. Pract.*, 7, 457–468.

Dhaliwal, G.K., Porporino, F., and Ross, R.R. (1994). Assessment of criminogenic factors, program assignment and recidivism. *Criminal Justice Behav.*, 21, 454–467.

Dodgen, C.E. and Shea, W.M. (1997). *Psychoactive Substance Disorders: A Comprehensive Resource for Clinicians and Researchers*. Florham Park, NJ: C & D Publications.

Douglas, K.S., Hart, S.D., and Kropp, P.R. (2001). Validity of the Personality Assessment Inventory for forensic assessments. *Int. J. Offender Ther. Comp. Criminol.*, 45(2), 183–197.

Doweiko, H.E. (1999). *Concepts of Chemical Dependency*. Brooks/Cole: Pacific Grove, CA.

Eisenberg, M. and Markley, G. (1987). Something works in community supervision. *Fed. Probation*, 51, 28–32.

Epperson, D., Kaul, J.D., and Hesselton, D. (1999). Minnesota Sex Offender Screening Tool–Revised (MNSSOST-R): Development, Performance and Recommended Risk Level Cut Scores. St. Paul: Minnesota Department of Corrections.

Fagan, J. (1990). Intoxication and aggression. In M. Tonry and J.Q. Wilson, Eds., *Drugs and Crime (Crime and Justice: A Review of Research*, Vol. 13). Chicago: University of Chicago Press.

Feldman, R.S., Meyer, J.S., and Quenzer, L.F. (1997). *Principles of Neuropsychopharmacology*. Sunderland, MA: Sinauer Associates, Inc.

Fisher, R.P. and Geiselman, R.E. (1992). *Memory-Enhancing Techniques for Investigative Interviewing: The Cognitive Interview*. Springfield, IL: Charles C Thomas.

Flynn, P.M., McCann, J.T., Luckey, J.W., Rounds-Bryant, J.L., Theisen A.C., Hoffman, J.A., and Koman, J.J. (1997). Drug dependence scale in the Millon Clinical Multiaxial Inventory. *Sub. Use Misuse*, 32(6), 733–748.

Flynn, P.M. and McMahon, R.C. (1997). MCMI applications in substance abuse. In: T. Millon, Ed., *The Millon Inventories: Clinical and Personality Assessment.* New York: Guilford Press.

Furman v. Georgia, 408 U.S. 238 (1972).

Gearan, A. 3-strikes laws' long sentences to get review. *The Plain Dealer,* (2002). p. A6.

Gottfredson, S.D., Wilkins, L.P., and Hoffman, P.B. (1978). *Guidelines for Parole and Sentencing: A Policy Control Method.* Toronto: Lexington Books.

Graedon, J. and Graedon, T. (1991). *Graedon's Best Medicine.* New York: Bantam Books.

Grinspoon, L. and Bakalar, J.B. (1992). Marijuana, in *Substance Abuse: A Comprehensive Textbook,* 2nd ed., Lowenson, L.H., Ruiz, P., Millman, R.B., and Langrod, J.G. (Eds). Baltimore: Williamson and Wilkins.

Grinspoon, L. and Bakalar, J.B. (1993). *Marijuana: The Forgotten Medicine.* New Haven, CT: Yale University Press.

Grinspoon, L. and Bakalar, J.B. (1995). Marijuana as medicine. *J. Am. Med. Assoc.,* 273, 1875–1876.

Grove, W.M. and Meehl P. (1996). Comparative efficiency of informal (subjective, impressionistic) and formal (mechanical, algorithmic) prediction procedures: the clinical-statistical controversy. *Psychol. Public Policy Law,* 2(2), 293–323.

Gudjonsson, G.H. (1992). The psychology of false confessions and ways to improve the system. *Int. Dig. Hum. Behav. Sci. Law,* 1(2), 49–53.

Gudjonsson, G.H. (1992) *The Psychology of Interrogations, Confessions, and Testimony.* New York: John Wiley & Sons.

Gudjonsson, G.H. and Peterson, H. (1991). Custodial interrogation: why do suspects confess and how does it relate to their crime, attitude, and personality, *Pers. Ind. Diff.,* 299–306.

Hall, H.V. (2000). Violence Prediction and Risk Analysis. Workshop Manual. Sponsored by the Pacific Institute for the Study of Conflict and Aggression.

Hall, H.V. and Pritchard, D. (1996). *Detecting Malingering and Deception: The Forensic Distortion Analysis (FDA).* Winter Park, FL: St. Lucie Press.

Hallfors, D., Cho, S., Livert, D., and Kadushin, C. (2002). Fighting back against substance abuse: are community coalitions winning? *Am. J. Prev. Med.,* 23(4), 237–245.

Hanson, R.K. (1997). The Development of a Brief Actuarial Risk Scale for Sexual Offender Recidivism. (User Report 1997-04). Ottawa, Ontario, Canada: Department of the Solicitor General of Canada.

Bibliography

Hanson, R.K. (1998). What do we know about sex offender risk assessment? *Psychol. Public Policy Law*, 4, 50–72.

Hanson, R.K. and Bussiere, M.T. (1998). Predicting relapse: a meta-analysis of sexual offender recidivism studies. *J. Consulting Clin. Psychol.*, 66(2), 348–362.

Hanson, R.K. and Thornton, D. (2000). Improving risk assessments for sex offenders: a comparison of three actuarial scales. *Law Hum. Behav.*, 24(1), 119–136.

Hare, R.D., Harpur, T.J., Hakstian, A.R., Forth, A.E., Hart, S.D., and Newman, J.P. (1990). The Revised Psychopathy Checklist: reliability and factor structure. *Psychol. Assess. J. Consulting Clin. Psychol.*, 2, 338–341.

Harris, G.T., Rice, M.R., and Quinsey, V.L. (1998). Appraisal and management of risk in sexual aggressors: implications for criminal justice policy. *Psychol. Public Policy Law*, 4, 73–115.

Hart, S.D. (2001). Violence risk assessment. Keynote Address, 11th European Conference of Psychology and Law, June 8, Lisbon, Portugal.

Hart, S.D., Hare, R.D., and Forth, A.E. (1994). Psychopathy as a risk marker for violence: development and validation of screening version of the Revised Psychopathy Checklist. In J. Monohan and H. Bedman, Eds., *Violence and Mental Disorder: Developments in Risk Assessment.* Chicago: University of Chicago Press, 81–98.

Hart, S.D., Cox, D.N., and Hare, R.D. (1995). *Manual for the Psychopathy Checklist: Screening Version* (PCL:SV). Toronto: Multihealth Systems.

Hartz, D.T., Fredrick-Osborne, S.L., and Galloway, G.P. (2001). Craving predicts use during treatment for methamphetamine dependence: a prospective, repeated-measure, within-subject analysis. *Drug Alcohol Dependence*, 63, 269–276.

Brethen, P. and Stimsom, J. (2002). Hawaii Conference on Methamphetamine "ICE" Epidemic.

Hays, C. (2002). Adult ADHD and Severity of Alcoholism: their Significance in Treatment for Alcoholism. Doctoral dissertation, Fielding Graduate Institute.

Hillbrand, M. (2001). Homicide, suicide and other forms of co-occurring aggression against self and against others. *Prof. Psychol. Res. Pract.*, 32, (6), 626–635.

Hoffman, P.B. (1994). Twenty years of operational use of a risk prediction instrument: U.S.P.C.'s salient factor score. *J. Criminal Justice*, 22, 477–494.

Hoffman, P.B. and Beck, J.L. (1985). Recidivism among released federal prisoners: salient factor score and five year follow-up. *Criminal Justice Behav.*, 12, 501–507.

Hoffman, P.B. and Stone-Meierhoefer, B. (1979). Post release arrest experiences of federal prisoners: a six year follow-up. *J. Criminal Justice*, 7, 193–216.

Honolulu Star-Bulletin (2002). Arrested males on "ice" top 35%, Honolulu outpaces 36 other big cities in its incidence of "ice" use.

Hubbard, R.L., Carddock, S.G., Flynn, P.M., Anderson, J., and Etheridge, R.M. (1998). Overview of one-year follow-up outcomes in the Drug Abuse Treatment Outcome Study. *Psychol. Addictive Behav.*, 11(4), 291–298.

In re Josslin, 1998 Ohio App. LEXIS 2008, 5/4/98.

In re Wilds, 997 Ohio App. LEXIS 4934, 10/24/97.

Inbau, F.E., Reid, J.E., and Buckley, J.P. (1986). *Criminal Interrogation and Confessions*. Baltimore, MD: Williams & Wilkins.

Kansas v. Hendricks, 521 U.S. 346, 358 (1997).

Karch, S.B. (1996). *The Pathology of Drug Abuse*, 2nd ed. Boca Raton, FL: CRC Press.

Kassin. S.M. (1997). The psychology of confession evidence. *Am. Psychol.*, 52, 221–233.

Kassin, S.M. (1998). More on the psychology of false confessions. *Am. Psychol.*, 53, 320–321.

King, M.S. (2002). Therapeutic jurisprudence in regional WA: the Geraldton Alternative Sentencing Regime. *Brief*, 29.

Kono, J., Miyata, H., Sadanobu, U., Yanagita, T., Miyasato, K., Ikawa, G., and Hukui, K. (2001). Nicotine, alcohol, methamphetamine, and inhalant dependence: a comparison of clinical features with the use of a new clinical evaluation. *Alchohol*, 24, 99–106.

Kopas, J. and Marshall, P. (1998). The offender group reconviction scale: a statistical reconviction score for use by probation officers. *Appl. Stat.*, 47, 159–171.

Laidler, K. and Morgan, P. (1997). Kinship and the community; the Ice crisis in Hawaii, in H. Klee, Ed., *Amphetamines Misuse; International Perspectives on Current Trends*. Reading, U.K.: Harwood International Publishers.

Lang, A.R., Goeckner, D.J., Adesso, V.J., and Marlatt, G.A. (1976). Effects of alcohol on aggression in male social drinkers. *J. Abnormal Psychol.*, 84(5), 508–518.

Leinwald, D. (2002). Dangerous club-drug knockoffs surge. *USA Today*, July 23, p. A3.

Linehand, M.M. (1993). *Cognitive Therapy of Borderline Personality Disorder*. New York: Guilford Press.

Linehand, M.M., Armstrong, H.E., Suarez, A., Almari, D., and Heard, H.D. (1991). Cognitive behavioral therapy with chronically borderline suicidal patients. *Arch. Gen. Psychiatr.*, 48, 1060–1064.

Lingeman, R.R. (1974). *Drugs from A to Z: A Dictionary*. New York: McGraw-Hill.

Locher, P. (2002). Meth bust. *The Daily Record*, February 16, pp. A1, A2.

Lockett v. Ohio, 438 U.S. 586 (1978).

Loftus, E.P. and Palmer, J.C. (1974) Reconstruction of automobile destruction: an example of the interaction between language and memory. *J. Verbal Learning Verbal Behav.*, 13, 585–589.

Loftus, E.P. and Zanni, G. (1975). Eyewitness testimony: the influence of the wording of a question. *Bull. Psychonomic Soc.*, 5(1), 86–88.

Lopez v. Davis, 186 F.3d 1092 (2001).

Lovett, A.R. (1994). Wired in California. *Rolling Stone*, May 5, pp. 39–40.

Lubinski, D. (1996). Applied individual difference research and its quantitative methods. *Psychol. Public Policy Law*, 2(2), 187–203.

Mann, J. (1994). *Murder, Magic and Medicine.* New York: Oxford University Press.

McCann, J.T. (1998). Broadening the typology of false confessions. *Am. Psychol.*, 53(3), 319–320.

McConaghy, N. (1999). Methodological issues concerning evaluation of treatment for sexual offenders: randomization, treatment drop-outs, untreated controls, and with treatment studies. *Sexual Abuse*, 11, 183–194.

McKetin, R. (2000). Cognitive Functioning and Psychological Morbidity among Illicit Amphetamine Users. Doctoral dissertation, University of New South Wales, Sydney, Australia.

McManus, R.F., Stagg, D.I., and McDuffie, C.R. (1988). CMC as an effective supervision tool: the South Carolina perspective. *Perspectives*, 4, 30–34.

Meehl, P.E. (1996). *Clinical versus Statistical Prediction: A Theoretical Analysis and a Review of the Literature.* Northvale, NJ: Jason Aronson (original work published in 1954).

Meloy, J.R. (1992). *Violent Attachments.* Northvale, NJ: Jason Aronson.

Meloy, J.R., Hansen, T.L., and Weiner, L.B. (1997). Authority of the Rorschach: Legal citations during the past 50 years. *J. Personality Assess.*, 69, 53–62.

Melton, G.B., Petrila, J., Poythres, N.G., and Slobogin, C. (1997). *Psychological Evaluations for the Courts: A Handbook for Mental Health Professionals and Lawyers*, 2nd ed. New York: Guilford Press.

Memon, A. and Kohnken, G. (1992). Helping witnesses to remember more: the cognitive interview. *Int. Dig. Hum. Behav. Sci. Law*, 1(2), 39–48.

Messina, N. (2000) Therapeutic Community Treatment Outcomes for Substance Abusers with Antisocial Personality Disorder. Doctoral dissertation. University of Maryland, College Park.

Messina, N., Wish, E., Hoffman, J., and Nemes, S. (2001). Diagnosing antisocial personality disorder among substance abusers: the SCID versus the MCMI-II. *Am. J. Drug Alcohol Abuse*, 27(4), 699–717.

Miller, M.M. and Potter-Efron, R.T. (1989). Aggression and violence associated with substance abuse. *J. Chem. Dependency Treat.*, 3(1), 1–36.

Milne R. and Bull, R. (1999). *Investigative Interviewing: Psychology and Practice.* New York: John Wiley & Sons.

Mistretta v. U.S., 488 U.S. 361, 396 (1989).

Monahan, J. (1981). *Predicting Violent Behavior: An Assessment of Clinical Techniques*. Beverly Hills, CA: Sage.

Montoya, A.G., Sorrentino, R., Lukas, S., and Price, B.H. (2002). Long-term neuropsychiatric consequences of "ecstasy" (MDMA): a review. *Harvard Rev. Psychiatr.*, 10, 212–220.

Morey, L.C. (1999). Personality Assessment Inventory. In M.E. Maruish, Ed., *The Use of Psychological Testing for Treatment Planning and Outcomes Assessment*, 2nd ed. Mahwah, NJ: Lawrence Erlbaum Associates, 1083–1121.

Morse, S.J. (2002). Uncontrollable urges and irrational people. *Va. Law Rev.*, in press.

Moston, S., Stephenson, G.M., and Williamson, J. (1992). The effects of case characteristics on suspect behavior during police questioning. *Br. J. Criminol.*, 32, 23–40.

Mount, M. and Perlini, A.H. (1995). The effects of source credibility and question working on witness recall: a case of the emperor's clothes. Paper presented at the 103rd Annual Convention of the American Psychological Association, New York.

Mulvey, E. and Lidz, C. (1985). Back to basics: a critical analysis of dangerousness research in a new legal environment. *Law Hum. Behav.*, 9, 209–218.

Mulvey, E. and Lidz, C. (1995). Conditional prediction: a model for research on dangerousness to others in a new era. *Int. J. Law Psychiatr.*, 18, 129–143.

National Institute on Drug Abuse (1991–1994). Final Report: Ice and Other Methamphetamines Use: an Exploratory Study. NIDA, summary and pp. 22, 125.

National Institute on Drug Abuse (1999). Methamphetamine Abuse Alert. *NIDA Notes*, 13(6).

National Institutes of Health (1998). Consensus Statement: Diagnosis and Treatment of Attention Deficit Hyperactivity Disorder. Available at consensus.nih.gov/cons/110/110_statement.htm#5_4._what.

O'Connor, B. and Kraus, D. (2001). Legal update. New developments in Rule 702. *Am. Psychol. Law Soc. News*, 21(1), 1–4, 18.

Ohio Revised Code, Section 2929.12 (d) (4).

Parker, S. and Block, M.K. (2001). The limits of federal criminal sentencing policy; or, confessions of two reformed reformers. *George Mason Law Rev.*, 9, 1001–1125.

Pirolli, P.J. and Mitterer, J.O. (1984). The effect of leading questions on prior memory: evidence for the coexistence of inconsistent memory traces. *Can. J. Psychol.*, 38(1), 135–141.

Quinsey, V.L., Harris, G.T., Rice, N.E., and Cormier, C.A. (1998). *Violent Offenders: Appraising and Managing Risk*. Washington, D.C.: American Psychological Association.

Reitman, A. (1998). Social psychology of false confessions: Bern's early contribution. *Am. Psychol.*, 53(3), 320–321.

Rice, M.E., Quinsey, V.L., and Harris, G.T. (1991). Sexual recidivism among child molesters released from a maximum security psychiatric institution. *J. Consulting Clin. Psychol.*, 59, 381–386.

Ritzler, B., Erard, R., and Pettigrew, G. (2002). Protecting the integrity of Rorschach expert witnesses: a reply to Grove and Barden (1999) re: the admissibility of testimony under *Daubert/Kumho* analyses. *Psychol. Public Policy Law*, 8(2), 201–215.

Ritzler, B., Erard, R., and Pettigrew, G. (2002). A final reply to Grove and Barden: the relevance of the Rorschach Comprehensive System for expert testimony. *Psychol. Public Policy Law*, 8(2), 235–246.

Rogers, R., Ed. (1997). *Clinical Assessment of Malingering and Deception.* New York: Guilford Press.

Rogers, R. and Wettstein, R.M. (1977). Drug-assisted interviews to detect malingering and deception. In R. Rogers. Ed., *Clinical Assessment of Malingering and Deception.* New York: Guilford Press.

Ruback, R.B. and Wroblewski, J. (2001). The federal sentencing guidelines: psychological and policy reasons for simplification. *Psychol. Public Policy Law*, 7(4), 739–775.

Saks, S., Saks, J., DeLeon, G., Bernhardt, A., and Staines, G. (1998). Modified therapeutic community for mentally ill chemical abusers: background, influences, program description, preliminary findings. *Substance Use Misuse*, 32, 1217–1259.

Sangiacomo, M. (2002). 3 dead infants, 30 years, no answers. *The Plain Dealer*, February 10, pp. B1, B3.

Saterfield v. Saterfield, 2001 Ohio App. LEXIS 2592, 6/13/01.

Schinka, J.A. (1995). Personality Assessment Inventory scale characteristics and factor structure in the assessment of alcohol dependency. *J. Personality Assess.*, 64(1), 101–111.

Sewer, J. (2002). Drug makers target farm storage tanks. *The Daily Record*, February 16, pp. A1, A2.

Shapiro, D. (1999). Legal milestones. *Bull. Am. Acad. Forensic Psychol.*, 20(1), 3, 17–21.

Snyder, A.G. (1998). The Neurocognitive Functioning of Dually Diagnosed Patients with Schizophrenia and a Substance Abuse Disorder. Doctoral dissertation. University of Houston.

State ex rel, Wright v. Ohio Adult Parole Authority, 75 Ohio State 3d 82, 661 NE 20 728 (1996).

State v. Burkholder, 1205 3d 205, 120BR 269, 466 NE 2d 176 (1984).

State v. Callahan, 2001 Ohio App. LEXIS 4633 (October 17, 2001).

State v. Cates, 2000 Ohio App. LEXIS 5387, 11/21/00.

State v. Cossin, 110 Ohio App. 3d79673 N.E. 2d 647 (1996).

State v. Gough, 2001 Ohio App. LEXIS 3331, 7/23/01.

State v. Hawkins, 120 Ohio App. 3d277 697 N.E. 2d 1045, 1997.

State v. Hughbanks, 1999 Ohio App. LEXIS 5789, 12/3/99.

State v. Hurd, 86 N.J. 525, 432 A.2d 86 (1981).

State v. Lewis, 1999 Ohio App. LEXIS 5485, 11/19/99.

State v. McNamee, 139 Ohio App. 3d 875745.n.2d 1147, 11/9/00.

State v. Perry, 1997 Ohio App. LEXIS 4309, 9/15/97.

State v. Ridgeway, 2001 Ohio App. 6057 LEXIS 6057, 11/21/01.

State v. Robinette, 80 Ohio St. 3d 234 685 N. 2d 762, 5/13/98.

State v. Signs, 1998 Ohio App. LEXIS 5468, 11/20/98.

State v. Trumbull, 1968 Ohio App. LEXIS 4268, 9/17/98.

State v. Wise, 1998 Ohio App. LEXIS 5121, 10/1/98.

Tobin, M. (2001). Dance-club drug spreads to the suburbs. *The Plain Dealer*, August 15, pp. A1, A8.

U.S. Drug Enforcement Administration Briefs and Background, Drug and Drug Abuse, State Factsheet, Hawaii. Available at www.usdoj.gov/dea/pubs/states/hawaii.html.

U.S. Sentencing Commission (2001). *Federal Sentencing Guidelines Manual*, 2001 ed.. The West Group, Washington, D.C.

United States v. Timothy J. Cline, 2001 U. S. Dist. LEXIS 12977.

United States v. Thomas Conne James, 257 F.3d 1173, 2001 U.S. App. LEXIS 15938.

United States v. Jaime Galvan Morales and Octavio Alvarez Ruelas, 252 F. 3d 1070, 2001 U.S. App. LEXIS 11836.

United States v. Pineda, 981 F.2d 569 (1st Cir. 1992).

United States of America v. Rafael Victor Torres Andrade, U.S. 10th Circuit Court of Appeals, 988100 (08/10/99).

Vogt, A.S. (2001). Comment: the mess left behind: regulating the cleanup of former methamphetamine laboratories. *Idaho Law Rev.*, 38, 251–290.

Wadler, G.I. (1994). Drug use update. *Med. Clin. North Am.*, 78(2), 439–455.

Weisgram v. Marley Co., 68 L.W. 4122 (February 2, 2000)

Weiss, N.L. (1998). Prevalence and Impact of Psychiatric Co-morbidity in Opiate Addicts. Doctoral dissertation. Yeshiva University, Los Angeles.

White, L.J. (1996). Review of the Personality Assessment Inventory (PAI): a new psychological test for clinical and forensic assessment. *Aust. Psychol.*, 31(1), 38–39.

Wright v. Ohio. Adult Parole Authority, 75 0s3d 82 661 N.E. 2d728 (1996).

Zakzanis, K.K. and Young, D.A. (2001). Memory impairment in abstinent MDMA ("ecstasy") users: a longitudinal investigation. *Neurology*, 56(7), 966–969.

Zickler, P. (2002). Methamphetamine abuse linked to impaired cognitive and motor skills despite recovery of dopamine transporters. *NIDA Notes*, 17(1), 1, 6.

Zimbardo, P., Haney, C., Banks, W., and Jaffe, D. (1972). The Psychology of Imprisonment: Privation, Power, and Pathology. Unpublished manuscript, Stanford University, Stanford, CA.

GLOSSARY

A

A posteriori: "From the effect to the cause"; from what comes after. Denotes an argument based on experience or observation.

A priori: "From the cause to the effect"; from what goes before. Denotes an argument that posits a general principle or admitted truth as a cause and deduces from it the effect that must necessarily follow.

Ab initio: "From the first act"; from the beginning, referring to the validity of statutes and so forth. In contrast to *ex post facto*.

Abnormal: Maladaptive behavior detrimental to the individual and/or the group.

Abrogate: To cancel annul or destroy; to repeal a former law by a legislative act or by usage.

Absence seizures: Petit mal seizures in children, shown by brief altered states of consciousness.

Absolute refractory phase: A period of complete unresponsiveness.

Acalculia: Impaired calculation abilities, more often associated with left parietal or occipital lesions.

Acapnia: A marked diminution in the amount of carbon dioxide in the blood.

Acceptance: An agreement to the act or proposal of another person.

Acetone bodies: Acetoacetic acid, β-hydroxybutyric acid, and acetone; found in blood and urine in increased amounts whenever too much fat in proportion to carbohydrate is being oxidized. Also called ketone bodies.

Acetylcholine (ACh): One of the best-known synaptic transmitters. Acetylcholine acts as an excitatory transmitter at synapses between motor nerves and skeletal muscles but as an inhibitory transmitter between vagus nerve and heart muscle.

Acetylcholinesterase (AChE): An enzyme that inactivates the neurotransmitter acetylcholine, thus halting its effects.

Achromatopsia: Impaired perception of colors due to cerebral dysfunction. Can be hemianopic or involve both visual fields.

Acidosis: Diminution in the reserve supply of fixed bases (especially sodium) in the blood.

Acquit: To set free or release from an obligation, burden, or accusation; to certify legally the innocence of a person charged with a crime.

Action: A formal proceeding or complaint brought within the jurisdiction of a court to enforce any right.

Action potential: Nerve impulse that flows along the membrane of the neuron. The membrane is receptive to potassium ions in the resting state and sodium ions when excited. The reversal in permeability causes the impulse.

Actuarial approach: Application of probability statistics to human behavior, as in insurance.

***Actus reus*:** "Guilty act"; a wrongful act. As opposed to guilty, *mens rea*.

Acute alcohol hallucinosis: State of alcoholic intoxication characterized by hallucinations.

Acute paranoid disorder: Psychoses characterized by transient and changeable paranoid delusions, usually related to an identifiable stressor and transient in nature.

Acute post-traumatic stress disorder: Disorder in which symptoms develop within 6 months of an extremely traumatic experience instead of entering the recovery state.

***Ad hoc*:** "For this"; for a special purpose or particular action.

Adaptation: Adjustment to a stimulus; also used to denote changes in the retina on exposure to different intensities of light. A progressive loss of receptor sensitivity as stimulation is maintained.

Adenohypophysis: *See* Anterior pituitary.

Glossary

Adequate stimulus: The type of stimulus for which a given sense organ is particularly adapted (e.g., light energy for photoreceptors).

Adhesion: Abnormal union of two surfaces as a result of inflammation.

Adipsia: A condition in which an individual refuses to drink.

Adjustment disorder with depressed mood: Moderately severe affective disorder behaviorally identical to a dysthymic disorder or depressed phase of a cyclothymic disorder but having an identifiable, though not severe, psychosocial stressor occurring within 3 months prior to the onset of depression.

Admissible evidence: Evidence that can be received by the court or judge.

Adventitia: The outermost covering of a structure that does not form an integral part of it.

Adversarial system: A legal system in which opposing parties contend against each other by presenting arguments and information in the interest of their clients. The judge acts as a decision maker. In contrast to the inquisitorial system.

Adversary process: Having two opposing parties. In contrast to an *ex parte* proceeding.

Adverse party: A person whose interests are opposed to the interests of another party to an action.

Adverse witness: A witness who gives evidence that is prejudicial to the party examining the witness at the time. Commonly refers to a witness whose testimony is prejudicial to the party that called the witness.

Afferent fibers/traits: Data going toward the brain through neuronal pathways from the peripheral area of the central nervous system.

Affidavit: A written or printed statement of fact, made voluntarily, signed and sworn before a person having the authority to administer such an oath (e.g., a notary public).

After potentials: Positive and negative changes of membrane potential that may follow a nerve impulse.

Aggregation theory: Proposed by Halstead, this theory held that discrete sensory areas within the cortex were joined by a multitude of cortical connections. The aggregation produces an integration of cortical function.

Aggression: Behavior aimed at hurting or destroying someone or something.

Agitation: Marked restlessness and psychomotor excitement.

Agnosia: Defect in object recognition not due to primary sensory system dysfunction.

Agrammatism: Speech deficits characterized by language abbreviation such as omission of articles, prepositions, and inflectional forms. Language is essentially reduced to substantives.

Agraphia: Disturbances in writing skills (not motor execution). Usually seen with aphasia.

Akathisia: A general motor restlessness together with elevated inner tension, subjectively reported by the patient.

Akinesia: Inability to move due to brain dysfunction.

Alarm and mobilization reaction: First stage of the general adaptation syndrome, characterized by the mobilization of defenses to cope with a stressful situation.

Albuminuria: Presence of albumin in the urine.

Alcoholic intoxication: State reached when alcohol content of the blood reaches or exceeds a legally prescribed level (0.08 to 0.1% or above in many jurisdictions).

Alcoholism: Dependence on alcohol to the extent that it seriously interferes with life adjustment.

Aldosterone: A mineralocorticoid hormone that helps maintain homeostasis in the concentrations of ions in blood and extracellular fluid.

Alexia: Inability to read due to brain dysfunction. Refers to total loss of ability to read due to a brain lesion, typically located in the posterior cerebral cortex.

Alexia without agraphia: Inability to read in the absence of other language deficit.

Alien hand syndrome: Also termed the "Dr. Strangelove effect," intermanual conflict between the two hands is seen, with patients learning to use their "obedient" hand to control the alien hand. Contralateral supplementary motor area (SMA) and corpus collosum lesions have been implicated.

Alkalosis: Increased bicarbonate content of the blood; may be the result of ingesting large amounts of sodium bicarbonate, prolonged vomiting with loss of hydrochloric acid, or hyperventilation.

Glossary

All-or-none: Refers to the fact that the amplitude of the nerve impulse is independent of stimulus magnitude. Stimuli above a certain threshold produce nerve impulses of identical magnitude (although they may vary in frequency); stimuli below this threshold do not produce nerve impulses.

Allesthesia: Sensation of being touched on the side ipsilateral to a lesion when contralateral stimulation was, in fact, presented.

Alpha motoneurons: Motoneurons that control the main contractile fibers (extrafusal fibers) of a muscle.

Alpha rhythm: A brain potential that occurs during relaxed wakefulness, especially at the back of the head; frequency 8 to 12 Hz.

Alzheimer's disease (AD): A degenerative disease characterized by the presence of neurofibrillary tangles and senile plaques. The disease is progressive in that it starts with memory and affect problems, then goes on to speech and motor problems, and eventually to an immobile and confused bedridden status. The disease lasts from 1 to 15 years.

Amblyopia: Reduced visual acuity not caused by optical or retinal impairment.

Amenorrhea: The absence of the menses.

Amicus curiae: "Friend of the court." A person who petitions the court for permission to provide information to the court on a matter of law that is in doubt, or one who is not a party to a lawsuit but who is allowed to introduce evidence, argument, or authority to protect his or her interests.

Amnestic syndrome: Inability to remember events more than a few minutes after they have occurred coupled with the ability to recall the recent and remote part.

Amoeboid movement: Movement of a cell by extending from its surface processes of protoplasm (pseudopodia) toward which the rest of the cell flows.

Amorphosynthesis: Loss of ability to synthesize more than a few properties of a stimulus. Multiple sensory stimuli cannot be simultaneously processed. Ascribed to parietal lobe dysfunction. Damage to part of one sensory system causing an inequality in the overall cerebral system. The hemisphere receiving the decreased stimulation due to damage now needs increased input to balance the level of awareness.

Amorphous: Without definite shape or visible differentiation in structure; not crystalline.

Ampulla: A saccular dilation of a canal. An enlarged region of each semicircular canal that contains the receptor cells (hair cells) of the vestibular system.

Amusia: A temporal lobe deficit associated with inability or reduced skill in perception of tonal patterns, individual tones, singing or humming to a rhythmical pattern, or even enjoying music.

Amygdala: A structure of a limbic system associated with flight/fight and other primitive responses. Located at the base of the temporal lobe. A group of nuclei in the medial anterior part of the temporal lobe.

Analgesia: Loss of sensitivity to pain.

Anaphylactic: Increasing the susceptibility to the action of any foreign protein introduced into the body; decreasing immunity.

Anarithmetria: Impaired primary calculation skills due to brain damage. Left hemisphere lesions are implicated.

Anastomose: To open one into the other; used in connection with blood vessels, lymphatics, and nerves.

Anergia: Decreased or absent motivation or drive.

Anesthesia: Loss of sensation.

Aneurysm: A dilation or bulging of a blood vessel that fills with blood. A sac formed by the dilation of the walls of an artery and filled with blood.

Angiogram: A technique for examining brain structure in intact humans by taking radiographic images after special dyes are injected into cerebral blood vessels. Inferences about adjacent tissue can be made by examining the outline of the principal blood vessels.

Angiography: Radiography of the head subsequent to injection of a radiopaque contrast medium into a major artery. Designed to enhance images of the cerebral vasculature.

Angiotensin II: A substance produced in the blood by the action of renin; may be involved in control of thirst.

Angular gyros: A cortical convolution on the parietal lobe, associated with speech functions.

Anions: Negatively charged ions, such as protein and chloride ions.

Anomia: Inability to name objects due to brain dysfunction.

Anomic aphasia: A fluent aphasia characterized by difficulty in naming objects or words. Comprehension and articulation may be unimpaired.

Anorexic: Lacking in appetite for food.

Anosmia: Absence of the sense of smell.

Anosodiaphoria: Unconcern over, but admission of an actual neurological impairment. *See also* Anton's syndrome.

Anosognosia: Denial of those affected with neglect syndrome that their paretic extremity belongs to them. Total ignorance with denial of obvious disability. Examples include Anton's syndrome with denial of blindness, and denial of amputation, amnesia, and hemiplegia. Usually accompanied by confusion or clouding of awareness.

Anterior aphasias: Primarily indicating a left frontal lesion, these include Broca's aphasia, transcortical motor aphasia, and supplementary motor area (SMA) disturbance.

Anterior cerebral artery (ACA): One of the two major vascular networks of the frontal lobes, the ACA and its branches feed the medial aspects of the anterior portion of the brain.

Anterior pituitary: The front lobe of the pituitary gland, which secretes tropic hormones; also called adenohypophysis.

Anterograde amnesia: Inability to recall life events from the time of a previous trauma or condition. Inability to learn and poor short-term memory are associated features.

Anterograde degeneration: Loss of the distal portion of the axon resulting from injury to the axon; also called Wallerian degeneration.

Antidiuretic hormone (ADH): A hormone from the posterior pituitary that controls the removal of water from blood by the kidneys; also called vasopressin.

Antigen: Any substance that, when introduced into the blood or the tissues, incites the formation of antibodies, or reacts with them.

Anton's syndrome: *See also* Anosognosia. Adamant denial of blindness, often associated with bilateral posterior cerebral vascular accident (CVA).

Antrom: A cavity, or chamber, especially one within a bone, such as a sinus; the pyloric end of the stomach.

Apathetico-akinetico-abulic behavior: Produced by massive damage to the prefrontal areas, among others. This syndrome is characterized by low drive and reduced motor output. Ongoing behavior may be disorganized. The effector aspect of action seems to be impaired in what has been termed the "pathological inertia of existing stereotypes."

Aperture: An opening or orifice.

Aphagia: Refusal to eat, often related to damage to the lateral hypothalamus.

Aphasia: Impairment in language understanding and/or production due to brain injury.

Aphemia: A poorly articulated, slow, hypophonic, breathy speech with no syntax deficits. Usually follows initial mutism and is associated with Broca's area lesions, or a subcortical undercutting of Area 44.

Apoplexy: A sudden loss of consciousness, followed by paralysis resulting from cerebral hemorrhage, or blocking of an artery of the brain by an embolus or a thrombus.

Appellant: The party who appeals a decision from one court or jurisdiction to another.

Appellate court: A court having jurisdiction of appeal and review.

Appellee: The party against whom an appeal is taken in a cause; the party who has an interest opposed to the setting aside or reversing of a judgment.

Apperceptive visual agnosia: The inability to synthesize or integrate visual input. Awareness of discrete parts may be intact. Inability to perceive meaning in or visually recognize objects, due to cerebral dysfunction, most likely in posterior areas. Patients act blind but can avoid obstacles, indicating preserved ability to see.

Apraxia: Refers to impaired goal-directed motor behavior in individuals with unimpaired comprehension and primary motor skills (e.g., coordination, strength).

Apraxia of speech: Known also as verbal apraxia or Broca's aphasia. Speech movement/articulation problems may include (1) articulation errors; (2) phoneme substitution; (3) greater latency of response; (4) greater trouble with initial than subsequent phonemes; (5) no major vocal musculature problems; (6) sparse output; (7) poor melody; and (8) articulation with much effort.

Apraxic agraphia: Deficit in forming graphemes when writing to dictation or spontaneously. Lesions are in the parietal lobe contralateral to the dominant (writing) hand.

Apraxic agraphia without apraxia: Preserved oral spelling with illegible graphemes in spontaneous and dictated writing. Normal praxis is apparent, including the ability to hold and use a writing instrument. Associated with parietal lobe lesions.

Glossary

Aprosodias: Deficits in the comprehension and expression of affect and emotion, traditionally associated with right hemisphere dysfunction.

Aqueduct: A canal for the conduction of a liquid; the cerebral aqueduct of Sylvius connects the third and fourth ventricles of the brain.

Arachnoid space: Allows for cerebrospinal fluid to move about the cerebrum. Filled with fibroid matter and considered one of the three layers of the meninges.

Arbitration: A method of resolving a dispute by using an impartial third party by whose decision both parties agree in advance to abide.

Arteriovenous malformation (AVM): Involving the frontal lobe preferentially and focally, AVMs are usually unrecognized until one or more episodes have occurred. Subsequent attacks by AVM hemorrhage widens the area of deficit.

Articulate: To join together so as to permit motion between parts; enunciation in words and sentences. Divided into joints.

Asphyxia: Unconsciousness owing to interference with the oxygenation of the blood.

Assertiveness training: A behavior therapy technique for helping individuals become more self-assertive in interpersonal relationships.

Association areas: Part of the cortex next to the motor or sensory cortex, involving an overlap of functions. Allows for integration of data; damage causes patterned rather than specific deficits.

Associative visual agnosia: Inability to recognize objects visually with intact ability to copy, draw, or match to sample.

Astereognosis: Inability to identify objects placed by touch in spite of intact appreciation of tactile sensation. Also called tactile agnosia.

Asthenia: Weakness.

Astrocyte: A star-shaped glial cell with numerous processes or extensions that run in all directions. Their extensions provide structural support for the brain and may isolate receptive surfaces.

Astrocytoma: Neoplastic disease arising from the astrocyte cells. Usually unencapsulated, intracerebral, and fatal.

Ataxia: Muscular coordination and balance problems due to brain dysfunction. A loss of the power of muscular coordination. Impairment in the direction, extent, and rate of muscular movement; often due to cerebellar pathology.

Athetosis: Slow, involuntary, twisting movements of the arms and legs. May occur either during movement or when at rest. Associated with lesions of the cortex and subcortex (especially globus pallidus and thalamus).

Atresia: Congenital absence, or pathologic closure, of a normal opening or passage.

Atrophy: A wasting, or diminution, in the size of a part of the body or brain.

Atropine: An alkaloid obtained from atropa belladonna; it inhibits the action of the parasympathetic division of the autonomic system.

Attention deficit disorder: Maladaptive behavior in children characterized by impulsivity, excessive motor activity, and inability to focus attention for appropriate periods of time; also called hyperactive syndrome or hyperkinetic reaction.

Attest: To bear witness to; to affirm as true or genuine.

Attribution theory: The theory of social psychology in which people explain causes of the behavior of others based on unseen or unrecognized qualities in themselves.

Auditory affective agnosia: Impaired ability to recognize or comprehend affectively intoned speech due to a cerebral disorder.

Auditory agnosia: Impaired hearing due to cerebral dysfunction with intact receptive abilities, as measured by audiometry or other means.

Auditory cortex: A region of the temporal lobe that receives input from the medial geniculate nucleus.

Auditory sound agnosia: Impaired ability to recognize nonspeech sounds due to cerebral dysfunction.

Auscultation: The act of listening for sounds within the body; employed as a diagnostic method.

Automated assessment: Psychological test interpretation by electronic or mechanical means.

Automatism: Producing without effort or delay material learned by rote in childhood for a given temporal period (e.g., alphabet, number series). Errors reflect attention, disturbances; nonacute condition–related errors may indicate significant memory dysfunction.

Autonomic nervous system: Part of the peripheral nervous system that supplies neural connections to glands and to smooth muscles of internal organs. Composed of two divisions (sympathetic and parasympathetic) that act in opposite fashions.

Autosome: Any ordinary paired chromosome as distinguished from a sex chromosome.

Autotopagnosia: Disorientation of personal space. Associated with left frontal aphasic signs. The subject is typically assessed for ability to touch, name, or imitate the examiner in touching body parts. Associated with parietal lobe damage.

Axon hillock: A cone-shaped area from which the axon originates out of the cell body Depolarization must reach a critical threshold here for the neuron to transmit a nerve impulse.

Axoplasmic streaming: The process that transports materials synthesized in the cell body to distant regions in the dendrites and axons.

Azygos: An unpaired anatomic structure; the azygos vein arises from the right ascending lumbar vein and empties into the superior vena cava.

B

Bailiff: An officer or attendant of the court who has charge of a court session in matters such as keeping order and having custody of the jury and of prisoners while in court.

Balint's syndrome: A syndrome consisting of (1) occulomotor apraxia, of focus from a near to a distant stimulus; (2) optic ataxia, shown by impaired visually guided movements; and (3) impaired visual attention in the absence of general attentional deficits, with initial random gaze until a stimulus is fixated upon.

Ballism: Uncontrollable violent tossing of the limbs due to basal ganglia dysfunction.

Ballistic: Classes of rapid muscular movements thought to be organized or programmed by the cerebellum. Contrast to ramp.

Bar: The entire body of attorneys, or the collective members of the legal profession.

Basal ganglia: Forebrain nuclei including those in the amygdala, caudate nucleus, claustrum, globus pallidus, and putamen. A group of forebrain nuclei found deep within the cerebral hemispheres.

Bases: Components of a DNA or RNA molecule. DNA contains four bases (adenine, thymine, cytosine, and guanine), a pair of which forms each rung of the molecule. The order of these bases determines the genetic information of a DNA molecule.

Basic neuroglial compartment: A level of brain organization that includes a single nerve cell with all its synaptic endings, associated glial cells surrounding extracellular space, and vascular elements.

Basilar artery: An artery formed by the fusion of the vertebral arteries; its branches supply blood to the brain stem and to posterior portions of the cerebral hemispheres.

Basilar membrane: A membrane in the cochlea containing the principal structures involved in auditory transduction.

Behavioral teratology: Impairments in behavior produced by early exposure to toxic substances.

Bench: A seat of judgment for the administration of justice; the seat occupied by the judge in court; the aggregate of the judges that comprise the court.

Berry aneurysm: A small sac formed by the dilation of the wall of a cerebral artery. The anterior portion of the circle of Willis is the site of about 90% of berry aneurysms.

Bifurcated trial: A two-phase trial in which issues are tried separately, e.g., guilt is determined in the first phase and punishment in the second, or in sanity cases, guilt is determined in the first phase and sanity in the second.

Bill of particulars: A written statement setting forth the demands for which a legal action is brought. Designed to inform the defendant of the specific information regarding the cause of action stated in the complaint.

Binocular disparity: The slight difference between the views from the two eyes, important in depth perception.

Bipolar neurons: Nerve cells with a single dendrite at one end of the nerve cell and a single axon at the other end. Found in some vertebrate sensory systems.

Bitemporal hemianopsia: Optic chiasm damage resulting in visual field loss in both temporal (as opposed to nasal) areas.

Blind spot: A place through which blood vessels enter the retina. Because there are no receptors in this region, light striking it cannot be seen.

Blindsight: Denial of recognition in the face of previous correct recognition and stimulus responses.

Blood–brain barrier: The mechanisms that make the movement of substances from capillaries into brain cells more difficult than exchanges in other body organs, thus affording the brain a greater protection from exposure to some substances found in the blood.

Glossary

Body schema: Body image.

Bolus: A rounded mass of soft consistency.

Bona: Good or virtuous.

Bradycardia: Abnormal slowness of the heart or pulse.

Bradykinesia: Motor slowing.

Brain stem: Thalamus, hypothalamus, ganglia, midbrain, hindbrain, and associated structures.

Brain stem reticular formation: Part of the brain stem involved in arousal.

Brandeis brief: A form of appellate brief that includes social science principles along with legal arguments. Takes its name from late Supreme Court Associate Justice Louis D. Brandeis, who used such briefs.

Brief: A written statement prepared by the attorney arguing a case in court, including a table of relevant cases, a summary of issues and facts, and an argument of law as it supports a litigant's position.

Broca's aphasia: An expressive speech disorder with relatively intact auditory comprehension. A nonfluent speech is noticed that is slow, labored, dysarthric, incomplete, and concrete. Agrammatism consists of missing grammatical words and inflectional endings. Considered an anterior aphasia.

Broca's area: An area in the frontal region of the left hemisphere involved in the production of speech.

Brown–Peterson distractor technique: Counting backward by twos or threes upon presentation of a verbal or nonverbal stimulus. Rehearsal is prevented by the counting.

Bruit: A sound or murmur heard in auscultation, especially an abnormal one.

Buccolinguofacial apraxia: An oral apraxia affecting voluntary movements of the larynx, pharynx, tongue, lips, and related suborgans in which simple, automatic movements are intact. Commanded tasks may yield deficits (e.g., no swallowing, laughing) in the presence of noncommanded, contextual responses (e.g., swallowing food after eating, smiling). Deficit in performing voluntary buccofacial motor activities (e.g., chewing, swallowing, raising eyebrows) with intact ability to perform reflexive movements with the same muscle groups.

Buffer: Any substance that tends to lessen the change in hydrogen ion concentration, which otherwise would be produced by adding acids or bases.

Burden of proof: In the law of evidence, the duty of a party to affirmatively prove a fact in dispute. The obligation of a party to convince the trier of fact as to the truth of a claim by establishing by evidence a required degree of belief concerning a fact. In civil cases, proof must be by a preponderance of the evidence. In criminal cases, all crime elements must be proved by the government beyond a reasonable doubt. In some equity issues and more recent decisions of the Supreme Court, the standard of proof is clear and convincing evidence.

C

Calcitonin: A hormone released by the thyroid gland.

Calculus: A stone formed in any portion of the body.

Calorie: A unit of heat. A small calorie (cal.) is the standard unit and is the amount of heat required to raise 1 g of water from 15 to 16°C. The large calorie (Cal.) is used in metabolism and is the amount of heat required to raise 1 kg of water from 15 to 16°C.

Canaliculus: A small canal or channel; in bone, minute channels connect with each lacuna.

Capgras syndrome: Involves the reduplication of relatives, friends, possessions, and the like, and is often viewed as a psychiatric, as opposed to neurological, problem. The target person, almost always a close relative, is considered an imposter.

Carcinoma: A malignant tumor or cancer; a new growth made up of epithelial cells, tending to infiltrate and give rise to metastases.

Case law: The sum of reported cases forming a body of law. The law of a certain subject as evidenced or formed by the adjudged case, as opposed to statutes or other sources of law.

Catabolism: Reactions in a plant or animal that result in the degradation, or exudation, of molecules.

Catalysis: Change in the speed of a reaction produced by the presence of a substance that does not form part of the final product.

Catalyst: Any substance that brings about catalysis.

Cataract: A loss of transparency of the crystalline lens of the eye or of its capsule.

Glossary

Catastrophic reaction: Intensely negative but temporary emotional reaction, associated with left hemisphere lesions. Often occurs when subjects are informed of their limitations or shortcomings, in response to task demands. A heightened sensitivity to one's limitations.

Caudal: An anatomical term meaning toward the tail end. Opposed to rostral.

Caudate nucleus: One of the basal ganglia with a long extension or tail.

Cell differentiation: The prenatal stage in which neuroblasts acquire the distinctive appearance of cells characteristic of a region of the nervous system.

Cell proliferation: The production of nerve cells.

Cellular fluid: *See* Intercellular fluid.

Central deafness: Hearing impairments related to lesions in auditory pathways or centers, including sites in the brain stem, thalamus, or cortex.

Central nervous system (CNS): The portion of the nervous system that includes the brain and the spinal cord.

Central sulcus: Known also as the fissure of Rolando, this sulcus divides the anterior from the posterior areas of the brain (frontal from parietal).

Cephalic: An anatomical term referring to the head end. Also called rostral.

Cerebellar cortex: The outer surface of the cerebellum.

Cerebellar fits: Not really seizures, these movements consist of periods of decerebrate rigidity. Associated with large midline cerebellar lesions.

Cerebellar syndrome: Due to a lesion in the cerebellum, ambulation is unsteady with side-to-side swaying. Equilibrium is adversely affected.

Cerebellum: A structure located at the back of the brain, dorsal to the pons; it is involved in the central regulation of movement.

Cerebral contusion: A brain bruise. Refers to superficial damage to gyri or other crests of the cortical convolutions.

Cerebral cortex: The outer bark or cortex of the cerebral hemispheres, which consists largely of nerve cell bodies and their branches.

Cerebral hemispheres: The right and left halves of the forebrain.

Cerebrospinal fluid: The fluid filling the cerebral ventricles.

Certiorari: "To be informed of." An action or writ issued by a superior court requiring an inferior court to produce a certified record of a particular case tried by the latter. The purpose of this action is to enable the higher court to inspect the proceedings to determine whether or not there were any irregularities. Most commonly used by the U.S. Supreme Court as a discretionary device to choose the cases it wishes to hear.

Cerveau isole: An animal with the nervous system transected at the upper level of the midbrain (between the inferior and superior colliculus). Contrast with the encephale isole.

Cervical: Pertaining to the neck region.

Chalazion: A small tumor of the eyelid; formed by the distention of a meibomian gland with secretion.

Character Disorder: *See* Personality disorder.

Cheiro-oral: Refers to the simultaneous twitching of the thumb and same-sided corner of the mouth. Occurs in epilepsy due to close proximity of motor execution zones for these body parts (i.e., the motor homonculus has its thumb in its mouth).

Chiasma: A crossing; specifically, the crossing of the optic nerve fibers from the medial halves of the retinae.

Child abuse: The infliction of physical damage upon a child by parents or other adults.

Child advocacy: A movement concerned with protecting the rights and ensuring the well-being of children.

Chlorpromazine: An antipsychotic drug, one of the class of phenothiazines.

Cholinergic: Refers to cells that use acetylcholine as their synaptic transmitter.

Chorda tympani: A portion of the facial nerve that serves as taste receptor in the anterior two-thirds of the tongue.

Choreic movements: Uncontrollable, brief, and forceful muscular movements related to basal ganglia dysfunction.

Chromidial substance: Pertaining to granules of extranuclear chromatin seen in the cytoplasm of a cell.

Chromosome: A body of chromatin in the cell nucleus that splits longitudinally as the cell divides, one half going to the nucleus of each of the daughter cells; the chromosomes transmit the hereditary characters.

Glossary

Ciliary: Relating to (1) any hairlike process, (2) the eyelashes, or (3) certain of the structures of the eyeball.

Cingulate bodies: Limbic system tissue above or superior to the corpus callosum.

Cingulum: A region of medial cerebral cortex lying dorsal to the corpus callosum. Also called cingulate cortex.

Circadian rhythms: Behavioral, biochemical, and physiological fluctuations during a 24-hour period.

Circle of Willis: A structure at the base of the brain formed by the joining of the carotid and basilar arteries.

Circumlocution: Often seen in fluent aphasia, the substitution of an incorrect word for another word. The substitution may itself demand a specific but unobtainable word, thus producing a convoluted output.

Circumventricular organs: Organs lying in the walls of the cerebral ventricles. These organs contain receptor sites that can be affected by substances in the cerebrospinal fluid.

Cistern: A closed space serving as a reservoir for fluid.

Civil: Of or pertaining to the state of the citizenry. Relates to an individual's private rights and remedies sought through civil action, in contrast to criminal proceedings.

Civil commitment: Procedure whereby an individual certified as mentally disordered can be hospitalized, either voluntarily or against the person's will.

Civil law: The body of law, concerned with civil or private rights and remedies, established by every particular municipality for itself; as opposed to the "law of nature."

Civil rights: The body of law pertaining to personal, natural rights that are guaranteed and protected by the Constitution, such as freedom of speech and press, freedom from discrimination.

Clarendon jury: In a procedure established by Henry II of England, at least 12 "good and lawful" men, reporting to the king's representative, were summoned as jurors to determine if a trial should be held and to decide actual innocence or guilt.

Clear and convincing: A standard of proof greater than preponderance but less rigorous than reasonable doubt. Proof that should leave the trier of fact with no reasonable doubt about the truth of the matters in issue.

Clear and present danger: A standard used to determine when one's First Amendment rights to freedom of speech and press may be curtailed. Pursuant to a doctrine in constitutional law, if necessary, government restrictions will be upheld to prevent grave and immediate danger to interests which government may lawfully protect.

Clinical neuropsychology: That which deals with the psychometric or other objective psychological methods in the assessment of higher cortical functions in humans.

Coactivation: A central nervous system control program that activates or inhibits the skeletal motoneurons at the same time as it alters the sensitivity of the muscle spindles.

Cochlea: A snail-shaped structure in the inner ear that contains the primary receptors for hearing.

Cochlear duct: One of the three principal canals running along the length of the cochlea.

Cochlear microphonic potential: An electrical potential produced by hair cells that accurately copies the acoustic wave form of the stimulus.

Cochlear nuclei: Brain stem nuclei that receive input from auditory hair cells and send output to the superior olivary complex.

Coenzyme: A nonprotein substance that is required for activity of an enzyme.

Cognitive dissonance: Condition existing when new information is contradictory to one's assumptions.

Collateral: Accompanying; running by the side of; not direct; secondary or accessory; a small side branch of an axon.

Colliculus: One of two pairs of structures on the dorsal midbrain. *See* Inferior colliculus, Superior colliculus.

Colloid: A state of subdivision of matter in which the individual particles are of submicroscopic size and consist either of large molecules, such as proteins, or aggregates of smaller molecules; the particles are not large enough to settle out under the influence of gravity.

Collusion: The making of an agreement between two or more persons with the purpose of defrauding another of his or her rights by the forms of law, or to obtain an object forbidden by law.

Coma: A state of profound unconsciousness from which one cannot be roused.

Coma vigil: Immobility and unresponsiveness with eyes open and moving, associated with posteromedial-inferior frontal and/or hypothalamic damage.

Common carotid arteries: Arteries that ascend the left and right sides of the neck. The branch that enters the brain is called the internal carotid artery.

Common law: The body of legal principles and rules of action that derives its authority from customs and general usage and rules of conduct existing among the people. In contrast to civil law. Originated in England.

Complaint: The original or initial charge by which a legal action is begun, naming a person by whom the offense was committed. In criminal law, a written statement containing the essential facts and legal theory on which the charge is based.

Complex cortical cells: Cells in the visual cortex that respond best to a bar of a particular width and direction anywhere within a particular area of the visual field.

Complex partial seizures: Epileptic seizures in which consciousness is altered (complex) and which are restricted or at least arise from a circumscribed area of the brain (partial).

***Compos mentis*:** Being sound of mind; mentally competent.

Compulsion: An irrational and repetitive impulse to perform some act.

Compulsive gambling: *See* Pathological gambling.

Compulsive personality: A personality disorder characterized by excessive concern with rules, order, efficiency, and work.

Computer assessment: Use of computers to obtain or interpret assessment data.

Computer axial tomography: A technique for examining brain structure in intact humans through a computer analysis of x-ray absorption at several positions around the head. This technique affords a virtual direct view of the brain.

Computer model: Use of computers to simulate psychological functioning.

Conciliation: The mode of adjusting and resolving a dispute through voluntary and unantagonistic settlement of the issues between opposing parties with a view toward avoiding litigation.

Concordance rates: Rates at which a diagnosis or a trait of one person is predictive of the same diagnosis or trait in relatives.

Conduct disorders: Childhood disorders marked by persistent acts of aggressive or antisocial behavior that may or may not be against the law.

Conduction aphasia: A constellation of behaviors produced by a lesion in the white matter fibers connecting the posterior/anterior portions of the brain (near the arcuate fasciculus). A severe repetition deficit is apparent relative to good auditory comprehension and expression of speech. A language disorder, involving intact comprehension but poor repetition of spoken language, related to damage of the pathways connecting Wernicke's area and Broca's area.

Cones: Receptor cells in the retina that are responsible for color vision. The three types of cones have somewhat different sensitivities to light of different wavelengths.

Confabulation: Production of bizarre, false, or unverifiable verbal/written responses, usually in association with amnesia. A close correlation exists between confabulatory tendencies and impairment in self-correction.

Congenital: Born with a person; existing at or before birth.

Consideration: The cause, price, or motivating factor that induces a party to enter into a contract.

Consolidation: A state of memory formation in which information in short-term or intermediate-term memory is transferred to long-term memory.

Conspiracy: A combination of two or more persons who propose to commit an unlawful or criminal act, or to commit a lawful act by criminal means.

Constructional disorders: Deficits in constructional tasks (e.g., drawing, assembling) in which the spatial form of the target object may be lost. Associated with pathology of the nondominant (nonspeech) hemisphere.

Contempt of court: An act or an omission that is calculated to obstruct or interfere with the orderly administration of justice or that is calculated to lessen the authority or dignity of the court.

Contingent negative variation (CNV): A slow event-related potential recorded from the scalp. It arises in the interval between a warning signal and a signal that directs action.

Contract: A binding agreement between two or more competent parties, based on mutual assent and made for a lawful purpose, which creates an obligation to do or not to do a specified thing.

Contralateral: Situated on, or pertaining to, the opposite side.

Glossary

Contrast sensitivity function (CSF): A psychophysical function determined by finding the contrast necessary for perceiving different spacings of dark and light bars. Used to measure spatial acuity of the visual system.

Contrecoup: Refers to the contusion (bruise) in the area opposite the point of impact (coup).

Conversion disorders: Neurotic condition in which symptoms of organic illness appear in the absence of any related organic pathology; previously called hysteria.

Coronal (plane): The plane dividing the body or brain into front and back parts. Also called frontal or transverse. The band of axons that connects the two cerebral hemispheres.

Corpus callosum: Intracerebral white matter connecting the right and left cerebral hemispheres.

Corpus delecti: The body or material substance of a crime that provides objective proof that a crime has been committed.

Corpus juris: A body of law. A term signifying a comprehensive book of several collections of law.

Cortical deafness: *See also* Cortical auditory disorder. Difficulty recognizing both verbal and nonverbal stimuli due to cerebral dysfunction. Most often associated with cardiovascular accident.

Corticotropin-releasing hormone (CRH): A releasing hormone from the hypothalamus that controls the daily rhythm of ACTH release.

Cortisol: A glucocorticoid hormone of the adrenal cortex.

Court martial: An *ad hoc* military court that is convened under the authority of government and the Uniform Code of Military Justice, that has penal and disciplinary jurisdiction in trying and punishing offenses committed by members of the armed forces. The type (e.g., general, summary, special) and composition vary according to the seriousness of offenses.

Cranial nerves: Originating from the brain, these are 12 pairs of nerves that transmit motor and/or sensory impulses to and from peripheral central nervous system sites. One of the three main subdivisions of the peripheral nervous system, composed of a set of pathways mainly concerned with sensory and motor systems associated with the head.

Cretinism: Reduced stature and mental retardation caused by thyroid deficiency.

Creutzfeldt–Jakob disease: A rare, transmittable (i.e., through a virus that has a 2-year incubation) dementia with a relatively short clinical course (9-month average). Similar to "mad cow" disease. Of cases, 10% may be inherited. Anxiety and memory loss first appear. Myoclonic jerking appears in conjunction with motor neurocerebellar, basal ganglion, or pyramidal tract lesions. Dementia with progressive rigidity and mutism are end-stage symptoms.

Criminal responsibility: Legal question of whether an individual should be permitted to use insanity as a defense after having committed some criminal act.

Cross-examination: The questioning of a witness during a trial, hearing, or deposition by the party opposing that which originally produced the witness to testify. Generally, the scope of cross-examination is limited to matters addressed in direct examination.

Crossed aphasia: Aphasic symptoms occurring, usually temporarily, in right-handed person with a right hemisphere lesion.

Cruel and unusual punishment: Punishment found to be unfair, shocking, or offensive to the ordinary person's reasonable sensitivity. The Eighth Amendment states that "excessive bail shall not be required nor excessive fines imposed nor cruel and unusual punishment inflicted."

Crystalloid: A body that, in solution, can pass through an animal membrane, as distinguished from a colloid, which does not have this property.

Culpable: Blame worthy; deserving of moral blame. Addresses fault rather than guilt.

Curare: A highly toxic extract that paralyzes muscle; it acts on the motor end plates.

Custody: The caring for, keeping, guarding, preserving of a thing or person. Implies responsibility for the protection and preservation of the thing or person in custody. When applied to a person, may mean lawfully authorized detention by means of restraint and physical control.

Cutaneous: Pertaining to the skin.

Cyanosis: A dark, purplish coloration of the skin and the mucous membrane caused by deficient oxygenation of the blood.

Cyclic adenosine monophosphate (cyclic AMP or cAMP): A second messenger involved in the synaptic activities of dopamine, norepinephrine, and serotonin.

Glossary

Cyclothymic disorder: Mild affective disorder characterized by extreme mood swings of nonpsychotic intensity.

Cytoarchitectonics: The study of anatomical divisions of the brain based on the kinds of spacing of cells and distribution of axons.

D

Dacrystic epilepsy: Seizures where crying is the predominant ictal event.

Damages: A monetary compensation that may be recovered in court by any party who has suffered a loss or injury to person, property, or rights as the result of an unlawful act or negligence.

Damages, actual: The amount awarded in compensation for a complainant's actual and real losses or injury that can readily be proved to have been sustained.

Damages, compensatory: A monetary award to the injured party strictly for the loss of injury sustained.

Damages, double (or treble): An award for certain statutorily authorized kinds of injuries in an amount two to three times the damages normally awarded by a court or jury.

Damages, nominal: A trivial sum awarded to a plaintiff in an action where there is no substantial loss or injury for which to be compensated. Or, in a case where there has been real injury, but the plaintiff's evidence fails to show its amount.

Damages, punitive (exemplary): Compensation in an amount greater than actual damages in cases where the wrong done to a plaintiff was aggravated by malice, violence, or fraud on the part of the defendant.

Damages, special (consequential): An award not arising directly or immediately from the act of a party, but only from the consequences or results of such an act.

De bene esse: Conditionally or provisionally; in anticipation of future need. Applies to proceedings taken provisionally and allowed to stand for the present but which may be subject to future challenges.

De facto: In fact, actually, in reality. Characterizes an officer, government, past action, or state of affairs that is illegal or illegitimate, but for all practical purposes, must be accepted.

***De novo* hearing:** A new hearing or a hearing for the second time in which the judgment of the trial court is usually suspended, with the reviewing court determining the case as though it originated in the latter court.

Decerebrate (rigidity): Extension and rigidity of the limbs caused by brain stem or cerebellar injury.

Deep dyslexia: Deletion of grammatical morphemes with the presence of semantic paralexias, due to cerebral dysfunction. The loss of grapheme-to-phoneme processing is seen during reading.

Default judgment: A decision of the court against a defendant because of his or her failure to respond to a plaintiff's action.

Defendant: The person from whom relief or recovery is sought in an action or suit. In a criminal case, the accused.

Defense: That which is offered and alleged by the party against whom an action or suit is taken, such as the lawful or factual reasons against the plaintiff recovering or establishing that which he seeks.

Delirium: State of mental confusion characterized by clouding of consciousness, disorientation, restlessness, excitement, and often hallucinations.

Delirium tremens: Acute delirium associated with prolonged alcoholism; characterized by intense anxiety, tremors, and hallucinations.

Delusion: Firm belief opposed to reality but maintained in spite of strong evidence to the contrary.

Delusion of persecution: False belief that one is being mistreated or interfered with by one's enemies. Often found in schizophrenia.

Delusion system: An internally coherent, systematized pattern of delusions.

Dementia pugilistica: The "punch drunk" syndrome. Symptoms associated with repeated head trauma include dysarthria, tremor, seizures, and frontal signs. Memory and concentration problems are marked.

Dendrites: Receptor structures of a neuron that project out in branchlike fashion. Extensions of the cell body that are the receptive surfaces of the neuron.

Dendritic branching: The pattern and quantity of branching of dendrites.

Dendritic spines: Outgrowths along the dendrites of neurons.

Dendritic tree: The full arrangement of a single cell's dendrites.

Deoxyribonucleic acid (DNA): A nucleic acid present in the chromosomes of cells containing hereditary information.

Dependent personality: A personality disorder marked by lack of self-confidence and feelings of acute panic or discomfort at having to be alone.

Dependent variable: In an experiment, the behavior that is measured to determine whether changes in the independent variable affect the behavior being studied.

Depersonalization disorder: A dissociative neurotic disorder, usually occurring in adolescence, in which individuals lose their sense of self and feel unreal or displaced to a different location.

Depolarization: A reduction in membrane potential (the inner membrane surface becomes less negative in relation to the outer surface); this is caused by excitatory neural messages.

Deponent: One who testifies to the truth of certain facts; one who gives a written state deposition; a witness.

Deposition: A witness's testimony taken under oath outside of the courtroom in question-and-answer form, reduced to writing and authenticated. Intended to be used at a civil or criminal trial.

Depressive disorder: Neurotic reaction characterized by persistent dejection and discouragement.

Depressive neurosis: Depression of intermediate severity with little or no evidence of personality breakdown or loss of contact with reality.

Depressive stupor: Extreme degree of depression characterized by marked psychomotor underactivity.

Derepression: The mechanism through which regions of the DNA molecule that are repressed from transcription become unblocked. This process allows for the selection of genetic information that will be utilized by a particular cell.

Dermatome: A strip of skin innervated by a particular spinal root.

Desensitization: Therapeutic process by means of which reactions to traumatic experiences are reduced in intensity by repeatedly exposing the individual to them in mild form, either in reality or in fantasy.

Deterrence: The premise that punishment for criminal offenses will deter that criminal and others from future criminal acts.

Dexedrine: An amphetamine drug; a stimulant used to curb appetite or elevate mood.

Dextral: Refers to right-handedness. Opposed to sinistral, or left-handedness.

Dialysis dementia: Chronic, degenerative intellectual problems (aphasia, memory difficulties), seizures, and motor signs (e.g., facial grimacing) seen occasionally as the result of long-term dialysis. The pathogenesis is unknown although the accumulation of aluminum in the brain has been implicated.

Dialysis disequilibrium syndrome: A consequence of the dialysis procedure itself, encephalopathy characterized by development of intermittent slowing speech, stuttering, and word-finding problems. Progression of dyspraxia, memory loss, concentration problems, and (occasionally) psychosis. Shifts in sodium and potassium are associated with the disorder.

Diapedesis: The passage of blood cells through the unruptured walls of the blood vessels.

Diaschisis: Reduction of neuronal activity in brain sites outside the immediate perimeter of the lesion. Associated with acute, focal conditions.

Diastole: The rhythmic period of relaxation and dilatation of the heart, during which it fills with blood.

Diathesis: A predisposition or vulnerability toward developing a given disorder.

Diathesis-stress model: View of abnormal behavior as the result of stress operating on an individual with a biological, psychosocial, or sociocultural predisposition toward developing a specific disorder.

Dichotic: Refers to studies where different stimuli are simultaneously presented to both ears and eyes, or tactilely to the subject.

Dictum (pl. dicta): A statement, remark, or observation of the law made by the court, not necessarily relevant or essential to the outcome of a case.

Diencephalon: The central core of the brain, which, together with the telencephalon, forms the cerebrum. Consists of the thalamus, subthalamus, hypothalamus, and epithalamus. The posterior part of the forebrain; it includes the thalamus and hypothalamus.

Differential reinforcement of other behavior (DOR): Behavior modification technique for extinguishing undesirable behavior by reinforcing incompatible behaviors.

Digitalis: The dried leaves of purple foxglove; used in the treatment of certain cardiac disorders.

Dilantin: An anticonvulsant medication often used in controlling epileptic seizures.

Diopter: The unit of refracting power of a lens; denoting a lens whose principal focus is at a distance of 1 m.

Diploid: Having two sets of chromosomes, as normally found in the somatic cells of higher organisms.

Diplopia: Double vision, due to eye muscle imbalance, metabolic disturbances, or other causes.

Direct examination: The initial questioning or examination of a witness by the party who originally called the witness to testify.

Directed verdict: A verdict ordered by the judge when, as a matter of law, the judge rules that the party with the burden of proof has failed to present a prima facie case. The judge orders the jury to return a verdict for the opposing party.

Disconnection syndromes: Disrupted neuronal transmission through the white matter that cuts cortical pathways, thus disconnecting a cortical area from the rest of the brain. Corpus callosum disconnections are the most dramatic.

Discovery: A pretrial procedure by which one party can obtain vital facts and information material to the case to assist in preparation for the trial. The purpose of discovery is to make for a fair trial and to allow each party to know what documents and information the opponent possesses.

Disinhibition syndrome: Inability to stop actions or impulses once initiated. Often attributed to frontal system deficits in exerting an inhibitory effect on ongoing mental or behavioral processes.

Disintegration: Loss of organization or integration in any organized system.

Disorganized schizophrenia: Subtype representing most severe disintegration of personality and poor prognosis for recovery; characterized by marked incoherence, silly or inappropriate responses.

Dissociation: Separation or "isolation" of mental processes in such a way that they become split off from the main personality or lose their normal thought–affect relationships.

Dissociative disorder: Psychoneurotic disorder characterized by amnesia, fugue, somnambulism, or multiple personality.

Distal: An anatomical term meaning toward the periphery or toward the end of a limb.

Diural: Daily.

Divergence: A system of neural connections that allows one cell to send signals to many other cells.

DNA: *See* Deoxyribonucleic acid.

Docket sounding: A meeting between the judges and attorneys for the purpose of determining the schedule of cases for a specific period of time.

Dopamine (DA): A neurotransmitter produced mainly in the basal forebrain and diencephalon that is active in the basal ganglia, the olfactory system, and limited parts of the cerebral cortex. For location of dopaminergic fibers.

Dopaminergic: Refers to cells that use dopamine as their synaptic transmitter.

Dorsal: An anatomical term meaning toward the back of the body or the top of the brain; opposite of ventral.

Dorsal root: Root at the back of the spinal cord.

Double-dissociation: Differential effects of lesions, allowing for comparison of both independent and dependent variables. Lesion x causes x but not y, whereas lesion y causes y but not x.

Double tracking: The simultaneous operation of two mental operations. Digits backward on the Wechsler Adult Intelligence Scale (WAIS), for example, calls for memory and reversing operations at the same time.

Down syndrome: A form of mental retardation associated with an extra chromosome.

Due process of law: The regular course of law as administered through courts of justice. In each particular case, refers to the legal proceedings in accordance with the rules and principles established in our legal system to enforce and protect private rights.

Duplex theory: A theory of pitch perception combining the place theory and volley theory. Volley theory operates for sounds from about 20 to 1000 Hz, and place theory operates for sounds above 1000 Hz.

Duplication of DNA: A process through which a cell duplicates (or replicates) its genetic information during mitosis.

Dura: First or outermost layer of the three layers of the meninges.

Glossary

Durham rule: The "irresistible impulse" test of criminal responsibility deriving from a 1954 decision of the U.S. Court of Appeals. States that a defendant is not criminally responsible if he suffered from a mental disease or defect at the time the unlawful act was committed if it is determined beyond a reasonable doubt that the act was a product of the mental disease or defect.

Duty: A legal or moral obligation or responsibility to perform an act or service.

Dyad: A two-person group.

Dynamic formation: An integrated evaluation of a patient's traits, attitudes, conflicts, and symptoms that attempts to explain the individual's problem.

Dysarthia: Refers to speech disorders based on peripheral motor deficits. The quality of speech is affected, as in hypenasality, breathy phonation, and stridor (flaccid paretic dysarthria), slow, low pitch, harsh and difficult phonation (spastic paretic dysarthria), or explosive speech (ataxic or cerebellar dysarthria).

Dysfluency: Difficulty in generating words.

Dysmetropia: Defects in the visual appreciation of object size discrimination. Also called "past-pointing phenomenon" (i.e., in finger-to-nose examination). Associated with cerebellar lesions.

Dysnomia: Word-finding disability. Shown by failure to correctly name objects or by choosing words that are "off center." Associated with temporal lobe dysfunction.

Dysphagia: Difficulty in swallowing.

Dysthymic disorder: Moderately severe affective disorder characterized by extended periods of nonpsychotic depression and brief periods of normal moods.

Dystonia: Prolonged abnormal posture as a consequence of involuntary muscle tension. Often a side effect of neuroleptic medication.

E

Echopraxia: The mimicking of another's motor movements. Indicates that extant motor problems are not due to lack of inactivity.

Ectoderm: The outer cellular layer of the developing fetus; this layer gives rise to the skin and to the nervous system.

Ectopic: Out of the normal place.

Edema: An abnormal accumulation of clear, watery fluid in the lymph spaces of the tissues. The swelling of tissue, especially in the brain, in response to brain injury.

Effusion: The escape of fluid from the blood vessels or the lymphatics into the tissues or a cavity.

Ego-dystonic homosexuality: Category of "mental disorder" in which the individual wishes to change his or her homosexual orientation.

Ejaculatory incompetence: A male's inability to ejaculate.

Electric synapse: Junctional region where the presynaptic and postsynaptic membranes approach so closely that the nerve impulse can jump to the postsynaptic membrane without being translated into a chemical message.

Electroencephalography (EEG): The recording and study of gross electrical activity of the brain recorded from large electrodes placed on the scalp.

Electrolyte: Any substance that, in solution, conducts an electric current.

Embolism: Obstruction, or occlusion, of a vessel by a transported clot, a mass of bacteria, or other foreign material.

Emotional inoculation: Therapeutic procedures designed to prepare persons who face stressful situations, such as surgery, by providing the person with adaptive techniques.

Empiricism: The philosophical view based on the belief that knowledge is acquired through experience and observation.

Empyema: The presence of pus in any cavity.

Encephale isole: An animal in which the brain stem is separated from the spinal cord by a cut below the medulla. Contrast with cerveau isole.

Encephalitis: A generalized viral infection of the brain's neurons or glial cell bodies.

Encephalomalacia: Cerebral tissue softening.

Encephalopathy: Brain degeneration.

Encoding: A process of memory formation in which the information entering sensory channels is passed into short-term memory.

Glossary

Endocrine: Refers to glands that secrete products into the bloodstream to act on distant targets; opposite of exocrine.

Endorphins: Neurotransmitters that have been called the body's own narcotics.

Endothelial cells: The tightly fitting cells that make up the walls of the capillaries in the brain.

Enhancement: Independent of behavior, the increase in activity of some posterior parietal neurons by motivationally important visual stimuli. Responses to those stimuli are enhanced.

Enjoin: To command or require that a person perform or desist from a certain act.

Enuresis: Involuntary passage of urine after the age of 3 years.

Enzyme: A protein that catalyzes a biochemical reaction.

Epicritic: Sensory experiences that can be located on the body of the organism and are of brief duration (e.g., a sharp pain in the foot). Opposed to protocritic.

Epinephrine: A compound that acts both as a hormone (secreted by the adrenal medulla) and as a neurotransmitter; also called adrenaline.

Episodic dyscontrol syndrome: Totally unprovoked violence associated with an aura, consisting of rising anxiety, headaches, illusions, numbness, drowsiness, and hyperacusis. The attack lasts 15 minutes to 2 hours and is very violent, often directed toward property or persons. May be due to temporal-limbic structure dysfunction. Associated features include hypersensitivity to alcohol, multiple traffic accidents, and sexual impulsiveness, the last rising to the level of forensic concern.

Episodic memory: Recall for events in one's life and experiences. It is therefore unique and anchored to distinct points in time and space.

Equilibrium potential: The state in which the tendency of ions to flow from regions of high concentration is exactly balanced by the opposing potential differences across the membrane.

Equipotentiality: Notion that a lesion anywhere on the cortex will produce equivalent deficits. This holistic approach was espoused by Lashley.

Equity: A system of law and courts administered according to fairness and justness. Based on a system that originated in England as an alternative to common law.

Estrogen: A hormone produced by female gonads.

Estrus: The period during which female animals are sexually receptive.

Eustress: Positive stress.

Evagination: A protrusion of some part of an organ.

Event-related potentials: Gross electrical potential changes in the brain that are elicited by discrete sensory or motor events.

Excitatory postsynaptic potentials (EPSPs): Depolarizing potentials in the postsynaptic neuron caused by excitatory presynaptic impulses. These potentials may summate to trigger a nerve impulse in the postsynaptic cell.

Exclusionary rule: The rule that defines whether evidence is admissible in a trial. In cases where evidence has been illegally obtained, it must be removed from consideration by the fact finders.

Exculpatory: Clearing or excusing a party from alleged fault or guilt.

Exemplary damages: A monetary award in an amount over and above what is required to compensate a plaintiff for a loss in a case where the wrong was aggravated by violence, malice, or fraud on the part of the defendant.

Exhaustion and disintegration: The third and final phase in the general adaptation syndrome, in which the organism is no longer able to resist continuing stress; at the biological level, may result in death.

Exner's area: Formally seen as a "frontal writing center," located at the base of the second frontal convolution. Lesions in this area produce agraphia.

Exocrine: Refers to glands that secrete their products through ducts to the site of action; opposite of endocrine.

Exophthalmos: A protrusion, or prominence, of the eyeball.

Experimental research: A research approach in which the experimenter manipulates the independent variable, controls outside conditions, and determines the effect on a dependent variable to test for causal linkages.

Expert witness: A witness who has special knowledge in a field, obtained from education or personal experience.

External validity: The degree to which experimental findings can reasonably be generalized to nonlaboratory situations.

Extinction: One of a stimulus pair simultaneously presented to different parts of the body visual fields, etc., is not perceived.

Glossary

Extinction to double simultaneous stimulation: Failure to report the stimulus presented to the contralateral side of a lesion upon bilateral simultaneous stimulation.

Extracerebral: Extrinsic to or outside of the brain hemispheres, for example, between the skull and the brain on one of the three layers of meninges.

Extrapunitive: Characterized by a tendency to evaluate the source of frustrations as external and to direct hostility outward.

Extrapyramidal system: A motor system that includes the basal ganglia and some related brain stem structures.

Extravasation: The act of escaping from a vessel into the tissues; said of blood, lymph, or serum.

Extrinsic: Originating outside of the part where it is found or upon which it acts.

F

5HT: *See* Serotonin

Fabrication: Relating imaginary events as if they were true without intent to deceive; confabulation.

Face–hand test: Touching the face simultaneously with another body part, particularly same-sided. Suppression or displacement of the more peripheral stimulus indicates possible parietal lobe dysfunction.

Facial nerve: A cranial nerve that innervates facial musculature and some sensory receptors.

Fasciculation: Localized contraction of muscle fibers, or an incoordinated contraction of skeletal muscle in which the fibers of one motor unit contract.

Feature detector model: A model of visual pattern analysis in terms of linear and angular components of the stimulus array. Contrast with spatial frequency filter model.

Felony: A crime of a more serious or harmful nature than a misdemeanor. Under federal law and many state statutes, any offense punishable by imprisonment for a term of more than 1 year or by death.

Fetal alcohol syndrome: Observed pattern in infants of alcoholic mothers in which there is a characteristic facial or limb irregularity, low body weight, and behavioral abnormality.

Fiduciary: A person having the duty to act in a relationship of high trust and confidence for another's benefit in the capacity of trustee, executor, or administrator.

Field properties: Characteristics of the environment surrounding a living system.

Finger agnosia: Inability to identify the fingers of one's own hand, or those of another person, due to brain damage.

Fistula: A pathologic, or abnormal, passage leading from an abscess cavity or a hollow organ to the surface, or from one organ to another.

Fixed action patterns: Complex preprogrammed species-specific behaviors triggered by particular stimuli and carried out without sensory feedback.

Flaccid: Relaxed, flabby, soft.

Flashback: The recurrence of a drug experience, usually in a negative manner, without further ingestion of the drug.

Flatus: Gas or air in the stomach or the intestine; commonly used to denote passage of gas by rectum.

Flexion reflex: Abrupt withdrawal of a limb in response to intense stimulation of the foot.

Flooding: Anxiety-eliciting technique involving placing the client in a real-life, anxiety-arousing situation.

Fluent aphasia: Speech difficulty with incomprehension, jargon speech, and other signs such as lack of awareness. Often associated with posterior lesions. Nonfluent aphasia is associated with anterior lesions and almost always involves expressive speech deficits.

Folia: Folds or convolutions of the cerebellar cortex.

Folie a deux: A psychotic interpersonal relationship involving two people; e.g., husband and wife both become psychotic with similar or complementary symptomatology.

Follicle-stimulating hormone (FSH): A tropic hormone released by the anterior pituitary that controls the production of estrogen and progesterone.

Forcible rape: An act of violence in which sexual relations are forced upon an unwilling partner who is over the age of 18.

Glossary

Forebrain: The frontal division of the neural tube that contains the cerebral hemispheres, the thalamus, and the hypothalamus. Also called the prosencephalon.

Forensic psychiatry: Branch of psychiatry dealing with legal problems relating to mental disorders.

Fornix: A fiber tract that runs from the hippocampus to the mammillary body.

Fovea: A cup-shaped depression or pit.

Fovea centralis: Small central pit in the retina, packed with cones, where vision is sharpest and color accuracy most developed.

Frontal amnesia: Difficulty in switching from one set of memory traces to another in the face of intact operating memory. "Forgetting to recall," as in disregarding instructions, is an illustration.

Frontal gait disturbance: *See* Magnetic apraxia and Utilization behavior.

Frontal inattention: A contralateral visual field defect caused by damage to particular frontal sites (arcuate sulcus in monkeys). Associated features may include conjugate deviation of the eyes and forced circling, the latter in the direction of the lesion.

Frontal psychosurgery: Includes leukotomies aimed at severing frontal-thalamic connections, orbital undercutting, for example, by placement of radioactive yttrium pellets in the orbital tissues, cingulomotomy, stereotactic destruction of focal sites, and topectomy, ablation of selected frontal areas.

Frontal "release" signs: These are primitive reflexes that long have been considered frontal signs. The grasp reflex is associated with midline frontal pathology. Frontal system problems are indicated by rooting, sucking, and snout reflexes indicating a brain stem diencephalic lesion.

Frye test: A test emphasizing the subject of an expert witness's testimony must conform to a generally accepted explanatory theory. Named after the case in which the determination was made.

Fugue: A neurotic dissociative disorder that entails a loss of memory accompanied by actual physical flight from one's present life situation to a new environment or less-threatening former one.

Functional psychoses: Severe mental disorders attributed primarily to psychological stress.

Fundus: The bottom of a sac or hollow organ; the farthest removed from the opening.

Future shock: A condition brought about when social change proceeds so rapidly that the individual cannot cope with it adequately.

G

Gambling: Wagering on games or events in which chance largely determines the outcome.

Gamma efferents: Motor neurons by means of which the central nervous system controls muscle spindle sensitivity.

Ganglion: A collection of nerve cell bodies. Also called a nucleus.

Ganglion cells: Cells in the retina whose axons form the optic nerve.

Gangrene: A form of necrosis combined with putrefaction; death of the tissue.

Gel: A colloidal system comprising a solid and a liquid phase that exists as a solid or semisolid mass; a jelly or solid or semisolid phase.

Gelastic epilepsy: Seizures where laughter is the predominant ictal behavior.

Gene: An ultimate, ultramicroscopic, biologic unit of heredity; self-reproducing; located in a definite position on a particular chromosome.

General adaptation syndrome: Reaction of the individual to excessive stress; consists of the alarm reaction, the stage of resistance, and the stage of exhaustion.

General paresis: A progressive mental deterioration due to syphilitic invasion of the central nervous system. Changes include deterioration of the entire range of mental

Gerstmann's syndrome: The symptom cluster of ocalculia, agraphia, left-right disorientation, and finger agnosia. Traditionally considered to involve the parietoccipital region of the brain.

Glabellar tap sign: The subject is tapped lightly just above and between the eyebrows to see whether blinking will normally and quickly habituate. Patients with Parkinson's disease will continue to blink with each tap.

Glial cells: Nonneural brain cells that provide structural, nutritional, and other support to the brain. Also called glia or neuroglia.

Glossary

Glioblastoma (multiforma): A neoplasm arising from the glial cells, characterized by a high degree of lethality and malignancy.

Gliomas: Brain tumors resulting from the aberrant production of glial cells.

Global alexia: Inability to read letters or words.

Global aphasia: Severe comprehension and articulation deficits associated with a large lesion of the entire perisylvian area of the frontal, temporal, and parietal lobes. Prognosis is grim.

Global stereopsis: Depth perception in the presence of ambiguous stimulus forms. Presumed to be mediated by right hemisphere and is differentiated from a stereoacuity.

Glossopharyngeal nerve: A cranial nerve that serves taste receptors in the tongue.

Glucocorticoids: Hormones released by the adrenal cortex that affect carbohydrate metabolism.

Golgi tendon organs: Receptors located in tendons that send impulses to the central nervous system when a muscle contracts.

Gonadotropin-releasing hormone (GnRH): A hypothalamic hormone that controls release of luteinizing hormone (or interstitial-cell-stimulating hormone). Also called luteinizing-hormone-releasing hormone.

Graded potentials: Potentials that can vary continuously in size; also called local potentials; contrast with all-or-none potentials.

Gradient: An ascending or descending slope. In the body, gradients are determined by the difference in concentration or electric charges across a semipermeable membrane.

Grand mal seizures: A type of generalized epileptic seizure that involves nerve cells firing in high-frequency bursts. These seizures cause loss of consciousness and sudden muscle contraction.

Grandfather clause: Certain legal provisions permitting those engaged in a business or profession before the passage of an act regulating them to receive a license, power, or privilege without meeting the criteria established for those new to the field.

Grievance: A denial of legal right or an injury, injustice, or wrong that is grounds for a complaint due to being unjust, discriminatory, and oppressive.

Growth hormone: A tropic hormone secreted by the anterior pituitary that influences the growth of cells and tissues. Also called somatotropic hormone (STH).

Guardian *ad litem*: A person appointed by the court to represent the interests of a minor or an incompetent person in a litigation and to act on the person's behalf until the conclusion of the case.

Guilt: Feelings of culpability arising from behavior or desires contrary to one's ethical self-devaluation and apprehension growing out of fears of punishment.

Gyri: The ridged or raised portions of a convoluted brain surface. Contrast with sulci.

H

Habeas corpus: "You have the body." A writ or order commanding the authority that is detaining an individual to produce the body of the detainee before the court to determine whether the detainment is lawful.

Health psychology: Subspecialty within the behavioral medicine approach that deals with psychology's contributions to diagnosis, treatment, and prevention of behaviorally caused physical illnesses.

Hearsay: A statement made during a trial or hearing that is not based on the personal, firsthand knowledge of the witness.

Hearsay rule: The regulation making a witness's statement inadmissible if it is not based on the witness's personal knowledge.

Heat of vaporization: The heat energy required to convert 1 g of liquid into a vapor without a change in temperature of the substance being vaporized.

Hebephrenic schizophrenia: Type of schizophrenia characterized by severe personality decompensation or disintegration.

Hematoma: An accumulation of blood within the meninges of the brain. Most often caused by head trauma.

Hematosis: The arrest of bleeding; the checking of the flow of blood through any part of a vessel.

Hematuria: The presence of blood in the urine.

Hemiparesis: Weakness on one side of the body.

Hemiplegia: Weakness or paralysis of one side of the body.

Hemispatial neglect: Neglect of the hemisphere contralateral to a lesion. Also termed visuospatial agnosia or neglect, unilateral spatial neglect, or hemispatial agnosia.

High-risk: Individuals showing great vulnerability to physical or mental disorders.

Hilus: A depression or pit at that part of an organ where the vessels and nerves enter or leave.

Hippocampus: Actively concerned with memory consolidation functions, located at anterior temporal lobe.

Histrionic personality: Personality pattern characterized by excitability, emotional instability, and self-dramatization.

Holistic: A systematic approach to science involving the study of the whole or total configuration; the view of human beings as unified psychobiological organisms inextricably immersed in a physical and sociocultural environment.

Homeostasis: Tendency of organisms to maintain conditions making possible a constant level of physiological functioning.

Homologous: Corresponding; having similar relations.

Homonymous field cuts: Loss of vision in the same part of both visual fields.

Homonymous hemianopsia: Loss of one half of the visual field in each eye, right or left sided (e.g., right temporal/left nasal; right nasal/left temporal).

Huntington's disease: A progressive, hereditary, dementing condition that affects the basal ganglia with atrophy of the frontal lobes and corpus callosum. Involuntary and spasmodic movements are associated features, along with declining cognitive and personality/social skills.

Hyaluronidase: An enzyme causing breakdown of hyaluronic acid in protective polysaccharide barriers, promoting invasion of cells and tissues by the invading agent; it is a spreading factor.

Hyperacusis: The perception of sounds as abnormally loud.

Hypergraphia: Overwriting, as when too many words are written in response to task demands.

Hyperplasia: The abnormal multiplication, or increase, in the number of normal cells in normal arrangement in a tissue.

Hypertrophy: The morbid enlargement, or overgrowth, of an organ or part, resulting from an increase in size of its constituent cells.

Hypnosis: Trancelike mental state induced in a cooperative subject by suggestion.

Hypnotherapy: Use of hypnosis in psychotherapy.

Hypnotic regression: Process by which a subject is brought to relive, under hypnosis, early forgotten or repressed experiences.

Hypochondriacal delusions: Delusions concerning various horrible disease conditions, such as the belief that one's brain is turning to dust.

Hypochondriasis: Condition dominated by preoccupation with bodily processes and fear of presumed diseases.

Hypophonia: Lowered voice volume. Contrasted to aphonia, or total lack of voice. The most common cause of both disorders is laryngitis.

Hypothalamus: Involved in homeostatic, motivational activities such as sexual activity, eating, drinking, and emotions, this structure is located in the limbic system, dorsal to the thalamus.

Hypothermia: Low temperature; especially a state of low body temperature induced for the purpose of decreasing metabolic activities and need for oxygen.

Hypotonia: The state of muscles tiring easily. Associated with cerebellar lesions.

Hypoxia: Refers to insufficient blood oxygen to the brain. Contrasted to anoxia, which refers to a total lack of blood oxygen to brain structures.

Hysterical amnesia: Loss of memory for emotional/psychological reasons without a known organic basis.

Hysterical disorder: Disorder characterized by involuntary psychogenic dysfunction of motor, sensory, or visceral processes.

I

Iconic memory: A very brief type of memory that stores the sensory impression of a scene.

Ideographic methodology: A method of study emphasizing the individual case and the uniqueness of each personality.

Glossary

Ideomotor apraxia: Simple execution of motor responses (e.g., hitchhiking sign, salute, whistling) is impaired or absent in the presence of intact comprehension. Implies deficits in planning and initiation. Associated with left hemisphere lesions.

Idiopathic epilepsy: A seizure disorder of unknown origin. Opposed to symptomatic epilepsy whose cause is known.

Illusion: Misinterpretation of sensory data; false perception.

Impeachment: A criminal proceeding against a public official before a quasi-political court. In regard to the testimony of a witness, to question the veracity of the evidence offered.

In bank (*en banc*): "In the bench." Refers to a court session in which the entire membership of the court participates in making a decision instead of the regular quorum or one judge and jury.

In camera: In chambers; in private. The hearing of a case before a judge in his private chambers, when all spectators are excluded from the courtroom, or when the judge performs a judicial act while the court is not in session.

In loco parentis: In place of a parent. A party charged to legally act in behalf of the parents.

In re: In the matter of; concerning or regarding. The usual method of assigning a title to a case in which there are no adversary parties.

In situ **research:** Research in which real-life social situations are the emphasis of study.

In vivo: Taking place in a real-life situation as opposed to the therapeutic or laboratory setting.

Inattention: Decreased/absent awareness of events occurring on the side of the body contralateral to the hemispheric lesion.

Incompetency: Lacking the physical, intellectual, or moral capacity or qualification to perform a required duty.

Independent variable: The variable in an experiment that is controlled or manipulated by the experimenter.

Indifference reaction: Denial, unawareness, or minimizing psychological/neuropsychological deficits, traditionally associated with right hemisphere lesions. Inappropriate elevated affect may be present.

Infarct: Impoverished or dead brain tissue associated with vascular occlusions.

Inferior colliculus: The auditory center in the midbrain; it receives input from the brain stem auditory nuclei and sends output to the medial geniculate nucleus.

Inflammation: A series of reactions produced in the tissues by an irritant; marked by an afflux of blood with exudation of plasma and leukocytes.

Informed consent: A person's agreement to the occurrence of a specified event based on a full disclosure of facts needed to make an intelligent decision.

Infra: Below, under, following; the opposite of *supra*.

Infundibulum: A funnel-shaped structure or passage. The stalk of the pituitary gland.

Inhibitory postsynaptic potentials (IPSPs): Hyperpolarizing potentials in the postsynaptic neuron caused by inhibitory connections. These potentials decrease the probability that the postsynaptic neuron will fire a nerve impulse.

Innervation ratio: The ratio expressing the number of muscle fibers innervated by a single motor axon. The fewer muscle fibers an axon innervates (the lower the ratio) the finer the control of movement.

Inquisitorial system: A system in which the judge, as the primary figure in a trial, conducts his or her own investigation. The judge generally maintains more control over the proceedings than in the adversarial system.

Insanity: A social or legal term indicating a condition in which a person is unfit and lacks legal responsibility or capacity due to mental illness. As stated in the American Law Institute Penal Code, "A person is not responsible for criminal conduct if at the time of such conduct as a result of mental disease or defect he lacks substantial capacity either to appreciate the criminality or wrongfulness of his conduct or to conform his conduct to the requirements of the law."

Insanity defense: "Innocent by reason of insanity" plea used as a legal defense in criminal trails.

Instrumental use of empirical data: The application of concrete social science information of concepts to a case.

Integration: Organization of parts (psychological, biological functions) to make a functional whole.

Intent: A state of mind (inferred from the facts or from a person's actions) showing purpose, design, or resolve to act in a certain manner.

Glossary

Intention tremor: Also called kinetic tremor, this anomaly occurs at the end of a movement. Contrasted to "rest" tremor, which occurs when no movement is present. A tremor that occurs only during a voluntary movement, e.g., when the person reaches out to grasp an object.

Interictal: Refers to behaviors/events between the time seizures occur. Adversive personality traits (e.g., irritability, obsessional traits) are associated features.

Intermediate coup lesions: Scattered areas of focal tissue damage in line with the point of trauma impact (coup) and possible terminal point of the damage (contrecoup).

Intermediate-term memory: A form of memory lasting longer than short-term memory, and requiring no rehearsal, but not lasting as long as long-term memory.

Internal carotid artery: *See* Common carotid artery.

Internal validity: A measure of the lack of confounding variables.

Interstitial policy making: Laws that may be "made" by judges when the issues in a case fall "between the gaps"—interstices—of previous decisions.

Intracerebral: Intrinsic to or inside of the brain hemispheres, usually referring to brain dysfunction caused by neoplasms or cardiovascular accidents.

Intracranial steal: Complicating the finding of an arteriovenous malformation (AVM) location, here blood is shunted away from normal brain tissue to the AVM site. Thus, the unaffected area may show evidences of neuropsychological deficit.

Intravascular: Within a vessel or vessels.

Intropunitive: Responding to frustration by tending to blame oneself.

Invagination: The pushing of the wall of a cavity into the cavity.

Involution: The return of an enlarged organ to normal size; retrograde changes.

Ion: An electrically charged atom or group of atoms formed by the loss or gain of electrons.

Ipsilateral: Same side; homolateral; opposed to contralateral (opposite side), bilateral (both sides), unilateral (one side).

Ischemia: Cutoff of blood flow to an area of the brain or body organ.

Ischemic infarction: A disruption of blood flow (infarction) creating dead or damaged tissue (infarct), resulting more from impaired or absent blood flow rather than from insufficient nutrients in the blood.

Isotope: An element that has the same atomic number as another but a different atomic weight. Radioactive isotopes, used clinically, usually refer to elements rendered radioactive by artificial means.

J

Jargon aphasia: A form of paraphasias that has no meaning to those who hear the sounds.

Judicial notice: The act by which a court, during a trial or while framing its decision, recognizes the existence and truth of certain facts that judges and jurors may take into consideration and act upon without proof because the facts are already known to them.

Jurisdiction: The authority and power by which courts and judicial officers hear and decide cases; the geographic area in which a court has authority.

Just-world hypothesis: The hypothesis stating that the world is fair and that victims deserve what happened to them and, therefore, do not deserve help.

Juvenile courts: A court system, established in the late 19th century, having special jurisdiction over delinquent, dependent, and neglected minors. Set up to treat youthful offenders separately from adults. The court acts in a parental, protective role.

Juvenile delinquency: Legally prohibited behavior, such as disobedient, indecent, or immoral conduct, committed by minors.

K

Ketosis: The condition marked by excessive production of ketone bodies in the body.

Kinesthetic: Pertaining to muscle sense, or to the sense by which muscular movement, weight, and position are perceived.

Kinesthetic afferentiation: Gathering data concerning one's own current muscle tone, body position, oral status, etc. Considered a function of the posterior association areas.

Glossary

Kinetic afferentiation: Integration of input from parietal–occipital tertiary zones, basal ganglia, and premotor areas producing sequential and integrated actions. Depends initially on kinesthetic afferentiation.

Kinetic apraxia: Disorganized transition of single movements (*see also* Apraxia, Echopraxia, Apraxia of speech). Associated with lesions in basal ganglia-premotor areas. Subordination of movements to intentions is impaired.

Kluver–Bucy syndrome: A condition manifested by hyperorality, hypersexuality, labile emotions, and inability to form new memories. Associated with temporal lobe or limbic system lesions.

Korsakoff's psychosis: A progressive dementia considered subcortical in focus and associated with a nutritional deficiency of vitamin B_1 (thiamine). The condition is considered secondary to alcohol abuse. Memory impairments are paramount with associated confabulation, blandness, and passivity. Hippocampus lesions have been associated with this condition. A memory disorder, related to a thiamine deficiency, generally associated chronic alcoholism.

Kuru: A slow virus of the brain, which produces trembling and, eventually, paralysis of the limbs.

L

Labeled lines: A view of stimulus coding stating that particular nerve cells are intrinsically labeled for particular sensory experiences such as cold, touch, pain, and so forth.

Labile memory: An early state of memory formation during which formation of a memory can be easily disrupted by conditions that influence brain activity.

Lacunar state: Multiple but small infarctions in the subcortical regions leaving lacunae. One of the end stages of hypertensive cerebrovascular conditions.

Laminar (form of organization): The horizontal layering of cells found in some brain regions.

Lateral: An anatomical term meaning toward the side; opposite of medial.

Lateral geniculate nucleus: Part of the thalamus that receives information from the optic tract and sends it to visual areas in the occipital cortex.

Lateral hypothalamus (LH): A hypothalamic region involved in facilitating eating.

Lateral inhibition: A phenomenon produced by interconnected neurons that inhibit their neighbors, producing contrast at the edges of the stimulus.

Law of effect: Principle that responses that have rewarding consequences are strengthened and those that have aversive consequences are weakened or eliminated.

Leading question: A question posed by a trial lawyer that is improper because it suggests the desired answer to a witness.

Lecithin: A monoaminomonophosphatide found in animal tissues, especially nerve tissue, semen, egg yolk, and in smaller amounts in bile and blood.

Legal fiction: An assumption of fact or a situation contrived by the law to decide a legal question.

Lethality scale: Criteria used to assess the likelihood of an individual's committing suicide.

Leukemia: A disease of the blood marked by persistent leukocytosis, associated with changes in the spleen and the bone marrow, or in the lymphatic nodes.

Level of aspiration: Standard by which the individual judges success or failure of his behavior.

Lexical agraphia: Impaired ability to spell irregular or unknown works with an intact ability to spell regular words. Associated with lesions in the parieto-occipital lobule.

Limb-kinetic apraxia: Complex/serial movement impairment in the presence of intact simple, repetitive movement. Brodman areas 4 and 6 are implicated in almost all cases.

Limbic system: Interconnected and primarily subcortial structures that are involved in emotional responses and memory.

Literal paraphasia: Production of off-target sounds with effortless articulation. Associated with postrolandic lesions.

Litigant: One who is party to a lawsuit.

Local circuit neurons: Small neurons that make contact only with neurons that are within the same functional unit.

Localization of function: The concept that specific brain regions are responsible for various types of experience, behavior, and psychological processes.

Glossary

Locked-in syndrome: Also known as deefferentiation; due to bilateral pontine lesions and characterized by aphonia and quadriplegia. The patient is aware of his or her surroundings.

Logical positivism: A philosophy that emphasizes the creation of knowledge and its verification through observation and experiment.

Long-term memory: An enduring form of memory lasting for weeks, months, or years.

Lumbar: Referring to the lower part of the spinal cord or back.

Lumen: The space in the interior of a tubular structure such as an artery or the intestine.

Luteinizing hormone (LH): A tropic hormone released by the anterior pituitary that influences the hormonal activities of the gonads. In males, this hormone is called interstitial-cell-stimulating hormone (ICSH).

Luteinizing hormone-releasing hormone: *See* Gonadotropin-releasing hormone.

M

M'Naughten rule: In most jurisdictions, the test applied for the defense of insanity. Under this test, an accused is not criminally responsible if he or she was suffering from a mental disease or defect at the time of committing the act and does not understand the nature and quality of the act or that what he or she was doing was wrong. To be considered "sane" and therefore legally responsible for the act committed, the defendant must know and understand the nature and quality of the act and have been able to distinguish between right and wrong at the time the offense was committed.

Macula: A spot.

Magnetic apraxia: Compulsive exploration of the immediate environment in the usual presence of intact comprehension skills. Forced hand grasping with difficulty "letting go" is an example. Prefrontal, mesial, and contralateral lesions are implicated.

Major affective disorders: Category of affective disorders in which a biological defect or other aberration renders a person liable to experience episodes of a more or less severe affective disorder.

Major depression (unipolar disorder): A severe affective disorder in which only depressive episodes occur.

Malaise: A feeling of general discomfort or uneasiness; an out-of-sorts feeling, often the first indication of an infection.

Malfeasance: The commission of an unlawful, wrongful act; any wrongful conduct that affects, interrupts, or interferes with the performance of official duties.

Malleus Malleficarum: Infamous handbook prepared by two monks dealing with the "diagnosis" and "treatment" of witches and witchcraft.

Mammillary bodies: Paired nuclei at the base of the brain slightly posterior to the pituitary stalk.

Mandamus: A writ or order issued from a superior court to a lower court or to a private or municipal corporation commanding that a specified act be performed. Used when other judicial remedies have failed.

Manic–depressive psychoses: Older term denoting a group of psychotic disorders characterized by prolonged periods of excitement and overactivity (mania) or by periods of depression and underactivity (depression) or by alternation of the two.

Masked fascies: An unblinking, bland, expressionless stare.

Masochism: Sexual variant in which an individual obtains sexual gratification through being subjected to pain.

Mass action: Proposed by Lashley, this notion stated that the degree of deficit shown by a lesion was a function of how much cortical tissue was destroyed.

Meatus: A passage, or channel, especially the external opening of a canal.

Medial: An anatomical term meaning toward the middle; opposite of lateral.

Medial geniculate nucleus: A nucleus in the thalamus that receives input from the inferior colliculus and sends output to the auditory cortex.

Mediation: A way of resolving disputes by using a third party to intervene between contending parties to bring them to a satisfactory settlement without resorting to litigation.

Medulla: The lowest part of the brain, also called myelencephalon.

Melokinetic apraxia: Deficit in speech, skill, and coordination of movement, usually confined to a small muscle group. Unilateral and contralateral to lesion in premotor area.

Memory traces: Persistent changes in the brain that reflect the storage of memory.

Meninges: Thin membranes on the brain dura mater, pia mater, and arachnoid, which provide a venous drainage system.

Meningioma: Neoplastic growth arising from the meninges.

Meningitis: Inflammatory disease of the meninges with associated signs of fever, headache, and stiff neck.

***Mens rea*:** A guilty mind; having a guilty or wrongful purpose or criminal intent.

Mental anguish: A compensable injury including all forms of mental, as opposed to physical, injury. In connection with a physical injury, includes the mental sensation of pain and accompanying feelings of distress, grief, anxiety, or fright.

Mesencephalon: The midbrain.

Mesmerism: Theories of "animal magnetism" (hypnosis) formulated by Anton Mesmer.

Messenger RNA (mRNA): A strand of RNA that carries the code of a section of a strand of DNA to the cytoplasm.

Metabolism: The sum of the chemical changes whereby the function of nutrition is affected; consists of anabolism, or the constructive and assimilative changes, and catabolism, or the destructive and retrograde changes.

Metamorphosias: Visual illusions where objects are distorted in size, shape, distance, and color. May occur with lesions anywhere in visual system, with substance intoxication, or in conjunction with psychological disorder.

Metencephalon: A subdivision of the hindbrain that includes the cerebellum and the pons.

Meter: A measure of length, 100 cm, the equivalent of 39.371 inches.

Methadone: An orally administered narcotic that replaces the craving for heroin and weans the individual from heroin addiction.

Microglia: Extremely small glial cells that remove cellular debris from injured or dead cells.

Microgram: One one-millionth of a gram, or 1/1000 of a milligram.

Micron: One one-millionth of a meter or 1/1000 of a millimeter.

Microtubules: Hollow cylindrical structures in axons that are involved in exoplasmic streaming.

Midbrain: The middle division of the brain. Also called mesencephalon.

Middle cerebral artery (MCA): The MCA and its branches are one of the two major vascular networks of the frontal lobes. The lateral convexity is fed by anterior branches of the MCA.

Milieu: The immediate environment, physical or social or both; sometimes used to include the internal state of an organism.

Millimeter: One one-thousandth of a meter; about 1/25 inch.

Misdemeanor: An offense less serious than a felony, typically punishable by a fine or short-term incarceration.

Misfeasance: The improper performance of an act a person has the right or duty to perform.

Misoplegia: A type of unilateral inattention where the lesioned individual, usually hemiplegic, exhibits a strong dislike for the affected limbs or portions of the body. Intense hatred resulting in self-mutilation may be expressed.

Mistrial: A trial that is terminated before its normal conclusion and declared invalid prior to the returning of a verdict. A judge may declare a mistrial due to an extraordinary event (e.g., death of a juror), for a fundamental, prejudicial error that cannot be corrected by instructions to the jury, or because of the jury's inability to reach a verdict (hung jury). In a criminal case, may prevent a retrial under the doctrine of double jeopardy.

Mitochondria: Organelles in the cytoplasm of cells; contain enzymes that make possible the reactions whereby energy is liberated from food and stored temporarily in the chemical bonds of ATP.

Mitosis: The process of division of somatic cells that involves duplication of DNA.

Model psychoses: Psychotic-like states produced by various hallucinogenic drugs such as LSD.

Modulation of formation of memory: Facilitation or inhibition of memory formation by factors other than those directly involved in memory formation. Also called modulation of memory storage processes.

Modus operandi: Manner or mode of behavior; a criminal's typical pattern of performing crimes.

Monopolar neurons: Nerve cells with a single branch leaving the cell body, which then extends in two directions — one end is the receptive pole, the other end the output zone.

Moot: A subject for debate; unsettled; undecided. A case is "moot" when a determination of a matter is sought that, when rendered, has no practical effect on the matter under dispute.

Moral nihilism: Doctrine that denies any objective or real ground for moral beliefs, and holds that the individual is not bound by obligation to others or society.

Moral therapy: Therapy based on provision of kindness, understanding, and favorable environment; prevalent during early part of the 19th century.

Motion: An application made to a court or judge, orally or in writing, requesting that a rule or order be given in favor of the applicant.

Motivational selectivity: Influence of motives on perception and other cognitive processes.

Motive pattern: Relatively consistent cluster of motives centered around particular strivings and goals.

Motoneurons: Nerve cells in the spinal cord that transmit motor messages from the spinal cord to muscles.

Motor aprosody: Inability to sing or to change pitch or voice tempo with intact ability to recognize melodies.

Motor cortex: A region of cerebral cortex that sends impulses to motoneurons.

Motor extinction: Increased contralateral limb akinesia when simultaneously using ipsilateral extremities, due to cerebral dysfunction.

Motor impersistence: Inability to maintain an initiated, voluntary (motor) behavior chain. Implies distraction due to interference factors. Common impersistences include lack of tongue protrusion, eyelid closure, mouth opening, breath holding, hand-grip pressure, and central gaze.

Motor neuron: Spinal cord neurons involved in movement that extend to effector muscle sites.

Motor unit: A single motor axon and all the muscle fibers it innervates.

Multi-infarct dementia: A vascular disease that has a progressive, stepwise course caused by multiple strokes and arteriosclerosis. Cognitive symptoms usually precede personality problems. Motor anomalies are distinctive of this condition and reflect subcortical involvement.

Multiple personality: Type of dissociative disorder characterized by the development of two or more relatively independent personality systems in the same individual.

Multiple sclerosis (MS): A degenerative condition involving deterioration of the myelin sheath on nerve fibers. This disease therefore affects primarily the white matter. Multiple cognitive and emotional deficits are noted. The rate of progression of MS is extremely variable.

Multipolar neurons: Nerve cells with many dendrites and a single axon.

Muscarinic: A cholinergic receptor (one responsive to acetylcholine) that mediates chiefly the inhibitory activities of acetylcholine.

Myasthenia gravis: A neurological disease characterized by easy fatigability and weakness of muscles.

Myelencephalon: A subdivision of the hindbrain; the medulla.

Myelin: The fatty insulation around an axon, formed by accessory cells; this improves the speed of conduction of nerve impulses.

Myelin sheath: A thin cover on the axons of many neurons.

Myelinization: The process of formation of myelin.

N

Narcolepsy: A disorder involving frequent, intense episodes of sleep, which last from 5 to 30 minutes, and can occur anytime during the usual waking hours.

Narcosis: Stupor, or unconsciousness, produced by some narcotic drug.

Narcotherapy (narcoanalysis, narcosynthesis): Psychotherapy carried on while the patient is in a sleeplike state of relaxation induced by a drug such as sodium pentothal.

Narcotic drug: Drug such as morphine, which leads to physiological dependence and increased tolerance.

Natural law: A philosophy that refers to a system of rules and principles for the guidance of human behavior; the system arises from the rational intelligence of humans. These rules are apart from enacted laws and stem from and conform to the entire human mental, moral, and physical constitution.

Glossary

Necker cube: An optical illusion using "rate of apparent change (RAC)" to differentiate normal from brain-injured individuals. Fewer and slower reversals are reported by brain-injured individuals, with damage associated with right hemisphere or frontal lobe lesions.

Necrosis: Local death of tissue.

Negative feedback system: A regulatory system in which output is used to reduce the effect of input signals.

Negativism: Form of aggressive withdrawal that involves refusing to cooperate or obey commands, or doing the exact opposite of what has been requested.

Negligence: The failure to exercise the degree of care that a reasonable person, guided by ordinary considerations under similar circumstances, would exercise.

Neocortex: The relatively recently evolved portions of the cerebral cortex.

Nerve growth factor: A substance that controls the growth of neurons of the spinal ganglia and the ganglia of the sympathetic nervous system.

Nerve impulses: The propagated electrical messages of a neuron that travel down from the axon to adjacent neurons. Also called action potentials.

Neural tube: A prenatal structure with subdivisions that correspond to the future forebrain, midbrain, and hindbrain. The cavity of this tube contains the cerebral ventricles and the passages that connect them.

Neurasthenic neurosis: Neurotic disorder characterized by complaints of chronic weakness, easy fatigability, and lack of enthusiasm.

Neuroblasts: Early forms of cells during the stage of cell migration.

Neurofibrillary tangles: Abnormal whorls of neurofilaments within nerve cells that are especially apparent in people suffering from dementia.

Neurofilaments: Small rodlike structures in axons that are involved in transport materials.

Neuroglia: "Nerve glue" or glia, these cells make up about half the volume of the central nervous system and provide structural and metabolic support to neurons. *See* Glial cells.

Neurohypophysis: *See* Posterior pituitary.

Neurological examination: Examination to determine presence and extent of organ damage to the nervous system.

Neuromodulators: Substances that influence the activity of synaptic transmitters.

Neuron: The basic unit of the nervous system, composed of a cell body (also known as soma or perikaryon), receptive extensions, and a transmitting extension (axon). A cell of the brain or spinal cord composed of a cell body, axon, and dendrites.

Neuron doctrine: A hypothesis that states that the brain is composed of separate cells that are distinct structurally, metabolically, and functionally.

Neuropathies: Peripheral nerve destruction.

Neurosecretory cells: Neurons that manufacture and secrete hormones.

Neurospecificity: A theory of nervous system development that states that each axon grows to a particular site.

Neurotic nucleus: Basic personality characteristics underlying neurotic disorders.

Neurotic paradox: Failure of neurotic patterns to extinguish despite their self-defeating nature.

Neurotic style: A general personality disposition toward inhibiting certain anxiety-causing behaviors; distinguishable from anxiety, somatoform, and dissociative disorders in that neurotic styles do not manifest themselves in specific, disabling neurotic symptoms.

Neurotransmitter: Biochemical substances that transmit information between neurons: *See* Synaptic transmitter.

Nicotinic: A cholinergic receptor that mediates chiefly the excitatory activities of acetylcholine.

Night hospital: Mental hospital in which an individual may receive treatment during the night while carrying on his usual occupation in the daytime.

Nigrostriatal bundle (NSB): A dopaminergic tract that runs from the substantia nigra of the midbrain to the lateral hypothalamus, the globus pallidus, and the caudate putamen.

Nihilistic delusion: Fixed belief that everything is unreal.

Nociceptors: Receptors that respond to stimuli that produce tissue damage or pose the threat of damage.

Node of Ranvier: A gap between successive segments of the myelin sheath where the axonal membrane is exposed.

Glossary

Nomadism: Withdrawal reaction in which the individual continually attempts to escape frustration by moving from place to place or job to job.

Nomothetic methodology: An approach in which the discovery of relationships between variables by studying large numbers of cases or events is emphasized.

Non compos mentis: Insane; not sound of mind. A very general term including all varieties of mental derangement.

Norepinephrine (NE): A neurotransmitter produced mainly in brain stem nuclei, also called noradrenalin.

Normal pressure hydrocephalus (NPH): A reversible condition involving obstruction of cerebral spinal fluid (CSF). Increased pressure leads to ventricle enlargement with the primary lesion in the midbrain reticular formation.

Nosology: The classification of diseases, including mental diseases.

NSB: *See* Nigrostriatal bundle.

Nucleotide: A portion of a DNA molecule composed of a single base and the adjoining sugar-phosphate unit of the strand.

Nucleus: An anatomical collection of neurons, e.g., caudate nucleus.

Nystagmus: Abnormal to and fro movements of the eye during attempts to fixate. Rhythmic oscillation of the eyeballs, horizontal, rotary, or vertical.

O

Occipital cortex: The cortex of the occipital (posterior) lobe of the brain.

Ocular-dominance histogram: A graph that shows the strength of a neuron's response stimuli presented to either the left or right eye. Used to determine the effects of depriving one eye of visual experience.

Ondine curse: A type of sleep apnea where automatic breathing during sleep is disrupted. Lesions of the reticulospinal tract have been implicated in this condition.

Oneirism: Prolonged dream state despite wakefulness.

Optic aphasia: Inability to name visually presented objects with intact recognition. Spared recognition is shown by demonstration of use or matching (pointing) to the object when named.

Optic ataxia: Inability to localize objects in space by visual guidance. Difficulty in shifting (stimulus boundedness) is an associated feature.

Optic chiasm: The site where optic neurons from the eye separate and cross over to the contralateral hemisphere. Located near the pituitary gland.

Optic radiation: Axons of the lateral geniculate nucleus that terminate in the primary visual areas of the occipital cortex.

Optic tract: The axons of the retinal ganglion cells after they have passed the optic chiasm.

Optokinetic system: A closed-loop system controlling eye movement and keeping the gaze on target.

Organ of Corti: A structure in the inner ear that lies on the basilar membrane; contains the hair cells and the terminations of the auditory nerve.

Orifice: Any aperture or opening.

Osmoreceptors: Cells in the hypothalamus that were thought to respond to changes in osmotic pressure.

Osmotic thirst: The response to increased osmotic pressure in brain cells. Contrast with hypovolemic thirst.

Ostium: A small opening, especially one that forms an entrance into a hollow organ or canal.

Overutilization anoxia: Occurring during epileptic seizures, a lack of sufficient oxygen secondary to the abnormal electrical discharges. Seen as due to the high metabolic rates during seizures.

Oxidation: The combining of food and oxygen in the tissues; chemically, the increase in valence of an element.

Oximeter: An instrument for measuring the oxygen saturation of hemoglobin in the circulating blood.

Oxytocin: A hormone released by the posterior pituitary that triggers milk let-down in the nursing female.

P

Pacchionian bodies: Small projections of the arachnoid tissue, chiefly into the venous sinuses of the dura mater.

Pain asymbolia: Loss of appreciation for pain, associated with left parietal lesions.

Glossary

Pain cocktail: A concoction of all the medication a pain patient is taking in a single liquid, which can be systematically controlled and reduced in strength.

Paleocortex: Evolutionary old cortex, e.g., the hippocampus.

Palilalia: Progressively more rapid and softer speech productions, ending in an indistinguishable mutter. Associated with bilateral frontal lesions or with subcortical structures.

Palpitation: Forcible pulsation of the heart perceptible to the individual.

Papilledema: Edema of the optic disk, associated with increased intracranial pressure.

Paradigmatic change: A new way of viewing the world.

Paradoxical sleep: *See* Rapid-eye-movement sleep (REM).

Parallel processing: Using several different circuits at the same time to process the same stimuli.

Paralysis: A loss of power of voluntary movement in a muscle through injury or disease of its nerve supply.

Paranoia: Psychosis characterized by a systematized delusional system.

Paranoid personality: Individual showing behavior characterized by projection (as a defense mechanism), suspiciousness, envy, extreme jealousy, and stubbornness.

Paranoid schizophrenia: Subtype of schizophrenic disorder characterized by absurd, illogical, and changeable ideas and hallucinations of grandeur and persecution.

Paranoid state: Transient psychotic disorder in which the main element is a delusion, usually persecutory or grandiose in nature.

Paraphasias: Errors in word usage associated with aphasia. Substitutions for a correct word may occur (e.g., "I ate night") or substitution for syllables (e.g., "I ate rupper"). Neologisms may occur (e.g., "I ate ronks").

Parasympathetic division: One of the two systems that compose the autonomic nervous system. The parasympathetic division arises from both the cranial and sacral parts of the spinal cord.

Paraventricular nucleus: A nucleus of the hypothalamus.

Parenchyma: The essential elements of an organ; the functional elements of an organ, as distinguished from its framework or stroma.

Parens patriae: Literally, "parent of the country." Refers to the role of the state as sovereign or guardian of such persons as minors and insane and incompetent persons.

Parkinson's disease: A degenerative neurological disorder involving dopaminergic neurons of the substantia nigra. A subcortical, progressive dementia that is primarily caused by neuronal degeneration of the basal ganglia, particularly the substantia nigra. There may also be cortical impairment. The three primary symptoms are tremor, rigidity, and bradykinesia. Egocentricity, irritability, and suspiciousness are common.

Partial seizures: Epileptic seizures arising from pathological foci that do not have widespread distribution. These include focal repetitive motor spasms and do not involve loss of consciousness.

Parturition: Giving birth to young.

Path analysis: Statistical technique that takes into account how variables are related to one another through time and how they predict one another.

Pathological gambling: Addictive disorder in which gambling behavior disrupts the individual's life.

Pederasty: Sexual intercourse between males via the anus.

Perceptual defense: A process in which threatening stimuli are filtered out and not perceived by the organism.

Perceptual filtering: Processes involved in selective attention to aspects of the great mass of incoming stimuli that continually impinge on the organism.

Perimeter: An instrument delimiting the field of vision.

Peripheral nerves: Neurons that lie outside the central nervous system.

Peripheral nervous system: The portion of the nervous system that includes all the nerves outside the brain and spinal cord.

Permanent planning: Placing children who are drifting through foster homes back into their original families.

Perseveration: Persistent continuation of a line of thought or activity once it is under way. Clinically inappropriate repetition.

Perseveration–consolidation hypothesis: A hypothesis stating that information passes through two stages in memory formation. During the first stage the memory is held by perseveration of neural activity and is easily disrupted. During the second stage the memory becomes fixed, or consolidated, and is no longer easily disrupted.

Personality disorder: A group of maladaptive behavioral syndromes originating in the developmental years and not characterized by neurotic or psychotic symptoms.

Perversion: Deviation from normal.

Petit mal seizures: A type of generalized epileptic seizure characterized by a spike-and-wave electrical pattern. During these seizures the person is unaware of the environment and later cannot recall what happened.

pH: The symbol commonly used in expressing hydrogen ion concentration; signifies the logarithm of the reciprocal of the hydrogen ion concentration expressed as a power of 10.

Phantom limb: The experience of sensory messages attributed to an amputated limb.

Phasic receptors: Receptors that show a rapid fall in nerve impulse discharge as stimulation is maintained.

Phlebothrombosis: Thrombosis of a vein without inflammation of its walls.

Phonological agraphia: Impaired ability to spell nonwords with intact ability for familiar words. Associated with lesions of the supermarginal gyrus or associated areas.

Phosphemes: Flashes of light caused by dysfunction of the auditory-visual association area. Visual hallucinations may also be produced, related or not to past experiences.

Photopic system: A system in the retina that operates at high levels of light, shows sensitivity to color, and involves the cones; contrast with scotopic system.

Phrenology: The belief that bumps on the skull reflect enlargements of brain regions responsible for certain behavioral faculties.

Pick's disease: Similar to Alzheimer's disease, here neuronic damage is typically confined to the frontal and temporal lobes. Personality changes usually precede memory loss. Affects twice as many women as men.

Pilocarpine: An alkaloid that stimulates the parasympathetic division of the autonomic nervous system.

Pitch: A dimension of auditory experience in which sounds vary from low to high.

Pituitary gland: A small complex endocrine gland located in a socket at the base of the skull. The anterior pituitary and posterior pituitary are separate in function.

Place theory: A theory of frequency discrimination according to which pitch perception depends on the place of maximal displacement of the basilar membrane produced by a sound. Contrast with volley theory.

Plaintiff: A person who initiates an action or legal suit. In a civil suit, the party who complains or sues.

Planum temporale: A region of superior temporal cortex adjacent to the primary auditory area.

Plea: In a legal action, the defendant's answer to the plaintiff's declaration.

Plea bargaining: In a criminal case, the process in which the accused and the prosecutor negotiate a mutually satisfactory disposition of the case subject to the approval of the court. Usually involves the defendant pleading guilty to a reduced punishment or offense or to a lesser number of counts in a multicount indictment.

Pleading: The formal allegations made by the opposing parties of their respective claims and defenses.

Pleasure principle: In psychoanalysis, the demand that an instinctual need be immediately gratified regardless of reality.

Plexus: A network, or tangle, of interweaving nerves, veins, or lymphatic vessels.

Pneumoencephalogram: A technique for examining brain structure in intact humans by taking radiographic images after a gas is injected into the ventricles.

Pons: A portion of the metencephalon.

Positive law: A system of rules and laws enacted or adopted by the government of an organized political community for the purpose of controlling the conduct of its people.

Positron emission tomography (PET) scan: A technique for examining brain structure and function in intact humans by combining tomography with injections of radioactive substances used by the brain. An analysis of metabolism of these substances reflects regional differences in brain activity. Computer-assisted radiographic procedure designed to analyze and track glucose utilization in the brain.

Postcentral gyrus: Involved in sensory mediation, this cortical convolution is located just posterior to the fissure of Rolando.

Posterior pituitary: The rear division of the pituitary gland. Also called neurohypophysis.

Glossary

Posthypnotic amnesia: The subject's lack of memory for the period during which he or she was hypnotized.

Posthypnotic suggestion: Suggestion given during hypnosis to be carried out by the subject after he or she is brought out of hypnosis.

Postpartum disturbances: Emotional disturbance of the mother associated with childbirth.

Postsynaptic potentials: *See* Graded potentials.

Post-traumatic amnesia (PTA): A form of anterograde amnesia seen as a postconcussional effect of head trauma. Correlates well with coma length and severity. Some retrograde amnesia may accompany PTA.

Post-traumatic stress disorder: Category of disorder in which the stressor is severe and residual symptoms occur following the traumatic experience.

Postural tremor: A tremor that occurs when a person attempts to maintain a posture such as holding an arm or leg extended, resulting from pathology of the basal ganglia or cerebellum.

Precedent: A previous judgment or decision of a court considered as an authority for deciding later identical or similar cases. Under the doctrine of stare decisis, case: which establish that a rule of law are authoritative and must be adhered to.

Precentral gyrus: Involved in the mediation of motor activity, this cortical convolution is located just anterior to the fissure of Rolando.

Precipitating cause: The particular stress that triggers a disorder.

Predisposing cause: The factor that lowers the individual's stress tolerance and paves the way for the appearance of a disorder.

Predisposition: Likelihood that an individual will develop certain symptoms under given stress conditions.

Pressor: Excited vasoconstrictor activity, producing increased blood pressure; denoting afferent nerves that, when stimulated, excite the vasoconstrictor center.

Presumption: An inference resulting from a rule of law or the proven existence of a fact that requires such rule(s) or action(s) be established in the action. Presumption can be irrefutable, such as the presumption of incapacity in a person under 7 years of age to act, or rebuttable, in which case it can be disproved by evidence.

Presumption of innocence: A principle of criminal law in which the government carries the burden of proof beyond a reasonable doubt for every element of a crime, with the defendant having no burden of proof to prove his or her innocence.

***Prima facie* case:** A case in which there is sufficient evidence for the matter to proceed beyond a motion for a directed verdict in a jury case or a motion to dismiss in nonjury trial; requires that the defendant proceed with his or her case.

***Prima facie* evidence:** Evidence that, in the judgment of the law, is good and sufficient to establish a given fact or a chain of facts making up the party's claim or defense. If such evidence is unexplained or uncontradicted, it is sufficient to sustain favorable judgment for the issue it supports; may be contradicted by other evidence.

Primary reaction tendencies: Constitutional tendencies apparent in infancy, such as sensitivity and activity level.

Privilege: A particular benefit or exemption enjoyed by a person, company, or class beyond the common ones held by other citizens.

Privileged communication: Statements that are made in a setting of legal or other professional confidentiality. Applies to certain persons within a protected relationship, such as husband–wife and attorney–client, who are legally protected from forced disclosure on the witness stand at the option of the witness.

***Pro bono publico*:** For the welfare or good of the public, such as when an attorney or other professional handles a case without compensation to advance a social cause or represents a party who cannot afford to pay.

Problem drinker: Behavioral term referring to one who has serious problems associated with drinking alcohol. Term is currently preferable to alcoholic.

Process (poor premorbid, chronic) schizophrenia: Schizophrenia pattern that develops gradually and tends to be long-lasting.

Prodrome: Behavioral/mood change preceding onset of a seizure. Prodromal signs may be apparent for several days before the seizure.

Progressive supranuclear palsy: An uncommon Parkinson-like condition that usually begins in the 50s with emotional liability, imbalance, and problems with downward gaze. A dementia develops with relative sparing of language and constructional abilities.

Projection neuron: Large neurons that transmit messages to widely separated parts of the brain.

Prosecution: A criminal proceeding to determine the guilt or innocence of a person charged with a crime. Refers to the state or federal government as the party proceeding in a criminal action.

Prosencephalon: *See* Forebrain.

Prosody: Rhythm, pitch, tempo, and similar characteristics of speech. Important in communication of affective content. Typically seen as a right hemisphere activity.

Prosopagnosia: Inability to recognize faces of those with whom one was previously familiar. Loss of ability to recognize unfamiliar faces is a variant of this disorder. Usually associated with right lesions.

Protocritic: A diffuse type of sensory experience (e.g., temperature) that is common to all homeostatic internal mechanisms. Cognitive processing does not lead to identifying a discrete place or duration for the sensation. Opposed to epicritic.

Proximal: An anatomical directional term meaning near the trunk or center; opposite of distal.

Proximate cause: An occurrence that, in a natural and unbroken chain of events, results in an injury and without which the injury would not have occurred. The event that is closest in the causal relationship to the effect.

Pseudo-community: Delusional social environment developed by a paranoid person.

Pseudobulbar state: Strong affective expressions to include laughing and crying, often simultaneously, but also incongruous to the stated feeling of the person. Associated with lesions of connecting pathways between the frontal lobes and lower brain structures.

Pseudodementia: A pattern of deficit behavior resembling organically produced dementia. Depression is the primary factor causing the intellectual suppression.

Pseudodepression: The major pathology involves the dorsal-lateral frontal convexity, severe bilateral frontal pathology, or severing of frontal-thalamic pathways. This is a pathology of reduced/absent motor responses (e.g., mutism, inactivity, helpless unconcern). The subject may be aware of his or her deficit.

Pseudohemianopsia: Lack of attention to visual stimulation from the contralateral side despite intact visual fields.

Pseudopsychopathy: The major pathology involves the orbital frontal areas and reflects motor excess (e.g., puerile acts, restlessness, bursting into motion, impulsive antisocial acts). The subject knows but cannot control the motor behavior.

Psychic cortex: Anterior portion of the temporal lobe that when stimulated produces recollection of previous experience (e.g., music, visual scenes). Temporal lobe tumors may produce hallucinations involving previous experiences.

Psychomotor epilepsy: State of disturbed consciousness in which the individual may perform various actions, sometimes of a homicidal nature, for which he or she is later amnesic.

Psychosexual dysfunction: Inability or impaired ability to experience or give sexual gratification.

Psychotogens: Substances that generate psychotic behavior.

Psychotropic drugs: Drugs whose main effects are mental or behavioral in nature.

Pterygoid: Shaped like a wing.

Ptosis: Drooping eyelid caused by a lesion to the oculomotor cranial nerve.

Pure agraphia: Writing deficits caused by brain damage in the absence of other significant language disturbance.

Pure word deafness: Inability to understand spoken words with an intact ability to read, write, and speak. Usually does not occur in isolation of other defects and is associated with cardiovascular accidents.

Purkinje cell: A type of large nerve cell in the cerebellar cortex.

Putative: Reputed or supposed.

Pyramidal cell: A type of large nerve cell in the cerebral cortex.

Pyramidal system: A motor system including neurons within the cerebral cortex and the axons that form the pyramidal tract.

Q

Quasi-experimental design: A research study in which the experimenter has partial experimental control over the setting and variables.

R

Ramp movements: Slow, sustained motions thought to be generated in the basal ganglia. Also called smooth movements. Contrast with ballistic.

Ramus: A branch; one of the primary divisions of a nerve or a blood vessel; a part of an irregularly shaped bone that forms an angle with the main body.

Random assignment: An experimental method that ensures that every subject has an equal chance of being selected for the experimental or control group.

Range fractionation: A hypothesis of stimulus intensity perception stating that a wide range of intensity values can be encoded by a group of cells, each of which is a specialist for a particular range of an intensity scale.

Rape: An act of violence in which sexual relations are forced upon another person.

Raphe nucleus: A group of neurons in the midline of the brain stem that contains serotonin, involved in sleep mechanisms.

Rapid-eye-movement (REM) sleep: A state of sleep characterized by small-amplitude, fast electroencephalographic (EEG) waves, no postural tension, and rapid eye movements. Also called paradoxical sleep.

Ratio decidendi: The principal ground or reason for a court's written decision. The point in a case that is essential to determining the court's judgment.

Reaction formation: Ego-defense mechanism in which the individual's conscious attitudes and overt behavior are opposite to repressed unconscious wishes.

Readiness potential: An electrical potential that occurs over widespread posterior regions of the scalp prior to the onset of a voluntary movement.

Reality assumptions: Assumptions that relate to the gratification of needs in the light of environmental possibilities, limitations, and dangers.

Reality principle: Awareness of the demands of the environment and adjustment of behavior to meet these demands.

Reasonable doubt: The degree of doubt required to justify an acquittal of a criminal defendant, based on reason and arising from evidence or lack of evidence.

Reasonable doubt standard: A standard beyond which guilt must be shown.

Receptive field: The stimulus region and features that cause the maximal responses of a cell in a sensory system.

Receptor: Nerve ending that receives a stimulus. The initial element in sensory systems, responsible for stimulus transduction, e.g., hair cells in the cochlea or rods and cones in the retina.

Receptor proteins: Substances at synaptic receptor sites whose reaction to certain transmitters causes a change in the postsynaptic membrane potential.

Receptor sites: Regions of specialized membrane containing receptor proteins located on the postsynaptic surface of a synapse; these sites receive and react with the chemical transmitter.

Recess: A short interval during a trial or hearing when the court suspends business without adjournment.

Reduplicative paramnesia: Associated with right parietal and/or frontal damage of a coarse nature. Involves relocating a place (e.g., hospital) to another place (e.g., one's home town).

Reflex: A simple, highly stereotyped, and unlearned response to a particular stimuli (i.e., an eyeblink in response to a puff of air).

Refractory: A period during and after a nerve impulse in which the axon membrane's responsiveness is reduced. A brief period of complete insensitivity to stimuli (absolute refractory phase) is followed by a longer period of reduced sensitivity (relative refractory phase) during which only strong stimulation produces a nerve impulse.

Regression: Ego-defense mechanism in which the individual retreats to the use of mature responses in attempting to cope with stress and maintain ego integrity.

Remand: To send a case back to the court from which it came to have further action taken on it there.

Remedy: The means by which a right is enforced or the violation of a right is prevented or compensated for.

Repression: Ego-defense mechanism by means of which dangerous desires and intolerable memories are kept out of consciousness.

Residual schizophrenia: Category used for persons regarded as recovered from schizophrenia but still manifesting some symptoms.

Resistance: Tendency to maintain symptoms and resist treatment or uncovering repressed material.

Glossary

Resistance to extinction: Tendency of a conditioned response to persist despite lack of reinforcement.

Resorption: The loss of substance through physiologic or pathologic means.

Respondent: The party answering a charge or the party contending against an appeal.

Resting potential: Potential differences across the membrane of nerve cells during inactive period. Also called membrane potential.

Retainer: A contract between an attorney and a client stating the nature of the service to be rendered and the cost of such services. By employing an attorney to act on their behalf, clients prevent the attorney from acting for their adversary.

Rete mirabile: A network of fine blood vessels located at the base of the brain in which blood coming from the periphery reduces the temperature of arterial blood before it enters the brain.

Reticular: Netlike.

Reticular activating system: Brain stem area that mediates level of arousal.

Reticular formation: A region of the brain stem (extending from the medulla through the thalamus) that is involved in arousal.

Retinaculum: A special fascial thickening that holds back an organ or part; helps retain an organ or tissue in its place.

Retrieval: A process in memory during which a stored memory is utilized by an organism.

Retroactive amnesia: A type of memory loss in which events just before a head injury are not recalled.

Retrograde amnesia: Inability to recall events previous to the onset of a trauma; recovery of remote events usually occurs first.

Retrograde degeneration: Destruction of the nerve cell body following injury.

Reuptake: A mechanism by which a synaptic transmitter released at a synapse is taken back into the presynaptic terminal, thus stopping synaptic activity.

Reverse tolerance: Situation in which a decreased amount of some psychoactive drug brings about the effects formerly achieved by a larger dose.

Rh antigen or factor: An agglutinogen, or antigen, first found in the erythrocytes of rhesus monkey, hence the Rh. Rh positive and Rh negative terms denote presence or absence, respectively, of this antigen.

Rhodopsin: The photopigment in rods that responds to light.

Ribosomes: Organelles that appear as dots lining the endoplasmic reticulum; they are the protein factories of cells.

Right: A power or privilege, enforced legally, giving a person control over the actions of others.

Rigid control: Coping patterns involving reliance upon inner restraints, such as inhibition, suppression, repression, and reaction formation.

Role obsolescence: Condition occurring when the ascribed social role of a given individual is no longer important to the social group.

Roots: The two distinct branches of a spinal nerve, each of which serves a separate function. The dorsal root carries sensory information from the peripheral nervous system to the spinal cord. The ventral root carries motor messages from the spinal cord to the peripheral nervous system.

Rostral: An anatomical term meaning toward the head end; opposite of caudal.

S

Saccades: Rapid movements of the eyes that occur regularly during normal viewing.

Saccadic suppression: The suppression of vision during saccades, which provides the viewer with perception free of these abrupt movements.

Sacral: Refers to the lower part of the back or spinal cord.

Sadism: Sexual variant in which sexual gratification is obtained by the infliction of pain upon others.

Sagittal plane: The plane that bisects the body or brain into right and left halves.

Saltatory conduction: The form of conduction seen in myelinated axons in which the nerve impulse jumps from one node of Ranvier to the next.

Schizo-affective psychosis: Disorder characterized by schizophrenic symptoms in conjunction with pronounced depression or elation.

Schizoid personality: Personality pattern characterized by shyness, oversensitivity, seclusiveness, and eccentricity.

Schizophrenia: Psychosis characterized by the breakdown of integrated personality functioning, withdrawal from reality, emotional blunting and distortion, and disturbances in thought and behavior.

Schizophreniform disorder: Category of schizophrenic psychosis, usually in an undifferentiated form, with a duration of less than 6 months.

Schizophrenogenic: Qualities in parents that appear to be associated with the development of schizophrenia in offspring; often applied to rejecting, cold, domineering, overprotective mothers or passive, uninvolved fathers.

Schwann cell: The kind of accessory cell that forms myelin in the peripheral nervous system.

Scotoma: A region of blindness caused by injury to the visual pathway.

Scotopic system: A system in the retina that responds to low levels of light.

Second messenger: A relatively slow acting substance in the postsynaptic cell that amplifies the effects of nerve impulses and can initiate processes that lead to changes in electrical potentials at the membrane.

Selective vigilance: A tuning of attentional and perceptual processes toward stimuli relevant or central to goal-directed behavior, with decreased sensitivity to stimuli irrelevant or peripheral to this purpose.

Sella turcica: A saddlelike depression on the upper surface of the sphenoid bone, in which the hypophysis lies.

Semantic agraphia: Deficit or loss of ability to spell or write with meaning, produced by brain damage to various sites.

Semantic memory: Memory for what is learned as knowledge. This recall therefore is considered "timeless and spaceless" (e.g., a number system, a foreign language).

Senile dementia: A neurological disorder of the aged involving progressive behavioral deterioration including personality change and profound intellectual decline.

Senile plaques: Neuroanatomical changes correlated with senile dementia due to the build-up of beta amyloid.

Sensorineural deafness: A hearing impairment originating from cochlear or auditory nerve lesions.

Sepsis: A morbid condition resulting from the presence of pathogenic bacteria. From septic.

Septo-hypothalamo-mesencephalic (SHM) continuum: One of three limbic mechanisms, the SHM continuum has distinct circuitry connecting the hypothalamus, the limbic midbrain area, and other sites. Only the prefrontal lobe has direct connections with the SHM continuum, out of the entire isocortex.

Serial lesion effect: The lessened severity of cerebral symptoms (e.g., due to diaschisis) when lesions are introduced in stages as opposed to all at once.

Serotonergic: Refers to neurons that use serotonin as their synaptic transmitter.

Serotonin (5HT): A neurotransmitter produced in the raphe nuclei and active in structures throughout the cerebral hemispheres; plays a role in the systems that control memory, emotion, and perception. A compound (5-hydroxytryptamine) found in the bloodstream that has vasoconstrictive properties.

Short-term memory: Memory that usually lasts only for seconds or as long as rehearsal continues.

Significant others: In interpersonal theory, parents or others on whom an infant is dependent for meeting all physical and psychological needs.

Simple cortical cells: Cells in the visual cortex that respond best to an edge or a bar of a particular width and with a particular direction and location in the visual field.

Simulation: An intentional imitation of the basic processes and outcomes of a real-life situation, carried out to better understand the basic mechanisms of the situation. In civil law, misrepresenting or concealing the truth, as when parties pretend to perform an act different from that in which they really are engaged.

Simultagnosia: The perception of one stimulus when two objects are presented. Often associated with inertia of gaze.

Sinus: A channel for the passage of blood; hollow in a bone or other tissue; antrum; one of the cavities connecting with the nose; a suppurating cavity.

Sinusoid: A blood space in certain organs, as the brain.

Situational stress reaction (acute): Superficial maladjustment to newly experienced life situations that are especially difficult or trying.

Glossary

Sleep apnea: A sleep disorder that involves slowing or cessation of respiration during sleep, which wakens the patient. Excessive daytime somnolence results from frequent nocturnal awakening.

Slow-wave sleep: Stages of sleep including stages 1 through 4, defined by presence of slow electroencephalographic (EEG) activity.

Socialized-aggressive disorder: Pattern of childhood maladaptive behaviors involving social maladaption, such as stealing, truancy, gang membership.

Sodium pentothal: Barbiturate drug sometimes used in psychotherapy to produce a state of relaxation and suggestibility.

Sodomy: Sexual intercourse via the anus.

Somatosensory agnosia: Loss of tactile recognition due to cerebral dysfunction in the presence of intact somatosensory receptive functions.

Somatosensory modalities: Refers to different types of body sensation (e.g., touch, pain, pressure). Distinguished from auditory and visual senses.

Somesthetic: Pertaining to somatesthesia, or the consciousness of having a body.

Somnolent mutism: Immobility and unresponsiveness with eyes closed, associated with mesencephalic–diencephalic lesions. Intense stimulation yields minimal responses.

Spasm: An involuntary, convulsive, muscular contraction.

Spatial acalculia: Spatial misarrangement of the numbers during arithmetic calculation with intact knowledge of correct principle. Associated with right hemisphere lesions.

Spatial agraphia: Deficits in spatial motor aspects of writing due to brain damage located in the nondominant parietal lobe. Frequently associated with the neglect syndrome.

Spatial summation: The summation of the axon hillock of postsynaptic potentials from across the cell body. If this summation reaches threshold, a nerve impulse will be triggered.

Special vulnerability: Low tolerance for specific types of stress.

Specific heat: The heat energy required to raise the temperature of 1 g of a substance by 1°C.

Spectrally opponent cell: A visual receptor cell with opposite firing responses to different regions of the spectrum.

Spinal nerves: The 31 pairs of nerves that emerge from the spinal cord.

Split-brain: Individuals who have had the corpus callosum severed, halting communication between the right and left hemispheres.

Squamous: Scalelike.

Stage 1 sleep: The initial stage of slow-wave sleep involving small-amplitude electroencephalographic (EEG) waves of irregular frequency, slow heart rate, and a reduction of muscle tension.

Stage 2 sleep: A stage of slow-wave sleep defined by bursts of regular 14 to 18 Hz electroencephalographic (EEG waves that progressively increase and then decrease in amplitude (called spindles).

Stage 3 sleep: A stage of slow-wave sleep defined by the spindles seen in stage 2 sleep mixed with larger amplitude slow waves.

Stage 4 sleep: A stage of slow-wave sleep defined by the presence of high amplitude slow waves of 1 to 4 Hz.

Star chamber: An ancient court of England that originally had jurisdiction in cases in which the ordinary course of justice was obstructed by one party to the extent that no inferior court would find its process obeyed. Abolished in modern jurisprudence.

Stare decisis: The legal policy of courts stating that once a principle of law is laid down, it will be adhered to and applied to all future cases in which the facts are substantially the same. Serves to ensure security and certainty of legal principles.

Static phase of weight gain: A later period following destruction of the ventromedial hypothalamus during which the animal's weight stabilizes at an obese level and food intake is not much above normal.

Statistical test of significance: A standard of probability stating that an experimental finding is significant if, by chance alone, it could have occurred fewer than 1 or 5 times in 100 occurrences. In the field of psychology, 5 times in 100 is usually the standard of acceptability for statistical significance.

Statute: An act of legislation by which a law is created, as opposed to unwritten or common law.

Statutory law: The body of law created by the legislature.

Statutory rape: Sexual intercourse with a minor.

Stellate cell: A kind of small nerve cell with many branches.

Stenosis: Narrowing or contraction of a body passage or opening.

Glossary

Stereoacuity: The ability to discriminate small differences in visual depth by point-by-point matching in the retinas.

Stereopsis: The ability to perceive depth, utilizing the slight difference in visual information from the two eyes.

Stimulus enhancement: The second stimulus in a pair adds rather than masks the neural effects of the first stimulus. Studies include those that present letters of one half of a word (first stimulus) and then letters of the remaining portion of the word (second stimulus).

Stimulus masking: A second stimulus leads into or masks a first stimulus if the trace of the initial stimulus is longlasting or otherwise sufficient. The target stimulus (e.g., letters of the alphabet) is interfered with by the masking stimulus (e.g., patterned line segments).

Stimulus persistence: Effects of external stimulation are lasting in the central nervous system, dependent on many factors. Stimulus persistence acting as an interference to new stimuli has been advanced to account for deficient perception in the older person.

Stipulation: An agreement made between opposing parties that certain facts or principles of law are true and applicable and will not be contested.

Stress-decompensation model: View of abnormal behavior that emphasizes progressive disorganization of behavior under excessive stress.

Striate cortex: A portion of the visual cortex with input from the lateral geniculate nucleus.

Strict liability: Liability without a showing of fault, as when a person, who engages in a hazardous activity, is totally liable for injuries caused by the activity even without negligence being shown.

Stricture: A circumscribed narrowing of a tubular structure.

Stroma: The tissue that forms the ground substance, framework, or matrix of an organ, as distinguished from that constituting its functional element, or parenchyma.

***Sub nom*:** Under the name. In the name of. Often used when the original name of a case must be changed due to a change in parties.

Subpoena: A command for a witness to appear at a certain time and place to testify in court on a certain matter.

Subpoena duces tecum: A command that a witness produce a specified document or record.

Substance-abuse disorders: Pathological use of a substance for at least a month, resulting in self-injurious behavior and biological dependence on the substance.

Substance-induced organic disorder: Category of disorders based on organic impairment resulting from toxicity or physiologic changes in the brain.

Substance-use disorder: Patterns of maladaptive behavior centered around regular use of substance involved.

Sulci: The furrows of convoluted brain surface. Contrast with gyri.

Superior colliculus: A structure in the midbrain that receives information from the optic tract.

Superior olivary complex: A brain stem structure that receives input from the left cochlear nuclei, providing the first binaural analysis of auditory information.

Supplementary motor area (SMA) location: Area 6 and partially area 7, anterior to paracentral lobule. Function: volitional (self-initiated) movements; perineal and leg movements are found in the medial extension of the motor homunculus. Considered also a secondary speech area.

Supra: Above, upon.

Supraoptic nucleus: A nucleus of the hypothalamus.

Synapse: An area composed of the presynaptic (axonal) terminal, the postsynaptic (usually dendritic) membrane, and the space (or cleft) between them. This is the site at which neural messages travel from one neuron to another. Also called the synaptic region.

Synaptic assembly: A level of brain organization that includes the total collection of all synapses on a single cell.

Synaptic bouton: The presynaptic swelling of the axon terminal from which neural messages travel across the synaptic cleft to other neurons.

Synaptic cleft: The space between the presynaptic and postsynaptic membranes.

Synaptic region: *See* Synapse.

Synaptic transmitter: The chemical in the presynaptic bouton that serves as the basis for neural communication. It travels across the synaptic cleft and reacts with the postsynaptic membrane when triggered by a nerve impulse. Also called neurotransmitter.

Synaptic vesicles: The small, spherically shaped structures that contain molecules of synaptic transmitter.

T

Tactile: Pertaining to the sense of touch.

Tactual hallucinations: Hallucinations involving the sense of touch, such as feeling cockroaches crawling over one's body.

Tardive dyskinesia: Abnormal involuntary movements involving the extremities or facial area (e.g., tongue, jaw, facial surface). Results as a late side effect of neuroleptic drug treatment and, in many cases, is irreversible. Involuntary movements — especially those involving the face, mouth, lips, and tongue — that are related to prolonged use of antipsychotic drugs, such as chlorpromazine.

Telecephalon: Consists of the cerebral cortex, corpus striatum, and medullary center. The frontal subdivision of the forebrain that includes the cerebral hemispheres when fully developed.

Temporal summation: The summation of postsynaptic potentials that reach the axon hillock at different times. The closer together they are, the more complete the summation.

Testosterone: A hormone produced by male gonads that controls a variety of bodily changes that become visible at puberty.

Tetany: Intermittent tonic muscular contractions of the extremities.

Thalamic syndrome: Disturbance of the senses with initial hemianesthesia, followed by a raised threshold to touch, pain, heat, and cold on the side opposite the lesion. The sensations may be extremely adversive when reached. Due primarily to a thalamic infarct.

Thalamus: The brain regions that surround the third ventricle.

Third-party beneficiary: A person who has enforceable rights created by a contract to which he is not party and for which he gives no consideration.

Thrombophlebitis: The condition in which inflammation of the vein wall has preceded the formation of a thrombus, or intravascular clot.

Thrombosis: The formation of a clot within a vessel during life.

Thrombotic stroke: Results from blockage or occlusion by blood or tissue particles or overgrowth. Forms most often where blood vessels branch.

Thrombus: A clot of blood formed within the heart or the blood vessels, usually caused by slowing of the circulation of the blood or by alteration of the blood itself or the vessel walls.

Thyroid-stimulating hormone (TSH): A tropic hormone released by the anterior pituitary gland that increases the release of thyroxin and the uptake of iodine by the thyroid gland.

Thyrotropin-releasing hormone (TRH): A hypothalamic hormone that regulates the release of thyroid-stimulating hormone.

Thyroxin: A hormone released by the thyroid gland.

Tinnitus: A ringing or singing sound in the ears.

Tolerance: Physiological condition in which increased dosage of an addictive drug is needed to obtain effects previously produced by smaller doses.

Tomogram: *See* Computer axial tomogram.

Tonic receptors: Receptors in which the frequency of nerve impulse discharge declines slowly or not at all as stimulation is maintained.

Tort: A private or civil wrong or injury, excluding a breach of contract, for which the court will provide a remedy in the form of an action for damages.

Toxicity: The poisonous nature of a substance.

Trabecula: A septum that extends from an envelope into the enclosed substance, forming an essential part of the stroma of the organ.

Transcortical motor (TCM) aphasia: Separation of general conceptual functions (posterior) from Broca motor output area (anterior). Lesions in the supplementary motor area (SMA) or in Broca's area. The patient can repeat words but has difficulty with comprehension and/or speech.

Transient global amnesia: A relatively brief (several hours to several days) amnestic condition with few neurological sequelae. Associated features include (1) a major symptom of anterograde amnesia, (2) some retrograde amnesia, (3) confusion and time/place disorientation, and (4) speech and orientation to person are unimpaired. There is usually a sudden onset and cessation with no prodromal symptoms or known cause.

Transient ischemic attacks (TIAs): Neurological deficits of sudden onset; less intense and temporary strokes that may precede thrombotic strokes. Last less than 24 hours by definition. About half of those who experience TIAs will have a major stroke.

Transient situational disorder: Temporary mental disorder developing under conditions of overwhelming stress, as in military combat or civilian catastrophes.

Transmethylation hypothesis: A hypothesized explanation of schizophrenia suggesting that the addition of a methyl group to some naturally occurring brain compounds can convert some substances to hallucinogenic agents, or psychotogens.

Transverse: *See* Coronal.

Tremor at rest: A tremor that occurs when the affected region, such as a limb, is fully supported.

Tremors: Rhythmic repetitive movements caused by brain pathology.

Trial: A judicial examination or determination, either civil or criminal, of issues between parties to an action.

Trigeminal neuralgia: Intense and sudden pain in area of a trigeminal nerve lesion. The episodic pain may be set off by light stimulation such as touching the skin.

Tropic hormones: Anterior pituitary hormones that affect the secretion of other endocrine glands.

U

Unconscious motivation: Motivation for an individual's behavior of which he or she is unaware.

Undifferentiated schizophrenia: Subtype in which the patient either has mixed symptoms or moves rapidly from one type to another.

Undue influence: Any wrongful or improper persuasion whereby the person's will is overpowered, thereby causing the person to act in a way he or she would normally not have acted.

Uniform laws: A body of written laws, in various subject areas, approved by the commissioners on uniform state laws, which are often adopted by individual states.

Unilateral apraxia: Apraxia affecting one side of the body. Sympathetic and callosal types have been postulated. The sympathetic aspect occurs when other functions are likewise impaired (e.g., right hemiparesis, left-hand apraxia) and Broca aphasia produced by left motor association destruction of callosal fibers.

Unipolar disorder: A severe affective disorder in which only depressive episodes occur, as opposed to bipolar disorders in which both manic and depressive processes are assumed to occur.

Unmyelinated: Refers to fine-diameter axons that lack a myelin sheath.

Unsocialized disturbance of conduct: Childhood disorder in which the child is disobedient, hostile, and highly aggressive.

Urticaria: Nettle rash; hives; elevated, itching, white patches.

Utilization behavior: Considered a type of magnetic apraxia, where the afflicted individual pursues a stimulus to grasp within a set of actively exploring the environment. Considered a strong frontal sign. Gegenhalten occurs when contact is made. Walking is then impaired when attempted, with leg stiffening and no movement.

V

Vaginismus: An involuntary muscle spasm at the entrance to the vagina that prevents penetration and sexual intercourse.

Vagus nerve: One of the cranial nerves.

Variant sexual behavior: Behavior in which satisfaction is dependent on something other than a mutually desired sexual engagement with a sexually mature member of the opposite sex.

Ventral: An anatomical term meaning toward the belly or front of the body or the bottom of the brain; opposite of dorsal.

Ventricles: Cavities in the brain that contain cerebrospinal fluid. The four cavities in the brain that contain cerebrospinal fluid. The choroid plexus produces the cerebrospinal fluid. Spaces within the brain, filled with cerebrospinal fluid, which provide support and cushioning for the brain.

Ventricular layer: A layer of homogeneous cells in the neural tube of the developing organism that is the source of all neural and glial cells in the mature organism. Also called the ependymal layer.

Ventromedial hypothalamus (VMH): A hypothalamic region involved in inhibiting eating, among other functions.

Venue: The particular geographic area in which a court with jurisdiction may hear and determine a case.

Verbal adynamia: Diminished speech spontaneity. There is slow speech initiation and/or reluctance to continue verbal output. Usually accompanies general apathy.

Verdict: The formal decision or finding made by a judge or jury on the matters or questions submitted for their deliberation and determination.

Vertigo: Dizziness, giddiness.

Vesicle: A small bladder, or sac, containing liquid.

Vesicles (synaptic): Small structures located at the end point (terminus) of the axon that are filled with neurotransmitter substances.

Vestibular: Pertaining to a vestibule; such as the inner ear, larynx, mouth, nose, vagina.

Vestibuloocular reflex: A rapid response that adjusts the eye to a change in head position

Viscosity: A condition of more or less adhesion of the molecules of a fluid to each other so that it flows with difficulty. A behavioral pattern characterized by stickiness in interactional contexts. Associated with frontal system damage.

Visual anosognosia: Denial of blindness caused by brain lesions. The subject attempts to behave as if the deficit were not present. *See* Anton's syndrome.

Voir dire: To speak the truth. The preliminary examination made by the court or by attorneys of one presented as a prospective juror to determine his or her competence.

W

Wada technique: Designed to assess which hemisphere is language dominant. Here, sodium amytal is injected into one carotid artery to deactivate an entire hemisphere. Changes in counting behaviors while the injection is in process indicate which hemisphere is dominant for speech and language.

Waive: To abandon or give up a claim or right.

Waiver: An intentional and voluntary surrendering or giving up of a known right.

Warrant: A document directing a public official to perform a particular act.

Weight of the evidence: The relative value of the credible evidence presented by one side balanced against the evidence presented by the other side. Indicates to the jury that the party having the burden of proof will be entitled to the verdict if the greater amount of evidence supports the issue.

Wernicke's aphasia: A fluent disorder with severe auditory comprehension and processing deficits. Empty speech, press for speech, and a moderate to substantial naming deficit are apparent. Considered a posterior aphasia.

Wernicke's area: A region of the left hemisphere involved in language comprehension.

White matter: Consists of densely packed conduction fibers that transmit neural messages between the cortex and lower centers (projection fibers), between the hemispheres (commissural fibers), or within a hemisphere (association fibers). A shiny layer underneath the cortex consisting largely of axons with white myelin sheaths.

Witness: One who testifies, under oath, to what he or she has seen, heard, or otherwise observed.

Word deafness: Also called pure word deafness. Here, nonspeech sounds are recognized but not spoken words. Usually produced by subcortical lesion disconnecting auditory input from auditory processing.

Work product: Work done by an attorney while representing a client, such as writings, statements, or testimony in regard to the attorney's legal impressions, tactics, strategies, and opinions, which are ordinarily not subject to discovery. Discovery may be obtained only when the party seeking it has a substantial need for the material to prepare his or her case and is unable to obtain the substantial equivalent of the material by other means without undue hardship.

Writ: An order issued by a court mandating the performance of a specified act, or giving authority to have it done.

X

X cells: Retinal ganglion cells that continue to respond to maintained visual stimuli.

Xanthrochromia: Blood cells in the cerebrospinal fluid with discoloration due to an abnormal somatic condition.

Y

Y cells: Retinal ganglion cells that respond strongly initially but rapidly decrease the frequency of response to a visual stimulus.

Appendix I

Treatment Facility Checklist

Date: _____

Facility Name: _____ Phone Number: _____

    Web site _____

Information Source: _____ Brochure(s) Requested _____

Physical Health
    M.D. (Internist, addictionologist, nonpsychiatric) on staff ___
    M.D. as above, consulting ___
    Nursing care provided ___

Psychiatric Coverage
    Psychiatrist on staff___
    Psychiatrist consulting___
    Psychotropic medication where needed___

Psychosocial Treatment
    Psychologist on staff___
    Psychologist___
    MA social worker___

Continuum of Care:
    Detox — On site___; Accessed elsewhere___
    Inpatient — On site___; Accessed elsewhere___
    PHP — On site___; Accessed elsewhere___
    IOP — On site___; Accessed elsewhere___
    Residential___

Dual Dx Treatment:
    Yes___No___

Treatment Philosophy:

12 Step (AA) only___
Rational Recovery (harm reduction) only___
Other Cog. Beh. Model only___
Mixed model
    AA and Cog. Beh.___
    AA and Psychoeducational___
    AA and other treatment___
    Any combination not including AA___

Payment Method:
_____
_____

Other Model (describe)
_____
_____
_____

Recreational/Occupational Rehabilitation
    OT/RT on site___; Consulting___; By referral___
    Vocational Rehab on site___; By referral___

Appendix II

Pacific Institute for the Study of Conflict and Aggression Statement of Purpose

The Pacific Institute for the Study of Conflict and Aggression is a nonprofit scientific and educational organization that addresses domestic, acquaintance, stranger, and institutional violence. The Pacific Institute focuses its training, research, and publication activities on conduct disorders, compilation of measures of malingering, deception, and distortion, cross-cultural violence factors, and development of the Violence Prediction Scale (VPS) in the U.S. and the Pacific Basin. Consultation services provided by the Pacific Institute include police training, criminal personality profiling, detection of malingering and deception, eyewitness identification and distortion, and conflict resolution and mediation intervention.

Members of the Pacific Institute Advisory Board include over several dozen distinguished professionals from all parts of the U.S. and from several foreign countries. Members represent many points of view in regard to etiology, evaluation, and intervention in violence and share the belief that increased knowledge of violence-related phenomena enhances understanding, contributes to effective intervention, and strengthens the relationship between professionals in this field and the public.

Listed below are members of the Pacific Institute Advisory Board:

Kenneth M. Adams, Ph.D., A.B.C.N., Clinical Neuropsychologist, University of Michigan Medical Center, Ann Arbor, Michigan

Dennis R. Baltzley, Ph.D., Industrial/Organizational Psychologist, Plantation, Florida

Sally H. Barlow, Ph.D., A.B.P.P., Assistant Professor, Brigham Young University, Provo, Utah

Tom Bevel, Police Detective, TBI-Forensic Consultation, Edmond, Oklahoma

V. Edwin Bixenstine, Ph.D., A.B.P.P., Clinical Psychologist, Bixenstine & Associates, Kent, Ohio

Randy Borum, Psy.D., Assistant Clinical Professor, Plantation, Florida

Patrick E. Cook, Ph.D., A.B.P.P., Forensic Psychologist, Tallahassee, Florida

Lloyd E. Dean, SAC, FBI (Retired), Threat Management Group, Inc., Louisville, Kentucky

Robert F. Eme, Ph.D., A.B.P.P., Clinical Professor, Illinois School of Professional Psychology, Rolling Meadows, Illinois

William E. Foote, Ph.D., A.B.P.P., Forensic Psychologist, Albuquerque, New Mexico

Charles J. Golden, Ph.D., A.B.C.N., Director, Center for Psychological Studies, Nova Southeastern University, Fort Lauderdale, Florida

Samuel T. Gontkovsky, M.S., Center for Psychological Studies, Nova Southeastern University, Fort Lauderdale, Florida

Harold V. Hall, Ph.D., A.B.P.P., Forensic Neuropsychologist, Psychological Consultants, Kamuela, Hawaii

Hua Han, Director, Program for Arms Control and Disarmament, Peking University, Beijing, People's Republic of China

Dayle L. Hinman, Special Agent, Tallahassee, Florida

Gary Jackson, Ph.D., Vice President and Director of Research and Development, Psychological Assessment Resources, Inc., Lutz, Florida

Michele L. Jackson, M.S., Center for Psychological Studies, Nova Southeastern University, Fort Lauderdale, Florida

Douglas Johnson-Greene, Ph.D., Clinical Neuropsychologist, University of Michigan Medical Center, Ann Arbor, Michigan

Phillip W. Johnson, Ph.D., A.B.F.P., Forensic Psychologist, Threat Management Group, Inc., Louisville, Kentucky

B.L.J. Kaczmarek, Ph.D., Professor of Neurolinguistics, Uniwersytet Marie Curie-Sklodowskeij, Lublin, Poland

Florence Kaslow, Ph.D., A.B.P.P., Clinical Psychologist, Palm Beach Gardens, Florida

James A. Marlow, Esq., Judge Advocate General, Sembach Air Force Base, Germany

Rosalie Matzkin, Ed.D., Lecturer in Films and Communication, University of Pennsylvania, Ogontz Campus, Abington, Pennsylvania

Sandra B. McPherson, Ph.D., A.B.P.P., Forensic Psychologist, Cleveland, Ohio

James I. Morrow, MGYSGT, USMC (Ret.), Substance Abuse and Trauma Counselor, Hilo, Hawaii

Angela Peterson-Rohne, M.S., Center for Psychological Studies, Nova Southeastern University, Fort Lauderdale, Florida

Joseph G. Poirier, Ph.D., A.B.P.P., Clinical and Forensic Psychologist, Rockville, Maryland

David A. Pritchard, Ph.D., A.B.F.P., Forensic Psychologist, Atlanta, Georgia

Reverend Jan Rudinoff, Minister, St. Michael and All Angels Church, Lihue, Kauai, Hawaii

Frank C. Sacco, Ph.D., Clinical Psychologist, Topeka, Kansas

Louis B. Schlesinger, Ph.D., A.B.P.P., Clinical Associate Professor, University of New Jersey, and Clinical Psychologist at Veterans Administration Center, East Orange, New Jersey

Lita L. Schwartz, Ph.D., A.B.F.P., Distinguished Professor Emerita, University of Pennsylvania, Ogontz Campus, Abington, Pennsylvania

Dingli Shen, Ph.D., Director, American Studies Program, Fudan University, Shanghai, People's Republic of China

Eugene Shooter, Ph.D., Clinical Psychologist, Washington, D.C.

Harley V. Stock, Ph.D., A.B.F.P., Forensic Psychologist, Plantation, Florida

Stuart W. Twemlow, M.D., Clinical Psychiatrist, Menninger Clinic, Topeka, Kansas

Leighton C. Whitaker, Ph.D., A.B.P.P., Adjunct Clinical Professor, Widener University, Wallingford, Pennsylvania

Errol Yudko, Ph.D., Assistant Professor of Psychology, University of Hawaii at Hilo, Hilo Hawaii

Appendix III

Verbatim History of a Crystal Methamphetamine Abuser

Introduction

I am an addict and a prisoner of drugs for "life." I am 39 now, and I was heavy into Crystal Meth, also known as "ICE," and also cocaine and pills (mostly downers). All the time I was high on drugs, I thought this was what life was all about. Then it became an addiction that I couldn't control. Failure was my way of life for many years when I was using drugs. It all started to go downhill from there. I caused myself much pain and suffering but, more so, to my loved ones, as well as innocent victims. This evil poison has caused me to do things I would never have done, had I not been caught up in it. Now, looking back at my life of drugs, I feel a lot of heartache for my actions. Also looking back from behind bars, I begin to see more clearly what is real.

This is why I wanted to put together this booklet, in hopes that I can help you, the beginner, hard core user, and all you parents, to understand the evils of drugs. This booklet will show how we, as addicts, think and act while we are on drugs. It will also help you as parents look for some of the "warning signs." Please read each page slowly and carefully and take all the writing personally. Try to feel it, understand it, and absorb it. Read it with an open mind and heart.

Battling the Monster

I remember the good drug experiences. I don't think about the bad experiences like being sick or going crazy when I didn't have any crack to smoke. I did almost anything to get more cocaine. I would manipulate people and I would try to control everything around me, no matter what the cost or who I hurt.

I used crack cocaine and a combination of drugs to help me to get away from the real world. I thought it would help me deal with my life. Crack cocaine at one point made me feel good until my body told me that I needed more crack to smoke.

My ability to love, care, and be responsible were sharply affected by my drug use. I was hurting, and I needed help but didn't know where to turn to. Some days the crack would bring me down. I would feel totally alone and abandoned. I found myself so strung out that I could no longer function as a human being. I would get to a point of paranoia and depression.

I guess I wanted the easy way out. So I started thinking about suicide. No matter how much I thought I was in control of the crack it always somehow brought me down. It defeated me every time. It was a losing battle. I could always get back my physical health but I always had a funny feeling when I wasn't using anything. It sure felt strange. The cravings were so intense that I became nauseated and sick until I couldn't stand it any more and would go and score some more crack.

I went through years of telling my wife it was going to be different this time. But it only got worse. I would try to change but sought very little help. This was the only way of life that I knew for many years. My pattern of abusing drugs was always the same. First the lying to loved ones and family then the stealing. It was a vicious cycle that I put myself and my family through every time. I had a difficult time giving up old habits and connections. I wanted to fit into society but never could because of my drug use. It was an uphill battle for me. The only way for me to win this battle was by either going to prison or death. Never in my wildest dreams did I envision this happening to me.

Losing My Soul

I developed a passion for ICE. It was my drug of choice. I would smoke for days then I would level off and no matter how much ICE I smoked, I couldn't get any higher. It would just keep me up. My body would ache for sleep and continue to lose weight, but my mind would race, and I would come to a point of paranoia and fear. When I smoked ICE for long periods of time, I would get extremely forgetful and would not be able to sleep. No matter what my wife or anyone told me about my drug problem I wouldn't listen. I still continued to insanely abuse ICE.

There were some days that I would kick back, watch my kids play, and wonder if I could stay clean just for one day. I could then have a chance for a quality life. I began thinking of how tired I was of living this kind of life. I was trapped by my need for the instant high to feel good.

I turned my life over to evil many times. I believe there is a demon inside all of us ICE users, and if given too much ICE for a long period of time it will one day turn ugly and evil.

I tried to stop using ICE on my own and went through the pain of withdrawal again. I felt lost, confused and even thought that my family deserted me. I would end up using the drug again. Sometimes I would even substitute ICE for another drug just to try to quit but it only prolonged the pain. I would devote all of my energy toward my desire to stay high with ICE.

People say that ICE is not as bad as smoking cocaine. When you smoke cocaine you have a mean head rush and ringing in the ears. Some first time users cannot handle the rush, so they turn to using ICE. When you smoke the ICE, there are no head rush and no ringing in the ears, so you think you can handle this drug. You continue smoking for a very long time.

ICE is a slow death process. You can smoke more and more till the ICE DEMON gets its evil claws deep into your soul. Then it's too late. You are doomed. With some other types of drugs, when I was without it I immediately began experiencing depression, hostility, anger, and stress, but as soon as I would score some more, I would mellow out and be happy. But with ICE, I was in a state of depression, hostility, anger, and in a stressful mood with or without the drug. You cannot escape this "ICE DEMON" once you start smoking. I was beaten.

The Plea

I am 39 years old, and I've been convicted of second degree murder. I'm incarcerated at Halawa High Maximum Security Prison. I was sentenced to life in prison with the possibility of parole. My minimum is 35 years and I see the parole board in the year 2002.

I'm in my cell that is 9' by 12' and I have to share it with another inmate. There's no place you can go and have quality time by yourself. As I lay here on my bed staring at my family's picture, I look at my three beautiful daughters and my lovely wife and ask myself "WHY?" How could I have been so stupid and allow myself to end up in a place like this?

I had everything going for me. I had my own business and things were progressing by the day and looking real good. My wife is a hard worker, supportive, and beautiful. My kids are the greatest. They bring joy and happiness into my life, even though I'm in here.

I never realized how blind a person can be. I guess for most of us it takes prison before we realize and see what we really had going for ourselves. For me now, just to see the outside and breathe the fresh air is a blessing. To be locked up in a place like this, I think, is the gateway to hell.

For me, I found the higher power in the "Man" upstairs and it helps me fight off the evil in this God-forsaken place. You have to be strong-minded and have a positive attitude to survive in this concrete jungle of hell.

I'm calling out to you, all my brothers and sisters of our island. Hear me out, please! Open up your eyes, ears, and mind before you start experimenting with the "CRACK MONSTER" and "ICE DEMON."

This is one of the few "poisons" that the devil has to offer us. It starts off pleasurable and the feeling is really good. But, trust me; it's not what it seems to be. Behind this mask of temptation is the devil himself waiting for us to do his dirty work for him. He rewards us with desperation and depression and we end up lying, stealing, physically hurting people, and even murder.

This is one of the ways I can contribute to you, the people of our island. By writing my true feelings and experiences, maybe I can at least help you, the parents, and our kids, understand the evils of using drugs. I was using drugs for over 20 years and for once in my life, I can feel sane and human again.

History

Also known as "speed" or "crank" methamphetamine is a synthetic stimulant developed by a Japanese chemist in the year 1919. It gives a feeling of euphoria (feeling of great happiness) and alertness and perception of improved self-esteem. It targets areas of the brain that control the emotions. But as it wears off, the abuser of the drug, especially after a several day binge, becomes easily agitated, on edge, and paranoid. Because they're emotionally burnt out, they respond with a "hair trigger." The crash is often deadly for the children, spouse, and friends of the drug abuser.

In the 1960s, doctors in San Francisco began prescribing meth injections for treatment of heroin addiction. Widespread abuse by students, and others, followed. While the drug became better controlled, illegal meth labs began to appear. San Francisco's Haight-Ashbury district became the heart of the worst abuse in the late 1960s.

In small, controlled doses, methamphetamine is used to treat obesity (overweight), increase attention span, narcolepsy (uncontrollable sleep), and depression. Doctors used to prescribe the drug to increase energy, decrease the need for sleep and elevate mood. It was also used legally by combat pilots who needed to fly through the night while staying alert for battle. Records have shown that astronauts used the drug to stay alert enough to make quick decisions at the end of long missions. Ex-President John F. Kennedy was known to have taken injections of this drug prior to key summit meetings.

Verbatim History of a Crystal Methamphetamine Abuser

It's a good stimulant, but Adolf Hitler, an abuser of the drug, used huge amounts of meth when he was in power to rule the world.

Treatment, education and reduction efforts worked, but some people continued to favor methamphetamine as a cheaper alternative to cocaine in the 1980s. Meth is a mixture of ephedrine, a common drug used for asthma and stuffy noses, and other chemicals found in gasoline, rubbing alcohol, pool cleaning supplies and drain cleaners.

In the mid-1980s, Philippines, Japan, and Korea took the "speed" (methamphetamine) one step further. It was purified to create what we now call "ICE" (crystal meth). There were two types of crystal meth — oil base and water base — and the cost is two to three times more than "speed" or "crack." Now it has plagued our beautiful island of Oahu.

Understanding

I am a chemically dependent person and will always be. I lack the "power" over my drug use. We, as addicts, are unable to predict the outcome of our actions while under the influence of drugs. A chemical dependent person is any person that is dependent on any type of drug such as coffee, tobacco, off-the-counter drugs, to the use of pot and crystal meth. This person is one that cannot control his or her craving for that type of chemical. The lack of will power! Another symptom of a chemically dependent person is that he or she sometimes can't stop using the drug when he or she wants to stop. We are all powerless over our dependency.

When we are under the influence, we miss out on what's important. We are too busy thinking where am I going to get the drugs and how? When we are using drugs, we think we are in control. We always justify our means. Here are some examples: "I use only on the weekends and special occasions, with my friends." "When I did use dope it wasn't much." "I only smoke pot, I don't use the hard stuff." "If I wanted to, I could quit at any time. Under the influence, we forget our responsibilities. Sometimes we don't plan on things happening the way we want them to. We forget the time and don't come home. We can't drive safely. We get pretty crazy at times and we usually do things we regret later.

When we first start out using, it's all fun and parties. It's a pretty neat experience. We think we are cool. But, after we keep on abusing our body and our mind, the drug begins to take over and we begin to listen to it. Then, it's the most important thing in our lives. When we are in this state we don't realize that this is a problem.

When we use drugs heavily, we cause our body to get rundown. We don't take good care of our body. We don't get enough sleep, and exercise. When we are high, we lack good judgment. We think we can solve problems, drive a car, and handle firearms. We sometimes think mixing drugs is pretty cool too. The combinations of drugs can be much stronger than we expect. Famous people, like River Phoenix and John Belushi, have died mixing and using a combination of drugs. They mixed heroin and cocaine (speedball). It can be deadly!

When we start using drugs, we tend to surround our entire life around it. We drift away from our family and our "true friends." When we are high, our behavior changes. We start to lie and steal from our family and friends. We don't even know that we are hurting them by our changed behavior. We lose all self-respect and self-esteem. It all goes down when we are using drugs.

When we are high, we tend to do more illegal things, like stealing, carrying weapons, driving while high, and even murder.

We waste more money when we are using drugs. We think we are in control. We spend every penny that we have on drugs. We also damage and hurt other people, because of what we steal, or by some injury we may have caused, whether we meant to or not.

We were, at one point in our lives, caring, loving, trusting, and honest people. We had goals and values in life. Now that we use drugs we become more selfish and less caring and we think more evil thoughts. As drug users, we put our trust into the drugs instead of our loved ones and friends. We lose faith in everything that we believed in at one time in our lives (wife, family, friends, and God).

My parents were always on my back about everything I did. They were always complaining about who I hung around with, the type of things that I wore, and the type of grades I brought home from school. They were always treating me like a little baby and never listening to what I had to say. They were always putting me down. They just didn't understand me. Sometimes I wished I wasn't born. Maybe if I had different parents, things would have been different. I don't know. Sometimes I had wished I was dead. I felt so lonely and so depressed. If I did die, would anyone really miss me?

These are some of the questions that go through our kids' mind when they are growing into the teen years. We must try to understand them, talk to them with respect, not as babies. They need lots of encouragement, not discouragement. We, as parents, need to communicate with our kids, talk with them, not talk at them. We have to give them lots of LOVE. We should be caring, open-minded and honest towards our kids and other people. We should also give them some responsibility and room to grow. If we don't learn to understand our kids, we may lose them to the evils of drugs.

Parents, these are some of the Warning Signs to look out for, if you suspect your kids are using drugs:

Glassy and/or redness of eyes
Loss of appetite and/or sudden weight loss
Craving for thirst
Lacking hygiene
Growing one fingernail extra long
Picking at skin on fingers
Acting more fatigued
Acting more energetic
Unpredictable mood swings
Depression setting in
Acting more irritable
Lying to cover-up
Forgetfulness and/or confusion
Being less responsible
Unpredictable, sudden outburst of anger
Crying for nothing and/or fits of laughter
Acting more secretively
Changes in friends
Lack of communication
Lacking in school or job performance
Always in need of money
Things being missing (money, jewelry, things of value)

If your kids have any or a combination of these Warning Signs, confront the problem head on! Don't hold back — if you do, you might lose your child to the evils of drugs. Always go with your gut feelings. Be there, sit down and talk "with" them. Show your child that you care and love them.

When your child starts using drugs they may start to feel good about themselves. This good feeling never lasts. So they end up using more drugs and the problem only gets worse. Two of the problems are peer pressure and curiosity. They are trying to fit in or to be cool.

Any type of drug paraphernalia is a sure sign of drug use. Here are some of the items you can look out for: any type of glass pipe with a bowl at the end or a straight tube, syringes and needles, razor blades, mirrors, cigarette rolling paper, matchbooks with the covers ripped off, Q-tip swabs, cottonballs, rum 151 alcohol, small decorative containers or small pill boxes, tweezers, tiny spoons, tiny plastic bags, and baking soda.

Also be suspicious of any type of pills, white or yellowish powder, herb or tea-like substances you cannot identify, any clearish form that looks like rock candy or Hawaiian salt. If you find any type of drugs, drug paraphernalia, or your kid admits to having a drug problem, seek help as soon as possible.

Sometimes when I look back at what I did to my family, friends, people I didn't know, and to myself, I feel a lot of pain, guilt, shame, sadness, loneliness, and fear. I think to myself, "Why go on?" When we feel this way, we think nobody cares. But they do care. All you have to do is ask for help or just ask for a "hug."

"I should just kill myself" — this is the easy way out for us drug users. We have to think hard and fight this feeling of hopelessness. We have to believe in ourselves and start thinking of others again. We are not losers! I BELIEVE WE ALL CAN MAKE IT!

For me, it helps a lot to talk about my addiction problem. They say that we who are users are sick people, we have a type of disease. I believe that one of the cures to this addiction is to believe in yourself and that you really have to want to stop using, for yourself.

Now I know my problem, I can try to deal with it one step at a time. First of all, I will have to be honest with myself and my loved ones. I have to clean up my act. I also have to distance myself from all drug friends and dealers. I have to admit that I have an illness, that I am an addict and take responsibility and action for my addiction. We are not alone in this quest for recovery. We have to learn to love ourselves first before we can love somebody. Drugs act as a magnet, it always attracts the bad elements.

If your child is using drugs or you suspect he/she is using, you can contact the school counselor, your doctor, the police department, and/or agencies....

Introduction to Corruption

1985, Crystal Methamphetamine, A.K.A. "ICE," is slowly creeping into the Hawaiian Islands, Oahu in particular. Oahu, "The Gathering Place," once known as one of the finest tourist attractions in the world is about to be devastated by this drug, "ICE."

I'm a "heavy drug user." The year again is 1985. I'm trying to quit smoking cocaine, but I find myself really suffering by this thought alone. I keep telling myself I can't maintain this lifestyle. If I do I'll lose my family. I'm already "losing my mind." So I ask myself,

"How am I going to quit this drug?"

Weeks later, I run into an old friend of mine. I tell him of my problem. He replies, "Brudda, just quit using cocaine and try this. This is what they call 'ICE.'" I was the type of user that preferred smoking the drugs rather than snorting it. And ICE was the perfect escape for me, so I thought.

I didn't have to go through the trouble of cooking the coke, buying the screens for the pipe, using rum 151 alcohol, cottons balls and baking soda. I actually felt that I was not only saving money, but time, which is so precious to a user. I didn't have to wait a long time to get high. So here I was thinking to myself that I would be saving money and time. My friend told me that I would be able to function at work, and in front of my family as well. Being able to face my family and using the drug at the same time was just the solution to all my problems.

So, I then proceeded to find out what this new drug was all about.

It was like the latest fad in town and I was the "biggest sucker." I was amazed that all I needed was the drug (rocks), batu pipe and lighter. I was spending fifty to a hundred dollars and it lasted me for two or three days. It was great! I could get high at home and even at work. Nobody would even notice. Ah, man, what a life! Boy, was I wrong!

Everything was fine for about a year. My wife even thought at first that I had quit using drugs. I held a steady job and I was bringing home my paycheck steadily like an average person. The quality of ICE was good and cheap. My habit was growing but was still under control, so I thought.

As time went on, ICE was being smuggled in from foreign countries such as Philippines, Korea, and Japan. This is when ICE earned its name "Batu." Batu is the Filipino name, literally meaning "rock," or "ICE." It comes in two forms, oil base or water base. With new varieties of ICE going around, such as "peanut butter," "apple" and "bubble gum," I found myself needing more of this poison.

I started buying eight-balls which is a total of 3.5 grams. At the most, this would cost me about $700.00. I would then break it down into papers, worth fifty to a hundred dollars each. By selling these papers I would double my money back and still have enough stash for me to smoke. I felt so invincible that nothing could bring me down, especially when you take downer too. I was "The Man!" But the monkey on my back was growing rapidly and telling me I still needed more, so I made my deals even smaller so I could smoke more, not knowing what I was becoming. I could feel it was getting worse, my addiction would soon get the best of me. And it did. I was doomed, but didn't know it.

The Hype

Thoughts ran wild in my head. "I've got to have more!" How do I get it? My heart is major throbbing. My hands filled with perspiration. I look at my stash, it's almost gone. I desperately start thinking of who, where, and how, can I get more stash for my dope.

Then I suddenly remembered someone having a safe in their home. No one will be at home; they're supposed to be at a party. What better time than now, broad daylight! Who would ever suspect it! I was so caught up in using this so-called "ICE" that I let the "hype" get to me. At this time I didn't care who I stole from. Stealing from your "own blood" is pretty much the lowest thing you can do, and the closest to describing, DESPERATE! And it was no chump change at that! The total estimate of jewelry and merchandise was around $10,000. (I made about $1,800 on the street).

As my needs grew rapidly for the ICE, I stole even more from my loved ones. It didn't matter who! At this point it was me, myself, and I; that was all that mattered. I ripped off my parents, wife, friends and even my children who I loved so dearly. It was anything for the "fast cash"! I couldn't control this craving I had inside of me. The ICE had full control over my mind, body, and soul.

Even the dealers were surprised and impressed at how good the quality of the merchandise I was boosting (stealing). They even made a list of things they wanted. For every item I brought in, such as jewelry (gold, silver, gemstones in any form), semi-auto handguns (22s all the way to 45s), even sawed-off shotguns, I'd get a certain amount of ICE for my goods. I didn't care what I sold, as long as I got high.

Planning

As I seem to step up a stage into this world I created, not even the President could bring me down. I entered a phase, full of false dreams and illusions. A phase that put me into the same category as men such as Al Capone, Machine Gun Kelly, etc. It was not so much of a gangster, but more of a Local Boy "Guardian-Angel," helping society get rid of the dealers. I eventually got this reputation, that I'm this "crazy guy" that likes guns, drugs, and will do anything to get what I needed. The dealers are even talking among themselves about me, so I used this so-called reputation to my advantage. I thought of dealers in the past, who ripped off users like me, by selling small deals for lots of money.

Basically those who had the drugs thought they were "GOD," and they had the power over others and me. It was now my turn to get even! All the hours of waiting at places they told me to meet them and never showed up, would all end soon! Shut them all down and do this island a favor. My main reason, I thought at the time, was to shut down these dealers because they don't care who they sold to. They even sold to intermediate school children. I've even seen kids as young as ten and eleven years old. At this point I knew I had to do something. I couldn't believe what I was seeing.

Getting Even

I start by making my list of dealers I want to shut down. I begin my equipment check which contains one 410-caliber sawed-off shotgun (shells filled with rock salt), a hunting knife, rope, pair of handcuffs, binoculars, ski mask, army fatigues, a dark shirt and make-up. I thought I was actually Rambo ready to go on my rampage. "Because they drew first blood." (Keep in mind that this is all still the thinking of the user, who thinks everything can be controlled by him).

I cruise around one of the dealer's house to check out what's going on in the area, who's coming and going. Being that I've already been up for 4 days, running low on fuel, my body weakens. I stop so I can refuel my body with some massive hits of my pipe and take some downers to settle my nerves. Now I'm all ready to take on the world. I freshen up. I start making my way to the house.

As I walk up to the front door and call, they let me in. I enter, with a hundred dollars, to pick up a quarter gram of ICE. As usual, it's another "rip-off" deal. I calm myself, remembering why I'm in there! I'm there scoping things out from the inside. I'm checking out how many people, children or dogs, type of locks on the doors and windows, and, most importantly, any weapons and alarms. It all checks out! I take my dope and make my way out the door, keeping in mind that I was again ripped off, but now, it's time to get even.

Now back in my car, I take more hits from my pipe, and start gearing up. The time is right; I start my plan of assault on the enemy. I go in and make my move. The feeling is unreal! I can't believe the "High!" My first hit is a successful one. Only two people in the house. I guess you can say I caught them by surprise! I made out with a lot more than I thought I would. Everything went smoothly, like clockwork. Nobody got hurt, and I got my stash. Most important, minus one less dealer on the street. The way I saw it, those that ripped people off and sold to young children deserved to be shut down (I could justify my means). There's a saying in the criminal world, "Never get too greedy." I didn't think much of the retaliation. I felt what I did was for all the right reasons. But I was wrong.

My Obsession

Time journeys on. It's 1989. Almost all my hits continue to be successful. I can't stop! So far I've been covering my tracks like a pro. I still continue to let the ICE manipulate me into thinking I am invincible! Time encourages me to move on to bigger and better riches (dealers).

This time I use — or rather, con — a friend of mine, John (as I will call him), without his knowledge. I use him to my advantage, being that he introduced me to my source of money for my bills, and dope for my high (unsuspecting dealers) for the next couple of months.

John and I have been partying for a week or so, no sleep for about 4 days now. John becomes delirious due to the lack of sleep. He starts talking about a big time dealer that sells to just about anybody with the "kala" (money). With my mind racing, and body drained, I start thinking everything out very closely and wondering, "Why, if these people are so big, don't they know the basic rule — Don't sell to anybody you don't know!" I know now that something must be wrong. These people must be desperate or have been up too long, "tweeking" on the dope. Taking the drug makes you lose focus and you become very vulnerable.

About three days later I decided to check these people out. I find out that they need to dump their stash so they can pick up a new load and make their people happy. Sure enough, it's an easy sell, no questions asked. Just in and out of the house. While I'm in, I scope out the scene and see that there are only four of them in the house, Big Daddy and three others. I tell them that I can dump some ICE for them, and can be back in about 3 hours. I show up a couple hours later for more. I did this so I look like a steady, worthy customer with a lot of cash. They loved it.

Now I'm in again, to pick up more dope. The same four are there. This time I ask them if I can use the bathroom. While I'm in the bathroom, I undo the lock to the window and screen. As I leave, I get a sense of trust from the dealer and his "Hui" (gang). They tell me I'm welcome anytime. I leave again with a grin on my face.

I drive my car 3 blocks away. There's only one way to the house and not without passing me first. I sit and relax for about an hour and take some hits from my pipe. I start getting ready for my mission and notice 3 cars coming my way. I recognize 3 of the men who were at the house. It's about two in the morning. Everything is quiet.

I'm all geared up and ready to make my move. I take another hit from my pipe and couple of deep breaths. Without thinking, I then make my move back to the house. I notice that all the lights are off except for the patio. I creep slowly into the front yard. Quietly I move like a "Ninja" to the side of the house where the bathroom is located. I take a peep through the bathroom window to see if anyone's in sight. It's clear! I lightly tap the screen to see if it's still loose. Sure enough, it's exactly the way I left it. I remove the screen and open up the window slowly.

The Big Score

I slide in like a snake on his attack. Without a sound, I start floating through the house like a cloud in the sky. I'm now 3 feet away from the patio where Big Daddy is facing in my direction. If ever he should awake, I'd be right in his view. So I quickly move to the side of the patio, out of his sight and taking a couple of deep breaths, trying to calm myself (I'm amping).

Now I get on all fours and pull my 22 semi (filled with 22 buck shots) out with the grace of Jesse James. I sneak up behind the couch where Big Daddy is sleeping. Completely shocked by my vision, I pause to check if what I'm seeing is for real. Lying in front of Big Daddy is a coffee table; there on the table was around a quarter pound of Shabu (ICE), 3 ounces of weed, and a koa bowl full of Valiums. I then quietly slip my black backpack off over my shoulder and move towards the dope with my gun pointed at Big Daddy. While putting the "treasures" into my bag, I grabbed the koa bowl of Valiums, but accidentally spill some on the table. Because of the noise Big Daddy awakes! With shock in his eyes and fear in my heart, I quickly jump towards him, still pointing the gun at him. I reach with my free hand and grab my backpack. Luckily, my face is covered. I then demanded cash, without hesitation he pulls out a wad of cash and I take it from him.

With my heart pumping wildly, perspiration dripping from my face, and fear in my eyes (what a feeling!), I slowly back up towards the door, open it, and flee as fast as a "jackrabbit" being chased by the fox.

Burnt Out

The mission was a successful one, but a very dangerous one as well. It's a blessing that I made it out alive. Now I think to myself, "Is this all worth it?" With all the dope and cash that I've ripped off, I have nothing to show for it. I'm tired.

This is a couple of examples of how far one will go to satisfy his needs to get high. In this case it was me. Sharing with you about the hits and being successful doing them, isn't what I'm trying to express to you. Believe me it wasn't always successful. I had my close calls and paid dearly for them. Being alive today, knowing where I was (ripping off), where I am now (prison), where I want to be (free), is the key to changing myself. And this, I would like to share with you from my heart, and hope that together we can help our keikis (kids) from making the same mistake.

Luckily, this is not Los Angeles or New York where we have to hide from flying bullets. This is HAWAII, our home of loving, caring, sharing, peace, and happiness, our ama (land). We don't have to be using drugs or killing one another to be recognized. Just showing love and appreciation for each other will be recognized greatly by many. People will want to be around you, as we share our love that we portray. Through our kind hearts, loving personality and Aloha we will be remembered always. We can do it! TOGETHER!

At Peace

When I gave myself to the Lord, the power of darkness that had plagued me and caused me so much heartache and pain slowly left. This evil feeling has not returned, and I know in my heart and soul that it never will. I don't really understand what has happened to me, but this I do know, something great, peaceful and magnificent has happened. All I know is that the Lord has done this great happening in my life. I don't care what other people say, all I know is that He has changed my heart, soul, and my life. I now feel at peace with myself, even in here behind these concrete walls of hell.

    Amen.

Appendix IV

Temporal Characteristics of Methamphetamine with Forensic Implications

Event	Typical Duration
Rush	5–30 minutes
High	4–16 hours
Crashing	1–3 days after high ends
Normal feeling returns	2–14 days after crashing ends
Binge	3–15 days
Withdrawal	30–90 days
Injected	Immediate onset
Smoked	5–20 minutes to take effect
Smoked	Up to 8 hours high
Smoked	12–36 hours half-life
Urinary excretion	Ends in 3–5 days
Psychosis	One third of patients show psychotic symptoms for more than 10 days
Recovery from psychosis	82% within a month after withdrawal
Sensitivity	Catecholamine agonists persist more than 3 months after discontinuation (animals) and to several substances (humans)
Tolerance	100 times increase (e.g., 5 to 500 mg) in a year
Psychosis	10% of patients show psychotic symptoms after 2 years
Recovery	Requires more than 5 years in 14% of cases (intravenous use)
Psychotic relapse	Single injection of methamphetamine may reactivate paranoid psychotic state, even after 5 years
Psychotic relapse	Psychotic state with frequent relapses continues for 8–22 years for some abusers, without methamphetamine reuse

Appendix V

Safety Tips for Approaching a Tweaker*

- Keep a social distance — preferably a 7- to 10-foot radius. Once a person has been identified as a potential tweaker, law enforcement officers should call for backup. Detaining a tweaker alone is not recommended.
- Do not shine bright lights at him. The tweaker is already paranoid, and if he is blinded by a bright light, the tweaker is likely to run or become violent.
- Slow your speech and lower the pitch of your voice. A tweaker already hears sounds at a fast pace and in a high pitch, and a side effect of the drug is a constant electrical buzzing sound in the background.
- Slow your movements. This will decrease the odds that the tweaker will misinterpret your physical actions.
- Keep your hands visible. Because the tweaker is already paranoid, if you place your hands where he cannot see them, he might feel threatened and could become violent.
- Keep the tweaker talking. A tweaker who falls silent can be extremely dangerous. Silence often means that his paranoid thoughts have taken over reality, and anyone on the scene can become part of the tweaker's paranoid delusions.

---

* *Source*: U.S. Department of Justice (1999). Training and Technical Support for Clandestine Laboratory Enforcement Programs. Office of Justice Programs, Washington, D.C.

Index

12-step
  as used in the matrix model 205, 208
  in the Middle East 21
  sentencing 132–138
5-HT *see* serotonin

A

Abortion 157, 159, 160, 162
Addiction potential scale 112, 123, 125, 126
ADHD *see* attention deficit hyperactivity disorder
Adolescent 22, 25, 29
Afghanistan 17
Aggression
  criminal responsibility 186, 190, 191
  dangerousness prediction 196, 198
  effects of MDMA 25
  effects of methamphetamine on 51
  humans 64, 67, 68, 78
  nonhuman animals 71–76
  sentencing 92, 107, 117, 118, 119
Alcohol
  criminal responsibility 181, 182, 188, 191
  custody rights 151
  diagnosis of methamphetamine use 59
  effects on the fetus 158–162
  evaluation 104, 107
  history of 3–6
  MDMA 26, 29
  methamphetamine 48, 50,
  sentencing 97, 100–101
  specific cases 120–125
  the Middle East 15, 19–21
  treatment 203, 205, 209
  treatment as a sentencing consideration 133–137
American law institute 182, 190
American society for addiction medicine 50, 132
Amphetamine
  aggression in humans 69, 78–79
  aggression in nonhuman animals 71–75
  diagnosis of use 124
  dominance in primates 76–78
  for treating obesity 17
  history 5–6, 9
  induced psychosis 58
  mitigation in sentencing 105, 111, 119
  neurotoxicity 41
  physiological effects 38–40
  poly-substance dependence 60
  specific cases 120, 126–127
Anhedonia 133, 171
Antisocial personality disorder 112, 123, 127, 179, 187
Anxiety
  as a symptom of methamphetamine abuse 55, 56, 59, 133
  criminal responsibility 183, 188, 189
  interrogation 169
  self medication 3
  specific cases 121
Aphrodisiacs 26
Appeals
  custody 152–157
  Daubert issues 87, 98
  death penalty cases 129, 130
  evaluation of defendants 100, 102, 103, 109
  Miranda rights 167
ASAM *see* American Society for Addiction Medicine
Attention deficit hyperactivity disorder 111, 122, 142, 188, 190
Australia 16, 78, 80, 146
Autoreceptors 38, 40

B

Barbiturates 26, 121, 142
Belgium 17
Benzodiazepines 26
Biphasic effects 74, 80
Bizarre mentation sub-scales 112
Brain damage 13

criminal responsibility 179, 181, 183, 189, 191
  MDMA 26
  specific cases 138
  the fetus 158, 160

C

Caffeine 49–53
Calcium 27, 37, 45
Calcium-dependent release 27, 39
Calcium-independent release 27, 39
Canada 16, 23, 24, 106
Cannabis
  history of 17, 19
  sentencing considerations 124, 127
  serotonin 29, 30
Capital sentencing 128
Cardiovascular 13, 14, 40
Catecholamines 38, 43, 45, 47
Center for substance abuse treatment 203
Central Asia 15, 18
Child protective services 120, 121, 151, 161, 162
Chlorpromazine 75
Chronic administration 73, 74
Clinical symptoms 55
Cocaine
  addictive qualities 41
  cross-tolerance 49–50
  delusions 57
  diagnosis 188
  epidemiology 13
  history of 3–4, 6, 8
  mixing with MDMA 19
  pregnancy
    effects on the fetus 158–162
    maternal rights 151–152
  reverse tolerance 58
  sentencing 101, 110, 112
  specific cases 120–123, 125–127
  treatment 203–204, 206–207
Coerced-compliant 168
Cognitive interview 110, 145, 176
Competency
  assessment instruments 170
  Miranda rights 167–169
  to confess 171
  to proceed 171–174

Comprehensive methamphetamine control act of 1996 102
Congress 4, 25, 29, 67, 102
Constitutional erosion 87
CPS *see* child protective services
Crack 6, 158, 162
Crank 6, 141
Crime control act of 1990 102
Crime
  amnesia of 194
  competency 172, 179–180
    mental state 182–184, 188–189
  death penalty 129,
  drug related 59–60, 131, 191
  evaluation of 113, 115
  false confessions 169
  organized 7–8, 16
  predisposition 85–86, 186–187
  sentencing 100–102, 109–110
  specific cases 118–120, 122, 123
  subcommittee 67
  trial in absentia 170
  use of a weapon 190
  violent 4, 68, 78–79, 144
Criminal behavior 110, 114, 123, 187, 191
Criminal justice
  belief in aggression causing effects of amphetamine 74
  contact with substance abusers 140, 141, 143
  evaluation 110, 112
  pre-sentence investigation 118
  sentencing 105
  State v. Ferguson 152
  the importance of treatment of substance dependence 131
Criminal responsibility 177, 179
  methamphetamine use 187–191
  methodology in determining 181–183, 185
Cross-reverse tolerance 49, 50
Csat 203, 209
Culture
  drug use patterns 21–22
  native American 156
  treatment implications 19
Czech republic 16

Index

D

Dangerousness prediction 195, 197, 198
Date rape 26
Daubert issues
  competency 182
  Daubert v. Merrell Dow Pharmaceuticals 87, 92
  expert testimony 88–91
  sentencing 105
  U.S. v. Rohrer 93
DAWN *see* drug abuse warning network
Death penalty
  special case of the 128–130
  state codes cases 99, 101, 113
Delirium 56, 57, 60, 61
Depression
  aggression 71, 78, 79
  case studies 123–125, 142
  criminal responsibility 188
  methamphetamine use 58–61, 203–204
  Middle East 22
Designer drug 41, 42
Detox *see* detoxification
Detoxification
  Haight-Ashbury outpatient model 207
  sentencing 133, 137
  treatment 6, 21, 132, 143
Diagnostic and statistical manual
  case studies 142
  criminal responsibility 185–188
  diagnosis of methamphetamine syndromes 59–61
  diagnosis of substance abuse versus methamphetamine abuse 48–51
  reporting to the court 116
Dispositional factors 196
Distractibility 171
Dominance hierarchy 76
Dopamine
  aggressive behavior 75
  control of levels 38
  fetal effects 161
  MDMA 27
  neurotoxicity 40
  symptoms of methamphetamine abuse 58
  tolerance 39
  treatment 207–208
Drope v. Missouri 171, 173, 174

Drug abuse warning network 9, 10, 25
Drug production 15
Drug trade 15, 16, 17, 18, 23
DSM-IV *see* diagnostic and statistical manual
Dual diagnosis
  case studies 124, 143
  Haight-Ashbury Model of Treatment 207, 208
  sentencing 135–138
Egypt
  methamphetamine use in 15–16
  treatment approaches in 20–23
Entrapment 85, 86
Ephedrine 5, 48, 49, 50, 58
Epinephrine 38, 42
Europe
  historical use of marijuana 4
  methamphetamine distribution 17–19
Exchange diffusion model 30, 39, 43
Executive function
  case studies 123
  competency 170, 173
  control of violence 115, 190, 191, 194
  methamphetamine's effects on 107, 111
  symptoms of methamphetamine use 58
Extreme emotion 149, 150, 191, 192

F

False confessions 44, 168, 175, 176
Feguer v. United States 170, 174
Fetus
  effects of cocaine on 158–159
  effects of methamphetamine on 160–162
  presumptions about methamphetamine use 153
  rights of 151, 156–157
Forensic assessment 113, 127, 144, 175
Fourth amendment 151, 153
Fowner v. United States 85
Frontal lobe 179
Frye v. United States 88

G

Gaza 15, 16, 22
Georgia court of appeals 157
Germany 5, 16, 17
Gulf War 18

H

Haight ashb, ury outpatient model 203, 207
Hallucinations
    amphetamine induced psychosis 60–61
    competency 170, 171, 189
    produced by amphetamine 6
    State v. Hughbanks 130
    symptoms of methamphetamine use 13, 55–59
    treatment 203
    use of methamphetamine despite knowledge of negative effects 42
Haloperidol 75
Hashish 17, 121
Hawaii 47f
    CPS 161
    history 6, 7, 8
    intermediate court of appeals 173
    methamphetamine use 41–42
    revised statutes 149, 171, 177
    sentencing 101
    State v. Kuhilia 179–180
    State v. Monte Louis Young 67, 181
    State v. Raquero 194
Heroin
    being overtaken as drug of choice by methamphetamine 13
    case studies 121
    history of use 4, 5
    sentencing 101, 105, 107
    use in the Middle East 15, 17, 21
HIV 9, 21, 83, 207
Hyperthermia 27, 58

I

Ibiza 17
Illinois teratogen information service 158
Immobility 72, 73, 75
India 16, 41
Indolamine 38
Interdisciplinary fitness interview 170, 175
Internet 13, 49
Interviewing 93, 109, 110, 168
Iran 98
    methamphetamine use 15–18
    treatment approaches 20–21
Ischemic stroke 47, 48, 62

Islam 15, 19, 20
Israel 15–18, 22

J

Judicial 21, 71, 198

K

Kia v. Long Island College Hospital 153
Kidnapping 122, 192
Kinder v. United States 85
Koran 20
Kurds 18

L

Laurelwood 139
L-dopa 50
Lockett v. Ohio 101, 146
LSD 121, 122, 125

M

Malingering
    competency 172
    diagnosis 111–112
    faking symptoms of 184
    forensic evaluation 107–108
    interview procedure 109–110
    State v. Hughbanks 130
Mania 57
Manslaughter 99, 149, 197
Maternal rights 152
Matrix model 203–207
MCMI-III *see* millon clinical multiaxial inventory
MDMA
    animal models of brain damage 160
    damage of serotonergic neurons 47
    memory deficits 111
    Middle East 17, 19
    myths about use 25
    neurotoxicity 26–29
    psychopharmacology 41–42
Memory
    effects of MDMA on 25, 28, 30
    effects of MDMA on low intellectually functioning males 41–42
    effects of methamphetamine on 58, 93, 170–171, 184

Daubert issues 90, 91–92
diagnosing dysfunction 109–111
case studies 127, 130
sentencing 189, 192
Mental health
case studies 118, 120
co-morbidity 143
competency 174
criminal responsibility 185
diagnosis of methamphetamine use 59
expert witnesses 51
long term effects of methamphetamine on 78
mitigation in sentencing 133
State v. Kuhia 179, 183
State v. Romel 187
the Middle East 15, 16, 19–21
treatment history 139–141
Merck pharmaceuticals 25
Methamphetamine
aggression
animals 71–76
humans 67–68, 78–80
child custody 153–155
competency 169–173
criminal responsibility
co-morbid disorders 188–190
deliberate distortion 182–186
heuristic model 191–194
history 187
pathological intoxication 177–181
current trends 9
dangerousness 195–196
death penalty 128–130
diagnosis of use
symptoms 55–58
syndromes 59–61
effects on the fetus 158–160
epidemiology 13
evaluation 103
expert testimony
Daubert issues 88, 90–94
U.S. Supreme Court 85–86
history of use in Hawaii 7–8
history of use in the U.S. 3–6
interview 109
legal issues in pregnancy 151, 152
malingering 107–108
Middle East
cultural aspects 19–20

geopolitical 15–18
treatment approaches 21
Miranda rights 167–168
mitigation in sentencing
federal 102
state 97–100
physiological effects 47–50
pre-sentence investigation 117–118
psychometrics 110–112
psychopharmacology 37–41
reporting to court 115–116
review of treatment center cases 139–143
rights of the fetus 156
risk analysis 104–106
similarities with MDMA 25–28
specific cases 119–123
TPI 114
treatment 203–207
treatment as a sentencing consideration 131–135
Methamphetamine-induced psychotic disorder 61
Mezzanatto 86
Michael v. Arizona 153, 155
Middle East
geopolitical interconnections 15–17, 19
substance abuse treatment 21–23
Millon clinical multiaxial inventory 112, 145, 184
Miranda rights 98, 130, 167–169
Mistretta v. U.S. 102
Mitigation in sentencing 97, 99, 103
mmpi
case studies 122–126
death penalty cases 126–127
evaluation of substance use 120–121, 184
treatment of axis I disorders 112–113
Monoamine oxidase 40
MPTP 26
Murder
aggression 67
coffee 50
criminal responsibility 177–179, 181, 184
mitigation in sentencing 93, 131, 141, 149, 192
rights of the fetus 157
Narcotics 15, 21, 68, 122
National Institute of Drug Abuse (NIDA)
fetal effects of methamphetamine 160
ice as a substitute for marijuana 8

marijuana 7
report on methamphetamine and sexual
    activity 9
report on treatment for
    methamphetamine abuse 131,
    203
National Institute on Drug Abuse 31, 131
Native Americans 156
Negative symptoms 55
Netherlands 17
Neurodegeneration 27
Neurons
    definition of 37
    dopaminergic 39–40
    neuronal injury 41
    post-synaptic 38
    pre-synaptic 42
    sensitization 47
    serotonergic 27, 28
Neurophysiology 37
Neurotoxic
    effects of MDMA
        on animals 25–26
        on humans 27
    effects of methamphetamine 40–41
Norepinephrine 38, 42
Northern African 15

O

Opiates
    history of 3–4
    the Middle East 21
    as neurotransmitters 38
    as predictors of aggressive behavior 107
    cross sensitization 188
Organic delusional disorder 179
Organic mental disorder 179

P

Pakistan 17
Palestine 16, 22
Panic 55, 56
Parkinson 26, 50
Pathological intoxication 177, 179, 180, 181
Personality assessment 112, 113, 116, 145
Placental abruption 159, 160
Plea bargaining 85, 86
Polydrug use

MDMA 28–29
    fetal damage 158–161
Pregnancy 155
    legal issues 151–153, 155, 156
    methamphetamine use 158–159,
        161–162
Pre-term delivery 159, 160
Psychological symptoms 58, 171
Psychosis 57–58
    competency 172
    criminal responsibility 188
    diagnosis 61, 185
    methamphetamine induced 5–6, 178
        long term 13–14
    treatment of 204, 207
Psychotherapy 17, 22, 25
Psychotic disorder NOS 181
Psychotic symptoms 61

R

Recall
    case study 122
    competency to proceed 167, 169, 173, 194
    expert testimony 93
    neurotoxic properties of MDMA 27–28,
        41
    State v. Melvin Hashimoto 171
Recidivism
    prediction of 116–118
    risk analysis 106–107
    sentencing 101, 104, 131
    violent 197
Red phosphorus 49
Reward pathway 42
Rogers criminal responsibility scale 189
Rorschach 113
Rule 702 88
Rural 9, 122
Russia 17

S

SASSI 17, 120, 121, 124, 127
Schedule I 17, 25
Schedule of affective disorders and
    schizophrenia 189
Schizophrenia
    axis III diagnosis 141
    caused by MDMA 25

Index

competency 130, 184
criminal responsibility 188–189
diagnosis of 6, 61
neuropsychological testing 111
sentencing 118
symptoms caused by methamphetamine 58, 178–179
SDR 169
Sensitization 40, 47, 52, 208
Sentencing commission 102, 103
Sentencing reform act 102
Serotonergic *see* serotonin
Serotonin
    fetal effects 160
    neurotoxic properties of MDMA 26–28, 47
    physiological effects of excitotoxic compounds on 38–39
SIDS 159, 160
Sixth amendment 87
Social exploration 72, 75, 78, 80
Sorrells v. United States 85
South America 3, 17
Southeast Asia 17
Spain 16
Spontaneous abortion 159, 160, 162
SSRI 122, 123
State of Ohio v. Gary Hughbanks 129
State v. Burkholder 101
State v. Cachola 93
State v. Freitas 177, 194
State v. Fukusaku 93
State v. Garringer 180, 194
State v. Hall 177, 194
State v. Holbron 178, 194
State v. Kane 174, 176
State v. Kuhia 179, 194
State v. Melvin Hashimoto 171
State v. Nuetzel 177, 194
State v. Paned 193, 194
State v. Romel 177
State v. Samson Pebria, Jr .167
State v. Sean Carvalho 197
State v. Silverio Soares 173, 176
State v. Souza 177, 194
State-dependent retrieval 169
Structural brain abnormalities 159
Supreme court
    competency 100, 170
    criminal responsibility 177, 180
    custody 152
    death penalty 128
    expert testimony 87–89
    methamphetamine 85
    sentencing 102

T

Terrorism 16, 18, 23, 131, 192
Thailand 16, 23
Thematic apperception test 113
Three strikes laws 101
Tolerance 50
    case studies 120–123
    competency 171
    criminal responsibility 188
    cross-tolerance 49
    memory 92
    mitigation in sentencing 125
    neuropharmacology 41
    prediction of dangerousness 195
    reverse tolerance 40, 49, 58
    to the anti-aggressive effects of methamphetamine 74
TPH 27, 28
Trailmaking test 111
Treatment 142
    as an option to prison 8–9
    case management 133–135
    case studies 123–127
    competency to confess 170–172
    court ordered versus self referral 137
    dual diagnosis 136, 138, 190
    during pregnancy 158, 161
    laurelwood 139
    Middle East 15–16, 19, 21–22
    NIDA guidelines 203
    of migraine with marijuana 4
    of Parkinson's Disease 50
    planning 132, 135, 136, 144, 205
    pre-sentence investigation 114
    reporting to the court 115–116
    sentencing 101, 104–106
    sentencing 118–121, 131–132
    strengths and weaknesses of clients 111–113
TPI 110
    with the Haight-Ashbury model 207–209
    with the matrix model 204–206

Tryptophan hydroxylase 27, 28, 33, 43
Turkey 17, 18
Tyrosine hydroxylase 27, 43

U

U.S. Supreme Court in *Dusky v. United States* 170
United States v. Adams 170, 176
United States v. Inadi 87
United States v. Mezzanatto 86
United States v. Russell 85
United States v. Wilson 170, 176

V

Vesicle 37, 39, 43
Violent behavior
    amphetamine induced psychosis 58, 122–123
    criminal responsibility 186, 192
    historical factors of 68

W

Weak base model 39
Wechsler adult intelligence scales 111
Wechsler memory scale 111
West Bank 15, 22
Wisconsin card sorting test 111
Withdrawal
    acute versus chronic administration 74
    case studies 180
    detox 136–137
    from methadone 153
    from pharmaceuticals 6
    from positive social contacts 121
    malingering 108
    methamphetamine induced psychosis 62
    neonates 159
    pharmacotherapy 50
    State v. Carvalho 197
    symptoms 58–60
    treatment 133
Working memory 28, 41, 46
World Trade Center 131
Wright v. Ohio 98, 101

X

XTC *see* MDMA